WOMEN AND THE POLITICS OF MILITARY CONFRONTATION

Palestinian and Israeli Gendered Narratives of Dislocation

Edited by

Nahla Abdo

and

Ronit Lentin

Berghahn Books
NEW YORK • OXFORD

Published in 2002 by

Berghahn Books

www.berghahnbooks.com

© 2002 Nahla Abdo and Ronit Lentin

Library of Congress Cataloging-in-Publication Data

Women and the politics of military confrontation : Palestinian and Israeli
gendered narratives of dislocation / editors, Nahla Abdo, Ronit Lentin.
    p. cm.
    Includes bibliographical references.
    ISBN 1-57181-498-2 (cloth : alk. paper) – ISBN 1-57181-459-0 (pbk. : alk. paper)
    1. Women, Palestinian Arab–West Bank–Social conditions. 2. Women, Pales-
tinian Arab–Gaza Strip–Social conditions. 3. Women, Palestinian Arab–
Lebanon–Social conditions. 4. Women–Israel–Social conditions. I. Abdo-Zubi,
Nahla, 1953– II. Lentin, Ronit.

HQ1728.7 .W65 202
305.42'095694–dc21   2002018414

British Library Cataloguing in Publication Data

A catalogue record for this book is available from
the British Library.

Printed in the United States on acid-free paper

Contents

PART II: ISRAELI JEWISH WOMEN

Acknowledgements

This project would not have been possible had it not been for the commitment and generous contribution of several Palestinian and Israeli scholars and activists. Our thanks go, first and foremost, to our contributors, whose stories of dislocation illustrate the price women pay for the politics of the Israeli-Palestinian military confrontation.

Sincere thanks are due to Alana Lentin for her editorial help on an earlier version, and Zeina Awad for her invaluable efforts at translating some of the Arabic material. Special thanks to copy editor Jaime Taber, production editor Vivian K. Berghahn, typesetter Shawn Kendrick and the production team at Berghahn Books, and in particular to our publisher, Marion Berghahn, who kept faith in the project.

Ronit Lentin would like to thank her lifelong friends Eli Aminov and Nitza Aminov for keeping her focused on the vicissitudes of Zionism.

Nahla Abdo would like to extend special thanks to Rosemary Sayigh for giving her a great gift – introducing her to Ronit – and to Sami, without whose generous support the time and effort spent on this project would have taken their toll on family life.

Contributors

Nahla Abdo is an Arab feminist and Professor of Sociology at Carleton University, Ottawa, Canada. She has published extensively on women and the state in the Middle East with special focus on Palestinian women. Among her publications are *Sociological Thought: Beyond Eurocentric Theory* (Canadian Scholars' Press, 1996), and *Sexuality, Citizenship and the State: Palestinian Experiences* (forthcoming, Syracuse University Press). She enjoys teaching and training in feminist theory and methodology. She contributed to the establishment of the Women's Studies Institute at Bir Zeith University and founded the Gender Research Unit at the Women's Empowerment Project/Gaza Community Mental Health Program in Gaza. She is currently working on a research project entitled 'Occupation and Women: Implications for the Public Sphere'.

Samia Costandi is a Montreal-based Palestinian-Canadian academic, educator, community activist and freelance writer. She is currently writing her doctoral dissertation and lecturing at the McGill Faculty of Education, Department of Integrated Studies in Education. Her dissertation deals with the use of narrative as a pedagogical tool for the teaching of values in education. She has lived between the different cultures of the Arab Middle East and the West. She taught in Lebanon at Beirut University College between 1983 and 1988 under the excruciating circumstances of the civil war. Samia's lived experiences are as valuable to her as an educator as her accumulated academic knowledge. She has always believed in praxis; her community work has been a reflection of her pedagogical views. In March 1999 she received the Helen Prize for Women for her work in the domain of the media as 'an articulate female Palestinian Canadian speaking truth to power', and in April 2000, she received the Margaret Gillett Award from the Center for Research and Teaching on Women at McGill University. She is currently writing a book about her life in Lebanon.

Souad Dajani is an American of Palestinian origin and a scholar and activist in the Boston area. She received her Ph.D. in sociology from the University of Toronto in 1984, and her MA and BA degrees from the

American University of Beirut, Lebanon. She has travelled frequently to Palestine and has lived and worked in the United States, Canada, Jordan, Lebanon, Cyprus and Abu Dhabi. She has extensive experience in public speaking. Her book *Eyes Without Country: Searching for a Palestinian Strategy of Liberation* was published in 1994 by Temple University Press.

Mona El Farra is a dermatologist practising in Gaza city. She was born in Khan Younis and moved later to Gaza city. She spent many years working with the Union of Health Work Committees in Gaza. She is an activist for the empowerment of Palestinian women and their social and health development.

Nabila Espanioly is the director of Al-Tufula Pedagogical Centre and Multipurpose Women's Centre in Nazareth. She has an MA in clinical psychology from Bamberg University in Germany, and is a feminist activist for human rights, Palestinian rights, women's rights and children's rights. She has published several books in Arabic in the field of early childhood education as well as articles in English, Arabic and Hebrew.

Esther Fuchs is Professor of Hebrew Literature at the Judaic Studies and Near East Studies Department at the University of Arizona, Tucson. She is the author of several books on Hebrew literature, including *Israeli Mythogynies: Women in Contemporary Hebrew Fiction* (State University of New York Press, 1998). She has also published poems in Hebrew on the experience of second-generation Holocaust survivors. She is the editor of a special *Shofar* volume entitled 'Women in Jewish Life and Culture' (1999), and of *Women in the Holocaust: Narrative and Representation* (University of America Press, 1999). Her latest book is *Sexual Politics in the Biblical Narrative: Reading the Hebrew Bible as a Woman* (Sheffield Academic Press, 2000).

Ronit Lentin was born in Haifa prior to the establishment of the state of Israel and has lived in Ireland since 1969. She is course co-ordinator of the M.Phil. in ethnic studies at the Department of Sociology, Trinity College, Dublin. She has published several novels and short stories in Hebrew and English, and in 1982 her *Conversations with Palestinian Women* was published by Mifras in Hebrew. Lentin is the editor of *Gender and Catastrophe* (Zed Books, 1997) and Europe and Middle East editor of *Women's Studies International Forum*. She has published extensively on the gendered link between Israel and the Shoah, feminist research methodologies, Israeli and Palestinian women's peace activism, and racism in Ireland. Her latest book is *Israel and the Daughters of the Shoah: Reoccupying the Territories of Silence* (Berghahn Books, 2000). She is co-editor (with Anne Byrne) of *(Re)searching Women: Feminist Research Methodologies in the Social Sciences in Ireland* (Institute of Public Administration, 2000) and (with Robbie McVeigh) of *Racism and Anti-racism in Ireland* (Beyond the Pale, 2002).

Hala Mannaa was born and still lives in Gaza city. She completed her BA in English from the Jerusalem Open University in Gaza. She has worked for several years with the Women's Empowerment Project at the Gaza Community Mental Health Programme and is currently working with the Women's Affairs/Gaza.

Rela Mazali is a bilingual English/Hebrew writer, and a feminist, anti-militarisation activist. Her latest book, *Maps of Women's Goings and Stayings*, was published in 2001 by Stanford University Press. She lives near Tel-Aviv with her partner and three children.

Isis Nusair grew up in Nazareth and received her undergraduate degree in social work from Tel-Aviv University in 1993. She was active in the Palestinian student movement and worked as a social worker and human rights activist in the Jaffa/Tel-Aviv area. She received her master degree in peace studies from Notre Dame University in 1995. Isis worked for three years as a researcher on women's human rights in the Middle East and North Africa at the Women's Rights Division of Human Rights Watch. She is currently a Ph.D. student in women's studies at Clark University.

Rosemary Sayigh, of British origin, is a resident of Lebanon and is married to a Palestinian. She began working in the Middle East as a teacher and journalist, and later studied anthropology and oral history, with a special interest in the Palestinians. She is the author of *Palestinians from Peasants to Revolutionaries* and *Too Many Enemies: The Palestinian Experience in Lebanon* (both published by Zed Books). She is currently working on a voice archive of Palestinian women's experiences of displacement.

Nadera Shalhoub-Kevorkian is a lecturer at the School of Social Work and the Faculty of Law, Institute of Criminology, both at the Hebrew University of Jerusalem. She has studied the Palestinian society in the West Bank, Gaza Strip and Israel and initiated the first hotline to service the Palestinian population in the West Bank and Gaza Strip. She is currently supervising the hotline services and social work department at the Women's Centre for Legal Aid and Counselling in Jerusalem. Her speciality is analysing the victimisation of women and children while focusing on subjects such as women and law; women in laws; cross-cultural models of intervention in dealing with female victims of abus;, women victims of abuse of power; women, violence, and social control.

Alice Shalvi was born in Germany in 1926 and educated in England. She has an MA in English from the University of Cambridge and a diploma in social work from the London School of Economics. In 1949 she made aliyah to Israel, where she was a lecturer in the English Department of the Hebrew University of Jerusalem between 1950 and 1990. In 1962 she completed her Ph.D. at the Hebrew University and became Associate Professor in 1971. She was the founding Chairwoman of the Israel Women's Network between 1984 and 1997. In 1996 Alice was appointed Rector of the Schechter Institute of Jewish Studies where she later served first as President and then as Chairperson of the Executive Committee. She is married and has three sons, three daughters and numerous grandchildren.

Ella Habiba Shohat is Professor of Media Studies and Women's Studies at the City University of New York, Graduate Center and Staten Island. She has lectured and published extensively on the intersection of post-colonialism, multiculturalism and gender. Her award-winning books include *Israeli Cinema: East/West and the Politics of Representation* (University of Texas Press, 1989), *Unthinking Eurocentrism: Multiculturalism and the Media* (with R. Stam, Routledge, 1994), *Dangerous Liaisons: Gender, Nations and Post-colonial Reflections* (co-edited, University of Minnesota Press, 1997) and *Talking Visions: Multicultural Feminism in a Transnational Age* (MIT Press in collaboration with the New Museum, 1999). Ella is a recipient of a Rockefeller fellowship, and has served on the editorial board of the journals *Social Text, Jouvert* and *Critique*. Her work has been translated into French, Spanish, Portuguese, Arabic, Hebrew, German and Turkish.

Gila Svirsky is a veteran peace and human rights activist in Israel. For six years she was the director in Israel of the New Israel Fund, and subsequently the director of Bat Shalom, the Israeli side of The Jerusalem Link: A Women's Joint Venture for Peace. During the first Intifada she served as chairperson of B'Tselem, Israel's foremost human rights organisation in the occupied territories. The year 2002 marks her fifteenth year standing on vigil every Friday as a Woman in Black. Since the al-Aqsa Intifada broke out in September 2000, she co-founded and helps co-ordinate the Coalition of Women for a Just Peace, a coalition of ten women's peace organisations in Israel.

Badea Warwar was born in Nazareth and immigrated to Canada in 1989. She received her undergraduate degree in English and women studies, and is currently finishing her Ph.D. in English literature at York University.

Nira Yuval-Davis was born in Israel and is Professor of Gender and Ethnic Studies at the University of Greenwich, UK. Her books include *Racialised Boundaries: Race, Nation, Gender, Colour and Class and the Anti-racist Struggle* (with Floya Anthias, Routledge, 1992), *Refusing Holy Orders: Women and Fundamentalism in Britain* (with Gitta Sahgal, Virago, 1992), *Unsettling Settler Societies: Articulations in Gender, Ethnicity, Race and Class* (with Daiva Stasiulis, Sage, 1995), *Gender and Nation* (Sage, 1997), and *Women, Citizenship and Difference* (with Pnina Werbner, Zed Books 1999).

Nahla Abdo and Ronit Lentin

Writing Dislocation, Writing the Self: Bringing (Back) the Political into Gendered Israeli-Palestinian Dialoguing

—⁓—

Introduction

Writing dialogically as a process of sharing not only our thoughts, but also our power, in a situation in which the power differential (between Israelis and Palestinians) is an obvious truism, has been our ongoing work as we toil to put this book together. In the panel titled 'Diversity in Editing' at which we were invited to speak during the Israeli Association of Feminist Studies and Gender Research conference dedicated to the crucial feminist issue of 'difference' held in Beit Berl College on 16 February 2000, we presented our thoughts about the concept of 'Shonout/difference' and the meanings of the concept among women, and particularly feminists. We attempted to contextualise the concept within the framework of our shared book and say something about the beginning of the project and about the centrality of autobiographical narratives as a feminist methodology to explore women's lives and in particular the construction of gendered selves in the process of nationalising histories. We also spoke about the difference between us in relation to political issues such as nationalism and women's place within nationalist projects. For obvious political reasons we presented the paper in English, despite the organisers' wish that we present in Hebrew. And for obvious political reasons (albeit different ones) our joint presentation, in which we spoke of the real difficulties of putting together a collection of narratives of gendered dislocation of Palestinian and Israeli women, met with a near-unanimous negative reception.

We both write about this experience in our separate essays, but this introduction is presented as a dialogue, one we have been writing to each other, across continents, via e-mail, for almost two years. Each section is named and dated. Dialogue between Palestinians and Israelis has never been harder than during the difficult days of the 2000–1 al-Aqsa Intifada. The least we can say about it is that we have continued to speak, continued to dialogue.

Nahla, 10 December 1999

As you know, Ronit, my initial hesitation in taking part in such a project has been whether the politics of the book in general meets basic common grounds of understanding Israel and Zionism. As you know, the first public encounter (discussion forum) between Palestinians and Israelis was the *Nightline* (Ted Koppel) ABC programme in which Hanan Ashrawi, Saeb Eireikat, and Haidar Abdel-Shafi met with the current mayor of Jerusalem and two other Israeli Jews just before the Oslo meeting. The fact that I cannot remember the names of the Israeli speakers is partly due to the role of national memory, which is selective and can easily delete names associated with fear, pessimism, and arrogance. Yet what has become very clear to me since then and throughout the Oslo meetings (it feels like hundreds of them) is the asymmetrical relation which is inherent in all of these 'talks'. This high or hard-level politics (i.e. male politics) is not very different from other forms of political 'negotiations', including those conducted among women and feminists. The Jerusalem Link, which epitomises political linkages between Palestinian and Israeli women, and which includes academics and feminists, is, I think, an equally feeble exercise. The failure of these forms of 'talks' or however one refers to them is that the talkers cannot stand on par with each other and are not negotiating from a basic common understanding of the identity and nature of the oppressor and the identity and nature of the oppressed.

It is possible to argue that no one can dialogue with the *state*, especially if it is as oppressive and complex as the Zionist state. But this is not the whole story. I cannot deny the presence – albeit rare and marginalised – of Israeli and Palestinian feminist activism, which is dialogical in nature and largely removed from power constraints. These attempts, however, operate in a less contradictory environment. You can find true dialogues and common work among Jewish and Palestinian feminists abroad and some within Israel itself. But I think it is almost impossible to expect the same from women who continue to live under direct Israeli occupation, oppression, and humiliation. It is almost impossible to find camp refugee women in Palestine or the diaspora who can accept the idea of dialoguing with the enemy.

I thought long and hard about the idea of dialoguing the introduction of the book. The questions that kept cropping up were: What is the meaning of dialogue? How does one dialogue an oppressive state? How does one dialogue Zionism? I kept asking myself if Zionism for you and in your experience is similar to the Zionism I experience and know! I know that for many European Jews, Zionism is the 'salvation army', is the 'nationalism', is the 'state', and is the 'refuge'. I also know that Zionism for me and for most Palestinians is the 'occupying and aggressive army', is the denial of our 'national identity', our 'anti-state' and the cause of our disposition and dispossession.

My first published dialogue was with Simona Sharoni, an Israeli Jew living in the United States, in an article called 'Middle East Politics Through Feminist Lenses: Dialoguing the Terms of Solidarity' (Abdo, 1993; Sharoni, 1993). Knowing Simona's anti-Zionist politics through her activist anti-racist work, I never thought of hesitating or even thinking twice when I was approached by *Alternatives* to 'respond' to her article.

But our book brings me to a new territory, namely claiming responsibility over Israeli contributors whose Shoah experience might cast Zionism in the very meaning that might be antithetical to that experienced by my people. My feminist, anti-racist and anti-classist stance prevents me from being in a position where I prioritise academic achievement over political commitment.

I know that we could have requested a feminist anti-Zionist position at the very beginning of the project. But I also realise that this is not exactly a proper thing to do because there are many feminisms and feminism itself is an on-going process. I myself have gone through different phases of development in my feminism, from nationalist feminism to a feminism critical of all nationalisms, including my own.

Mature political feminism, which is the product of the emergence of many critical feminist voices from the margins – Blacks, Asians, Middle Eastern, Native, Palestinian and Jewish etc. – has undoubtedly opened more doors for critical thinking and more space for 'white' politics to acknowledge and unlearn their 'whiteness'. It is the power of the idea of reaching out from a strong position, which empowers the marginalised and turns my fears, worries, and uncertainties into powerful tools expressing presence, identity, and voice.

Our introduction, which will serve as the feminist, political, ideological and social context for all contributions (whether it will truly represent every contributor or not), I think, is what is going to make the difference. Although I am sure some of the contributions, perhaps most, will be of great value in the path of reaching out, the introduction, I hope, will lead the way. I wrote all of the above thinking I was writing the introduction. When I reached the end of the last paragraph I realised I have not yet begun. I am thinking of starting the introduction with the title 'Unlearning Zionism'. What do you think?

Ronit, 13 December 1999

I had the idea of editing a book about the experiences of dislocation of Palestinian and Israeli women because of my interest in how diasporic and occupation experiences impact women as gendered beings. I had just read the work of Homi Bhabha (1994) and I was attracted by his idea of an 'inter-national' space for counter-narratives (where the hyphen is not only the space for commonalities but for subversion as well) and felt that our voices, the voices of anti-nationalist feminists who have been affected by diasporicity of any kind, is one form of counter-narrative to the masculinist, nationalist narration of nation, and in particular to the Zionist narration of nation, which, in the course of inventing itself (see Anderson, 1983), constructed a series of 'nativist' foundational narratives.

Because women are often excluded from the story of nations and because of the important work done by Israeli feminists (mostly outside of Israel) such as Simona Sharoni (1993), Nira Yuval-Davis (1982, 1997) (but also within Israel, for example Erella Shadmi, 1992, and others) and by Palestinian feminists (also mostly out of Palestine) such as Souad Dajani (1994), Nahla Abdo (1994),[1] and others, I wanted to collect these gendered narratives as one response to the hitherto exclusively mascu-line-militarist narrations of nation, on both side of the equation.

Another reason that I wanted to work on this project was my com-mitment to autobiographical personal narratives as a crucial way of learning about the construction of gendered selves in the process of nationalising histories. My own work, on the gendered relations between Israel and the Shoah, or Holocaust (Lentin, 2000), centres on Zionism as a masculine construction that, in the process of creating itself, silenced and feminised not only the Palestinians, but also the (Jewish) diaspora, the Shoah and its survivors. I say clearly in all my work that I do not think anything can be written about Zionism or Israel in isolation from the Israeli occupation. I actually subtitled my book *Re-occupying the Territories of Silence*, arguing that occupation and territories are central to any theorisation of Zionism. I employed per-sonal narratives of Israeli writers who are daughters of Shoah sur-vivors, and my own autobiography, to which the silence about the Shoah, but also about the dispossession and occupation of Palestini-ans, was central, at least until 1967. Using autobiographical personal narratives to break the conspiracy of silence seemed to me a powerful feminist methodology to give voice to a voiceless, female experience of dislocation.

Very soon after I sent out a call for papers on various e-mail lists, I was ticked off by a woman who became one of the contributors to this book; she said that editing such a book without a Palestinian co-editor was tantamount to a re-colonisation of the lives of Palestinian women. With my politics, anti-Zionist, feminist, anti-racist and all that, I was embarrassed that I had to be told this obvious truth.

As you know, Nahla, we have been dialoguing by e-mail for months now and have moved from formality to as much closeness as e-mail permits, because we are both working hard to challenge our own understandings of nationalism and the effect of silencing and erasure. However, though challenging Zionist occupation and its results for Palestinians, both in Palestine and in the diaspora, is, for me, the central point in making sense of women's experiences of exile, migration, dispossession, and diasporicity, we must, as you say, also challenge other nationalisms and ask whether feminism and nationalism are compatible in our lives and in the lives of our contributors.

I am a committed anti-racist. I spend most of my waking time in Ireland today not only as a university lecturer whose brief is the sociology of racism and nationalism, but also as an anti-racist activist, in the face of Ireland's increasingly visible racism towards asylum seekers and other indigenous and incoming 'aliens'. I feel we must approach this project from an anti-racist, anti-classist premise. However, realising that Zionism – and this is not easy to write, even though I am an avowed anti-Zionist Israeli – is *racist* means that in the dialogue between us, and between our contributors through their various essays, there can be no real equality. Because, despite the fact that some of the contributors, myself included, have a recent family history as Jewish refugees in Nazi-occupied Europe, in Israel-Palestine we belong to the occupiers and you to the occupied. Indeed, as you say, Zionism and the existence of the state of Israel as a Jewish state have different meanings for you and for me.

But there is also a class element – the essays we shall end up with will, necessarily, be written by women with access to education and cultural capital and may not, therefore, represent the lives of refugee women and working-class women. Although several Palestinian contributors are writing about their experience as, and work with, refugee women, issues of representation must not be glossed over.

The challenge is almost too daunting. But in order for it not to paralyse us, you and I must not fall into positions of moral superiority (of the occupied) or guilt (of the occupiers) but address them as honestly as we can, despite the pain involved.

Nahla, 10 January 2000

Unmasking the Zionist settler project in Palestine is a first step in understanding the processes that have led to Palestinian women's dispossession, dislocation, and diasporic existence. This process involves two simultaneous tasks. The first involves the deconstruction of the Zionist myth of 'solving the problem of people (primarily European/Ashkenazi Jews) without land by settling them in a land (Palestine) without people'; the second requires the reconstruction of the reality of Zionism as materialised in the form of the Jewish state of Israel.

These tasks, as we both know, have been invariably attempted by several Palestinian and anti- or non-Zionist, mainly male, academics and authors (Said, 1979; Zureik, 1979; Hadawi, 1988; Shafir, 1989; Marshall, 1995; Peled and Shafir, 1996, among others). A feminist deconstruction of these tasks has also been attempted, albeit largely separately, by both Palestinian feminists (Abdo, 1991, 1993; Dajani, 1994) and anti-Zionist Jewish feminists (Yuval-Davis, 1982; Shohat, 1988; Gottlieb, 1993; Sharoni, 1994; Lentin, 2000; see also Abdo and Yuval-Davis, 1995). What is original in our project is our approach, our attempt at unmasking Zionism from a gender or, rather, feminist perspective of Jewish and Palestinian feminists for whom Zionism has constructed and shaped their life experiences differently, both as Israeli and as diasporic citizens. Also specific to the approach we bring into this project is our attempt at interrogating the classed and gendered construction of Palestinian nationalism and the classed, gendered, and racial construction of Zionism and its materialised form of the Jewish state. The method we chose, namely, dialoguing these differences and constructions, will, I hope, produce a bridge or a new pathway for more Palestinian and Jewish Israeli women to walk onto with less fear hanging on from the past and present and more hope towards a better future, particularly for Palestinian women.

ZIONISM, RACISM AND THE PALESTINIAN NATIONAL ASPIRATIONS To be honest, due to my experience as a Palestinian in the diaspora and a citizen of Israel, I admit that my feminism, while anti-nationalistic, has not been anti-national. Being anti-national would have rendered me indifferent towards the Zionist or the Israeli racist and nationalistic exclusion and oppression of the community of women and men I belong to. As argued elsewhere (Abdo, 1991), Zionism is a nationalistic exclusivist and exclusionary movement, which when institutionalised in the state of Israel was expressed in policies and practices of racial discrimination and national exclusion. The racism and colonialism of the Jewish state was my experience not only because it ruined the lives of about 80 per cent of 'my' people during the 1948 Nakba, or because it continues, since 1967, to subjugate millions of Palestinians in the Occupied Territories of the West Bank and Gaza (not to mention other occupations of the Golan Heights and Southern Lebanon), but also, and perhaps more poignantly, because of my very national identity as a citizen of the state.

For most of my life as a Palestinian (with Israeli citizenship), I was always reminded that I have no place or space in my own homeland, reminded I was inferior to the non-Palestinian (Jewish) citizens of Israel, all of which was done not in the name of a straightforward patriarchal rule against women, but rather against 'me' as a member of an 'inferior', 'backward', 'subjugated', and 'alien' nation. My very presence and belonging has often been denied. The overwhelming obsession of the Jewish state with my national identity, expressed, among other ways, in the confiscation of land, the Judaisation of Palestinian land (see Abdo in this volume), the imprisonment and silencing of critical voices, the distortion of our history in textbooks at schools, the denial to Palestinian citizens of equal access to labour, education, political and other areas of the public sphere, had the impact of subsuming my feminist identity under my national one.

When at elementary schools we were forced to decorate the classrooms to celebrate Israel's birth and march in the streets singing in a language which my mother still does not understand, songs which glorify Israel; when even, as teenagers in high school, we were forced to deny our Palestinian belonging and punished if we drew our flag in public, and were denied poetry and literature written even by Palestinian citizens of the state, such as works by Mahmoud Darwish and the late Tawfeeq Zayyad, we were in fact encouraged, if not forced, to adopt our Palestinian nationalism blindly and unquestionably. Growing up in Nazareth, going to schools which were basically rented rooms in different places, having to suffer the cold of the winter and the heat of the summer, denied any simple facility other non-Palestinian (Jewish) citizens took for granted, be it playgrounds, labs, libraries and so on; having to study under the light of a small lamp (as electricity shortage in Nazareth was the norm rather than an aberration); having to travel long distances at a young age to bring water from Mary's-well (as water shortages were also common) – we knew we had to study hard and work twice as hard as Jewish Israeli citizens did to achieve high education. And then the real moment strikes you, as an adult who completed high school successfully and is ready for university education, you begin to realise that you cannot take this subject: it is connected with Israeli security; you cannot take another one: it is reserved for those who serve in the army. You cannot, cannot, and cannot. But adulthood brings also its internal revolutionising consciousness and the ability to face silencing with voice and subjugation with resistance.

Nahla, 23 January 2000

That was a small part of my experience of Zionism. I resented and rejected Zionism as a national movement because for me it meant the opposite of everything libratory. Logically, one could not conciliate between a movement that is colonial, settler, and aggressive in nature, yet claims to be liberating and freeing. How could the Algerian national movement fighting French colonialism, the South African national movement fighting apartheid, and the Palestinian movement fighting Zionism be compared, let alone equated with Zionism?

As elaborated elsewhere (Abdo, 1994), Palestinian nationalism, in contradistinction to Zionism, is a liberatory movement with the potential for opening up a space for social justice and gender issues. Zionism, on the other hand, is the force which suppresses and subjugates the very existence and identity of the Palestinians. It is this very context, both lived and experienced, which shaped the development of my national identity. This is my adulthood, which was experienced as a Palestinian, an Arab, an 'Israeli' citizen. Who was the Palestinian during the 1960s and 1970s, particularly after Israel had lifted the military rule over its Palestinian citizens? Was she an Arab? An Israeli? An Arab Israeli? An Israeli Arab? A Palestinian Arab? A Palestinian Israeli? The list goes on! It depends on who you ask! We were hardly asked who we are or how we would like to define (identify) ourselves. As people denied their own national identity, we were nonentities, referred to in the Israeli official statistics as 'non-Jews' or 'others', and sometimes as Muslims, Christians, Bedouins, and Druze. The latter, incidentally, were altogether removed from any Arab context. It is interesting to note also that not all of us Arabs were even considered Arabs. The Eurocentric and Orientalist character of Zionism has often equated Arab with Muslim. Christian Arabs were Christians only and not Arabs. I often found it frustrating as a university student in Israel to have to prove to Jewish friends and colleagues of mine that I am an Arab with a Christian background. Ironically, though, later on in life, I had to justify to my own people my right to marry a Palestinian Arab who is from a Muslim background.

The national question undoubtedly occupied – and continues, albeit not fully willingly, to occupy to a certain extent – a big part of my life. During the mid- and late 1970s in Israel, much of my energy as an activist, whether at the university or outside, was spent reaffirming my identity as a Palestinian. The national struggle was accepted – for women – by Palestinian society as a legitimate struggle and field of involvement. Women activists, especially in the late 1970s, while not abundant, were quite visible. The late 1970s were a particularly active era, especially for Palestinian university students, who waged a struggle against their forced enrolment in the Israeli security system. During that time the state came up with a new law forcing all students, including Palestinians, to act as the security force on entrances and exits of university buildings. The logic was the fight against 'terrorism'. While

Israeli Jewish students, themselves members of the military establishment, would do the service with machine guns in their hands, Arab students were ordered to do the same but without weapons ... they were not trusted to carry weapons! Arab students who refused to do the service were threatened with being thrown out of the university. Resistance to the 'national security' order along with other politics waged by students resulted in several Arab students being detained and/or jailed. I was one of these students. Without going into this experience here, it suffices to say that for political prisoners, Israeli jails are inhumane to say the least. In detention as well as jail, Israeli officials break and ridicule any and every human rights law, every international convention and every ethical or moral principle and code known to humanity.

It is not surprising, as I have mentioned earlier, that this experience has created favourable conditions for prioritising nationalism over gender issues, for making me more a 'Palestinian' than a gendered being, a woman. This experience was partly strengthened further and partly shaken during the 1980s, particularly in the late 1980s during the Intifada.

Ronit, 7 February 2000

Nationalism ... big sigh ... what can I say? If we agree that nations are 'imagined communities' (Anderson, 1983), something which we may not agree on of course, then we must ask whether the recent resurgence of Palestinian nationalism has been imagined mostly (merely?) in response to (Zionist) oppression? Has it been imagined in relation to oppression in the same way that Zionist nationalism might have been imagined in response to anti-Semitic oppression in nineteenth-century Europe?

But why do I find myself wishing to defend something that I do not believe in? Perhaps it is because I see more similarities than differences between Israeli (Jewish) and Palestinian nationalisms, both allegedly aiming at constructing autonomy, independence, self-determination. There are, of course, many differences too, but as a feminist, I cannot but argue that nationalism is conceived by and for men (Anderson's 'horizontal brotherhood'), without taking into account either the experiences of women, or their active participation in national liberation struggles. Souad Dajani (1994), for instance, argued that during the 1987–93 Intifada, in which women played a central role, there was a serious backlash against Palestinian women, many of whom vowed not to go in the footsteps of their Algerian sisters, who were sent back home after playing such a central role in the independence struggle against the French.

My critique of nationalism also stems from my understanding of Zionist nationalism as a masculine construction, in which the 'new Hebrew' was male, and in which diaspora Judaism was feminised, in contrast with Israeli nationalism. Various Israeli feminist scholars (e.g. Dafna Izraeli, 1981; Deborah Bernstein, 1992) have interrogated the role women played in the early years of Zionism and attempted to explode the gender equality myth. What most of them failed to do, however, was to make a direct link between the colonising nature of Zionism and its gender-oppressive nature. I wonder to what extent Palestinian feminists, as Dajani proposes, can incorporate the social (gender) agenda into the national agenda. Or must that pose a split in these feminists' subjectivities, as you suggest, between your feminist selves and your national selves?

'Identity', as has been argued by many (e.g. Stuart Hall, 1992), is a process, rather than fixed and ahistorical. Aware of the challenges issued by majority world and black feminists (e.g. Ahmed, 1982; Mohanty, 1991) to Western feminism in relation to being discursively constructed as a unitary 'woman' and to Western feminism's prioritising gender as the uppermost category of analysis, I agree with you that gender is not always the main factor in our intersection of subordinations. Our identities are gendered, raced, ethnicised, but, as you argue so forcefully, also nationalised. I take on board your nationalism, but where is mine? Do I still have a nationality? A nationalism?

In 2000 I taught a student-led seminar discussion on nationalism and feminism, which opened with the student asking participants to indicate whether nationalism was dominant in their country, and whether they identified with their country's nationalism. When it came to me, although I have lived in Ireland for the past 30 years, I answered in relation to Israel, that yes, nationalism was dominant in 'my' country, and no, I not only did not identify with Israeli nationalism, I had been engaged in struggling against it since 1967. Another student, a young woman also born in Israel, but living in the United States for the past few years, also answered in relation to Israel, and her answer was similar, although less adamant than mine. We then mused aloud about why we chose Israel as 'our' country, rather than Ireland or the US. There is no rational answer, I suppose. Israel is 'mine' in a variety of ways, mostly to do with family, love and hate, anger, frustration, passion, shame, guilt, struggle. Ireland is also 'mine' – in that I am a citizen, and a critical one at that – but it is not 'mine' in any way like Israel, my loved-hated (m)other-land, is. In a feminist conference on women, war, and peace in Zagreb in 1996, I argued that because Israel is 'mine' in all those complex and multilayered ways, I must take responsibility for its deeds and misdemeanours. Responsibility, but not blame. A Serb woman also present at that conference argued against me owning up to that belonging, to that responsibility. For her, a lesbian feminist activist, Serbia could never be 'hers' after the atrocities of the Bosnian war. And she refused to assume responsibility. Interestingly, although the Serb participants were eventually allowed to join the conference after being detained on the Croatian border for several hours, the only participant prevented from attending the memorable conference – despite all efforts by Daphna Golan, the former director of Bat Shalom – was the Palestinian participant, the peace activist Jihad Abu Zneid, whom the Israeli authorities did not allow to travel to a women's peace conference because she did not possess the right papers (see Abu Zneid, 1997).

It is because I assume that responsibility that this dialogue is more painful than I had imagined it would be when I suggested writing this introduction as a dialogue. Because in engaging with our entwined respective autobiographies, about which we really do not yet know enough, I must take responsibility for your jailing, for your pain, for your anger. But I cannot take them away. And my own pain of loss and dislocation pales in comparison – here goes that guilt I was cautioning myself against earlier. Because my dislocation was not caused by your people, but yours has been caused by mine. Because your pain is my responsibility, but mine is not your responsibility.

But I am becoming emotional. Is it in preparation for our first meeting next week, when we will present our preliminary thoughts about editing a collection across diversity in the Israeli Association for Feminist Studies and Gender Research in Beit Berl? I must confess I feel anxious about the meeting. You have kindly invited me to Gaza as your guest, which is as it should be – me being your guest, rather than you being mine. You have also insisted on delivering your part of the presentation in English or Arabic, although the organisers stipulated they preferred us to speak in Hebrew. It is a dilemma, but I feel we should both not speak Hebrew, despite the organisers' wishes. At every step of the dialogue new issues arise, not only around diversity, but also around identity construction and power relations, some more explicit than others.

In the year between the last contribution and the following contributions, we continued to speak, by e-mail, about practical matters relating to various essays. Some months were quieter than others; we were away from our desks, doing other things. Then, in September 2000, with the beginning of the al-Aqsa Intifada, our e-mails became different; we mostly passed on to each other electronic communications of various lists. You sent me the enraged, raging communications of Palestinians, women and men, about the Intifada, and I sent you, less frequently, e-mails from Israeli feminist organisations such as Bat Shalom and New Profile who, after a short period of confusion (see Lentin in this volume), began working in earnest to oppose the continuing occupation and the suppression of Palestinian populations, and in particular the violent attacks by the Israeli police and armed forces on Israel's Palestinian citizens in October 2000. We continued to talk, but our dialogue was different as we deliberated the way forward with this book. We asked all the contributors to update and amend their essays in light of the Intifada. Some Israeli contributors decided to drop out; others responded that they could not revise, and their essays had to be included as written prior to the 2000–1 events (although in the end most did revise). Some Palestinian contributors never responded, others decided not to contribute in light of the resistance to co-operation with Israelis on any project, others wrote their essays only after the al-Aqsa Intifada broke out, and others again updated their contributions. You and I continued our dialogue, but a major theme was our disgust, if not surprise, at the self-silencing of Israeli feminists, most of whom – together with other Israeli intellectuals – lined up with Barak's government. We wondered whether we should continue to write our introduction in dialogue style and finally decided that this was the best way.

Nahla, March 2001

No problem, Ronit … we will continue the dialogue style.

After reading my essay, you responded, 'You were right, Nahla, about the silencing that Jewish feminists employ against Palestinian feminists or even Jewish feminists who do not think like them!'

I think that the main reason for the strategy of silencing employed by Jewish feminists, I must say, both in Israel and in the West, is the ease with which Israeli and Jewish feminists of the Zionist ideology have internalised Zionist practices and continue to intentionally and consciously conflate 'people', 'government', and the 'state' in one, and turn this one into the sole ontology of Jewishness.

These women are mentally conditioned to equate Jewishness with Zionism and people with the state. Zionist hegemony has made it impossible for them to see this institutionalised ideology as what it really is. Zionism, for most Jewish feminists, is seen as a religious taboo that no one can touch, investigate, question, let alone criticise. For many, Zionism is equal to nationalism, and if you betray your nationalism, you betray your people and delegitimise your very existence. Criticising Zionism for them thus becomes tantamount to self-destruction! By religiously refusing to touch this taboo (Zionism), these feminists are giving a clear message: *We choose to be blind about Zionism no matter what anybody else thinks.*

This blindness and unwillingness to disentangle people from government-state makes it difficult for them to see Zionism as an ideology of settler-colonial power, and thus necessarily oppressive, exclusionary, and racist. Apartheid as a regime, as the state, was also ingrained in the very mentality of most white settlers in South Africa. It took a real shaking off from the outside to begin to shake the oneness of individuals and regime in South Africa. It will take a real shaking off, a real Intifada in the mentality of Israeli and Jewish feminists, to change their position on Zionism and on Israel as a racist regime, and allow them to begin to think of Jewish identity in separation from the Jewish state.

I am amazed, if not totally baffled, by the notion that women who call themselves feminists – and some even are identified as progressive – are still so weak intellectually that they cannot shake off their own oppression from within.

Our experience of speaking together at the February 2000 Israeli feminist conference in Beit Berl is just one example of what I am saying. Remember how some Israeli self-defined feminists tried to *violently* silence me and make me shut up, because of my insistence on contextualising my speech, because I was trying to analyse the historical framework within which my experience has unfolded. Of course, as a Palestinian citizen of Israel my experience was one of living under a racist state that tried its utmost, through laws, policies, and practices, to exclude me and my people from the wider socio-economic, political, and cultural rights owed to us as Israeli citizens.

My shock and real astonishment was at knowing that Israeli feminists were open to knowledge, to new ideas, new theories, and new methods of research, but that all this knowledge came from the West. They were willing to go anywhere to build 'sisterhood' with women abroad, but *they knew nothing about women living in their midst, in the same cities they live in.* They did not know anything about Palestinian women living in 'their' own country!

This state of not knowing your own neighbour, this state of blindness to issues that are very close to you physically and geographically, is not a benign matter at all. It is, I believe, a conscious decision on their part to ignore the Palestinian 'other' within.

Another reason why I was appalled by the reaction of the Israeli feminists to my presentation was because I expected them to be better informed than Western (Canadian) Jewish feminists, many of whom have never ever been to Israel yet defend Israel blindly. The fact, however, is different. Apparently, Jewish feminists in the West can be potentially more open to cleansing their minds from all forms of racism and oppression, including a serious attempt on the part of an increasing number to renounce Zionism as a form of racism.

Anti-Zionism must not be conflated with anti-Semitism. Throughout my life in Israel and despite all my criticisms of Zionism as implemented by Israeli state racism, and in spite of all my friends and colleagues' criticisms of the same state, none of us has been accused of anti-Semitism. I always thought, as a member of the Semitic people, that no one could identify me against my 'self'! To my greatest surprise, that was not my experience in exile. In North America, anti-Semitism is turned into a label used left and right by some groups at the sound of any criticism against the state of Israel.

The last section in my essay in this volume is entitled 'The Changed and the Changer'. I borrowed this subtitle from an article written about twenty years ago by Sherry Gorelick, a Jewish feminist activist. Gorelick, a sociology professor at Rutgers, decided, after the 8 March 1983 celebration of International Women's Day in Toronto, to study the events around that day. She titled her article 'The Changer and the Changed: Methodological Reflections on Studying Jewish Feminists' (Gorelick, 1989). Gorelick came to visit me for an interview which I reluctantly gave, asking for anonymity and refusing her the use of a tape recorder. To refresh my memory, while writing these words I decided to call Sherry Gorelick. She reminded me of my fears at the time and said that I was so scared I told her that 'walls have holes'!

My negative reaction to Sherry, who later became a good friend, was based on the bitter 'silencing' experience I went through during the 8 March event of the same year. The theme of that day was colonialism and national struggles in the hottest areas of the world at the time: South Africa, El Salvador, and Palestine.

Unanimous support for the South African speaker! Unanimous support and solidarity with the El Salvadorian struggle! And for the presentation on Palestine, a standing ovation by the majority, while havoc was unleashed by a very small number of Jewish feminists, apparently influential in the feminist organisation in Toronto. During my presentation, I read a poem by Mahmoud Darwish condemning Zionism for its dispossession of the Palestinians, the grabbing of their land, the destruction of their physical and cultural existence. Zionism at the time was declared by the whole world, except South Africa and the US, to be a form of racism. So I was not alone in describing Zionism as racist and making sure that I differentiated between Judaism and Zionism.

No matter how scientific, objective, and reasonable I tried to be and was sure I was, a handful of Jewish feminists were 'outraged', I was told, and went out angry, furious and some even in tears! The next day I received all kinds of messages from friends speaking about how 'awful' I was, according to some of those women. Worse yet, I was accused of being anti-Semitic and at least one article to that effect was written about me in a local newspaper.

For many years after that event, I was unable to understand what the hell had happened there. How dare these Jewish women call me anti-Semitic? Do they not know that I am as Semitic as they? Do they not know that I know Israel better than all of them combined? Do they not know that of all of them, I was the only one who knew the Hebrew language, and that I read Israeli press more often than all of them combined? What was this fury all about?

I realised much later that most of them knew that I came from there and that I knew more than they did about real life there, but none of that was important to them. In fact, they could not have cared less about who I am and what I represent, what my feminist ideas were or what I was standing for or calling for. All they cared about was that I, a Palestinian woman, dared to tell them the state they supported was racist; that they should distance themselves from the state which claimed to represent them; that they were wrong in supporting a state like Israel. Putting it differently, all these Jewish feminists were outraged that someone, and a Palestinian at that, had *challenged* their very beliefs, their very ideals, the very foundation of their moral existence!

It was the challenge – the shaking off, the Intifada which my talk had potentially engendered in them – which was most threatening to them. The challenge seemed so strong because it had the potential for real change, the potential for changing them into something different.

We all know that the *new*, the *different*, and the *unknown* is almost always very threatening and causes real fear. It takes special courage and brave souls to take up the challenge and undergo the shakeup from within.

Shakeup, or Intifada from within is what Amy Gottlieb has gone through, partly influenced by the events of that day. In an article entitled: 'Not in My Name: A Jewish Feminist Challenges Loyalty to Israel' (1993), Gottlieb recounts in detail the events of the day and attests to the difficulty and complexity of having to come out as anti-Zionist.

Maybe Israeli feminists need to get outside of the Israeli society, which tends to be a breeding ground for more and more right-wing fanatics and racist forces, like the current prime minister and his aides. Maybe they need to unlearn their conscious state of ignorance and arrogance and learn how to disentangle themselves from the State, how to save their *humanity* as women, as human beings, and refuse to turn into cheap political tools used by the State to justify its own colonialist and expansionist interests. Maybe they need to read Sherry Gorelick; maybe they need to read Amy Gottlieb, maybe they need to read Nira, Ronit, Ella, Simona, etc., more than Sharon, Barak, Peres, Rabin, and all of these statesmen.

What do you think?

Love for now, Nahla

Ronit, 30 March 2001

For me, trying to make sense of the ferocious repression of the Palestinians during the 2000 Intifada inevitably means making links with my understanding of the Holocaust. On 13 and 14 March 2001, I organised an international conference in Dublin titled 'Re-presenting the Shoah for the Twenty-First Century'. The keynote speaker was Zygmunt Bauman, whose seminal work *Modernity and the Holocaust* (Bauman, 1989) was central to my beginning to make some sense of the Shoah in relation to my own work. Bauman's argument centred on the indivisibility of morality. His argument as to the victimised becoming victimisers was powerful. The Bible, he reminded his listeners, has a 'Thou shalt not kill' edict, but no edict 'Thou shalt not be killed'. Therefore survival, at any price, tends to be valorised above morality in the way we memorise and commemorate the Shoah. The Israeli contributors to the conference were scandalised. Had Bauman not heard the phrase 'He who comes to kill you, thou shalt kill him first', they asked. Bauman was not dissuaded by their argument. For him, the possibility that your enemy might kill you does not mean you should kill him first. He insisted that 'killing one person is where the calamity of humanity lies'.

Bauman's argument is far more complex than my representation of it (see Bauman, 2000). What I took from the interchange was, yet again, the refusal by most Israelis to separate the historical fate of the Jews, and the Shoah in particular, from the moral permission Jews allegedly have to victimise their contemporary 'enemies' and the permission they give themselves to view Israelis as the victims of Palestinian oppression and violence without comparing this victimhood – sometimes translated into the real fear of mothers for their children in relation to 'suicide bombs', for instance – to the Israeli victimisation of the Palestinians.

My friend Rela Mazali of 'New Profile – the Movement for the Civilisation of Society in Israel', a strong feminist voice struggling against militarisation and oppression (and a contributor to this volume), sends me endless e-mails, which keep me abreast of Israeli feminist peace activism and keep my spirits up. One such recent mailing was Yehudit Harel's e-mail to the *Alef* electronic list (16 March 2001). Harel, a bereaved Israeli mother and a daughter of survivors, criticised the ongoing manipulation of the Shoah and thus the memory of the six million victims in order to minimise the atrocities committed by Israelis: 'As a daughter of a family exterminated in Auschwitz, I am deeply ashamed that we, the descendants of the survivors, are directly responsible for the catastrophe of another people, their uprooting and ongoing suffering. Moreover, even now – 52 years after the *Nakba* and the establishment of our state – when we could try and make up for the evils done in the past, we are incapable of taking the right actions and instead we continue the brutal oppression of the Palestinian people, including war crimes'.

On 28 March 2001 Rela forwarded a mailing from Hajo G. Meyer, a German-born Auschwitz survivor Jew who, like Bauman, quoted Rabbi Hillel as saying 'What is hateful to you do not do to your fellow' and compared Israeli tactics with Nazi 1930s tactics. These tactics include: acting on previous national humiliation (the Germans in relation to the Treaty of Versailles, the Jews in relation to the traumatisation of the Shoah); the second class citizenship status of the Jews in Nazi Germany and the Palestinians in Israel; the racialisation and differentiation of Jews in Germany and Palestinians in Israel. Meyer quoted an interview with former prime minister Ehud Barak in *Ha'aretz*, 2 February 2001: 'It is because of the Arab character of discourse that their culture does not contain the concept of compromise. Compromise is apparently a Western concept for settling disputes'; and 'In any event they [the Israelis who wanted peace] see that their [Arab] neighbours are not benign. Not part of Western culture'. Meyer also noted that whereas German Jews reacted to their discrimination with meekness, Israeli Palestinians in 2001 are fighting back. However, this difference, he insisted, does not justify their discrimination. Finally, he compares the confinement of Jews to ghettos and the Palestinians to the 'occupied territories' (where Barak has contemptuously called Palestinian areas 'cantons', *Ha'aretz*, 11 January 2001).

Meyer said that his pain was caused by the realisation that 'my own people humiliate the Palestinians day after day in very similar ways, in spite of the wisdom of Rabbi Hillel (not to do unto your friend that which you would not want done to you). This shameful behaviour of the Israelis, Meyer reminded his readers, is vividly described in a shocking article by *Ha'aretz* journalist Amira Hass that ends with the words 'look at yourselves in the mirror and realise how racist you have become....'

Rela's e-mails are 'useful' to me as I recycle them into articles and essays, and forward them to interested Irish and international colleagues, while Rela and her Israeli colleagues continue to do the oppositional work on the ground. I write to her on 29 March 2001, after she writes to say she is glad her mailings serve our joint political aims:

Dear Rela. Yes, your material is 'useful' – if 'useful' is the term for the recycling of mails by 'progressive' Israelis – many of my Israeli friends in London and elsewhere (and also non-Israelis who call themselves 'progressives') spend their time shuffling e-mails – forwarding, writing protest e-mails to government ministers and to President Bush.... Yes, I know all this is 'good work'. But when one reads about the children killed during the Intifada (for instance, in Gideon Levy's articles under the collective title 'The Twilight Zone', in *Ha'aretz*), or when one sees the horrific destruction in Qalqiliah and Gaza yesterday as retaliation for the car bombs – I wonder if all we are doing is massaging our bruised egos, bruised because our own humanity is punctured by these 'evil deeds', while it is people like you and Gila (Svirsky) and others like you, who are putting their bodies where their mouse is (I mean computer mouse, not a spelling mistake for 'mouth'), not us who merely shuffle e-mail messages, who are doing the work Israelis need to do.

And while we ('progressive' Israelis) congratulate ourselves on our 'good work', our Palestinian sisters view us with increasing cynicism, as is demonstrated by the e-mail you forwarded to me on 28 March 2001 from Zeina, responding to the declaration of solidarity with Palestinian women posted by *Bat Shalom*. 'Give it up for all of them warrior princesses' was the subject line of that e-mail. How understandable, and how desperately sad, and, to an extent, how ultimately hopeless.

Love, Ronit

Ronit, 9 May 2001

This is probably my last instalment in our dialogue-introduction. We are well into the reign of Israel's most hawkish prime minister, Ariel Sharon, elected by a large majority despite (or is it because of?) his responsibility for the 1982 invasion of Lebanon and the ensuing massacres in Sabra and Shatila, among many other 'exploits' condemned worldwide. Sharon continues Israel's punitive economic siege and military operations against Palestinian towns, villages, and refugee camps; so far they have killed more than 400 civilians – the most recent being the four-month old baby girl Iman Hejjo of Deir al-Balah refugee camp – and injured 13,000, many of whom are children.

We have both written these instalments – and our continuous e-mail correspondence – from the depth of our multiple diasporic positionalities, yet hopefully, without constructing an ideal homeland, as exiles are often given to do.

Last week I returned from a visit in Haifa to celebrate my mother's eightieth birthday. I was afraid of marring the family reunion by arguing about politics, although Mother and I had made a tacit agreement years ago not to argue about our opposing politics. In your wisdom, you advised me to avoid political arguments with my family; after all, you counselled generously, this was my mother's big day. It was indeed a great reunion as children, grandchildren, relatives, and friends expressed our love and respect for Mother. But echoes of political strife did penetrate the family gathering when my brother, who has been living in the US for thirty years, expressed his disgust with the Palestinian

Haifa city councillor who wanted to change the name of Zionism Avenue back to its original Arabic. 'What does that dirty Arab think?' my usually mild-mannered brother said. When my daughter pointed out that 'that dirty Arab' was a citizen of Israel and a Haifa city councillor, he retorted, 'But this is *our* country'. She did not ask why he was not living in 'our country', but this is hardly the point. The deep involvement (even in the form of utter rejection) with Zionism persists beyond the boundaries of the state, as my brother and I demonstrate.

I was not prepared, however, for Mother's birthday falling during the week of Independence Day. This accentuated the contradiction, for this oppositional diasporic daughter of the Zionist dream, between politics and reality. The streets were festooned with blue and white flags; Mother hurried to fly her flag before I returned from a visit to Jerusalem, saying jokingly that she knew that I 'would not have allowed her' to fly her flag had I been at home. I timed my comings and goings so that I would not be on the street during the sirens commemorating Israeli soldiers who 'fell' in Israel's wars (no chance of commemorating Palestinians thus 'fallen') – I could not countenance the enforced public silence when the sirens sounded and feared public censure if I broke that silence. The dilemmas for an anti-Zionist living in Israel are myriad; it was again made obvious how much easier it is to be oppositional abroad. But more importantly, I was made aware time and again how much more difficult it is to live as a Palestinian under occupation and closure, or as a second-class Palestinian citizen of Israel, than to oppose Zionism from the comfort of my Dublin-based computer.

Yet on another level, during that week when, apart from fireworks and military-style televised independence celebrations, there were also several car bombs and the resultant house demolitions and air raids, I was again aware of the delicate balance between sanctimonious approval of anything Palestinian and the possibility of retaining a critical stance – which means, among other things, being able to critique both Israeli *and* Palestinian nationalisms – and a feminist anti-nationalist stance, even as I abhor Israeli apartheid and racism (terms which have begun being publicly used by Israelis since the outbreak of the al-Aqsa Intifada and the resulting heavy-handed oppression).

After the initial confusion and self-silencing, the Intifada and the resulting oppression have occasioned protests and criticism by a growing number of Israelis, inside and outside the academy, inside and outside the feminist movement. Despite my experience at the Bar Ilan conference, where my paper on the links between the silencing of Shoah survivors and the silencing of the real story of the dispossession of the Palestinians during the 1948 war won near universal censure (Lentin, 2001), there is now a growing number of meetings and conferences in which the politics of protest take centre stage.[2] The Israeli feminist magazine *Noga* devoted a large section of its Spring 2001 edition, subtitled 'Bilada, Bilada' (Her homeland, her homeland), to a series of articles by Palestinian women from the occupied territories and Israeli feminist peace activists under the title 'Don't Say We Didn't Know' (*Noga*, 2001). Feminist peace activism is more visible than ever (see Svirsky in this volume), although the very term 'peace activism' is problematic. I prefer to call it political activism, even if this more general term does not denote the complex, radical, and specific nature of this activism, which includes vigils against the ongoing closure and economic siege, and against racism and apartheid; condolence visits to relatives of Palestinian victims; the rebuilding of demolished Palestinian houses; food distribution in the occupied territories under closure, etc.

However, there is a deep dichotomy between the Israelis doing this work and the alignment of the majority of Israelis – on both sides of the political spectrum – against the Palestinian Authority, whom they accuse of instigating the al-Aqsa Intifada and thus 'betraying' the Israeli political left, and negating the 'concessions' offered by Ehud Barak's government. Israelis – particularly on the left of the political map – insist that the acts of oppression and wanton destruction of Palestinian homes and villages are acts of self-defence, and even those who supported the 'peace process' (as expressed by the Oslo Accords) are mobilising now against the Palestinians' right of return – a serious bone of contention in the Israeli left, but otherwise a broad-ranging consensus among Israelis who maintain a victimhood stance.[3]

But more than anything else, I am struck again and again by the escapist indifference of the majority of Israelis not only to the suffering of Palestinians under occupation, but also to the future of the so-called 'peace process'. Most left-leaning Israelis find it easy to dissociate themselves from the government of Ariel Sharon, who insists that nothing has changed, that he would not give back territories, nor dismantle any settlements (Shavit, 2001: 18–22). It is harder for them to criticise the so-called 'left' government of Sharon's predecessor, Ehud Barak, who was allegedly prepared to make widespread 'concessions' to the Palestinians (not realising the humiliating nature of such 'concessions' …).

But the hardest for 'progressive' Israelis is to criticise Palestinian nationalism, the Palestinian Authority, or Yasser Arafat, who, despite his efforts to collude with Israel in stopping the uprising, is, according to Egypt's President Hosni Mubarak, powerless even to condemn the targeting of Israeli civilians because of the resentment felt by ordinary Palestinians over Israel's heavy-handed economic and military measures against Palestinian civilians (Jansen, 2001: 13). Eli Aminov, my old friend from the days of Matzpen, is one of the few radical Israelis who dare mount such criticism from the left. He argues that the 'legal entity handed over to the PA as part of the Oslo Accords is a de facto state ... an apparatus of coercion and oppression which safeguards the interests of the Palestinian bourgeoisie'. According to Aminov, all the territories and assets transferred to the PA still fail to alter its nature, which, he insists, is dictated by the needs of US imperialism and supported by the CIA and the Israeli security forces. Moreover, Aminov argues, the PA is consolidating its socio-economic position with the help of Israel, which, while effectively enforcing the closure of the territories, is enabling the free movement of goods that benefits the monopolies granted by Arafat to his supporters at the expense of Palestine's poor (Aminov, 2001: 29).

This has nothing to do with the truism that victims do not lie but oppressors always lie, as you have pointed out. However, reading Aminov (who has been my political 'left marker' for decades), I remember you pointing out to me the gap between rich and poor and between privileged and oppressed during my visit with you in Gaza. I remember your anger about gender inequalities in Gazan society, where violence against women is often the result of the men being oppressed and humiliated not only by the Israelis, but also by social inequalities within Palestinian society. And I think about how 'white guilt', self-censorship, and adherence to a sense of 'political correctness' often stop us (me included) from engaging in a fully honest political exchange, made more difficult by my diasporic positionality.

Contemporary diasporic practices, as Clifford (1994) points out, cannot be reduced to (and must therefore transcend) the nation-state or global capitalism: 'while redefined and constrained by these structures, they also exceed and criticise them: old and new diasporas offer resources for emergent "postcolonialisms"' (Clifford, 1994: 302). Clifford points out that anti-Zionist diasporic visions (as I argue in my book; see Lentin, 2000) are not simply rooted/routed in a narrative of return to a literal Jewish nation in Palestine despite a common (Jewish) history of victimisation by scientific racism and anti-Semitism. But, I would add, nor should they simply accept the narrative of Zionism's victims uncritically if the ultimate goal is not merely the establishment of a Palestinian state side by side with Israel, as yet another nationalist project with all its attending political, social, and gender inequalities, but rather turning Israel from an exclusively Jewish state – and the putative Palestine from an exclusively Palestinian state – into a secular democratic state 'of all its citizens'.

It is not easy for me to say all this to you, particularly as I am constantly angry about Israeli racist oppression, about the blanket destruction of Palestinian homes and villages and the loss of innocent lives, including the lives of children and babies (and let me make quite clear that I deplore the self-appointed 'feminist' critics for blaming

Palestinian mothers for allegedly sending their children to the front line, and implicitly for their children's murder by the Israelis). On the other hand, I am also angry about the PA, which, as Aminov argues, is strategically colluding with the Oslo Accords, the sole aim of which is the preservation of the Jewish state.

All this makes my part of the dialogue particularly painful, leaving me more confused and pessimistic than ever before, not only about the prospects for 'peace' (will there ever be true peace, or can we at best expect some sort of 'agreement', I wonder?), but also about my impossible position as an oppositional Israeli diasporic feminist.

Nahla, 15 May 2001 (or the fifty-third Memorial of al-Nakba)

Before I reflect on issues that seem to be somewhat troubling for you, because you do not know how I will react to them, namely, your criticism of 'my' nationalism and especially the PA, I would like to comment on two points you made earlier: the frustration of people like Zeina, and the bravery of people like Amira Hass. Let me say at the outset that the difference between the two resides in neither who is braver, nor who is more frustrated. The real difference is one of power differential, dictated by the ethnicity/nationality/religion of each. Zeina, whom you quote as saying: 'Give it up for all of them warrior princesses', is, I believe, the very same Zeina who has helped translate parts of a contribution in Arabic submitted for our book, and she is the same woman who is working closely with anti-Zionist Jewish feminists here in Canada. Knowing her well, I think that she, not unlike most, if not all of us Palestinian activists and feminists, is frustrated by the lack of adequate action by Israeli (Jewish) feminists. A daughter of a refugee mother born in Lebanon, she sees the devastation of Palestinians by the Israeli military machine while the whole world watches in inaction. Like most of us, she receives the news about the crimes of Israel's Prime Minister Sharon along with the deafening silence of Israeli (Jewish) society at large, and its feminist movement in particular. Like us, she is unable to understand how the Israeli government can get away with its atrocities without an international outcry!

Secondly, I truly believe that all the Zeinas of Palestine wish to follow Amira Hass, and cry out loud: 'Look at yourselves in the mirror and realise how racist you have become'. They/we want to scream like Hajo G. Meyer, the German-born Auschwitz survivor Jew you quoted earlier, and tell the Israelis and the whole world that what Israel is doing is out of 'HATE', out of 'racism', and similar to 'what the Nazis have done'. But they/we cannot do it. We are Palestinians and as such, not allowed to name things as they are! Meyer can say it, Hass can say it, and many other Jews can say it, but not Palestinians! Not Arabs!

They/we are forbidden to say it; not only by Israel or the Jews, but also by the Christian, guilt-ridden West. If they/we say it, they/we will be immediately branded as anti-Semitic and automatically discredited. Just a couple of weeks ago, the *Toronto Star* published an article by Michele Landsberg, a veteran Canadian Jewish feminist, whose previous articles I used to admire, especially those critiquing women's position under the yoke of Muslim dictatorships such as the Taliban regime. But Landsberg, like most Jewish feminists in North America, employs two different standards when it comes to the Middle East: one apologetic to Israel and to Zionism, and the other critical of the rest of the world. Her resentment of the UN conference scheduled by the Non-Allied Movement that took place in August 2001 in South Africa, which was to consider a resolution equating Zionism with racism, made her utter all sorts of sweeping generalisations; she ridiculed the United Nations and even made what amounted to racist remarks about Arabs, Muslims, and almost everybody involved. All this was done to solidify her fervent defence of Israel and Zionism.

I was particularly shocked by the extent to which Landsberg was ready to go in order to defend not the historical sufferings of the Jews, but rather, the state (Israel) and its racist ideology (Zionism). In an attempt to show how Israel is allegedly more democratic than all Arab countries, she says: 'Almost all the Arab countries base their citizenship laws on native parentage. Foreigners don't have a prayer of becoming citizens; Israeli Arabs, in contrast, while often discriminated against, are citizens and have elected members of the Israeli parliament'. How outrageous! Palestinians in Israel, who are the indigenous people of historic Palestine are turned by Landsberg into immigrants, while the overwhelming Jewish population of Israel, who *are* immigrants and settlers, are made into 'indigenous' people! For a Canadian like Landsberg, this is like saying that 'Natives in Canada should be grateful that the European white settlers have accepted them in their midst and given them some rights'. Elsewhere in her article Landsberg concludes that 'the destruction of health, homes, jobs and infrastructure on *both sides* is incalculable' (emphasis added). In addition to the grave historical inaccuracies in her article, Landsberg adds: 'To keep their people primed for endless war, Palestinians have inculcated racist hatred of Jews and of Israel in school texts, official newspaper articles and leaders' pronouncements, in language so hideous it would have made Goebbels grin' (see *Toronto Star,* 29 April 2001, A2).

The danger here, it must be stressed, lies not so much in the sickening content of such erroneous, false, and rather racist public statements, but more importantly in the fact that the Zionist pro-Israel lobby can easily find listening ears and receptive arms to publish and publicise all sorts of propaganda, including racist utterances, and get away with it, while the Zeinas of Palestine or the Arab world must swallow their pride silently! Landsberg's article, consciously or not, can only add fuel to the already existing hatred and contempt for Arabs, Muslims, and Palestinians in the Judeo-Christian West.

Still, I must admit that your struggle as an anti-Zionist Jewish feminist must be equally frustrating, perhaps even more difficult, if different. I know it. I experienced it when I used to stand in solidarity with my Jewish anti-Zionist 'Women in Black' friends on the streets of Toronto, protesting the Israeli invasion of Lebanon. I have seen the hatred in the eyes and faces of many Israeli or pro-Israeli Zionists towards anti-Zionist Jews and especially feminists. Nonetheless, it is these 'marginal' but honest voices of peace and change which can lead the way.

About the position you were 'afraid' was going to make me angry, namely, your criticism of the PA, let me begin by saying that my critical position on the PA is widely publicised. Because of the need for reform and change within the Palestinian Authority, I decided to publish my work in a venue accessible to most Palestinians. Hence my choice of *The Journal of Palestine Studies*. The article (Abdo, 1999) presents a clear challenge to the PA (since Oslo, Palestinians have debated the national representativeness of the 'Authority', and most Palestinians prefer the term 'Authority' over 'National Authority') for its failure to deliver the long-promised democratic governance pledged throughout the national struggle and especially during the first Intifada, and its failure to truly represent the Palestinian 'national' collective. In particular, the article blames the Authority for the lack of transparency, professionalism, and accountability in its governance. It reminds the Authority of the general disappointment it has generated among many sections of Palestinian civil society, especially women, objecting to the patronage system it employs in appointing high officials and holding the Authority responsible for the deterioration in women's position, among other things.

While that article was very clear about the almost total economic and political dependence of the Authority on Israel and the United States, this dependency, I argued, would only lead to other forms of subjugation, including the realms of the social, gender, and cultural. The article also points to the Authority's economic mismanagement and its reluctance to abide by the very laws it has established. Without going into more detail on a position already made public, let me say that I concur with many of the points made by your friend Aminov. Finally, my critical stance on the Palestinian Authority, which, by the way, was developed soon after my field visit in 1994, continued through different means, such as letters, petitions, etc. Just yesterday, I signed a petition put up by *Miftah* (a democratic platform directed by

Hanan Ashrawi) criticising existing mismanagement, and the lack of transparency by the various legislative bodies.

Having said that, however, I think I can still separate nationalism, as in a national liberation movement, from institutionalised national-ism or state-nationalism. In my 1991 article, after a field visit to the 'women of the Intifada', where I witnessed their work, courage, enthu-siasm, and commitment to change, I was optimistic, like them, about a better future, and trusted they would be rewarded at the hands of the state-in-process. This hope, unfortunately, has begun to dwindle grad-ually since then. Like me, several other Palestinian feminist authors have begun to launch clear criticisms of the semi- or quasi-state and demand their due rights. In fact, for the past six years or so, it has become clear to me that my critical feminist identity is more important than my national one. It is for this reason I chose to concentrate my work with refugee women not on issues of 'nationalism', but rather on issues directly related to their development and freedom, such as their right to education, jobs, public life, and a life without violence, domes-tic or otherwise. This was also the reason for my heavy involvement in helping to establish a gender research unit, in training women – mainly refugees – in the methods of doing feminist research, and in doing, with them, field visits and interviews in the refugee camps.

Nonetheless, you probably have noticed a 'nationalist' tone, which seems to be directing some of my writing in this introduction as well as in my essay. This tone, I admit, is an expression of the spontaneous – albeit real – reaction I have developed since the Second Intifada. My 'nationalism' here is not in defence of the Authority; it is not in defence of the feeble, lame, and dependent entity; it is not in defence of the Palestinian male patriarchy, which continues to oppress my fellow sis-ters. My nationalism, rather, is an expression of my support of the ongoing popular movement, which is using all means (stones, demon-strations, sit-ins, protests, petitions) to resist Israeli colonialism; it is an expression of my deep involvement, from thousands of miles afar, in this legitimate movement as it struggles against Israeli military occu-pation. Deep inside, I realise the difference between Arafat's regime and the people in the streets. I understand the difference between the involvement of the Authority and the involvement of many sectors of civil society. I also understand the spontaneity with which many chil-dren take up stones and throw them at Israeli soldiers in a gesture to rid themselves of the foreign enemy.

You probably will be surprised to hear that I also understand the involvement of most of the police and security forces. You might ask how I can justify this, knowing that this force is part of the Authority and operates under its orders. Well, the overwhelming rank-and-file police and security forces are made up of young men (few women), as young as eighteen years-old. Many of them were the 'children of the stones' of the first Intifada; most have found themselves unemployed and unemployable; many were forced to quit school as their lives and the lives of their families were interrupted during the first Intifada; those who are employed are hardly trained and mostly underpaid. A couple of days ago (13 May 2001) five of them were assassinated when an Israeli missile hit their car. They were between nineteen and twenty-three years old! Like many others, these young men left their families in the Gaza Strip looking for work in the West Bank, and for over one and a half years were prevented, by the Israelis, from going back to visit their families, many of whom are refugee camp dwellers and live in utter misery.

I fully recognise that the 'national unity' which exists among the very different and differentiated people involved in the Intifada is both constructed and somewhat artificial. There is little, if any, common interest or outlook between, for example, Hamas and the secular forces, whether among Fateh or the Communist Party; between most men and women involved; between the national bourgeoisie, some of whose interests have been hit, but who are still living an advantageous lifestyle, and the camp dwellers whose homes have been destroyed and whose sources of survival have dwindled to near-starvation levels. I fully recognise that nationalism, as an ideology, is blind to gender, class and ethnic/religious affiliation, if not totally biased towards the rich, male and powerful. I know this, I have written about this, and I believe in this. In this sense, I am sure that my 'nationalism' is not blind nationalism. Yet I strongly defend the 'movement' currently going on, on the streets of Ramallah, Gaza, Beit Hanoun, Jabalya, Khan Younis, Nablus, etc. I strongly defend the struggle against Israeli settler colonialism, the anti-colonial movement against occupation and against the foreign invasion of their land, homes, and space. If my struggle with, support for, and almost total identification with what is happening in the streets of the Occupied Territories appears as nationalism, it is also because of the strength of 'feelings' and the almost 'real' emotions, as Benedict Anderson said, that are brought out by the loss of, and the fight for, cultural and material existence.

You suggest a long-term strategic solution in the area, or an answer to the current conflict. Your solution addresses the fundamental problems of the region, as well as the problems of Israeli racism, expansionism, and occupation; it also deals with Palestinian dependency, marginalisation, and lack of democracy. This solution or answer is 'the establishment of a democratic secular state for both peoples'. I do not disagree with this solution at all. It is probably the best solution to our trouble-ridden region. This solution, by the way, is not new; it was adopted by the Palestinian left many years ago and is still, for some, the only viable solution. In fact, Palestinian intellectuals have debated the shape of the future solution for some time now. For some, the solution resides in the establishment of an independent Palestinian state alongside Israel with the right of refugees to return to their homeland; for others, the solution resides in 'One State, Two Nationalities' or a binational state; and for others, it is the 'Democratic Secular State for all Citizens'. All of these options have been developed epistemologically and are still debated.

The reality, however, is that millions of Palestinians continue to live under military occupation and experience aggression and oppression more than they experience life itself! The status of this people is more ontological than epistemological. As the Arabic saying goes, *illi eedoh bil-mayy mish zayy elli eedo bil-nar* (literally, those whose hands are in water are not the same as those whose hands are on fire). Living under daily blockage, bombardment, siege, subjugation, and fear is what marks the daily experience of most Palestinians under occupation. Under these conditions people tend to see the struggle as immediate and one-dimensional. Occupation forces causing death and devastation; settlements causing reduced living opportunities and diminishing possibilities for growth; joblessness, poverty, and misery. The solution to all this, for people living it, is to rid themselves of the direct foreign force, of Israeli occupation and onslaught. All they need now is 'freedom' from occupation. These people did not choose Oslo, nor did they freely elect all or most of the Authority. Their instant reaction was: *any Palestinian leadership, but not Israel!*

The failure of Oslo and its resultant Authority to deliver has been felt by a growing number of Palestinians in the occupied territories, yet the greed and constant expansionism of the more powerful oppressor, Israel, has overshadowed Palestinian internal frustration and contradictions; hence their overwhelming focus on the external enemy. While this is not a justification for, nor an attempt at legitimising the existing Authority and its undemocratic structures, it is an attempt at understanding the ontology of the occupied.

The occupied might try, however relentless is their struggle, to free themselves from the yoke of the occupier and perhaps succeed, but we must not burden them with the task of also freeing their occupier from the latter's own oppression. A democratic secular state is a long-term project that requires readiness and commitment to such a solution on the part of Israeli Jews. Where are the Israeli-Jewish secular democratic forces – I mean forces, not individuals? Where is the Israeli anti-racist, anti-Zionist movement – I mean movement, not individuals? Where is the Israeli anti-militaristic state campaigns – I mean campaigns, not individuals? In a heavily militaristic garrison like Israel, there is hardly a civil society, let alone a serious resistance to this state! Remember our earlier frustration as we lamented the absence of critical feminist voices that would take a truly democratic decision and not speak the state language? Remember our earlier aggravation at the deplorable marginalisation of the forces of true peace and justice in Israel?

Your suggested solution is just too good to be true, practical, or appropriate at this point in the relations, or rather lack of relations, between your people and mine. It needs more legs to stand on, and at least one leg has to be expressed through the emergence of Israeli Jewish voices calling for justice, humanity, freedom, and equality, voices that are made loud enough to be heard beyond the national borders. Yes, there needs to be trust between us, but not the Oslo-type trust or the earlier Sadat-type trust. A new form of trust must be genuinely articulated between Arabs in general and Palestinians in particular on the one hand, and ordinary Israeli Jews, people at grass-roots level, on the other. As it stands, Palestinians do not trust Israelis, and vice versa.

I believe we need a new Intifada in the Israeli streets, where women, men, and children would come out of their secure nets and sheltered lives and begin to notice their neighbours; begin to feel that their 'shelter' and 'security' are artificial and temporary as long as this 'security' is based on the violation of others, while their 'sheltered life' is at the expense of another people's deprivation. Incidentally, these differences are not just across the national borders, that is, between Israel and the Palestinian occupied territories of the West Bank and Gaza. They are also within their own borders, within Israel itself. This is the racialised and ethnicised reality of Israel proper.

Will Israeli (particularly, Ashkenazi) Jews take up the task? Will the haves risk their comfort to share with the have-nots? Even if, one day, they were attacked by amnesia and decided to carry the torch of freedom and democracy in the region, do you think they would be allowed? Let's not forget that the whole Middle Eastern region consists of dictatorships, monarchies, autocracies, and theocracies. Not only that, they are what they are, and in most cases in spite of the will of their peoples – because of the position and role they seem to be required to play within the global system. In this era of globalisation where the nation-state as a concept is immaterial altogether, let alone whether or not it is a democratic state, I am doubtful about this ideal solution!

But giving up, as you well know, is the last thing on the mind of activists. Our belief in dialogue at the grass-roots, intellectual, and at the activist levels remains the only path towards realising true peace and tranquillity amongst our peoples. Let's forge that path and carry on with our mission.

Love, Nahla

A Note on the Order of the Essays

Part I of the book is devoted to the Palestinian contributors. Because of the multiplicity of exiles, dislocation, dispossession, and refugeeism, some of our contributors have also reflected on their experiences in the West and North America (for example, the essays by Abdo, Dajani, Fuchs). The best way to place authors and articles in order is to divide the contributions according to place of exile. It is important to point out that almost all contributors, Palestinians and Jews, have multiple experiences of dislocation and exile. Some of these are by choice, but in most cases, particularly in the case of Palestinians, these exiles are forced. Despite the spatial and temporal differences among the Palestinian contributors, all seem to be united around one particular moment of history, namely, the catastrophic impact al-Nakba has engraved in their lived memory. No matter who the recorder of this part of the history is – young or old, academic, activist, or a member of an NGO – one thing is crystal clear for all: al-Nakba is the historical beginning and point of departure for our 'national', 'cultural' identity. Nonetheless, each section or category is historically specific, while each contribution speaks of a unique experience.

Exile in Lebanon

This section presents the experiences of Samia Costandi, Rosemary Sayigh, and Souad Dajani. Rosemary Sayigh, a wife and mother of Palestinians, has almost a lifelong experience of living with, working with, and advocating the rights of Palestinian camp refugees in Lebanon, while Souad Dajani and Samia Costandi have gone through the culture of dislocation in Beirut. They lived and absorbed the culture of al-Nakba and were witnesses to their own and their parents' suffering as the latter went through forced expulsion from Palestine. These contributions also speak of Israeli atrocities during the invasion of Lebanon in 1982 and recount the horror undergone by Palestinians during the massacres in Sabra and Shatila.

Home as Exile: Living under Israel's Racialised Rule

This section deals with the experiences of women whose parents were internally dislocated and moved from one city or village to another within the state of Israel after its establishment. These include Isis Nusair, Nabila Espanioly, Badea Warwar, and Nahla Abdo. The contributions here are particularly poignant in that the contributors, like the rest of this sector of the Palestinian people, have long been marginalised and, until lately, cast out of the configuration of 'the political solution'. These essays reveal the delicate struggle of identity undergone by Palestinians in Israel: the struggle between, on the one hand, maintaining their cultural and national identity, on the ruins of which the Jewish state was established, and, on the other, their struggle to achieve social, civil, economic and political equality as citizens of the state.

Life under Occupation: West Bank and Gaza Strip

This section articulates experiences of exile and dispossession in the Israeli-occupied territories of the West Bank and Gaza Strip. Contributors to this section include Nadera Shalhoub-Kevorkian, Mona El Farra, and Hala Mannaa. Shalhoub-Kevorkian, who is originally a Palestinian citizen of Israel, has lived and worked in the West Bank for the better part of her adult life. Both El Farra and Mannaa live in Gaza city. Contributions in this section represent the agony, fear, and frustration experienced by the contributors as all have lived and are still living the Intifada and suffering from daily Israeli raids and bombardments. While each of these contributors provides a unique experience, they all detail the severity of present life as expressed by destruction of homes, including refugee homes, uprooting of trees, destruction of roads and other infrastructural foundations, restriction of movement, and death on a large scale.

Part II, devoted to the Israeli-Jewish contributions, will be divided according to the place of exile, and to the nature of the contributors' political and academic activism.

Exile as Home

The three contributors who have made Israel their home after a lifetime of dislocation are Alice Shalvi, whose experience as a refugee from Nazi Germany brought her first to England and then to Israel, where she became one of the leaders of mainstream Israeli-Zionist feminist and peace activism; Rela Mazali, who tells the story of her mother's dislocation and her own multiple childhood experiences of strangerhood, and of the lessons she has learnt from this multi-locationality which has led her to feminist anti-militarisation activism; and Gila Svirsky, who writes about her present-day radical feminist anti-occupation politics and activism and who has also chosen Israel as her home.

Exile as an Oppositional Locus

Nira Yuval-Davis, who has chosen to live in Britain after a lifetime of anti-Zionist activism, apart from her political activism, is also a major academic commentator on the broader issue of the intersection of gender and nation(alism). Ella Habiba Shohat, whose trajectory from Iraq to Israel to the United States has made her an outsider *extraordinaire*, critiques Zionism from the point of view of its (Arab) Jewish victims. Hers is one of the strongest voices bringing the Mizrahi experience centre stage.

Existential States of Exile

For the two final contributors to the Israeli section, Esther Fuchs and Ronit Lentin, being daughters of families of Shoah survivors has shaped their diasporic trajectories. Fuchs experiments with turning her life story into the subject of her identity search beyond Zionism and Judaism, and Lentin uses her writing, both fictional and academic, to chart her trajectory from 'ordinary' Israeli to diasporic Jew with anti-Zionist politics.

Notes

1. See also the special issue 'Women in the Conflict', *Palestine-Israel Journal of Politics, Economics and Culture*, vol. 2, no. 3, 1995.
2. Two examples are the Annual Conference of the Israeli Anthropological Association, 6–7 May 2001, in which, among other panels, there was a discussion of the 1948 massacre at Tantura, as well as several papers dealing with militarism and multiculturalism; and the Militarism and Education conference, organised by New Profile in association with the Hebrew University School of Education and the Kibbutzim Teachers' Training College, 29–31 May 2001.
3. See, for example, a letter (dated 30 April 2001) by the Israeli ambassador to Ireland, insisting that 'despite reports to the contrary, Israel only *returns fire in self-defence ...* (yet) we are constantly being told that we must not defend our lives and homes'. See also Michael Warshavsky's challenge to the peace camp spokespersons and novelists Amos Oz, A.B. Yehoshua and David Grossman, who have now rallied against the Palestinians' right of return (Warshavsky, 2001: 25–6).

References

Abdo, Nahla. 1991. 'Women of the Intifada: Gender, class and national liberation'. *Race and Class* 32 (4): 19–35.

———. 1993. 'Middle East politics through feminist lenses: Dialoguing the terms of solidarity'. *Alternatives* 18 (1): 29–41.

———. 1994. 'Nationalism and feminism: Palestinian women and the Intifada – no going back?' In Valentine M. Moghadam (ed.), *Gender and National Identity: Women and Politics in Muslim Societies*. London: Zed Books.

———. 1999. 'Gender and politics under the Palestinian Authority'. *Journal of Palestine Studies* 27 (2): 38–51.

Abdo, Nahla, and Nira Yuval-Davis. 1995. 'Palestine, Israel and the Zionist settler project'. In Daiva Stasiulis and Nira Yuval-Davis (eds.), *Unsettling Settler Societies: Articulations of Gender, Race, Ethnicity and Class*. London: Sage.

Abu Zneid, Jihad. 1997. 'Women, children and housing rights: The case of the occupied Palestinian territories'. In Biljana Kasic (ed.), *Women and the Politics of Peace*. Zagreb: Centre for Women's Studies.

Ahmed, Leila. 1982. 'Western ethnocentrism and perceptions of the harem'. *Feminist Studies* 8 (3): 521–33.

Aminov, Eli. 2001. 'When Father returned from Tunis'. *Kan* [Here] 2: 29.

Anderson, Benedict. 1983. *Imagined Communities: Reflections on the Origin and Spread of Nationalism*. London: Verso.

Bauman, Zygmunt. 1989. *Modernity and the Holocaust*. Cambridge: Polity Press.

———. 2000. 'The Holocaust's life as a ghost'. In Robert Fine and Charles Turner (eds.), *Social Theory after the Holocaust*. Liverpool: Liverpool University Press.

Bhabha, Homi. 1994. *The Location of Culture*. London: Routledge.

Bernstein, Deborah S. (ed.). 1992. *Pioneers and Homemakers*. Albany, NY: SUNY Press.

Clifford, James. 1994. 'Diasporas'. *Cultural Anthropology* 9 (3): 302–38.

Dajani, Souad. 1994. 'Between national and social liberation: The Palestinian women's movement in the Israeli-occupied West Bank and Gaza Strip'. In Tamar Mayer (ed.), *Women and the Israeli Occupation: The Politics of Change*. London: Routledge.

Gorelick, Sherry. 1989. 'The changer and the changed: Methodological reflections on studying Jewish feminists'. In Alisson M. Jaggar and Susan Bordo (eds.), *Feminist Reconstructions of Being and Knowing*. Brunswick, NJ: Rutgers University Press.

Gottlieb, Amy. 1993. 'Not in my name: A Jewish feminist challenges loyalty to Israel'. In Linda Carty (ed.), *And Still We Rise*. Toronto: Women's Press.

Hadawi, Sami. 1988. *Palestinian Rights and Losses in 1998*. London: Saqi Books.

Hall, Stuart. 1996. 'Who needs identity?' In Stuart Hall and Paul Du Gay (eds.), *Questions of Cultural Identity*. London: Sage.

Izraeli, Dafna N. 1981. 'The Zionist women's movement in Palestine, 1911–1927: A sociological analysis'. *Signs* 7 (1): 87–114.

Jansen, Michael. 2001. 'Arafat seen as powerless to curb Intifada'. *The Irish Times*, 9 May: 13.

Landsberg Michele. 2001 'Iran's plan to revive smear against Israel is sick'. *Sunday Toronto Star*. 29 April: A2.

Lentin, Ronit. 2000. *Israel and the Daughters of the Shoah: Reoccupying the Territories of Silence*. Oxford and New York: Berghahn Books.

———. 2001. 'To remember, to forget: Gendering the silences in the relations between Israeli Zionism and the Shoah'. Paper presented at the Gender, Place and Memory in the Modern Jewish Experience, 2–4 January, Bar Ilan University, Ramat Gan, Israel.

Marshall, Mark. 1995. 'Rethinking the Palestine question: The apartheid paradigm'. *Journal of Palestine Studies* 25 (1): 15–22.

Mohanty, Chandra T. 1991. 'Under Western eyes: Feminist scholarship and colonial discourses'. In Chandra T. Mohanty, Anne Russo and Lourdes Torres (eds.), *Third World Women and the Politics of Feminism*. Bloomington and Indianapolis: Indiana University Press.

Noga. 2001. 'Do not say we didn't know: Testimonies of Palestinian women from al-Aqsa Intifada'. *Noga* 40: 14–32.

Peled, Yoav, and Gershon Shafir. 1996. 'The roots of peacemaking: The dynamic of citizenship in Israel, 1948–93'. *International Journal of Middle East Studies* 28: 391–413.

Said, Edward. 1979. *The Question of Palestine*. New York: Viking Press.

Shadmi, Erella. 1992. 'Women, Palestinians, Zionism: A personal view'. *News from Within* 8 (10–11): 13–6.

Shafir, Gershon. 1989. *Land, Labour and the Origins of the Israeli-Palestinian Conflict, 1882–1914*. Cambridge: Cambridge University Press.

Sharoni, Simona. 1993. 'Middle Eastern politics through feminist lenses: Toward theorising international relations from women's struggle'. *Alternatives* 18 (winter): 5–28.

———. 1994. 'Homefront as battlefield: Gender, military occupation and violence against women'. In Tamar Mayer (ed.), *Women and the Israeli Occupation: The Politics of Change*. London: Routledge.

Shavit, Ari. 2001. 'Oto Sharon' [The same Sharon]. *Ha'aretz Magazine*, 13 April: 18–22.

Shohat, Ella. 1988. 'Sepharadim in Israel: Zionism from the standpoint of its Jewish victims'. *Social Text: Theory, Culture, Ideology* 19–20: 1–34.

Warshavsky, Michael. 2001. 'The right of return: A challenge to the peace camp'. *Kan* [Here] 2: 25–6.

Yuval-Davis, Nira. 1982. *Israeli Women and Men: Division behind the Unity*. London: Change International Reports, Women and Society.

———. 1997. *Gender and Nation*. London: Sage.

Zureik, Elia. 1997. *The Palestinians in Israel: A Study in Internal Colonialism*. London: Routledge.

PART I

PALESTINIAN WOMEN

ONE

Exile in Lebanon

Samia Costandi

A Narrative of Dispossession

As a Palestinian dispossessed woman, I came from the desolate streets of Beirut to Montreal seeking a higher education. Beirut had begun to be resurrected during the late eighties, and did not fully come out of the turmoil of its civil war until the early nineties. I had been trained in philosophy in my undergraduate years. After my divorce, I went back to my former university and procured an additional diploma in teaching English as a second language; concurrently, I taught ESL there for five years between 1983 and 1988 in a special programme to underprivileged students competing for scholarships.

Teaching in the environment of war, bombardment, and the threat of being kidnapped is an experience that has moulded me into the kind of teacher I am. Personal and collective experience of hardship raised our consciousness and sealed our commitment as a community of teachers and learners.

At McGill, I changed my major from TESL to philosophy of education in my pursuit to find meaning in the midst of both the complex and the absurd. Since my education had always been in English, and had always been at Western institutions, I did not find it alienating to enroll at McGill, except for the culture of the university itself, which was quite conservative. I was a single mother with two young boys aged eight and ten. I was determined to make my mark on society here, whether as a female voice representing those who were silenced back home, or as an educator who was seriously engaged in pedagogical issues in Montreal.

My dispossession began when I was born, in Cyprus, to two very young Palestinian parents. My father, Kamel Costandi, was from Jaffa in Palestine proper (what is today Israel), and my mother, Violet Nasser, from Birzeit in the West Bank. My father worked at the Near East Broadcasting Station in Cyprus as a radio producer. Palestine had been formally occupied two years before their marriage.

The first languages I spoke were Arabic and Greek. In the aftermath of the invasion of the Suez Canal, my father and his Arab colleagues resigned from the Near East Broadcasting Station, and my parents left for England. There, my father worked with the BBC Radio's Arabic department, and was invited to join them permanently and obtain the British passport. He declined; my parents took the decision to head back to the Arab world since they did not feel it was right to impose on their children a life in Europe away from their Arab heritage.

British colonialism in Palestine notwithstanding, my relatives in Beirut found my interlocution with them in my Oxbridge accent absolutely delightful when I landed there as a five-year old. I had gone through two years of preschooling and kindergarten in London before my arrival. The coloniser had succeeded to embed in us an ambiguous attitude towards his presence amongst us in Palestine: it was a love-hate relationship with the British, the residues of which I carry to this very day.

* * *

Living in Beirut for thirty-something years was both delightful and disconcerting. Beirut was at once familiar yet foreign, close yet distant, palatable yet sour.... Beirut seduced you but did not live up to the hospitality it promised. Palestinians were a mercurial presence in Beirut, they were at once there and not there, existing yet not, recognised yet disenfranchised, welcomed yet barely tolerated. It all depended on what kind of Palestinian you were.

If you lived in the camps, you were doomed to a faceless and nameless existence. Camp residents were not allowed travel documents besides the paper which unequivocally stated that they were Palestinian refugees. That document effectively deprived them of every civil, legal, and humanitarian right imaginable. They were not allowed to work outside the camps and were abused and discriminated against wherever they went. They were beaten and put in jail without cause or due process of the law.

If you were lucky to have escaped that anomalous oppressed existence, then you paid your dues in any profession you had. In order to function and travel you would have procured the Lebanese passport because either you were a Christian Palestinian – as we were – or because you were a successful, wealthy, influential Muslim Palestinian; in both cases, you put in much hard work and lots of money hoping that the system would not cheat you. Some got cheated, like Yusuf Baidas, a Palestinian millionaire who was destroyed financially in a cold-blooded calculating manner when Lebanese officials thought he was getting too big for his britches and might become president of Lebanon. Although this man had served Lebanon immensely, the way he was disposed of was ruthless. (A scheme was devised whereby rumours were spread about the availability of cash at the Intra Bank which he owned. Thus, people rushed to cash their money. He had the equivalent of the money in gold in Kuwait; he rushed to bring it to Beirut, he needed a bracket of twenty four hours or something like that to bring the gold by plane. The government did not give him that bracket of time, and closed in on the bank). On a lesser scale, tax collectors harassed middle class businessmen like my father by presenting fraudulent documents requiring them to pay their taxes twice over.

Despite the fact that we lived outside the camp, in the heart of Beirut near Hamra Street, I did not feel protected beyond the confines of the four square kilometers surrounding my home and the inside of my school. I had no Palestinian communal existence besides my extended family, my friends, and my parents' friends. My paternal family all lived in the familiar area of Ras Beirut, as did one maternal aunt. It was safe enough for me to walk to their houses, and Beirut has a funny way of being friendly and safe despite its alienating and vicious politics. For one thing, you do not generally face the same problems you face in urban North American cities, such as child kidnapping and child abuse.

In spite of that friendliness and familiarity, my security blanket was shredded at an early age: I always felt the great loss that was passed on to me by my parents. During long drives in my parents' car, either to the mountains or to the suburbs where my paternal aunt lived, I would see and hear both my parents crying in the car as soon as a Fairouz song came on the air. The song that made the tears fall like a stream feeding an arid garden was the song entitled 'Raji'oun' (We will return).

At first I marvelled. I was in awe of that curious 'thing' which could incite in both my parents so much emotion. It must be quite a serious matter that pushed my two role models to shed their defences particularly in front of me. I was the eldest child, and as I became more privy to these difficult moments, I also became very sad. I gradually realised that this was not a passing summer cloud, but a gloomy big black winter cloud that carried within its folds torrents of strong wind and heavy rain. I felt special, however, to be allowed into the secret space of parent vulnerability.

When I inquired, my parents answered me. They explained about Palestine, this exotic lovely place where there were orange groves and gardens, where life was beautiful, where they were born and grew up. I felt privileged to take a peek into something so precious that they felt so strongly about. My two younger brothers at the time were treated like real children; they were not impacted by these moments. The fact that I was the only girl did not help divert the attention away from me, which had both its good and bad points.

My parents held the beacon for me and expected me to follow suit from a young age. They had very high hopes and dreams for their daughter. It was no ordinary daughter who recited Shakespeare at the young age of five. Perhaps she might become a famous orator, a writer, an actress (something they did not necessarily encourage as a career for a woman in the Arab world – ironically, my Dad was a producer and director), a great politician, a leader of some sort. Perhaps the piano drills that I was obliged to engage in daily spoke of future promises too. Under all circumstances, Samia was not going to be simply an ordinary girl who followed an ordinary path, get married and have many kids. She was a career woman!

Those perceptions change you as a female. Herein lie the seeds of feminist thinking: the identification with roles other than the traditional ones of motherhood and keeping house as a dutiful wife. Not that those roles were denigrated in any way in Palestinian communities, nor in the Arab world – absolutely not, and certainly not in our home. My mother was the 'Queen'! That was the title my father bestowed on her. Her word was sacred, her opinion was highly valued, she was a full partner in my parents' marriage; she was also his confidante and advisor in the business part of the work domain.

However, both my parents made it clear to me from a young age that I was a special person, a person with gifts. Whether it was writing poetry and reciting it, or playing the piano, or being an A student, all of those things seemed to be preparing me for some extraordinary mission in my life. I carried that sense of specialness within me all my life. At sixteen, I broke under the burden. I did not want to be special any more; I wanted to be just another mischievous kid, a silly brat who was trivial and unnoticeable!

Up to the age of fourteen, before the inception of the Palestinian revolution, I was unable to come to terms with my identity, and it was a source of great confusion for me, a constant worry at a very young age. When other girls were busy choosing what dolls to play with and what dresses to wear, I was preoccupied with *who I was*. I read avidly, I read every single book I could lay my hands on. It came to the point where, during holidays, my mother had to buy me a book per day.

When I was in elementary school, I was always making an effort to speak the Lebanese dialect. For some reason, Lebanese people made fun of the Palestinian dialect, and I could never figure out why. Perhaps it was the camps that surrounded the city that fed that attitude, the spectacle of shacks lined up without any proper sanitation where children played in the sewage paths. This had become the source of our 'shame'; it was a glaring statement of our defeat as a people, a symbol of our disempowerment, our dehumanisation, and our inability to negotiate a better deal for ourselves in the aftermath of our 'Nakba' of 1948.

I would be on the phone in my parents' living room speaking to a colleague, and you could not differentiate my accent from any Lebanese girl's accent; there was no trace of a Palestinian accent in my dialect. My mother would pass by and laugh, she would say to my Dad, 'I cannot believe how this kid speaks the Lebanese dialect. Look at the way she switches between Palestinian and Lebanese!' It was a complete denial of that other part of me, the part my parents left in Jaffa and the West Bank. It was as if these two worlds of Palestine and Lebanon could not collide!

Make no mistake, however: the moment our parents told us that we were going to journey in our car across the Syrian and Jordanian deserts to the West Bank for the summer to see my mom's family, to enjoy the company of our maternal uncles, aunts, and cousins who arrived from different parts of the globe, it was sheer ecstasy! There was a celebration at home for at least a week before the event. In retrospect, we basked in the sunshine of those summers for at least another six months after the reunion.

Since my paternal aunt was the principal of the school I attended in Beirut, I was protected from cynicism and mockery as a Palestinian kid. I was not just any kid; I was the elementary principal's niece. I always marvelled at how my aunt, Dalal, retained her Palestinian accent and was not self-conscious. My classmates knew I was Palestinian, and I would certainly have declared that proudly had anyone asked me, but no one did. It was not a topic you brought out into the open, it was almost as if it were an accusation. Thus, I did not speak the dialect openly because no one else in my school environment did, and I certainly did not want to be singled out. In my heart, I felt that Palestinian Arabic was closer to the literary Arabic; I felt it had a richness and fullness to it.

I experienced a split: there was the Palestinian Samia who travelled with her family to the West Bank almost every summer, who felt she belonged there, who utterly enjoyed the reunions with her cousins, the long talks, the fun and laughter, the stories and lore, who even fell in love with a sixteen-year-old boy when she was thirteen under the shade of those lovely pines. That was the happy Samia who was filled with warmth and love, energy and excitement. You could also find the happy Samia within the enclaves of her home in Beirut, with her parents and brothers, with her paternal cousins who lived in the same city. Our home was like an oasis in the middle of a desert of identity-less dunes....

On the other hand, there was the melancholy Samia who felt that her life was hijacked, whose presence in Beirut she believed to be temporary, transitory, whose existence there was artificial, superimposed as if by some fluke, transparently inauthentic. It was a forced existence, an existence of negation, of discomfort, of disease, of vulnerability, disempowerment, and disenchantment. It was a post-colonial existence that denied her roots, that taught her the history of England instead of Palestine and Lebanon, that made Henry VIII and his wives more accessible to her than her grandparent's orchard. It made Wordsworth and Coleridge more important than the foremost Palestinian poets Mahmoud Darwish, or Samih el-Kassem, or her mother's first cousin, Kamal Nasser – poet, writer, PLO spokesperson. It was an oppressive schooling aimed at alienating people.

The most alienating thing about that kind of post-colonial education is that you are made to feel guilty if you are not grateful that you are getting the best education possible from that Eurocentric world. To begin to even doubt the value of that education was a great leap forward. I was very lucky I had nationalistic parents who were politically very clear about their identities: they were two displaced exiled Palestinians who were adamant about making that reality clear to everyone around them, particularly if that someone happened to be foreign, specifically British. I did not grow up with any illusions politically, and for that I am grateful. My parents could identify intellectually with the European culture and thought, but they were emotionally distant from it, which made things easier for me. Hence my strong sense of Palestinian identity.

* * *

The moments of joy for me in Beirut were the ones I lived with my paternal uncles, aunts, and cousins. My paternal grandfather was a teacher, and the only image I have of him is one of an overwhelmingly serious man of stature and character, sitting in an armchair, wearing his red 'tarbush'. My favourite uncle was Uncle Emile, my father's youngest brother, who took me with him to the American University campus to show me off as the most audacious child under ten with a career ahead of her matching Greta Garbo's! We had a lot of fun together. One of my maternal aunts, who still lives in Beirut, was also very special to me, Aunt Lily, whom we called Florence Nightingale, or Lily of the Valleys, for the aroma of compassion she spread around her. Her only daughter, Hala, remains to this day a substitute for the sister I never had, and my best friend.

My childhood was also specifically characterised by a very special relationship with my paternal grandmother, who for me was the most lovable character one could encounter. Every Friday afternoon, I would come from school, throw my schoolbag nonchalantly at my mom's doorstep, and literally run two streets down from our house to my grandma's house to give her non-stop hugs and kisses. She would be waiting for me while she was cooking in the kitchen, standing there with her back hunched from the misery of displacement, hard labour, and years of anguish in diaspora. She used to cook my favourite meals, which obviously no one could emulate. It was the way she made those dishes, the special flavour induced by mindfulness and great love that was the magic she mesmerised us with.

My adorable and beautiful mom, Violet, was always gracious in extolling the virtues of her mother-in-law, and encouraging the bond between me and my grandma. Her eyes sparkled when I used to come home and tell her how much I loved my grandma. Violet was so beautiful that, it was said, when she walked down the streets in Birzeit before her marriage to dad, all the young men would line up to watch in utter captivation!

When I was growing up, I thought my father, Kamel, was the most brilliant man I will ever know. He taught me to appreciate great literature, Dostoyevsky and Tolstoy, as well as Charles Dickens and Charlotte Brontë, Khalil Gibran, and many great Arab writers and poets with whom I have lost contact today. He taught me how to appreciate great music, both Beethoven and Umm Kulthoum. To this day, I still believe my father is the man with the most comprehensive spirit I have ever known. This great man knows how to cry when he hears a great piece of music or feels sad for a fellow disempowered human being. This is one thing that has impacted my life and my brothers' in many ways: he taught us that a man is still a man if he sheds tears of compassion. He and Mom taught us the art of loving and giving.

We had heard it said often by anyone who visited our home in Beirut that its space was like a temple, a place filled with joy!

But my parents were not flawless, nor were they invincible. Sometimes, we got fed up of hearing how much they did for us, how much they sacrificed for their children, how hard they worked, and how we must follow their example. That Protestant ethic of hard work really made us feel guilty!

Whenever we passed by the camps, my parents wept. They were upset and would begin to speak about the dehumanisation of the Palestinian people. It was a constant topic of discussion in our house. All you had to do was push the button, and the question of Palestine would be on the table. This carried on for years and years.

Our home was always a meeting place for artists, writers, intellectuals, poets, and many a Palestinian hero who came to take shelter for lunch or dinner while travelling across the Middle East spreading the message of the revolution or seeking hiding from some oppressive Arab regime.

It was in my parents' living room that I learnt the art of interlocution and debate. I watched as the adults discussed and would venture, as I approached adolescence, to give certain opinions; I would test the impact of my ideas on the guests in the room, it was my training site. I would defer to my parents later for comments.

* * *

It was in my parents' living room that I met the great Palestinian poet Mahmoud Darwish in person and watched him in awe as he spoke. His nervous constitution exuded the neurosis and existential angst of a poet in every way. It was in my parents' living room that we mourned my maternal uncle Kamal Nasser, who was assassinated in his home in Beirut in 1973. On that ominous night he sat down to write a piece of poetry in commemoration of a Lebanese poet for an event taking place the next day. He had to face his killers alone. My parents used to joke with him and say, 'Kamal, you are a poet, you cannot shoot!' Apparently he did shoot in self-defence and even injured one of them.

Kamal was the most charismatic character I have ever met. He was soft-spoken and lovable in every way, charming and funny, eloquent, entertaining, and very attractive. Women fell in love with him all the time. He was a poet, an orator, a great thinker and writer, one of the few Christians in the leadership of the revolution. He was nicknamed 'The Conscience' because he was loved by all; he could go into any meeting of any faction in the PLO (of any ideological bent) without an invitation.

When he was found crucified in his home – he was actually laid down in a crucified position by the Israelis before rigor mortis set in – this represented to me the death of joy and the victory of misery in the world. It was as if the sun had been hidden from the face of the earth forever! The wailing and laments of my parents terrified me on that early morning when they got the final news from PLO people who had called at four in the morning, looking for him in the homes of relatives before they went up to his apartment. It was as if his fellow commandos were still hoping against all odds that he had not been sleeping at his home; they were terrified to go into his apartment and be faced with the cruel truth.

But finally they did go. They found him lying in a pool of blood, riddled with bullets in his chest, his mouth, and the fingers of his right hand. It was all highly symbolic: the heart that feels, the mouth that speaks, and the fingers that write! His left side had also been injured by a hand grenade thrown at him as the invaders entered his house.

In my parents' living room a committee was formed which met over a period of a year and published two books: a collection of Kamal Nasser's poetry and a collection of his prose. My father recreated artistically a vocal production of a cassette on which Uncle Kamal read poetry. My father took the cassette to his studio, refined the voice technically to the resonance of Kamal's voice, and inserted music with the reading. Today, I am perhaps one of two people who have a copy of that record. When you hear it, it seems as if my father and Uncle Kamal had produced the cassette together. There is a very strong spiritual presence on that recording.

* * *

The turning point in the question of the development of my identity came after 1965, particularly after 1967. This was a period of complete transformation for all of us. Not only was the question of being Palestinian brought out into the open, but also it became a source of great pride. We embraced that fully. I was kicked out of school for one day for inciting a demonstration after Israeli planes attacked the Lebanese airport in 1968. My parents could not imagine that their goody-two-shoes had done that!

My brothers were attacked in high school in the early seventies due to their overt stance in support of Palestinian rights. One of my brothers, Raja, actually got slashed with a knife on his head – and thankfully it was not a major injury. Paradoxically, this brother feels more Lebanese than Palestinian. Nabil, on the other hand, feels very Palestinian, and has suffered deeply from the psychological trauma of exile. Today he is a priest residing in England.

The resurrection of Palestinian identity took place in the aftermath of the inception of the Palestinian revolution. The Palestinians were celebrating. Not only was our identity and nationhood a source of pride, but we were also happy to declare it in the streets, on rooftops, through loudspeakers, and on radios. When we carried arms to defend ourselves and to fend off the attacks of our oppressors, we regained our dignity and our integrity. We earned respect and recognition from other peoples of the world. Although we are still far from being legally recognised as a nation-state, those years in Beirut from 1965 until 1982 were formative years in the development of our nation. We came a long way, from 'mere refugees slumped in camps and forgotten by the world', to a legitimate and recognised people with adequate formal and legal representation. We began to wield power and to negotiate with the top leaders of the world.

My first activist speech was in 1968 in Hyde Park in London (I have an ambivalent relationship with England that will haunt me forever). We had travelled with my parents to enjoy a holiday while dad produced some television programmes in London. On a Sunday afternoon, we took a cab to Hyde Park. I had heard much about it, all sorts of anecdotes. When we disembarked from the taxi, I immediately saw the Palestinian flag ruffling in one corner of the park that was not too far from us. A force propelled me, as if by sheer magnetism, to head in that direction at utmost speed.

I was drawn so quickly that when my father finished paying the taxi driver and looked around, he could not see me. 'Where is Samia?' he asked my mother. And my mother, who had been watching closely, smiled and said, 'You want to know where Samia is, just look up there!' He could not believe what he saw; it had taken me literally less than a minute to reach the Hyde Park Palestinian corner. Remember, this was the first time in my life that I had seen the Palestinian flag ruffle anywhere without liability! I immediately sized up the situation: a young man with a kaffiyeh wrapped around his head was speaking in broken English and no one was listening to him, although there was a large crowd there.

I thought that the crowd would definitely be more attentive to the question of Palestine if I, a Palestinian young woman wearing a miniskirt, went up to the podium and addressed them. This is exactly what happened. I asked the co-ordinator to let me climb up there, and someone said, 'But she is not on the programme1' Another said, 'Just let her go up, damn it!' As I climbed the steps I could hear the loud noises in the crowd subside until they became whispers; finally those whispers disintegrated into total silence as I began speaking. You could literally hear a pin drop. I introduced my speech with, 'Golda Meir says there are no Palestinians, they never existed. Well, she is lying, they do. I am a Palestinian'.

When I began telling the story of the Palestinian dispossession, someone in the crowd said that I did not look like a refugee to him. So others in the crowd shut him up, and I explained that factor of not looking like a refugee quite carefully. I spoke about the hundreds of thousands of exiled Palestinians who were living back home in tents and shacks, totally forgotten by the world. I clarified that I was one of a lucky minority whose parents had miraculously avoided that. Imagine the experience of having to be apologetic about not living in a camp! Part of the anguish of dispossession is that of the guilt harbored against that backdrop of our people living in camps. One felt like a traitor, that one's credibility and authenticity was undermined as a result of that.

The Hyde Park incident was a memorable experience. A few Israeli young people were standing and wanted earnestly to talk about a peaceful solution and about returning the West Bank to the Palestinians! But that was in the old days and my father did not think it was a good idea that I speak to them, so we simply left. What an irony, what a paradox, to be negotiating that very same item of withdrawal from the West Bank today in 2001, and unsuccessfully!

* * *

My husband and I divorced in 1982 in Beirut, and he remarried in September of the same year after the massacres of Sabra and Shatila. The leader of the revolution, of whom he was one, had exited Beirut in the aftermath of the Israeli invasion. His swift remarriage left indelible scars on my psyche, for my marriage to him had had much to do with my marriage to Palestine, my revisitation of my roots, my allegiance to my nation, and my conviction of a moral ideal. My husband married a woman who had already been known to us as the wife of a member of his organisation; they had two kids. She had frequented our house as a guest with her husband and children over the span of a whole year.

I felt so completely cheated. This was the ultimate metaphor for betrayal, a betrayal that sunk its claws deep into my flesh. This was not the way the myth was supposed to unfold. I had literally uprooted myself from my own community and alienated my parents and my friends when I married him. Despite the fact that we were both Palestinian, and that my family respected and valued him, we came from different backgrounds. My family lived in an urban area of Beirut; he lived in the Palestinian ghetto, where the camps were concentrated. Marrying him in the throes of a love affair was a big political statement on my part. Sometimes he made me feel guilty for who I was, where I grew up, for not having lived in a camp, for having studied in Western schools. He did not recognise my intellectual, psychological, and emotional dispossession as a Palestinian. He had a narrow vision of dispossession that centred on the material.

I had difficulty relating to people in his environment on certain levels, even though I cherished and respected them, and with my author's curious mind examined their characters and delighted in their humour and diversity. I had to adopt another persona that suited his work and his milieu. After making what I beheld as many sacrifices, I felt abandoned. He was not present in my life, his was only a formal presence. I was not a full partner, nor was he intending to make me one. For years I tried to deal with this. It was paradoxical that the man I chose to be the father of my children, and who was supposed to be one of the 'liberators' of our country, would turn his face away from his own family and act like an oppressor. His excuse was that he loved me enough to let me go, since he knew that we could not be happy together.

My ex-husband and I shared moral ideals, shared a vision of a liberated Palestine and a commitment to articulating the civil, moral, and legal rights of our people. However, we differed on the ways we envisaged this could be done. I was an educator with an idealistic vision, and he was a military leader with a will of iron, a stubbornness and patience that served him very well in his work. He was a generous, warm-hearted, principled, and honest man whose most striking quality was his courage and determination in the face of adversity. He was compassionate enough to release one of his prisoners from the Phalanges party when he saw a picture of the boy's mother in a Lebanese magazine with a caption reading 'Return my son to me'. He sent the prisoner to his mother with a letter and a brief history of Palestine, including an explanation of what the war was about. On the other hand, he could be ruthless too. He was feared greatly by friend and foe alike. To him, the personal was communal and the communal personal. From my perspective, his boundaries were flawed: my sense of the personal was private, and privacy was sacred. Members of his organisation would call him at four in the morning for any reason, and he would allow it. To me, there were clear demarcation lines that could not be crossed except in cases of emergency. This issue was a great source of distress for both of us since it problematised our family life greatly.

The historical socialisation process had taken its toll on both of us. I tried to compromise, and he would not change his ways. He was a patriarch in a patriarchal society; he was a warrior with a clan encircling his life on a daily basis. The day-to-day living became extremely difficult. I felt that my life was becoming completely subsumed by his – in fact, I became another of his accolades. Although we had weathered many storms together, we could not hold the marriage intact: the contradictions outweighed the commonalties. Despite the fact that we had faced near-death experiences together, including the frightful blowing up of the building our family home was located in with three hundred kilos of TNT, which we survived only accidentally since we were not there, he felt that the only way to work out our disagreements was to sever the relationship completely. I felt that the love, the camaraderie, and the history we had together warranted communication, taking a moratorium on the marriage, and deep reflection on the consequences of our differences for the benefit of our children. He disagreed. I, of course, had no choice. It seems that the historical and political changes that the Middle East underwent reflected many of the changes that people went through. In the case of Lebanon, there was a surge of identification with the Palestinian resistance which encompassed hundreds of thousands of people. It is ironic that Lebanon turned out to be the country that gave the most to the revolution in terms of the loss of life and of livelihood. Thousands of Lebanese martyrs who came from the poorer classes, mostly Muslim Lebanese but certainly some Christians too, gave their lives as martyrs for the revolution as well as for a new Lebanon. The revolution had promised to create a new society based on democracy, equity, freedom, and parity of the classes. Even though those dreams were not fulfilled and those ideals were not reached, there exists today a bond between the Palestinian and Lebanese peoples that will stay cemented by the common struggle forever. I find it paradoxical that the smallest country in the Arab world, and the one with the least resources materially, a beautiful country of tourism and services, ended up being the one that became a spearhead for change in the Middle East. It is also a greater irony that at the hands of the courageous southern Lebanese people, Israel received its first official defeat ever when its troops were expelled from the South of Lebanon in the year 2000.

Years after our divorce, when my ex-husband and I met, he acknowledged his mistakes and spoke about his unforgivable immaturity, and the rashness and arbitrariness of his past actions. He also acknowledged his psychological abandonment of me, and his not having lived up to my expectations of him. Although he has always provided materially for his boys within the parameters of his ability, he feels haunted by what he considers our sons' dispossession, their having lived in a Western rather than an Arab society. The paradox is, however, that he also feels good about his sons being citizens of a Western *democratic* society, rather than an Arab oppressive one. Today, he encourages his sons to partake in the privilege of living in a democracy and not to take it for granted. 'If I was living in Canada', he says, 'I would not settle for less than becoming prime minister! You are so lucky to be living in a democracy'. He speaks with respect of my intellectual work in front of our kids and with his friends.

The story of my marriage was one of a loss I had never envisaged and had to adapt to. This was the basis on which my feminist thinking, though not my feminist experiences, began. It was in Montreal, through my readings at university, my interaction with colleagues, and the maturation of my thinking that I began to understand my life as a Palestinian woman, and to give coherence and credence to my struggles as a female.

My experiences sometimes baffled me; I wanted to put them in context, to assign meaning to them, and to understand the nuances and the multi-hues that coloured them. I had always felt that I was authoring the story of my life, and that I was responsible for putting its parts together. I attempted to create my own path, despite the fact that the larger part of the narrative of dispossession was imposed on us as a people, and more so as women.

There had always been an autobiographical bent to my thinking: I always felt driven and impassioned by my ideas and values. I felt that I was on a mission, that there were reasons my life was taking the turn that it did, and that on this journey I was assigned a task, to obtain a boon for my society.

The drive, passion, and determination helped my work, both the academic and the communal aspects of it, which have always been merged because I believe in *praxis*. My father's training me to recite Shakespeare at four years of age abetted any doubts I may have nurtured about my abilities as a teacher and public speaker. It was wonderful to have a father who celebrated having a daughter. I was hired as a part-time lecturer in my department at McGill and worked there over the past ten years. There was something about having a voice that was so empowering, so fulfilling, and I used that voice wherever I could.

Political and social consciousness notwithstanding, women did not have full access back home in Lebanon's patriarchal society. It was in and through the traditional roles of mother, teacher, and perhaps writer that women articulated their views. Despite the fact that many women joined the revolution, fought side by side with men, and had much to do with organising political cells, there were few outspoken women in society who challenged the existing status quo. In addition, there was much fear of the reprisals that had been witnessed against anyone who had a strong voice. Many men and their families were assassinated in their very homes because they spoke out. A few women who stood out courageously were also assassinated in the streets and in their homes. Hence the value and importance of my newly found freedom in Canada.

When I spoke at conferences, on radio, on television, at workshops, when I challenged professors at the university, I felt that it was not only my voice that was speaking, but the voices of the hundreds of women I had left behind back home, who had no power and no access, who were silenced in the most vicious of ways.

Most of the time, my voice heralded my ideas instead of the other way round. I was unstoppable: I wanted the world to hear about Palestine, about the women in the refugee camps, about their strength and their resilience, about their terrible grief and their incredible courage. I wanted everyone at McGill and in Montreal to hear about the grave injustices that had been, and continue to be, committed against my people. I wanted them to know how the West had stolen the innocence from our children's eyes, quelled the flame in their hearts, and stultified their minds.

I wanted Westerners to know that to fulfil the yearnings of one group of people they cannot steal the dreams of a whole nation, of the millions of refugees in the camps who had lost everything, their land, their dignity, their integrity, their livelihood, their education, and their future.

I wanted them to see what I had seen back home and to hear the narrative of the PALESTINIAN WOMAN, and so I recounted Herstory:

- I am the mother, the giver, the friend, the mentor, the helper, the builder, the partner, the wise one, the one who carries the brunt of the suffering of my people in every way imaginable. I weep for the martyrs and cook for the living. I don myself to please my husband at night and slave to feed my children during the day. I am fully present, and I make the decisions on a daily basis that keep my family from falling into the bottomless pit.
- The narrative of my life is dictated to me, yet I walk the path with dignity and pride. I nurture my own sense of security with the strength of my imagination, with faith and determination. In the early rainy days of the revolution, with no end in sight and a hostile world ejecting us off the shores of civilisation, I was the one to keep our community together, to weave the quilt of nationhood with strong threads.
- Like a long-lost hero coming out of a forest, my comrade, the commando, arose and fought the dragon. I was the heroine beside him, ahead of him, guiding him with my wisdom, encouraging him with my words, and singing to him in the stealth of the night as we made love. I held the gun and fought when he fell. I ululated when they carried him to his final resting place. I held the torch and led him on the path towards liberation.
- I took over the beacon when my child could not see her father anymore. I am a fortress of strength, and a well of compassion. I am the

treasurer of secrets; I am the storyteller, and the dancer on the horizon of victory.

- You were not there, my North American sister, when the American-made Israeli Napalm and cluster bombs ripped the children of my community apart. You did not see the homelessness of people within their own skin as they glared at an alien body while their mind's eye crossed to Hades in resignation, waiting for sweet imminent death to arrive in haste and end the suffering.

- I am walking down the streets of Beirut. It is desolate and gloomy, with raking images of a revisited horror. Could it have been a nightmare? How many times do a people have to go through occupation, oppression, and dehumanisation? No, this is it; this is what being Palestinian is all about. The smell of burning flesh, commandos having to eat cats during the siege of the camps in Beirut, the women being sniped to death as they went to buy food for their children.

- The earth has not dried yet, nor will it soon, from the blood of our martyrs. To this day, the trenches in the West Bank connect with the trenches in the South of Lebanon, with the trenches in Gaza, with the protesting voices in London, Washington, Los Angeles, Berkeley, and Montreal.

- I am walking the streets of Montreal with my head wrapped in my hijab and tears streaming down my ravaged face. This was not in the cards my North American friend, my husband was not supposed to befriend another woman and leave me and my kids to suffer. I have no sister and no cousin to speak to. I am filled with a sense of shame....

- I am walking the streets of Montreal, my North American sister. My heart is pounding and I am exhausted. I have carried the bags of food from metro to metro, from one bus stop to another; I am tired and spent. I am a labourer with no wages, someone enslaved in the patriarchal system of my society. I have no identity, I am faceless and nameless. I am so-and-so's wife, and so-and-so's mother. I have no right to disagree.

- I am walking the streets of Montreal and I see a familiar face. Could it be him? No, it cannot. I walk speedily, I run, I reach the crossroad, I look both ways ... I lost him. But why am I surprised, he was always a dream, an idea, a fictional character, somehow.

- Back home, my mother's bosom would have held my anguished head, and her wise words would have comforted me and given me strength.

- Who will allay my fears? Who will abate my anguish? Can my North American sister understand? How so, when she has never seen a child killed for no reason, or a mother beaten in front of her children by a soldier? How so, when she has never seen a man tortured, a house demolished, a tree uprooted in spite?

- How will my North American sister understand when she has never seen a baby stolen from its mother's bosom, or a young woman slaughtered like a sheep?
- Yet, in the writings of my North American sisters, I found an explanation for the oppression. How mystifying. How awesome, but that is the crux of it, the universality of our humanity, of our femaleness, of our experiences. I guess you have to be somewhat distant, as my sisters here are, in order to be able to analyse, to dissect, to interpret the larger picture.
- We speak a common language, my North American sister, even though our dialects differ. In your books I have found an explanation for the words dominator and dominated, oppressor and oppressed. We share an understanding of the conspiracy that fuels wars and creates genocide in order to feed the arms industry. We share a struggle to undo the marriage between patriarchy and capitalism, and other 'isms'.
- In the poetry and stories of my Arab sisters I have found comfort and consolation. I dipped my pen in the welter of their experiences and I have felt at home in diaspora, despite my dispossession.
- My mother's garden has always beamed with colour. Her green thumb has always been a metaphor for survival, for resistance, for resurrection. So will my garden continue to bloom until the end of time.
- I am a feminist, a feminist, a feminist, a feminist, a Palestinian Canadian feminist …

And so I revert to my immediate existence, to my concrete presence here as Samia. I am a walking paradox of contradictions. I stand between two cultures, the Middle East and the West. Being on the periphery helps me fend off the onslaught of the oppressor from all sides of the prism of dehumanisation. I master the language, thus I use the *word*. I walk alone because I understand what being whole is about, yet I feel lonely because I have been deprived of my extended family, my childhood friends, the rich folklore of my community, its lore, its mythology, its song and dance, it poetic atmosphere.

I am dispossessed like my sister back home, yet my dispossession is especially bitter. The advantage my Palestinian sister back home has over me is that she can share her dispossession with her other sisters, whether that be in the camps, in the cities, or in the villages. She can find consolation and comfort in the communal narrative.

I learnt the History of the oppressor; I read His books, His poetry, and His philosophy. I was deprived of learning the history of my culture and my people. Yet I learnt it through osmosis, sitting on the steps of my great aunt's house in Birzeit in the West Bank, where I breathed the air of my country, the smell of jasmine and fruit trees, and watched the beautiful sunsets through the branches of the cedars and the pines.

I sat there like a dutiful student absorbing what nature was teaching me. The smell of the earth is still fresh in my nostrils, and the fresh air still invigorates my heartbeats. I heard the stories and myths from my aunts, uncles, and grandmothers. We are a great nation of storytellers. I listened as if I was listening to the gods; every word was sacred and every detail was important to remember.

Today, in May 2001, I still hold the key to my grandfather's house. My life has been like a journey against an upward stream. I may not have been able to live in my country, but I have made sure that I will be buried there, as I have already instructed my children. Although the prospect of building a home in Palestine and living there for the rest of my days seems remote, I still nurture an intense yearning to go and spend a few summers in Birzeit, perhaps teach at Birzeit University for a while.

My twenty-three-year-old constantly battles the world and is anguished about his identity. My twenty-year-old romances the world in many ways. I bask in the sunshine of my sons, and together they are a metaphor for both my dispossession and my empowerment. I carry my pain with dignity and fight oppression zealously; on the other hand, I re-create the story of my life with faith and hope, and continue to plant seeds towards rebirth along the less travelled road of my life.

I will carry on despite all odds. It is the quality of the journey, not the destination, that makes the difference. I will continue to push the boundaries and to create new spaces for our Middle Eastern and Western cultures to meet. Whether or not we reach liberated Palestine in our lifetime becomes irrelevant. What is relevant is that the pen is mightier than the sword, and that women are the ones who will finally lead humanity on the path of liberation from manifold forms of oppression.

Feminists must create the spaces necessary for the meeting of minds, and for the healing of wounds in bleeding hearts. We understand that peace is a comprehensive concept, and that without justice peace is impossible. Peace is a process, a verb, not a noun.

Only in my full humanity can I encounter the 'other', and in the eye of the hurricane lies the dormant rainbow.

Rosemary Sayigh

Remembering Mothers, Forming Daughters: Palestinian Women's Narratives in Refugee Camps in Lebanon

—ɯ—

Introduction

A fruitful theoretical starting point for those concerned with national independence struggles, state formation, and the part played in them by women and gender is Yuval-Davis and Anthias (Yuval-Davis and Anthias, 1989). The different forms taken by women's centrality in state- and nation-formation as defined by these writers clearly points to the likelihood of contradiction between active/participatory and passive/symbolic forms. (Yuval-Davis and Anthias, 1989: 7). Chatterjee's study of anti-colonial nationalisms is another important theoretical reference (Chatterjee, 1993). This writer sets the participatory/symbolic contradiction within a larger one between the 'programmatic' and the 'thematic' in anti-colonial nationalisms, the former action-orientated and modernising, the latter epistemological and moral (Chatterjee, 1993: 36–53). Another member of the subaltern studies group, Radhakrishnan, has elaborated this basic theoretical insight in the field of gender, noting the way anti-colonialist national movements force themselves, in their quest for 'cultural authenticity', into an ideological 'bind' by dichotomising between female/home and male/political domains (Radhakrishnan, 1992: 85). We need to see how this contradiction works out in particular cases of national struggle not only to throw light on the contradiction itself, but also to compare the forms it takes in the subjectivities of male and female members. Another aim – since women seldom have direct, unmediated relations with states or national movements – is to discover what structures – families, communities, political parties, religious sects – intervene either to block or to facilitate their movement towards what Hammami and Johnson have usefully termed 'active citizenship'. (Hammami and Johnson, 1999: 325). My essay draws primarily on life stories recorded with women from Shatila camp between 1989 and 1992, but also from my own life as 'cultural traveller', a foreigner married to a Palestinian, a visitor to the camps turned anthropologist.

From the beginning I was struck by the strength of the women of the camps, their ability to cope with large families and harsh life conditions. I loved camp women's talk, even before I understood it, so expressive in the way it involves face, hands, and voice, so different from speech in classical Arabic. Gradually I became fascinated by their aesthetic and performative skills as storytellers. So the decision I took in 1989 to record the life stories of a small sample of women from Shatila camp for a doctoral dissertation arose from an essentially subjective and emotional beginning.[1] In spite of these roots in personal desire, and in spite of the doubts I have about the autonomy of the life story, especially when solicited by a Westerner from members of a refugee community, I believe that recording Palestinian refugee women's life stories is justified theoretically and politically. The telling of a life story brings into existence a 'self' that reflects history, culture, and overlapping collectivities (Passerini, 1987).

Though women's struggle within the Palestinian national struggle has given rise to a growing literature, almost all of this has focused upon leading figures and political party women,[2] with Peteet (1991) and Najjar (1992) as rare exceptions. The problem with the testimonies of leading women is that the priority they assign to the national narrative suppresses the personal and the domestic (Stanley, 1996; Fleischmann, 1996). Far from the discourse of state or party, non-élite women's narratives unselfconsciously crisscross the (politically constructed) boundary between 'public' and 'domestic', narrating the national *through* the personal, revealing the penetration of families by politics, and politics by families. Non-élite women also narrate the *local*, a crucial level of social organisation that nationalist testimonies omit. Further, whereas leading or politicised women may be tempted through nationalism to minimise problems that Palestinian women face as women, 'ordinary' women tend to be more outspoken, and their testimonies are more likely to reveal tensions between national discourse and women's experiences within the movement, or in their families. Marginally mobilised, women of the camps express nationalism in their own fashion, as well as their own kind of 'feminism', case-specific and non-theoretical.

In this essay I draw out of the Shatila life stories what they tell about the mother/daughter relationship over time in camps in Lebanon. The mother/daughter relationship has been neglected by scholarship on Arab and Middle Eastern families, which have focused on the relationship between mother or father and oldest son. Though based on numerous practices, such as the naming of mothers after the oldest son, and the importance for women's status of giving birth to sons, this culturally sanctioned focus has deflected attention from less obvious ties between related women, which have importance at different levels – household economies, extended family ties, neighbourhood relations, and the political system (Joseph, 1983, 1993). Hilma Granqvist unusually drew attention to women's 'marriage policies' in her main Artas study, through which out-marrying women tried to marry their daughters back into their family or village of origin, or bring wives from them for their husband's household. (Granqvist, 1935: 96). A second reason for interest is the existence of two distinct discourses in Palestinian milieus, one around the importance of producing sons, the other about the positive values of having daughters, a dissonance that undoubtedly reflects debates about gender values linked to exile experience. A third reason is curiosity aroused by my observation of the diametrically opposed outcomes of this relationship, with some mothers transmitting patriarchal customs with almost punitive force, while others are their daughters' allies in loosening constraints. In some cases nationalist activism has been transmitted from mothers to daughters; in others, mothers have kept their daughters at home, deprived them of education, and married them off in early adolescence. Theorists of the family and the state from Engels onwards have posited a correspondence between political and family regimes, and there is strong ground for suggesting that the relationships between refugee mothers and daughters have political implications for a future Palestinian state and society.

How did my foreignness, cultural 'baggage', attributes, and limitations affect access to Shatila, selection of speakers, their responses, and my interpretation? Discussions of 'positionality' tend to focus on researcher attributes – nationality, class, gender, marital status, age. More important in my view are the research community's categories for classifying 'strangers', based on its political situation, historical experience, needs, and culture. As refugees and as nationalists, Palestinians feel the need to 'speak to the world' through foreigners. Furthermore, political and material support for Palestinians as refugees have come from multinational sources. Yet foreigners have also been experienced as enemies and spies, creating a fear of 'strangers' that was at a peak at the moment when I began work in Shatila, soon after the massacres of September 1982. Access to the community and eventual acceptance as 'outsider/ insider' was achieved through existing connections with Umm Khaled and *Ustadh* (teacher) Ahmad, respected members of the research community. Perhaps it helped that I was married to a Palestinian, and mother of Palestinian children, but far more important was my local identity as 'friend of Umm Khaled'. My foreignness, gender, and age all helped me to cross Lebanese Army checkpoints, but among my attributes perhaps age and married status were the most positive factors, since mature women could speak to me frankly, which they might not have done if they had assumed that, unmarried, I was sexually inexperienced.

Yet access is seldom the hardest part of research. Within the politics of my study approach there was a basic conflict between advocacy for the refugees as an oppressed national collectivity, and my feminist readings and interests. I had to consider that feminism may be a 'strong language' (Asad, 1986: 156) that distorts other cultural epistemologies. Yet, locally, nationalism was a 'strong language' that over-rode women's discourse. The debate within the Palestinian women's movement over feminism – Western ideology or universal issue of human rights and democracy? – became part of my own inner dialogue. Life stories appeared a promising method precisely because they subdued my feminist focuses and forced me to listen for meanings in the speakers' own renderings. Though choice of speakers was based in my own visiting network, and was thus arbitrary and unrepresentative in the resistance movement sense of including all the factions, I worked with members of the community on issues of selection and interpretation. Collectivising the project was ruled out by the period in which it was carried out, one of insecurity, arrests, and internal conflict (Sayigh, 1996).

Camps as Context: Change and Resistance to Change

Lebanon has been unique as a host for Palestinian refugees, with the refugees always seen as a security issue and threat. The mass of destitute refugees, mainly rural in origin and Sunni Muslim in sect, were subject to strict zoning and army control. Legal restrictions produced high unemployment and out-migration rates (mainly of young men), and stunted occupational development. Under Chehab (1958–64) the camps came under Army Intelligence control; in 1969 a camp uprising paved the way for the transfer of the resistance movement from Jordan to Lebanon. As a''liberated zone' for the armed struggle movement, the camps became targets of attack – Israeli, Lebanese, Syrian – subjecting their populations to continual violence, displacement, and loss.

Rural Palestinian families in exile in Lebanon faced a total transformation of their political and material conditions. Sarhan identifies seven main forces for change: (1) separation from landed property; (2) dispersion of the *hamula* (clan); (3) individual dispersion; (4) growth in size of kin units; (5) growing socio-economic differentiation; (6) growing cultural heterogeneity; and (7) the death of elders: factors that combined to weaken hamula solidarity (Sarhan, 1991). Gender and honour ideology that had sustained clan solidarity in Palestine became vested in the household family, the camp community, and ultimately the 'Palestinian people' (an exilic construct); these shifts allowed women some margin of manoeuver, while poverty and dispersion weakened patriarchal control.

Exile brought three main factors for change in Palestinian women's lives: free education, wider employment openings, and – after two decades – national movement mobilisation. UNRWA (the UN agency established in 1951 to administer the refugees) provided free schooling to all refugee children between the ages of six and sixteen, and from the beginning most girls in camps attended, at least to the end of the primary level. The Lebanese economy generated jobs for women in urban services, commerce, and industry, as well as construction and agriculture. However, refugee women usually left the workforce once their families found other sources of income, for example when men got jobs in the Gulf. Later, in the 1970s, the PLO generated training courses and job openings for women, seen by camp families as 'national work', therefore acceptable. Interviews I carried out with women from Shatila in the early 1980s suggested that it was not earning income that altered their status in families but rather the knowledge and self-confidence they gained through entering the public domain.

In spite of sharing a common history, language, and culture with the Lebanese, Palestinians of the camps experienced the host society as alien. Though over time segments of it became familiar, through politics, business, employment, and eventually marriage, relations have always fluctuated. More than elsewhere in their diaspora – except in Israel – Palestinians in Lebanon configured themselves in opposition to the host society. Women and gender ideology figured centrally in this construction of Palestinian-Lebanese 'difference', with multiple effects for women, such as the reinforcement of 'protection' through space restriction. Early coercive marriage continued in many families, though not in all. A negative effect of exile was that, since the Lebanese environment was perceived as alien and aggressive, the entire camp community focused on women's behaviour, condoning 'honour crimes' and hiding them from the Lebanese authorities. A study of women carried out in Burj al-Barajneh camp in the early 1970s showed their hopes that the resistance would bring change to their lives. (Khalili, 1981).

At the level of camp households and domestic labour, several unobtrusive shifts occurred which changed the composition, management, and relationships between women members. In rural Palestine, girls were married out in early puberty, and compound households were managed by the senior woman through her daughters-in-law (Granqvist, 1931: 44). However warm the tie might be, the mother/daughter relationship had slight structural or economic significance in rural Palestine. Refugee conditions brought structural and relational changes: the compound household tended to separate into nuclear households; girls tended to marry at later ages, sometimes managing to prolong their education, hence spending more time in the parental household; housewives relied more on the help of adolescent daughters than on daughters-in-law (now concerned with their own households), or on usually distant female kin. Over time, the majority of camp households were managed by single housewives aided by their daughters. Some daughters stayed at home for several years before marriage, and some did not marry. Even when daughters married, mother/daughter co-operation continued, since the majority preference was for marriage within the camp. In cases of sickness or childbirth, or if husbands were unemployed or suffered an accident at work, such help between related women was crucial to household survival. Prolonged by exile conditions, the mother/daughter relationship was also a crucial channel of transmission of knowledge of Palestine. Young refugees who had never seen their village knew mainly from their mothers of its setting, fruits and vegetables, families, stories.

Another exile-based change is important here: the transformation of the camp into 'moral communities', sites exemplifying 'Palestinian difference'. Others might consider them slums, but their people were proud of conformity to traditions of *karm wa sharf* (generosity and honour). Given women's behaviour as the touchstone of the moral health of the collectivity, this – combined with the gradual shift to the 'one household/one housewife' pattern – made mothers more personally responsible for their daughters, and more accountable to the community for their behaviour. The reputation of a family, neighbourhood, whole camp, or – later – resistance group would be discussed in terms of the behaviour of its *banat* (young unmarried women). Mothers were judged in terms of their skill in raising daughters with the essential female virtues – modesty, self-control (*rakiza*), and truthfulness (*sadiqa*). Any scandal involving girls would spread immediately throughout a camp, involving a 'collectivity of mothers', an intercommunicative, rule-upholding group that actively intervened in the public domain.[3]

Refugee Mothers: Commemorations, Omissions, Critiques

Umm Imad was one of two speakers who described their mothers spontaneously, with detailed descriptions and anecdotes, and in commemorative mode.[4] Both her parents figure prominently in her memoirs, but anecdotes about her mother are more affectionate and more carefully configured. Here is a typical passage:

> She was very tidy, very neat. For example she would take a piece of material to the sewing woman, and when it was finished she brought it home and sewed the hem over again. And she'd make the buttons stronger so they wouldn't fall.... I remember she had a little shelf in the kitchen on which she

put the razor, toothpaste, and such things. Our sheets, everything, she embroidered them. When she went visiting there was in her bag a needle and thread and something to embroider. She learnt this from her mother.

Many women praised their mothers for their home-making ability, but Umm Imad praised her mother for unusual qualities such as not trying to keep her ignorant of sex. Close proximity in camps with people from other villages, 'strangers', and the need for girls to 'mix' in school and on the streets, produced new parental control methods – closer supervision, warnings, or sometimes explanation:

Once our neighbour told my mother, 'Tell Samira to leave, we want to talk'. My mother said, 'Let her stay. I want my daughters to know everything. If you give a girl freedom and teach her the difference between right and wrong, she won't make mistakes. But if you tell her, 'This is forbidden, that is a sin!' she will want to try it'. My mother was always talking to me and explaining things to me. We children never lied to her.

Zeina praised her mother in similar terms:[5]

Our mother didn't want us [daughters] to be afraid: 'If you behave properly, if you tell me about everything you face outside, there's nothing to fear'. And I – maybe because I was the youngest of the girls – used to play more outside with my friends in the streets. My older sisters didn't like me playing outside but my mother said, 'Leave her alone, she's still young'. I don't remember a day when she said, 'Don't go there; I'm afraid for you because you are girls'. There was confidence. [When] we were in school, for example, if people [men] talked to us on the road, we always told her. If young men 'threw words' at us she'd say, 'Don't answer them, don't worry about it. Walk alone. It's up to the girl to oblige others to respect her'.

Zeina contrasts her mother positively with other mothers in Shatila camp who wouldn't allow their daughters to go to political meetings. Her mother had already been involved in Palestine through her husband and cousin, both *munadileen* (strugglers). She knew how to conceal weapons:

The things he [cousin] wanted to hide he brought to my mother. She was someone who could keep a secret. He [cousin] was followed by the Deuxième Bureau. Once they came to search our house.... I remember I was young, they came, I was sitting on the bed, they pushed me aside to search there. They didn't find anything.... Later we asked her where she had hidden them? She said that she had wrapped them in a blanket and hidden them in the ground in our small garden. It seems she had experience.

Both Umm Imad and Zeina had inherited a repertory of stories of Palestine from their mothers, some political, others anecdotes of daily life. Zeina related:

She told us real stories, not fables (*khurafiyyat*). She told us about my father, how he used to fight the British, how he was pursued, and ran from building to building, and escaped them. One night he wanted to sleep in the quilt. She took off the quilt to wash it. He said, 'I want to sleep in the quilt'. She said, 'Yes, if God wants'. He said, 'Whether God wants or not, *I* want to sleep in the quilt tonight'. That night the British came and took him, and he stayed six months in prison.

Like many women's stories, this one appears to contrast men's wilfulness with women's intuition. Zeina's mother sensed that it would be dangerous for her husband to sleep in a quilt – harder to throw off – but she could not disobey him. He got his way, and was captured by the British.

Umm Imad had incorporated her mother's stories about Palestine into her unusually fertile memory, retelling them to her own children when they were young, and now – in the dingy 'squat' the family had fled to after the last 'Battle of the Camps' – telling them to me, along with her stories of growing up in Ain Helweh camp. I was fascinated by the minutiae of their relationship: how her mother had helped her out when the first child was born; how she had once brought Umm Imad's favourite dish, still warm in the saucepan, from Ain Helweh to Shatila; how Umm Imad had sent one of her daughters to live with her mother to help her out. Umm Imad said of her, 'Anyone who sat with her thought she was educated. She was very sociable, she loved jokes and laughter'. Her death had been 'the worst thing that happened in my life'.

Through the stories they told, the food they cooked, their accents and proverbs, their singing of lullabies and *ataba'* (dirges), the mothers of women too young to remember Palestine formed a direct link with the land and with specific regions. Zeina:

> My mother used to visit Palestine in the early days, frequently, and for long periods. She told us about work with olives and the wheat harvest. She worked on our own land. Throughout the fifties people used to bring oil from their own and, via Jordan. Mother went alone, to visit her family.

Both these speakers eulogised their mothers (killed during attacks on the camps). Umm Imad said of her mother, 'She was great, a model of a Palestinian woman'. Zeina: ' I consider [my mother] an ideal mother in relation to other Palestinian women. She learnt to read and write, she had ambition. She always made her children enthusiastic for education and patriotism and home'. Words like theirs are often spoken about women of the 'generation of Palestine', those who suffered expulsion from Palestine and the early years of exile, when material conditions were harshest. Both Umm Imad and Zeina had married at relatively late ages (22 and 25 years, respectively); the affection and richness of their descriptions of their mothers surely owes much to this long period of co-residence, as well as the love of Palestine they shared.

Yet the life stories also reveal other feelings towards mothers: implicit criticism, ambivalence, outright hostility. Poverty created mother/daughter tensions, for example by increasing discrimination in favour of boys, or through maternal anxiety for their daughters' reputations. Nationalist movement mobilisation was even more important in generating conflict between girls and their parents. Dalal, the youngest speaker, began her life story with the scar of gender discrimination:[6]

> My mother favoured the boys, she loved the boys more than the girls. For example, she discriminated in food, she used to bring liver for my [older] brother but we ate ordinary food. My brother got new shoes quite often whereas they didn't give us such things. What I liked best was to get sick so as to feel loved. She'd cry over me and bring me everything I wanted.

Like most women of her age group, the 'generation of the revolution', Dalal had gone through sharpest conflict with her mother over nationalist activities. In the following quotation we see how marriage is posed by parents as the 'final solution', one that cannot be questioned or evaded:

> My mother completely refused that I should work with young men. She wanted me to marry so that she could relax. Every day she kept telling me, 'You've got to marry. As soon as someone comes along, that's it!'

Dalal questions not only her parents' upbringing and societal gender norms, but also – paradoxically – the effect of the resistance in spoiling her femininity. Her narrative displays strong ambivalence towards her mother, beginning with blame for conventional gender attitudes but ending with praise for her moral teaching:

> After [my parents] died we went on living the same way. Nothing changed. For instance, no strange man entered our house. Staying out at night was forbidden. We lived according to the rules. My mother's way of raising us influenced all of us, as an atmosphere. Deep inside we knew what is forbidden, what is permitted. My mother taught us all the essential values.

Such ambivalence may be interpreted as rooted in the rapid fluctuations of Palestinian history in Lebanon, and the discursive debate over values that such fluctuations give rise to. Because of its cultural and symbolic resonance, no topic generated more heated debate in the camps during the resistance period than gender. Indeed, this continued to be so up to the time when I was recording the life stories, from 1989 to 1993.

Among speakers who did not spontaneously describe their mothers was Umm Noman, whom I'd first met in a resistance office.[7] In a visit made after recording her life story, I asked about her mother. She had been a very religious woman, very respected. Had she told Umm Noman anything about marriage? No, there wasn't time, her engagement had come about very suddenly, when she was fourteen. The story is revealing of the relationships and calculations involved in arranged marriages:

> [My husband] respected my mother, he spoke to her so that she would approve of him, she liked him, that's why she didn't oppose him. Before him, someone else asked for me and my mother said I was too young. But she didn't oppose Abu Noman. (Did she ask your opinion?) Yes, she asked. I said, Whatever you wish, I gave the decision to her. I put the responsibility on my mother.

The marriage had evidently not been a happy one. Umm Noman had had twenty pregnancies, but in spite of this she was still active with the Women's Union when I recorded with her. I asked, had her mother been 'active'?

> No, she wasn't. She was a housewife only. She didn't have anything to do with such things, i.e. politics. Because of her pilgrimages and her faith, she used to avoid politics. She didn't have a national role.

In contrast to the rich descriptions of their mothers given by Umm Imad and Zeina, Umm Noman was reticent, giving minimal answers to my questions about her mother. It was clear that she didn't want explicitly to blame her mother, or to suggest that they had not been on good terms, but it was equally clear that their relationship had been cool. Though they had lived in nearby camps in the Beirut area, visits between them had been rare. This in itself was unusual. I recall my first Shatila friend, Umm Khaled, who, during a lull in the fighting during the invasion of 1982, had piled all the children into a taxi and crossed the Israeli lines between Beirut and Sidon to look for her mother in the wreckage of Ain Helweh camp. 'There is no one dearer than the mother' she told me later, as sufficient explanation.[8]

The degree of hostility expressed by one of the speakers, Umm Marwan, towards her mother was unusual, given the habitual respect for parents.[9] It was made even more unusual by the fact that we were recording in a family setting, with her mother present. It was an occasion of reconciliation after many years of severed relations (*muqaat'a*).[10] Umm Marwan reached the central point of her story after the briefest of introductions:

> I was married at the age of seventeen. When a girl marries, her husband takes responsibility for her and lightens the burden on her family. I was married to a sick man, from the beginning. Because she wanted this. I married him, and he was sick, he had a heart problem. She wanted him because he was a relative. I wanted someone who was not a relative. Our married life was difficult, we remained four years without children. It was life and not-life.

Umm Marwan had not been allowed by her parents to benefit from free UNRWA schooling. Her rebellion grew out of coercive marriage, an experience common to women of her generation, but unlike most, she had taken opportunities offered by exile – the jobs available in urban areas – to cut ties completely with her natal family after being widowed, and had brought up her five children in rare economic and social independence.

Anger at their parents for not having allowed them to go to school recurs in the narratives of many older women, both those of the 'generation of Palestine' and those of the 'generation of the catastrophe'. Usually it was fathers who had blocked their daughters' education, but sometimes it was the mother. Here is another testimony, expressed with unusual bitterness:

> [My mother] was a backward woman, she seemed to come from three hundred years ago. I told you she was selfish. They sent my brothers, who were much younger than me, to school. But my sister and me, no. I went and begged my mother. I told her, 'Mother you want me to help you, bake, wash dishes, bring you water – I'll do it all'. But she said No to school. I asked her, 'How shall I live?' She told me, 'As I lived, you will live'.[11]

To summarise, most speakers recalled their mothers positively, often as a model for themselves, or for all Palestinian women. This was more particularly the case when both the speaker and her mother shared nationalist feelings. Two strong ideological references impose such sentiments: religion and nationalism. 'Religion', one speaker told me, 'says "your mother, your mother, your mother, then your father"'. Celebration of 'our heroic peasant mothers' was also part of resistance discourse, particularly in those sectors responsible for mobilising women. This could account for some of the piety expressed towards mothers, but I would argue that exile and refugee camp conditions changed the mother/daughter relationship, stretching and complexifying it, and altering its content. Thus it was mainly mothers who were recalled as telling their children about Palestine, or as embodying Palestine in their use of language, clothing, food preparation, or style of mothering.

Talking about Daughters

It was not to be expected, given the generic orientation of life stories towards the past, that the Shatila speakers would talk about their daughters. Nor was it likely that they would spontaneously discuss the upbringing of daughters, or problematic relationships with them, or their feelings towards them; these I sometimes heard about in subsequent visits. But speakers sometimes listed their children, or used their births as markers of historical events. Recently, in work in the West Bank and Gaza, I noticed a difference between women's life stories there and the earlier ones recorded in Lebanon. Women in the West Bank and Gaza usually gave only their sons' names, or sons' names first followed by their daughters', regardless of birth order. With Shatila speakers there was no such discrimination: daughters' names were given in their birth order, and daughters were included when telling of children's achievements in education or professional careers, or when telling of losses. A possible explanation of this difference is that in Lebanon many single women worked (and work) to support ageing parents, and many widows work to support families. The importance of women's economic contribution is a widely acknowledged fact that recurs in daily life conversations.

Yet contradictions between customary attitudes and recognised fact abound. For example, Umm Sobhi[12] wanting to illustrate for me the extent of her despair in exile, said:

> If we die here we find no one to bury us. I had an operation about three months ago. I didn't cry because I was sick but because if I died there was no son beside me. My only son is far; *he is the only one among six daughters. I have no one.*

An example of what appears to be a contradiction is given by Umm Noman, who had brought up her sons to be politically active like herself, but said this about her daughters:

> I don't like my daughters to work outside [the home]. I'm against this. Unless she has a good position. We are Arabs, we have principles, but things you see nowadays are not in conformity with principles. When the girl goes out to work, it could happen that a guy who's not worth a franc but is a bit good-looking, he takes her out and she becomes 'exposed'. Look, we as Palestinians, we don't own anything, we don't have land or property, we have nothing. What can we still own? A little dignity.

This passage illustrates perceptions of the Lebanese environment by Palestinians of rural origin as a source of corruption. Further, it points to young women as the vulnerable sector, those who must be protected, not so much for their own sake as for the sake of 'dignity'. We should not expect Umm Noman to make explicit her concern for her daughters' future marriages, nor the link between her daughters' reputation and her own status. Instead, she expresses the dominant popular conviction that though national struggle involves men and women equally, part of this struggle is to preserve women's role in reproducing national culture and morality.

Gender conservatism and silence about daughters are still common among older women of rural origin. It is possible that age and education as well as social status make a difference to the way women phrase and enforce the control of junior women. Umm Ghassan, a member of the 'generation of Palestine', unschooled, surprised me by the vehemence of her complaints against her husband.[13] Yet her answer to my question about the upbringing of daughters was among the most conservative I received.

Whereas several other mothers emphasised the importance of explanation, Umm Ghassan evoked the older method of silence: 'They [daugh-
ters] *must know without being told* what is forbidden and what is
permitted'. A Palestinian colleague who listened to Umm Ghassan's tape
commented on the effectiveness of silence in terrorising girls as they
approach adulthood.

Dalal's description of her mother's upbringing is probably quite typical of widely used ways to terrorise girls into self-vigilance:

> My mother's way of raising us influenced all of us, not just me. [She] taught
> us the essential values, like washing our hands before eating, brushing our
> teeth, that God is one, not to be greedy. She taught us that if a girl turns out to
> be dirty (*wassakha*), her family will kill her. Such-and-such a girl was killed
> because she loved someone. She used to tell us these stories to teach us.

Umm Marwan was one of the few life storytellers who integrated
daughterhood and motherhood into a coherent narrative. Indeed, two
themes, anger against her mother and love of her children, dominate
and shape her story. In an eloquent passage suffused with rural metaphors of fertility, she tells how having children compensated her for an
unhappy marriage:

> At the beginning of a life, a young man and a young woman, love, fun, life – I
> didn't have that. Emotions died. Days passed and I didn't experience these
> things.... The children that came to me – how can I explain to you? – it's like
> when you have a small plant, maybe it'll live, maybe it'll die. Then you see it
> make many shoots and grow. In spite of the suffering of work, the fatigue, it's
> like having a flower garden, you are proud of it, you say, 'Tomorrow it will
> grow and have flowers'. It gives you hope and a goal. The things you couldn't
> do yourself, you see them in the eyes of your children.... This compensates
> you for the life you couldn't have.
>
> When I came home from work I stayed with my children. We would sit
> together and tell each other what had happened to us during the day. Because
> the world is like a forest, there are evil people and good people. So you have to
> teach your children (e.g. not to steal).... I wanted to raise them in my own way.

In a passage whose interest lies in the light it throws on the close links
between motherhood, children, and community values around women
and sexuality, Umm Marwan talks about work:

> I worked. I did any job except what would hurt my dignity, for the sake of my
> children. My children carry my flag, my respect. I respect myself for my chil-
> dren's sake. I gave up everything for them.

The thematic of Umm Marwan's story leads, not surprisingly, to the
elaboration of the difference between her upbringing and the way she
brought up her daughters:

They all went to school, and three went to university....[14] The girl should learn everything. Yes! Because she mustn't depend completely on a man. Maybe he'll turn out no good, maybe he'll tell her, 'Get out!' Is she going to beg?! Is she going to work as a maid?!... She has to study, she has to learn a profession.... She has to be independent.

The idea of women working outside the home has been a highly charged one for camp Palestinians. As we would expect, Umm Marwan is a strong advocate of women working, yet certain parts of her life story reproduce central elements of Arab gender values, for example the idea that women must bear the weight of special scrutiny, that 'eyes are fixed on women'. They should work, but they must discipline themselves to exclude promiscuity:

Work isn't shameful. It is life. I encourage women to work and to struggle. There are obstacles that face woman but she can overcome them.... She should be controlled because eyes are fixed on women ... she shouldn't play ... she must respect her house, and respect herself. Perhaps she doesn't like her husband, she might see someone who pleases her better. No matter what, she must forbid herself – to protect her house and her children.

As a woman who had suffered from coercive marriage, Umm Marwan adopted a different marriage policy with her own daughters:

They were free to make their choice. But first of all I refused marriage for them before twenty years. No! It's refused. She must finish her studies. Afterwards she'll be mature, old enough to decide. If she meets someone, let her bring him home, we'll talk, exchange ideas. I don't want them to marry according to my will.

We see here the outline of a parent/child relationship reformed in both senses of the word, one of 'give and take', where parental authority is modified without challenging its moral necessity, and where the community constraints on female sexuality are sustained. This essential relationship between community, mother, and daughter is symbolised by the *badli baidha* (white dress) which Umm Marwan introduces towards the end of her story, the dress she has had made for her youngest daughter to wear at her wedding. Umm Marwan conducted the marriage negotiations just as a father or family elder would have done and, embedded in the telling of the marriage arrangements, the white dress is clearly a matter of pride, a sign of her daughter's proper upbringing, and even more, perhaps, of her own success in achieving community norms of parenting in spite of poverty and a hard life.

Umm Marwan's criticisms of certain aspects of Palestinian gender practices – failure to educate girls, coercive marriage, male rights to divorce, opposition to women working – were the most forceful that any of the eighteen Shatila speakers expressed. Yet she took pains to place limits on her critique. Beginning with suffering and rebellion, her narrative ends on a note of triumph. Her pride and self-worth challenges a feminist analysis. Have patriarchal gender rules been preserved? Or have they been re-formed? Has Umm Marwan revealed to us a 'women's discourse' that implicitly critiques and subtly undermines male privilege? Or has she incarnated for us a link between mothering, daughters, and community status that the oppression and impoverishment of Palestinians continue to reinforce?

Conclusion: Twelve Years Later

Here is how I would have ended this essay before the new Intifada: Is the importance of the mother/daughter relationship revealed in the Shatila life stories uniquely a product of conditions of exile, or could it be a much wider characteristic of Arab family life that has been missed only because it is unmarked in dominant discourses of scholars and of Arab society? I would argue, based on observation as well as the life stories, that the mother/daughter relationship in Palestinian rural society has always been emotionally central to women's lives, but that it has been repressed by the imposing structural and cultural weight of the patrilineage. Indisputably, however, conditions in exile – particularly the weakening of the patriarchal hamula – gave greater space for this relationship to develop, and endowed it with new political and ideological potentialities.

When the Resistance movement came with its message of mass struggle, women's response was immediate and strong, but was largely frustrated by opposition from heads of families (or mothers speaking in their name). Stories of women's experiences during the resistance period generally attribute differences in their political activism to individual characteristics ('strength' or 'weakness'), or to family ideology ('conservative' or 'progressive'). Examination of household structural factors might yield a different analysis. Without survey data as backing, I would argue that even though most young women had to struggle with their mothers, mother/daughter alliances were still a major factor enabling some younger women to move into the public domain, legitimating their presence there through the guarantees they offered of a 'proper upbringing', and thus contributing to the 'active citizenship' that has marked Palestinian women in general, deeply altering the nature of the public domain.

Another time, another language! Writing now (February 2001), so many years after the recordings, as refugee camps in Gaza and the West Bank are being shelled, I interrogate myself regarding my role as medium. Could I have done more, done better, to communicate these stories to the world? Why should Palestinian suffering continue? Now I question my academic purposes, my musings over the relationship between nationalism and feminism, my professional concerns as a writer to frame and analyse their raw words to become 'testimonial literature'. Now, even the radicalism of doing research in a refugee camp appears suspect and false. How much harder it would be to live their lives instead of merely writing about them. And live such lives with enough heart left to take in ignorant strangers!

Souad Dajani

Yaffawiyya (I am from Jaffa)

I always feel rather uncomfortable at the prospect of public disclosure, and at any rate it is hard to separate my personal narrative from the political biography of my people. I am also a bit uneasy with the selfishness involved in the act of writing – of having the luxury to do so while my nation is under siege. So I would like to resort to the form of a letter to tell my story. I address this note, 'Dear friend from Yaffo', to some generic 'other' who has replaced me in my homeland and to whom I have always wanted to say these words. I know this isn't entirely fair: I have invented a stereotype of a person who cannot respond to what I say. Yet I do want to peel and explore the layers of my life as a Palestinian in exile with this person. Perhaps my voice will resonate with others who are determined to seize control over the dissemi- of their nations. Perhaps my story will mirror others' experiences and dilemmas in finding a 'self' in a world that rejects their identities.

Dear friend from Yaffo,

The other day I was shopping at the local Star Market when a sign caught my eye: 'Jaffa Oranges, $ 0.79/lb. with card'. I could feel myself bristling: 'The gall of it! *My* oranges 'WITH CARD'?' Then I remembered they were not my oranges. Besides, I could just imagine how people would react if I made a claim to them. How would *you* react? I walked away with a dismissive shrug: 'More likely they were grown on some pesticide-infested farm in California. Jaffa oranges indeed!' As I walked by I caught a whiff of them, and that authentic flowery-citrusy scent reaching my nostrils transported me....

Now, here's the mystery: Tell me, how could the scent of these oranges take me back to relive a time and place I have in fact never known? Is

Palestine imprinted on my soul? Are the sights, sounds, and smells of Jaffa encoded in my genes? How else could I *know* what I've never experienced? How is it I can close my eyes and *feel* the breeze, know exactly how warm it is, and how gently or urgently it blows? You live there now, yet *I* smell the salt of the sea intermingling with the citrus in the air. I smell that peculiar smell of musty walls and walkways, of history and generations of people who once inhabited that ancient place. I hear the swish-swosh of the waves; I hear the voices of people, both living and dead. I hear footsteps on the concrete paths – no, not your footsteps, but the muted echoes of those who passed before in this very place. I feel the warmth of the sun; I shiver slightly when a shadow falls over me. I wonder if a ghost – maybe that of my grandfather – just caressed my skin.

I gaze over Yaffo with my mother's eyes. I can see it through her, the way it was, the way she lived more than fifty years ago, before I was born, before I was even conceived, before you made your home there, before your people renamed it 'Yaffo'. Simultaneously, I am here and I am there. Who is to say what is real? Is my physical body the measure of life and being? Is it my spirit? I – the cynic, the *kaffirah* – experience my own body as disembodied. I traverse time and space in a vehicle that is not my body, and I find myself puzzled and confused as to who 'I' am.

Let me tell you a bit about my past. Two events shaped my life and my experience of 'exile' – for I cannot decide whether 'dislocation' or 'exile' best describes my situation, or if they are synonymous and overlap. I'm not sure I can make sense of the difference. Events seem to converge and fuse together as my parents' lives spill over into my own. Both events I am talking about are critical markers in the Palestinian experience as well: the 1948 catastrophe (Nakba) and the 1982 Israeli invasion of Lebanon.

I was not even present at the former, for I was born in Detroit in 1953, far from the shores of the troubled land that was Palestine. I was not personally thrust into physical exile, as were my parents. I was not a direct witness to the violent wrenching of their possessions, their homes, their patrimony, and their very homeland, right from under their feet. I did not share their fate of being cast adrift into a hostile, rejecting world – a world that for the most part defined them as illegitimate interlopers and liars. I was born of parents whose very existence your people made into a fabrication and a myth. No wonder, then, that a sense of exile is branded on my soul and has stayed with me all my life. Growing up this way was strange: I suppose it gave all of life a surreal quality, and made me wonder whether even to believe in my own existence.

I spent my formative years in Beirut. I was almost eight years old – the eldest of four children, two girls and two boys – when we left the US in 1960. My youngest brother was born in Beirut in 1966. My parents wanted to raise us in an Arab country. They especially wanted their two elder daughters to be brought up Arab rather than American. We had many relatives in Lebanon waiting for us – most had fled Palestine in 1948. I guess my parents longed to recapture, in exile, a sense of the community they had lost.

Paradoxically, Israel's 1982 invasion of Lebanon, the horror that cast me personally into physical exile and marked my own acquaintance with dispossession, was also the pivotal event that snapped me out of a sense of my own disjointed life. At least, that was how it seemed at the time. I finally became aware of belonging to a Palestinian nation. I realised how fundamentally intertwined my fate is with the fate of my people. All at once, the myth of individualism that as a good American I had so readily absorbed, was shattered for me. I was no longer the arrogant, smug American who could thumb her nose at the world. At the mercy of Israeli warplanes, I was merely another Arab, another Palestinian. The planes that bombed us day after day didn't care who I was. Were you a soldier there? A pilot? Did you know or care where the bombs fell?

I was jolted into awareness that as a Palestinian I do not have the luxury of walking out of my own skin. I cannot escape my identity even if I wanted to. My personal story is a political biography as well. I learnt quickly that it isn't the colour of my skin that gives me away; I can seek temporary shelter and anonymity in the nondescript olive of my skin. But my name is like a siren call: 'Souad Dajani' definitely Arab, and in-your-face Palestinian at that. No one can mistake or evade the 'Dajani' as anything but Palestinian. My name unabashedly confronts those Jews who took away my homeland with the reality of my existence, and hence with their act of dispossession. You did not participate in stripping Yaffa away from my parents, but are you among those who would deny me a right to it now?

It is strange that with an identity so public, I still find myself reluctant to write. It is not that I am afraid of inviting hostile reactions – even from you. I expect it comes with the territory. But perhaps I am too private, and dread the self-disclosure involved. Perhaps a measure of angst is missing right now. Do you remember once asking me, 'What will you do with your life if the Israeli/Palestinian conflict is ever resolved?' Well, it hasn't been solved, but after three long years of hand-to-mouth existence in very exploitative part-time teaching positions, I have finally found a job I enjoy. Because of that, one dimension of my sense of exile seems to have been eased. Perhaps I hesitate to write because I am concerned about appearing self-serving. So many tragedies have befallen people around the world! You've followed the news, how in the spring of 1999, Serbs brutally tried to empty Kosovo of its native Albanian population. Did that hit close to home? Then in the fall, Indonesian forces scorched East Timor and left it in ruins. And since mid-1997, Ethiopia has expelled hundreds of thousands of Eritreans in the 'forgotten' war of the Horn of Africa.

I suppose little has changed in fifty years: The tragedies Palestinians endured are replicated around the world today. I feel the trauma of the victims, especially of the refugees created by recent conflicts. I shudder for them, yet I feel helpless and cynical. Fifty years hence, these dispossessed people too will be writing their stories, shedding their tears, their pain of exile intermingling with ours and with all those dispossessed before and since. It is too overwhelming and paralysing to think about. I find myself spinning in my tracks, in the same closed circle in which the very act of writing appears a meaningless luxury.

Over the years, I have come to realise that exile is multi-layered. Just when I think I have solved the mystery and arrived at the core of my being, I find another layer to peel. Exile has to do in part with 'choosing' to live at a geographical distance from a homeland that is simultaneously mine and not mine. What can I say about that? How much of it is a choice, after all? You once asked me, 'Well, why don't you go live in Ramallah in the West Bank?' I told you then, 'I don't want to hate'. Were you satisfied with that answer when it doesn't satisfy me? I felt speechless at the time, because it seemed so amazingly simple, yet so complex. I cannot go 'home' because I am not Jewish. But because I hold an American passport, no Arab country can be my true home. And Ramallah is not my home either, because – I come from Yaffa.

If that is not enough, the experience of *living* exile comes simply (?) from being a Palestinian, being a woman, being single, being ... approaching ... middle age. I wonder if these pieces can ever be connected, whether there is a place to plant roots rather than uproot, and if I will ever find home. My existence is a patchwork of exile and dislocation. I reside in Boston, my soul floats over Yaffa, and my mind is preoccupied with Palestine. And my heart ...?

With all that, what is dislocation? Does that mean like a joint? An elbow? A hip? Don't those heal? Is it that after a certain point, dislocation sets in as a new way of being, a way of life? Is that all one can wish for? To reconcile, rather than relocate? Why should I experience being Palestinian very much as an exile, and exile upon exile at that? Why is it that what set it in motion was more like an earthquake than a dislocation? As though, in the space of a single moment, the ground shifts and heaves, and when we next blink and look around, we are left standing on ground that wasn't even there just a short moment before. The effect is unnerving, unbelievable, permanent; it scars us for generations. There is no way back.

Is dispossession the defining moment? I did not experience the dispossession of Palestine firsthand, yet I feel that loss in every part of my life. 'Dispossession' – disposed of, as my parents and their generation were; disposed to, as an attitude perhaps – one could put on or discard as needed. After all is said and done, there is a 'pose', a way of being in the world, a way of relating to self and others. I pose in front of that camera, waiting, with a frozen smile on my face, for the shutter to click so I can resume my life. It never does.

A woman's heart in a Palestinian body, and a Palestinian heart in a woman's body: My fragmented, dislocated, and displaced existence cries out for acknowledgement, recognition, and redress. But what if these are not forthcoming? Am I to spend my life in some disembodied purgatory? Does my existence depend on others to declare it – me – real?

Can you understand this eternal dilemma of the dislocated? I feel frozen in an existence where time stopped at the hour of exile. Yet I am breathing in a time that continues to tick on, as though unaware of or unsympathetic to the ever widening gap between then and now, and the irreconcilability of these two worlds. I am unnerved by the sensation of skin being pulled and torn apart in two different directions. Which way am I looking? Which way should I go? Do I have a choice?

I know what you must think of my parents and me, indeed, of all Palestinians. You think Palestinians are a people irrationally consumed by hate and anger. Well, you are wrong. Let me tell you that what is most striking about Palestinians of a certain age: their bewilderment. Yes, their bewilderment!

I see this bewilderment in my mother, in my aunts and uncles, and in friends and relatives who lived through the actual experience of having their own homeland ripped away from them. In what must have seemed to them as the blink of an eye, they watched this homeland claimed by Jews, by your people, and denied them forever. The experience is as fresh and raw today as it was over fifty years ago. I still hear my parents speak about Palestine in the present tense as a living experience. Then suddenly they catch themselves and their bewilderment makes them gape. Stunned yet again, they *know* Palestine is lost to them, but they are mentally unable to grasp this loss or come to terms with it. What has befallen them is simply too inconceivable and unbelievable to have really happened. None of the mind games in the world, the ones that people have so often played to cope with tragedies and disasters, ever worked here. My parents, like everyone belonging to the last living generation of Palestine, remain simply incapable of grasping the enormity of what has befallen them. So they exist, in some limbo of past-present and perennial bewilderment.

One of my aunts, a *khalto*, died recently – the eldest of my mother's sisters. She'd been living in Abu Dhabi for the last twenty-five or so years. She was around eighty-three or eighty-four years old when she died. She was a patient, gentle, and loving person who left behind children, grandchildren, and even several great-grandchildren. I don't even know them all! My aunt had a tough life after their exile in 1948. She, her husband, and their kids settled in Nablus. Her husband died shortly after the youngest of her seven children was born. I first met that branch of my family in 1960 or 1961, after we left the US for Lebanon. We used to travel by car to the West Bank to visit our relatives (it was still under Jordanian rule). I remember my aunt's house, high on a hill. I remember playing with my cousins.

I used to watch my aunt and her only daughter doing the housework, seeing, but not understanding, the rather poor conditions in which they lived. I had heard stories of their earlier life in Jaffa, but I was still too young to understand the significance of the change. As you know, we settled in Beirut, and I think we saw them only once more before your country occupied the West Bank (and Gaza Strip) in 1967. I don't remember the year, but my aunt later suffered a stroke that left her partially paralysed on one side of her body. She must have been in her early fifties by then. She did walk – shuffle – but could not use one of her hands. Her kids grew up. Her daughter – my cousin – got married and settled in the Gulf. In time, her brothers also left Nablus to study or work, and my cousin finally got her mother out of Nablus and settled her in Abu Dhabi. That's where I last saw my aunt, when I worked in Abu Dhabi for a year before moving to Canada to complete my studies in 1977.

I was very sad at her passing. My cousin, of course, was devastated. Talking to her over the phone, all the way to Abu Dhabi, really brought home the impact of distance, the tragedy of exile, of permanent dispersion. I was stung by a deep sense of impotence, of not being able to be with my family, of not being able to have a 'normal' life that encompasses family. I didn't know whether I was more upset at my aunt's passing as a *person*, or sad at the loss of history. She is another one of the generation of Palestine who is gone. It made me realise how our heritage, our history, is flowing away from us, and I can't stem that flow.

A friend of mine in Boston also lost an uncle recently, and she reacted in much the same way: To her, this uncle embodied the living history of Palestine. She and I often talked about how we could preserve the memory of Palestine. How could we keep this memory alive and real? More vexing, how could we transmit the immediacy of it to the next generation, to kids who are living a totally different world? How would we make it relevant and vital to them? How do we, the exiles who never *lived* in Palestine, keep it alive for others?

I can anticipate your reaction. 'Why keep it alive when it does not exist anymore?' After all, you'd say, we Palestinians can find 'twenty-two Arab states' to choose from, or we can be content with the 'better' life we can make for ourselves in the West. I think you know the answer to that too, and can tap into your own Jewish history to appreciate it. Can you accept the analogy?

Let me tell you more about my heritage. I am determined to keep it alive and real and reclaim it someday. We have a family tree hanging in my parents' home in Canada. It traces a long line of Dajanis – dating back several hundred years. My mother, Leila Abdullah Dajani, and my father, Rashid Munib Dajani, were both born in Jaffa, Palestine. Distant cousins, they are descendants of several generations of Dajanis born and raised in Palestine. My mother and her family lived in the Ajami quarter of Jaffa. They were quite wealthy by standards of the day; they lived in a large, luxurious house and owned orange orchards – yes, the famous 'Jaffa oranges'.

My maternal grandfather had remarried after the death of his first wife (my mother's aunt), with whom he had had two children. He and my grandmother, Najibeh, went on to have another seven children, the youngest of whom is my mother. My mother never knew her father; he died in 1926, only three days before she was born. I never met my grandmother either; she died while we were in the US. I remember my mother crying when a letter came with the news. I must have been six or seven years old at the time. How could I have understood the significance of my roots being ripped away?

As was customary among families in the early 1900s, my grandparents shared a huge house with their extended family. On one floor, my mother lived with her parents and siblings, and on another, my grandfather's brother lived with his family. Both brothers owned the land and the orchards with their orange groves. My mother can still describe, and in the most minute detail, what her home looked like – expensive furnishings, paintings on the walls (original oil paintings from Europe), dishes and silverware, shelves lined with books, and even a piano. She says that my grandfather was the first man in Palestine to own a car – and have a chauffeur! My mother talks of her father as a kind and generous man who treated her mother well. He bought her fur coats from Europe, took her on outings in the new car, and always behaved towards her with the utmost caring and respect.

I admit I have some mixed feelings about the wealth and, especially, the fur coats. But I feel it is important to reveal these details about my mother's life. For one thing, it should dispel the notion that all Palestinians lived in squalid, nomad-like conditions, with no real ties to the land or a sense of belonging to their country. And telling my mother's story may shock you into a genuine understanding of their exile. My parents awoke one day to find themselves dispossessed of all they had. Worse, they were plunged into a life where all around them they heard it said their lives were nothing but lies that belonged to the dustbin of history, never to be retrieved or reclaimed. Palestine – Israel – henceforth was 'the state of the Jewish people'. Don't people wonder, when we utter the word 'Palestinians'? Surely they must originate from a place (once) called Palestine?

My mother and her family fled the fighting in 1948. They sought refuge with relatives in Tripoli, in Northern Lebanon. Like countless other Palestinian families who tell and retell the events of their exile, I must have heard the story of their departure hundreds of times. For all these Palestinians, it is as fresh and raw today as it was over fifty years ago. Thinking that they would escape the worst of the fighting and return home when things had calmed down, my mother, her mother, and the rest of the family packed weekend suitcases. My elderly aunt (the second in line), now over eighty years old and living in Abu Dhabi, still nags at me to find her a copy of the book she was reading when she left Yaffa. It was called *The Five Stepping-Stones*. She says, 'I left it lying face-down, on my nightstand at home. I want to know how the story ends'.

Well, we know how this story ends. The state of Israel is declared, the borders are sealed, and my parents, along with all the hundreds of thousands who fled or who were violently expelled from Palestine, are forbidden from returning. My mother lost her homeland – forever. A pause, a freeze in time – in a time that would inexorably tick on – and I came into being in Detroit. Oh, did I tell you that my parents were married and left for Detroit, where my dad went to study? That's how we ended up in the US.

And what about you? When did you arrive in Yaffa? Where did you come from? Whose home did you inhabit? Was it ours? Did you marvel at your 'luck' at finding a fully furnished house to inhabit? Did you wonder what must have possessed people to abandon such a home? Did you wonder where we were, how we felt then, how we must feel today? Because you are Jewish, you got my home, and my homeland. That is how I came to be born in exile. Yet, whether I chose to or not, I would still grow up being Palestinian.

Let me piece together the rest of my story. I went on to study at the American University of Beirut (A.U.B.). I will skip the details, except to say I was in Beirut during the civil war years of the mid-1970s. After graduating with my masters degree in 1976, I left Lebanon to continue my studies in Canada, arriving there in 1977 after other stops on my journey in exile. Inevitably while in Beirut, I had experienced the tension of being Palestinian in a Lebanese society and being a woman in a male-dominated and somewhat restrictive one. I was also quite outspoken and independent in my beliefs and way of thinking. That got me into no end of trouble, especially with my family. But I knew no other way to *be*.

I returned to Beirut in the fall of 1981 to collect information for my doctoral thesis. I was invited to teach sociology at A.U.B. It was a wonderful experience, despite lingering tensions in the country. Many of my students belonged to political factions, but I never wanted to know if they carried arms or fought in militias once they left campus. Early in the second semester, I started hearing rumours about an imminent Israeli invasion. Were you aware of these plans? Were you being trained to fight?

June 1982: Israel indeed invaded. For someone who had been in Beirut during the peak of the Lebanese civil war, Israel's invasion was still unparalleled in its horror, its violence, and its brutality. How did *you* imagine it was for us? We were totally terrorised by the indiscriminate bombing, and utterly helpless against warplanes raining death upon us. If we asked 'Why?' we were told that as 'civilians', we should not be living among 'terrorists'.

We lived in West Beirut, opposite the Fakhani area on the other side of the Corniche Mazraa (one of the main thoroughfares linking East and West Beirut). Because of its proximity to Palestinian refugee camps and residential areas, our neighbourhood quickly became unsafe. We abandoned our home. My parents and youngest brother sought refuge in the Hamra area, in the home of someone who was away at the time. I holed up at the American University of Beirut Hospital, where my sister was studying medicine. I spent most of my waking hours in a daze, walking aimlessly up and down the corridors with a transistor glued to my ear.

I remember how after each round of bombing, cars and ambulances would converge on the scene to pull out the dead and injured. Bodies would be tossed haphazardly into vehicles, and cars would then rush off in every direction. Often, this meant that families did not have a clue where their sons, daughters, husbands, wives, and parents had been taken – or even if they were alive. At the hospital where I stayed, I would see the aftermath: people running up and down corridors, pulling at their hair, crying, screaming, 'Oh, my son!' 'Oh, my husband!' 'Oh, my mother!' Everywhere, I saw frantic and hysterical people. Thinking of it still sends shivers down my spine. I could not cope with the human anguish. I would retreat into the surgical wards full of people – those with missing limbs, exposed guts, torn bodies. Blessed silence! These patients were anesthetised; they could not scream.

With all the death and destruction around me I began to understand, to wake up – as though roused from a deep sleep – and consciously identify myself as Palestinian. Until then I had unconsciously grown into a rather acquiescent American, internalising Western notions of individualism and responsibility. I truly believed people were responsible for their own fate and that if they worked hard, they would 'make it'.

How naïve and misled I was! The invasion shocked me into a different reality. Did your warplanes know or care that I was a young woman, teaching, working on a Ph.D., and an American to boot? Did your bombs ever distinguish me from the 'refugees' your country was bent on eliminating? I am ashamed how brainwashed I was then – believing that Americans were somehow 'deserving'. Ironically, Israeli bombs snapped me into an awareness of what others around me had known all along: as Palestinians, Lebanese, Arabs, Muslims, we were not individuals with our own lives and cares, but collectively branded; our lives were expendable. I learnt that my American passport meant nothing. I learnt that as a Palestinian, I would never be safe, personally secure, or able to control my own destiny, until my people were safe. I'll bet this was not your intention. Surely it was not your politicians' intentions to make passive Palestinians like me aware of our Palestinian identity and determined to struggle for it! What an irony of war! How many new Palestinian militants and nationalists did your 1982 invasion create?

I vowed that if I got out alive I would do what I could to struggle for Palestinian rights. A few weeks later I left Beirut (a tale for another time). When I returned to Canada, I found myself consumed by hate and rage. I was incensed at life going on normally around me in Toronto while Beirut was up in flames. I was enraged by the media's lies about the carnage there. I was mad, mad! But I was alive; and so another 'radical Palestinian' was born.

I have never quite recovered from the trauma of that invasion. I still get startled when jet fighters screech through the sky, and I jump at sudden loud noises. The years have dulled some of the rage, and a lot of the hate, but not my attachment to Palestine. It took several years for me to make the next logical leap, and to understand that for Palestinians to be safe, Jews have to be safe too – but not one at the expense of the other. And not – as the Oslo peace process prescribes – by Palestinians accepting what your own countrymen and women surely never would, a mere 1 per cent of their original homeland, and a scattered 11 per cent of the lands at that. Today, 1.2 million Palestinians are citizens of the Israeli state. They 'co-exist' among about five million Jews. Yet they are unequal in their own land. Another 2.8 or 2.9 million Palestinians inhabit the West Bank and Gaza, where the Jewish settler population – including East Jerusalem – has topped 400,000.[1] On both sides of a fast disappearing 'Green Line', your people wield power and control. Some of you want to 'separate' from us, in the form of 'two states'. Tell me, do you sincerely believe what is going on is a blueprint for two states?

I visited in June 1999 (after an absence of six years) and was shocked by the changes. I saw the way Oslo had unfolded on the ground of the West Bank and Gaza, establishing 'facts' in the form of settlements and so-called 'bypass' roads that, far from removing the occupation, have entrenched it even further. I couldn't believe my eyes at how many settlements have sprouted and expanded in the area. And how huge so many of them have become! Maale Adumim, once a tiny outpost, is a city now. It extends all the way from just outside Jericho on the east to the towns bordering Jerusalem on the west. Once its expansion is complete, it will permanently cut off the northern West Bank from the south. Have you been to the West Bank lately? Did you notice how the Palestinian areas of 'self-rule' are mere pockets in a sea of Israeli control? Did I ever tell you of the day I had to go to Jerusalem to keep an appointment? I had barely left the outskirts of Ramallah when I was stopped at an Israeli checkpoint and a soldier said, in a very deliberate tone, 'Welcome to Israel!' I thought to myself, 'This is *peace*? The "state" of Ramallah, the "state" of Nablus, the "state" of Jenin, the "state" of Bethlehem – how are all these scattered and fragmented bits of territory ever to add up to a functioning state?'

It seems your countrymen and women want it all, refusing to give up *all* the areas occupied in 1967. What is it that you accept for us and want to impose on us? Is apartheid okay, and we can call it a 'state' if we like, as long as it doesn't touch you or your life, or threaten your privilege as a Jew? Tell me, in your heart of hearts do you believe human beings are the same, be we Jewish or Palestinian? Can you acknowledge and accept our claim to Palestine as being as worthy and legitimate as you proclaim your own? *It is our homeland too*, and for better or worse, it is also the only country we two peoples have. What should we make of it?

Frankly, if things were reversed and I was on the 'winning' side, I don't know if I would have the guts or the morality to confront my unearned entitlement and give it up, or share it. But as things stand, the situation is untenable and outrageous. How can one people claim an exclusive right to a homeland that is not exclusively theirs, and attempt to permanently control, oppress, subdue, and confine the other people who have legitimate claims to that same land?

After my own long journey in reflection and activism, I have come to believe there is only one solution to our dispossession, exile, and disloca-tion: A single secular democratic homeland and state for both Palestini-ans and Jewish Israelis. I know that most Israelis shudder at the notion of a single state. How do you feel about it? Don't you think my parents have a right to claim their home, and I have a right to claim my patrimony? How long will your people try to deny us that right?

In talking to you this way, am I placing national rights over and above gender equality? What about my own very real sense of dislocation and exile as a woman? I have to admit that since 1982, the sense of being part of a collective Palestinian identity has predominated. Israeli warplanes and bombs didn't distinguish between men and women, and I emerged from that experience feeling the Palestinian identity itself was under attack and had to be saved. That doesn't mean I ignore my gender: After all, I can no more pry away my female-ness than I can my Arab-ness. I am rudely reminded of these interlocking identities almost daily. And you men (yes, I lump you together) – Israeli Jewish and Palestinian alike – keep finding ways of turning us into scapegoats for your political deci-sions and activities. I remember one visit to the Dome of the Rock in Jerusalem with one of my cousins. It was in the late 1980s, during the Intifada, and a Palestinian man walked up to us and began shouting angrily at me. He was berating me for not wearing a headscarf, and he went on and on about how Palestinians were being defeated because we had violated our 'traditions' and succumbed to foreign customs. It was a twisted logic, but quite telling. I have heard a similar logic coming from the 'other side', when two Jewish Israeli women whom once I encountered insisted they had 'no need' of feminism in Israel because women could join the army!

I have paid a high personal price for affirming both my identities as a Palestinian and a woman. And I can't say I've enjoyed more acceptance in one society than another. Whether it's Lebanon, Jordan, or the US and Canada (to mention a few of the places where I've lived and worked), either one or both of my identities have been problematic. In the West, I have come across feminists and so-called progressives who have wanted me to leave my Palestinian heritage behind and speak out as a 'sister' against all the evils of Arab male patriarchal domination. In the Arab world, they give lip service to their support of the Palestinian cause but frequently discriminate against Palestinians in practice. And being a woman? I think Arab society is confused and vacillating over women's roles: I've lived all the extremes, from the most respectful and circumspect, to being degraded and viewed as the mere property of men. No wonder I am unable to put down an anchor in any society and call it home. I – as a symbol of womanhood and Palestine – make people squirm.

So, friend from 'Yaffo', I could go on. But let me end with this. As long as I refuse to accept my dispossession and exile, you too will have no peace. Your life, like mine, will be dislocated and torn. You will constantly be searching for ways to patch up the 'original sin' of your presence in my homeland, and I will be watching you closely and seeking my way back home.

Yours truly,
Yaffawiyya,
Souad

Postscript: I finished writing this letter in January 2000, well before the fateful events of September 2000. Were my last words prescient? The Second Intifada seemed to embody my last warning: Palestinians would not forget nor abandon their homeland.

Whether this revolt signalled the beginning of the final battle for Palestine, or whether it would be crushed to erupt again at a later date, the essential 'fault lines' have been irreversibly exposed. Israel's overwhelmingly brutal use of force tore the veil of hypocrisy off 'Oslo' and destroyed the illusion of the occupation being over. More important, the primal nature of this conflict has been peeled down to its bitter roots.

Jews wrested the Palestinian homeland from its people by force, and will – have to – ward off confronting that original sin. This, I believe, underlies the Israeli Jewish willingness to use extreme force against Palestinian civilians and the obscenely racist remarks about Palestinian parents willing to send their kids into the street. It also explains the rush to establish an apartheid-like system to distance Israelis as much as possible from the living reminder of that 'sin'. Too many Israeli Jews, and indeed other Jews, simply believe they are a superior people, a different and more deserving species than the Palestinians. In that way, they can rationalise both their original dispossession of the Palestinians and all manner of carnage against them now. But why would they have to go this far if there wasn't a niggling sense of guilt and sense of wrongdoing? It is a vicious cycle that won't end: As long as Palestinians exist to remind them of what they did, Israeli Jews will attempt to destroy that reminder. And the harder they clamp down, the more they will be scrambling to reconcile morality with their vicious deeds. This will only beget more racism and bigotry, and fuel and rationalise the need for even more violence. Palestinians haven't been innocent in all this either, and I dread the day we will have to face our own internal rottenness. Meantime, so it goes.

I've been asked several questions about both my essay and the 'position' I've taken in recent months. About my essay, 'Why don't you speak more directly to the voice of a woman – as one who is dislocated and dispossessed?' Maybe I am too dislocated from myself right now. I can't. This is my voice. 'Is the 'friend from Yaffo' in my letter a male?' Yes. 'Is he a real person?' To be honest, 'he' is a composite of several people I have met along the way, but with whom I can no longer be in dialogue. About my position at this time, 'Why can't you acknowledge the need for a safe place for Jews in a separate Jewish state?' Because Jews will never be safe if they persist in denying Palestinians a right to their own homeland, and when Palestinians do return to their homeland, there will no longer be a Jewish state. Until my friend from Yaffa acknowledges and accepts these realities, and does what needs to be done for the sake of a truly just peace, I cannot dialogue.

My people's fate, and his, will likely be forever intertwined. I hope we won't find ourselves in an eternal death trap.

Boston, Massachusetts
December 2000

Notes

'Remembering Mothers, Forming Daughters'

1. My earliest visits were to Dbeyeh camp, north of Beirut, where relatives of my husband's lived, originally from Al-Bassa (erased) in northern Galilee. Later, in the early 1970s, I did fieldwork in Burj al-Barajneh camp, using oral testimonies to write Palestinian history (Sayigh, 1979). In the autumn of 1982, after the war, I began visiting Shatila camp, writing an oral history of the camp (Sayigh, 1994), and a doctoral dissertation, 'Palestinian Camp Women's Narratives of Exile: 'Self', Gender, National Crisis', University of Hull, 1994.
2. Najjar gives a comprehensive bibliography, though now slightly outdated (Najjar, 1992).
3. During the PLO period, senior women were known to go to the Abu Ammar to protest against 'honour killings'. In my time in Shatila, a group of mothers went to the school director because boys jostled girls at the entry. Compare with Arab immigrant communities in France (Andezian and Streiff-Fenart, 1983).
4. Umm Imad, born in 1946, in Akka, married in 1968. 'Umm' means mother; Imad is the name of her oldest son. This is how married men and women are named in popular Arab milieus. All the names used in this essay are fictitious.
5. Zeina, born in 1949, somewhere in South Lebanon, married in 1974.
6. Dalal, born in 1965 in Sabra, unmarried.
7. Umm Noman, born in 1937 in Kabri (Galilee), married in 1951.
8. Umm Khaled was born in 1948, on the way from her parents' village near Safed to Lebanon.
9. Umm Marwan, born in 1938 in a small village near Akka, married in 1956.
10. I have heard of quarrels between brothers leading to long or permanent alienation, but rarely between related women.
11. This comes not from the Shatila life stories but from another set published in 1998/99 in a Beirut journal, *Al-Raida*, 16 (83–4): 48.
12. Umm Sobhi, born in 1941 in a small village near Haifa, married in 1958.
13. Umm Ghassan, born in 1930 in a small village near Akka, married in 1945.
14. The word 'university' is used here as a euphemism for post-secondary training.

'Yaffawiyya (I am from Jaffa)'

1. For data on population trends and settlement building in the occupied territories, see 'Report on Settlements in the Occupied Territories', Foundation for Middle East Peace, www.fmep.org; and Palestinian Academic Society for the Study of International Affairs, www.passia.org.

References

'Remembering Mothers, Forming Daughters'

Andezian, Sossie, and Jocelyne Streiff-Fenart. 1982. 'Relations de voisinage et controle sociale'. *Peuples Mediterraneens*, January–June: 22, 23.
Asad, Talal. 1986. 'The concept of cultural translation in British social anthropology'. In James Clifford and George Marcus (eds.), *Writing Culture: The Poetics and Politics of Ethnography*. Berkeley: University of California Press.

Chatterjee, Partha. 1993. *Nationalist Thought and the Colonial World*. London: Zed Books.

Fleischmann, Ellen. 1996. 'Crossing the boundaries of history: Exploring oral history in researching Palestinian women in the Mandate period'. *Women's History Review* 5 (3).

Granqvist, Hilma. 1931 [1935]. *Marriage Conditions in a Palestinian Village*. 2 vols. Helsinki: Soderstrom.

Hammami, Rema, and Penny Johnson. 1999. 'Equality with a difference: Gender and citizenship in transitional Palestine'. *Social Policies* (fall): 314–43.

Joseph, Suad. 1983. 'Working-class women's networks in a sectarian state: Political paradox'. *American Ethnologist* 10 (1): 1–22.

———. 1993. 'Connectivity and patriarchy among urban working-class Arab families in Lebanon'. *Ethos* 21 (4): 452–85.

Khalili, Ghazi. 1981. *The Palestinian Woman and the Revolution*. Beirut: PLO Research Centre. [Arabic]

Kandiyoti, Deniz (ed.). *Gendering the Middle East: Emerging Perspectives*. London: Tauris.

Najjar, Orayb. 1992. *Portraits of Palestinian Women*. Salt Lake City: Utah University Press.

Passerini, Luisa. 1987. *Fascism in Popular Memory: The Cultural Experience of the Turin Working Class*. Cambridge: Cambridge University Press.

Peteet, Julie. 1991. *Gender in Crisis: Women and the Palestinian Resistance Movement*. New York: Columbia University Press.

Radhakrishnan, R. 1992. 'Nationalism, gender and the narrative of identity'. In Andrew Parker et al. (eds.), *Nationalisms and Sexualities*. New York: Routledge.

Sarhan, Bassem. 1991. 'Structural change in the Palestinian family'. *The Journal of the Union of Palestinian Writers* (Damascus) 22: 16–29. [Arabic]

Sayigh, Rosemary. 1979. *Too Many Enemies: The Palestinian Experience in Lebanon*. London: Zed Books.

———. 1994. *Too Many Enemies: The Palestinian Experience in Lebanon*. London: Zed Books.

———. 1996. 'Researching gender in a Palestinian camp: Political, theoretical and methodological problems'. In Deniz Kandiyoti (ed.), *Gendering the Middle East: Emerging Perspectives*. London: Tauris.

Stanley, Jo. 1996. 'Including the feelings: Personal political testimony and self-disclosure'. *Oral History* 24 (1): 60.

Yuval-Davis, Nira, and Floya Anthias (eds.). 1989. *Woman-Nation-State*. Basingstoke: Macmillan.

Two

Home as Exile

Isis Nusair

Gendered Politics of Location: Generational Intersections

—ᚖ—

I went back to my hometown Nazareth in late December 1997 to conduct a comparative analysis of the socio-political experiences of three generations of Palestinian women, citizens of Israel, from 1948 to1998 for my dissertation. It was my first long stay at home since I started my graduate studies in the United States in 1993. The first inter-generational group I interviewed in Nazareth in mid-January 1998 was my family. I interviewed consecutively my mother, aunt, grandmother, and cousin.

The 'Beginning': My Grandmother (Rahija Farah)

I spent the morning of 17 January 1998 talking to my grandmother in Arabic about her life experiences, how she defines herself, and her memories of the first years of the creation of the state of Israel. I sat next to her and wrote down every word she said. My grandmother recounted:

> In 1948, I was twenty-seven years old. George was eleven months old, and I was six months pregnant with Siham.Before 1948, people were simple. In 1947 when the British left, the revolution took place. Your grandfather was a policeman with the British, and they [the Jews] asked him to leave his job. There were one hundred and fifty policemen; they kept fifty and fired one hundred. He was with the communists, and they told him that he might get his job back, but they never took him back. He had a retirement allowance from the British, and for five years he was without a job. It was an extremely difficult period (*inharaina fiha hariy*). I sold my gold. Afterwards, he worked in construction and his hands used to bleed.
>
> When they first came there was a patrol, and there was curfew during the day and at night. The curfew would be lifted for two hours a day. Between

1948 and 1950 they gave us a very hard time (*nashafu riqna*). If you wanted to go somewhere, to Haifa for example, you needed a permit from the military governor. Men were without work; only those who had permits could work. One afternoon your grandfather wanted to go to the neighbours to play cards, and they ordered him to remain inside. Refugees came [to our neighbourhood] from Ma'aloul and El-Mjaidel, and they had nothing. We had some stored food and I used to help out [the refugees]. We needed someone to help us, though.

When the Jews came in May 1948, we were asleep. During the occupation night, a man from the Fahoum family came to our house, and called on your grandfather to bring his rifle and follow him. That night, my brother-in-law came with his wife and kids. They lived in the centre of town and there was more fear there than here [in the market area]. At two in the morning your grandfather left for Saffourieh to fight. The Jews threw a bomb at them, and it made a hole in the ground. As he was running, he fell and sprained his ankle. In the morning he came home. The man from the Fahoum family fled with his family to Lebanon. The British stood with the Jews and gave them rifles. During the first and second weeks they warned people to hand in their rifles. Your grandfather hid his rifle instead of throwing it in the well.

The nuns started to distribute clothes and food to the refugees and widows at the Baptist school. They said, 'Come and we'll give you some food'. We were shy and felt like beggars. I used to carry the aluminium pot and they would give us milk. The nuns liked me a lot and used to add butter in the milk for cooking. The missionaries helped out. During the first four to five years [of the creation of the state of Israel] we had a very hard time (*shufna fiha nujum el-duhr*). After the kids grew up, time was running, and God knows how we survived.

In 1952, I worked in the cigarette factory. Michel, my youngest [and fifth] child, was two years old. I was supposed to be a teacher. The kids were young and people were shy. After a few months the cigarette factory closed down, and I was without a job. I hated the Jews because everything in our lives was turned upside down.

I define myself as an Arab Palestinian.... Israel is better for us; we have rights and they help us. If only the politics were different and they would love the Arabs. They are good if you do not get close to them. We did not see much in Nazareth, especially us, the women. No Jew lived in Nazareth. I did not come and go. I had small kids to care for. They used to give me a hard time when I wanted to see my brother and sister [in Jordan], and the Abu-Saleh family [the family of her brother-in-law in Jerusalem]. I could not see them for ten years. I did not interfere in their [the Jews'] business; I did not have any interaction with them.

The communists were fighting back, and it was not my business. I wanted to care for my children. It is enough that your grandfather ruined our lives (*kharrab baitna*). They used to treat the communists badly (*yhrqo dynhin*). They never jailed your grandfather. During the beginning of the occupation, the communists used to have a meeting once a month. We were unable at the time to pay the electricity bill, and they wanted to have a meeting at our place. I asked them not to have meetings at our place, because we could hardly afford to eat. Your grandfather was very committed to communism, and I was angry with him for that. After ten years we got used to them [the Jews].

I was twenty years old when I got married. I was sixteen when I graduated from school. After graduation, I went to Beirut, to study for six or seven months, after which I taught at St Joseph school in Acre for six or seven months. My mother did not allow me to go back to Acre and get the education certificate; she was afraid that I would become a nun. I was not daring (*fitha*), and I had pride (*'izzat nafs*). Now I regret it. At the time, if you got engaged you were required to quit school. During the British Mandate, married women used to work at the post office or as teachers. I had a chance to work at the post office, but my family would not allow me. If you wanted to work, you had to challenge your family, and if you were timid you missed your chance. I got engaged to a guy from the Danial family, but we did not get along. At age eighteen, I was learning to sew at Umm Emil's. Your grandfather was a policeman in Gaza, and we were engaged for one and a half years before we got married.

Your mother wanted to be a teacher and her father did not want her to continue her education. The day she was supposed to go for an interview in Tel-Aviv to be a teacher, she got engaged. Your mother, God bless her, is smarter than those who had graduated from universities.

Before the Jews came, I was the best off in the neighbourhood. Your grandfather worked as a policeman, and we were doing well economically. When I was fifty-one I had a stroke. I had had [high] blood pressure since I was thirty-six. There was too much fear, tension, and worries (*ra'abe wa-mumaqateh*). I was sick from what we went through and from the changes that took place. In 1971, your grandfather was injured at work [construction site], and he could no longer work. He got a monthly allowance from the National Insurance and our situation improved.

After about two hours we ended our conversation. I heated my grandmother's lunch. She insisted that I drink some lemonade before I leave, and asked me to come back and stay with her that night. My grandmother had lived on her own since my grandfather's death in 1995. By the time I arrived at her place at about midnight, I found her unconscious. I called an ambulance, but it was too late. She had suffered a heart attack and died that night at her home at the age of seventy-seven.

The Loss of My Grandmother: A Last-Minute Glimpse into Her Life

The sudden loss of my grandmother was overwhelming, and that close encounter with death was horrifying. She is gone. I will never see her nor talk to her again. I will never be able to ask her any more questions about who she was, and how her experiences shaped and were shaped by the political changes around her.

Many questions still haunt me regarding the death of my grandmother. Was it the questions that I asked, or the memories that our conversation brought to her mind that contributed to her death? Was she so overwhelmed by what was left unsaid that only death would liberate her from the traumas and burdens of the past? Was it just a coincidence, implied by a friend who once told me: 'Consider her last words a present. She shared part of her life with you'.

I will never know what went through my grandmother's mind after the interview. I can never ask her for clarification nor for more details. The life story of my grandmother, as well as the life stories of the majority of Palestinian women of her generation, will remain absent from the official history books and academic analyses. They are the 'invisible and marginalised' whose story does not count. They are the 'reproducers of society', but not necessarily recorded as the 'makers of history'.

Writing this essay is a personal search for meaning, and a means to understand the continuity and discontinuity between the lives of my grandmother, my mother, and myself. The intersection between our generations is the focus of this essay.

The 'Beginning': My Mother (Elham Nusair)

I spent the morning of 16 January 1998, the day before I spoke with my grandmother, talking to my mother in Arabic about her life experiences, how she defines herself, and her feelings towards the state of Israel. I sat across the table from her and wrote every word she said. My mother recounted:

I define myself as a Palestinian Arab living in the state of Israel. I respect the state's law and order but do not consider myself to be an Israeli.

During the period between 1949 and 1966, people (*el-nas*) were without jobs. They needed permission from the military governor to work. They [the Jews] took the land from Nazareth to build Nazareth Illith. People started to demonstrate against land confiscation. They did not know what was going to happen, and they were afraid for their daughters. My father was a policeman with the British. After the British left, he was without a job. We were kids, and my mother had to sell her gold and the house furniture. They got him out of his job because he was a communist. My mother worked in the cigarette factory for seven or eight months. Fear and poverty is what I remember about that period. My father used to cry. Afterwards, he worked as a construction worker. His feet used to swell, and blood would drip from his feet and hands.

The refugees who came from Ma'aloul lived opposite our house. People received them well. Their kids went to school and people thought that it was a short and passing period. People were confined (*mahsura*). They were afraid that new people were coming to our neighbourhood. They accepted the refugees but did not know what would happen. There were no Jews in Nazareth. The military governor was in El-Qashle [a hilly area in Nazareth], and the police department (*maskubiyya*) had a Jewish administration with an Arab police force [at the centre of the city].

When I was thirteen [in 1957] there were demonstrations against land confiscation. People started to organise against the occupation. My brother was jailed during the students' demonstrations. Three years later, I was engaged and got married. The Jews were modern, and people [Palestinians, citizens of Israel] were afraid that their daughters would become loose. The main reason for my early marriage was fear and poverty.

During the 1967 war, people had hopes that the situation would improve. We heard the news about the defeat (*hazima*). That allowed people [Palestinians, citizens of Israel] to accept their destiny. They lived with the state of Israel and allowed it to do whatever it wanted to them. They gave up, and except for the political parties no one was organising. In six days they occupied all of the Arab countries. There was no hope, and whatever we heard on the radio during the Abdel-Nasser period was pure demagogy.

They [the Jews] did not bother us nor interfered in our affairs. No Jewish family lived in Nazareth. People continued in their way of living. We lived as if in a ghetto, without openness to the outside world. There were few opportunities for education. After 1967, the situation improved, and the economy improved. People started to work to improve their social condition. In the beginning they were closed off and later there was more openness.

It is hard to compare fifty years ago to today. The gap is very large. People modernised under Israel more than they did in the Arab countries. I support that. The daily life has improved. People accepted the occupation, and until today I still consider it an occupation. Only when Palestinians receive full rights and justice will I belong to the state of Israel that is not Jewish. We are residents and not citizens. Before 1967, there was no oppression. After 1967 we understood that the state is expansionist. It is an oppressive state that believes in something on behalf of another people [the Palestinian people]. They took the land from us without a fuss (*'ala el-saket*). People did not resist, as if they were in shock not knowing what would happen next.

As a mother I suffer for the death of the Palestinian and the Jew, because a human being is a human being. I am in pain because the occupier has everything and the weak have nothing. I see power and weakness, and justice is lost in between. I brought up my kids to understand what goes on around them, and not to give up. I am not satisfied, because I can do more than this. I did not do anything for myself. I worked for my family and kids. I am trying to change but do not know how.

The Israelis never scared me. I consider them an occupying and cruel people. They know what is theirs but do not recognise the rights of the other (*bie'arfu illi el-hin wa-la bi'arifu illi 'alaihin*). I do not know much about them except from what I see on television, and from our friends in Tiberius. Our generation, the generation of the occupation, suffered the most. Before [1948], people were satisfied, and it was a closed society. We grew up under occupation. We grew up in fear and terror of the unknown. Your dad was strict, and I believe that I gave up. Our generation gave to you what we could not get. I see my success in your generation, and that is my only consolation.

The Communist Party resisted all along, and they had a women's organisation. People started to work in factories, and workers' unions and local councils were being established. After 1967, there was work and people with their own initiative improved their situation. Television had an impact. They also lifted the military rule, and we had a chance to go out and see the world (*nitla' winshuf el-dinya*).

The occupation affected us. We could not finish our education. People were afraid of something that they did not know what it was. For fifty years now we have been going on the road of development. Still, if Israel had not come the development process would have been better. The state of Israel is an occupying state, and it became more obvious after the 1967 occupation [of the West Bank and Gaza]. It is an arrogant and militarised state that does not want peace. I live in a state where I am not satisfied with anything it does. I feel marginalised and have no influence. I do not feel I belong to their political parties. I belong to the *jabha* (Democratic Front for Equality and Peace), and not to the communist party because I am not a communist. Violence and dominance are seen and felt on a daily basis. I did not experience it directly, except through the television and radio. I do not like the violence on both sides.

I do not believe that I have a healthy marriage, despite my being satisfied with it. I believe that I was deprived of my childhood and adulthood, and I blame the occupation for that. The lack of jobs caused violence in the family. My father was short tempered. He was violent with my mother and older brother. He was not too violent, though. He stayed at home without a job and without authority (*nofouz*). People were neither happy nor relaxed.

I should have finished my education. Opportunity came and your father did not want to wait. My mother more than my father, wanted to marry me off. My father said, 'She is still young, leave her alone. What do you want from her?' My mother would say, 'I cannot continue to take responsibility for her'. I found it a way to escape from this life to a better one. I was a coward.

I am against the oppression of the Jews. I want them to live with us in dignity and justice. I am against violence and oppression, and do not believe that God gave them this land. There is no connection. It has to be a state of all its citizens. Other than this, neither they nor their God has anything to do here.

Demarcation Lines

As each interview had minimal intervention on my part, it was left for my grandmother and mother to determine the content and structure of the interview, and to construct a meaning through their memory and narrative. The interview is a moment in time and place. It is a reflection of how my grandmother and mother perceived their experiences, and the ways they wanted to present them to the 'outside world'. The only demarcating lines were those which enclosed the period covered in the research project (1948–98). Both my grandmother and mother took the year 1948 as a point of reference, and both eloquently presented the complex intertwining between the public and private spheres of their lives.

According to Sizoo (1997: 6), the question of how women 'face, negotiate, and shape the social space of their environment needs to be looked into from a time perspective as well as a cross-cultural place angle'. Sizoo wonders about the changes that we see over a certain period of time in a given 'geographical context (multi-generational or 'vertical' perspective)' and how a 'particular period in which a generation experiences a certain environment makes a difference (intergenerational or 'horizontal' perspective') (ibid.: 6). Life narratives, concludes Sizoo, are a translation of a perception of events, and are intuitively analytical. They can be selective and full of contradictions.

Fifty Years After: National Symbols, Statehood and Assertion of Power

My research coincided with Israeli celebrations of fifty years of independence, and the Palestinian commemoration of fifty years of catastrophe (*nakba*). As a Palestinian, second-class citizen of the state of Israel, I found myself in a new position. I am the outsider from within, and the insider from the outside.

On Israel's fiftieth Independence Day I wrote in my journal:

The Air Force planes flew above our heads. Their voice was loud and overbearing. I glared at the sky and contemplated the celebrated power and asserted presence of the Israeli Air Force in my life. I spent the day with my family in our house in Nazareth. Life continued as usual. The only difference was that it was neither Sunday nor a 'holiday', and still my father, brothers, and sisters-in-law were off work. I guess it was a national holiday for the Jewish population of Israel, while Palestinians knew and were reminded (in case they forgot) that they were excluded from it.

I spent the day flipping through the Hebrew newspapers, Ma'ariv, Yediot Ahronot, and Ha'aretz. I looked for a glimpse or a mention of my/our presence. I looked for anything that I could relate to or identify with. The only article I could find was an article in Ha'aretz about a Jewish kid (now a professor at Tel-Aviv University) who was brought up by his communist parents on the margins of Israeli society.

A Canadian team was in town filming a documentary about the celebrations (or lack thereof) of Israel's fifty years of independence. My father told me that he saw the team filming in the old market in Nazareth. I could imagine them trying to capture the moment of 'life as usual' in Nazareth's old alleys, where parallel realities stand hand in hand. One reality is constructed and imposed by the state of Israel regarding its creation and independence, and the other is deconstructed and subverted by Palestinians who continue with their lives as usual and as they have been doing for the last fifty years.

On the afternoon of 'Independence' Day, the same Canadian team interviewed various members of my family (including myself) at my aunt's house in Nazareth about our thoughts and feelings on that day. I remember looking around and feeling suffocated by that dry but strong sense of isolation in a ghetto called Nazareth.

Palestinian Memory and National Symbols

During the first half of 1998, various activities commemorating the Palestinian Nakba took place in Nazareth and the Galilee area. Women were mostly absent, not only from organising these events but also from being represented in them. Even the local newspaper articles in *Kul-al-Arab, Fasl-Almaqal*, and *Al-Itihad* that attempted to register women's stories focused on women as mothers of martyrs and bearers of the Palestinian history. There was no analysis of the gendered politics of power in the Palestinian community itself.

According to Moghadam (1994: 2): 'the representation of women assumes political significance, and certain images of women define and demarcate political groups, cultural projects, or ethnic communities. Women's behaviour and appearance – and the acceptable range of their activities – come to be defined by, and are frequently the subject of political or cultural objectives of political movements, states and leaderships'. Moghadam adds that in so many contemporary political movements, women are assigned the 'role of bearers of cultural values, carriers of traditions, and symbols of the community' (ibid.: 4). The ideology of nationalism, argues Abdo (1994: 150), is a 'strong force capable of using, misusing, and abusing its female participants. Nationalism in general promotes a specific discourse on women. In this discourse, women are identified as maintainers and reproducers of "national soldiers, national heroes and manpower"'. Nationalism, she adds, can also be used as a potential force for gender and social liberation.

October 2000

I was born in 1967, the year Israel occupied the West Bank and Gaza. I learnt from an early age to associate my birth with war. I grew up in Nazareth, and, like many girls my age, I had to abide by the gendered restrictions imposed on my life. From an early age I started questioning why I, unlike my three brothers, had to help my mother with the housework, and why my society was so preoccupied with 'feminine beauty'. In fourth grade, watching Jordanian children singing their anthem on a television broadcast from Jordan, I first understood that we have neither a national anthem nor a flag, and I cried. At age fourteen I read in Arabic my mother's copies of Nawal El-Sa'adawi's the *Hidden Face of Eve* and *Woman and Sex*.

In 1982 Israel invaded Lebanon. During the war heavy trucks loaded with tanks used to pass through our town to be delivered to Israel's northern border, and military planes used to roar above our heads. Our schoolteacher would sarcastically say that they were on their way to distribute sweets to the people of Lebanon. I kept a war journal since war was part of my daily life. I listened to the news about the war on the radio before and after school, and watched the news on television in the evening. At the time, I was still too young and timid to participate in the demonstrations in Nazareth against the Sabra and Shatila massacres.

In high school I questioned the absence of Palestinian history and literature from our school curricula, and designed, in response, my own curriculum. I used to hide Ghassan Kanafani's stories in my schoolbooks to avoid being scolded by my mother for not 'studying'. My experience growing up in Nazareth revolved mainly around my family and school. When I went to pursue higher education at the Hebrew University in Jerusalem (and later at Tel-Aviv University), my sheltered Nazarene world was shattered. I realised that Nazareth was not the world, and the education I received in its private schools was second-class in comparison to that of Israeli Jewish students. As a child and teenager growing up in Nazareth, I always knew my 'place'. I felt I belonged to my hometown though not to the Israeli collective. While growing up in Nazareth, within the limits of my place, I found it easy sometimes to ignore this location and continue living as if Nazareth was all there was.

In 1989, a year after I moved to Tel-Aviv University, I started working to pay for my education and gain economic independence from my family. I worked with the blind, the elderly, in a house for women prisoners, and at a human rights organisation. I was active on campus with the Arab Student Committee and leftist Israeli Jewish groups in protesting against the occupation of the West Bank, Gaza, and Lebanon. In 1993, I received a scholarship to study peace studies in the United States of America. I never thought that I would ever leave *liblad* (the country) to study abroad. My family was very supportive of the idea, but when I decided a year later to stay in the United Sates to pursue a Ph.D. in women's studies, my parents were hesitant. It was surprising coming from them, they who had had no chance to finish their high school education and who, as a result, were always encouraging my brothers and me to study. My grandmother was more forthcoming and wondered whether by continuing my education I would become too 'old' to get married.

I spent the years between1993 and 1997 luxuriously studying feminist practice and theory. Those were the years of the Oslo peace process and its euphoria. In October 2000, I was still living, working, and studying in the United States.

In October 2000, the curtain fell. There were no more illusions or pretence, and peace and justice were not part of the 'new' equation. Power was the sole language of the moment. In October 2000, when Palestinians, citizens of Israel, protested against their treatment as second-class citizens in Israel and expressed solidarity for the rights of the Palestinian people in the West Bank and Gaza to live in dignity and freedom from occupation they were crushed. In one week of demonstrations, thirteen

Palestinian citizens of Israel were shot and killed by Israeli police and border patrol units, and hundreds were injured and arrested.

I had naïvely thought that Palestinians, citizens of Israel, were no longer orientalised, 'othered' and treated like a fifth column with an identity crisis by Israel's state institutions (including academic research). It was horrifying to read in Israel's major Hebrew newspapers during the early weeks of October descriptions of 'them' as an internal threat and a fifth column. Fifty-two years have passed and we are still at square one, a threat. I was terrified of what could happen next, since a rational mind cannot explain this excessive and brutal use of force.

I am finishing the last sections of this essay a few days after Israel's celebrations of its fifty-third Independence Day, and seven months into the Second Intifada. During these seven months, Israeli abuses of Palestinian human rights in the West Bank and Gaza have become the norm. Here I am in the United States of America, following closely what is happening at home through talking to my family, and reading on-line the Arabic and Hebrew newspapers that are published in Israel. The paradox of being there and here at the same time makes my self-imposed exile meaningless, and makes the connections between these two locations stronger.

By late October 2000, it was time to break away yet again from my sheltered life, and reach out to the community around. As a taxpayer in the United States, I was implicated, whether I wanted to admit it or not, in funding the Israeli occupation of the West Bank and Gaza. By November 2000, I was active in two political groups in the Washington, D.C. area, one focusing on Arab American feminist issues, and the other on United States tax-funded aid to Israel.

Gendered Politics of Location: Generational Intersections

Both my grandmother and mother related to the year 1948 as a demarcating event in their lives. In 1948, my grandmother's life was turned upside down. My mother would subsequently bear the results of that new situation of poverty and fear of the unknown. My grandmother acknowledged during our conversation that she had had limited contact with the state of Israel, and that she was mostly confined in her experience to the private sphere. My mother reflected a similar experience when she said that her main contact with the state of Israel was through radio and television. My grandmother acknowledged that the state of Israel treated the elderly well, and provided social services. 'If only they would treat the Arabs better', she said. My mother related to the state as oppressive and expansionist, and acknowledged that although the situation of Palestinians, citizens of Israel, has improved over time, it was they, not the state, who facilitated this. Both my grandmother and mother were very clear in terms of their relation to the state. They felt, although in different ways, isolated, marginalised, and oppressed.

I, on the other hand, despite having experiences different from my grandmother's and mother's, feel the same way that they do towards the state of Israel. Israel embodied the 'other' for my grandmother and mother. It was hard for me to deal with this 'othering' language during the interview. I could not exactly tell if my grandmother and mother were othering the state of Israel in return for its continued othering of them, or if they were simply referring to the state of Israel in mythical and general terms. The interaction of my grandmother and mother with the 'other' was very limited. My grandmother did not know the Hebrew language. Although she recognised that everything in her life was turned upside down as a result of the creation of the state of Israel, she acknowledged that after ten years she got used to 'them' and hence continued to live her life in Nazareth as if nothing had changed. My mother interacted with the new reality of post-1948, and recognised the constraints that it imposed on her life. The fact that I left my hometown and went to the university, a site that is predominantly Israeli Jewish, deconstructed any myth of the other that I might have had. I interacted on a daily basis at the university and at work with the state's institutions and people.

While my grandmother blames the occupation for turning her life upside down, and while my mother blames the occupation for the loss of her childhood and adulthood, both take responsibility for their life choices. My grandmother's timidity and pride, according to her, prevented her from challenging her family, while my mother considered her marriage a cowardly escape. It was honour and fear that prevented my grandmother from continuing to work as a teacher, and it was honour and fear (compounded by the horrors of war) that drove my mother's family to allow her marriage at age sixteen. Both admit that they did not resist the gendered limitations and constraints imposed on their lives sufficiently.

I was not fully aware of the continuity between the experiences of my grandmother, mother and myself until I wrote this essay and attempted to understand our lives in relation to each other. Now I can see that I was able to resist the constraints in my life because of them. It is the continuity between our three generations compounded by education and political activism, that helped me carve an alternative path and challenge the gendered limitations in my life. After more than fifty years of resistance on different fronts, I keep wondering how many more generations it will take to move another square away from the politics of occupation.

Nabila Espanioly

Nightmare

Initial Reflection

'Death to the Arabs ... death to the Arabs!' a voice shouted outside my window. Although I had been in a deep sleep after a very long day, instinct made me run to the window to see the dozens of cars, civilian cars, passing in the street below and shouting this slogan. My entire body began to shake, even more so when two minutes later I saw the police passing by.

Another night of nightmares, which had become routine since 28 September 2000. But this night, the nightmare was so real that it felt as if they were coming to get me.... It felt as if they were preparing a new attack on my town, Nazareth, the way they had the night before. It felt like a new pogrom was being cooked up.

I, a Palestinian woman, am living in the Jewish city Nazareth Illith (a town built in the 1950s over the lands of Nazareth and the surrounding Arab villages), even though I consider myself a Palestinian Nazarene who works, lives, and was born in Nazareth. I consider Nazareth 'my town', and Nazareth Illith 'my place of residence' – somehow schizophrenic, but this is not the only problem.

I am a Palestinian who was born after the Israeli state was founded. My family was able to stay in its hometown – Nazareth – unlike the thousands of Palestinians who had been thrown out of their homes and villages in 1948. Thrown out of their homes and into the neighbouring Arab countries, they are now known as 'the refugees'. This total destruction of 480 villages occurred not centuries ago, but only fifty-three years ago.

The children of that time are the grown-ups of today. They are the living memory of our history. But who is not?

We are all living memories of the 'Via Dolorosa' that as individuals and as a people we live through daily. We are the living oral history because most of the written history doesn't tell our story; therefore I decided to write this essay to contribute to the written history, my recounting of what became known as the 'Jerusalem Intifada', or 'al-Aqsa Intifada', and the protest of the Palestinian citizens of Israel in support of that event.

Seeing Sharon (Israel's current prime minister) enter al-Aqsa – the Temple Mount – with his entourage of protectors harmed not only the feelings of the Muslims among us Palestinians, but all of us – Christian, Muslim, and secular (like myself). The visit was intended to provoke, intended to deliver the political message 'we are the power, and it is we who decide what belongs to us'. Al-Aqsa is a symbol of Jerusalem, and has a political meaning as well as a religious one.

Following Sharon's provocation, the Palestinians in the occupied territories of 1967 and under the Palestinian Authority (PA) rose up against the Israeli occupation. They were mobilised by Sharon's visit and long-standing negotiations for a place meant to be shared by the Palestinians from the areas occupied in 1967. The Palestinians who lived in Palestine up to 1948 (historic Palestine) and who today are in the diaspora or in refugee camps, perceive Palestine as wholly their own. Nevertheless, they made a very brave compromise when they accepted the state of Israel as a reality and were ready to negotiate with it on the terms of establishing their own state. They have to face an Israeli negotiating policy which says 'what we have (occupied in 1948) we own, and what we occupied in 1967 we want to share with you'.

The negotiations are not on the division of Palestine into two states—the Palestine of 1946/47, which ended with the founding of the Jewish state with an enlarged border (exceeding the ones in the UN's 1947 division plan)—but rather on the division of the occupied territories of 1967.

The political frustration of the Palestinians was increased by economic and social frustration under the PA, which remained totally dependent on Israeli decisions. Even Arafat can't leave Gaza if Israel decides not to let him.

The accumulated frustration triggered by Sharon's visit to al-Aqsa broke out as outrage against the Israeli occupation.

We, the Palestinian citizens of Israel, witnessed the brutality of Israel's reaction to the children and youths who were throwing stones. We witnessed Mahmoud Aldurra killed in cold blood whilst lying in his father's arms. We witnessed a twelve-year-old child facing a tank, but in complete contradiction to the similar picture of the Chinese student in Tiannamen Square, which had caused a worldwide reaction, this child was forgotten by the media. We, Israel's Palestinian citizens, went out to protest (by the way, we were joined by some Jewish women) and we were shot at, gassed, and injured, with thirteen dead, 540 injured, and thousands more suffering from gas inhalation. The Jewish women were ignored and the killing and injuring continued.

In this situation, what remains for someone like me – a peace activist, feminist, politically involved woman and psychologist – to do? What was my role? What could I do? I was injured and furious, angry, frustrated, and in pain. I participated in the demonstrations, called on journalists to raise our silenced voices, cried and wept with the mothers and sisters of the injured and the martyrs, informed whoever wanted to be informed, struggled for my place at the funerals of the martyrs when some fundamentalists wanted to send me to the back of the lines, behind the men. I stayed there, as if to keep my place under the sun, and shouted even more fervently than before 'Oh you martyrs, rest in peace, we will continue the struggle': *'ya Shaheed, irtah irtah, ehna minkamel el-kifah'.*

Coming back to work after several days of strikes and police brutality in our streets and in our homes, how could I continue? What should I be doing? Open a hotline to support children, parents, and teachers when there was no other psychological support available? Not enough. Write a guide for teachers on how to deal with the issue in their classrooms? Not enough. Write a guide for parents, work with parents, and listen to mothers in Nazareth weeping over how their houses were invaded by police and how their sons or daughters can't sleep now? And, three months later, how their children still keep a knife under their pillow and can't sleep without it?

All that, and thinking of my brothers and sisters who have lived through all the days of October, all the days of November, December, January, February ... up until the present day, under curfew and experiencing daily violence and attacks. What do their children feel? Fear? Panic? What? And how does a child deal with fear?

Over the radio a Jewish mother tells how her child chose a Superman outfit to wear to a carnival: she explains that her son deals with his fear by wanting to feel powerful. What about the Palestinian child? How does he deal with his fear? No, he does not have a cape to be 'Superman', but he does act like one. He goes out to throw stones. He deals with his fear by being a hero. He learns to solve problems through violence. Then he comes home and acts out his learning, and a new circle of self-destruction begins, which, as women, we must experience on our bodies as wives or sisters ... for how long?

Still more poignant are the effects of Israeli militarisation upon society, especially the women, and the racist attitude that is becoming part of daily life in Israeli society.

The next morning, after the shaky night, I was going down in the elevator and I met a Jewish neighbour dressed in army uniform. I asked him if he had heard the shouting in the night? 'No, what shouting?' he replied. I: 'Death to the Arabs'. He: 'Oh no, I did not'. Why should he? I am the Arab here, and I am the one who felt that they were coming up to my apartment....

These initial thoughts, experiences, and feelings touched on different issues which I would like to elaborate on in this essay: the Palestinians in Israel and their struggle; the peace movement in Israel; the women's peace movement and Jewish and Palestinian women working together; racism in Israeli society; and the internal conservative forces in Palestinian society in Israel.

The Palestinians in Israel and Their Struggle

The Palestinian citizens of Israel now comprise 18 per cent of the total population of the state of Israel. These are the Palestinians who have been able to remain within the borders of the state of Israel since its foundation in 1948. They were able to stay in spite of the plan to expel them all to the neighbouring Arab countries. Various wings of the Zionist armed forces at the time, which later became the Israeli armed forces, conducted several massacres (the first was Deir Yassin on 9 April 1948, to be followed by others), demolished houses, destroyed 480 Palestinian villages all around the country, destroyed the infrastructure, and exiled the Palestinians, forcing them to become refugees in Arab countries.

We who were able to stay or were born after the state was founded had to live under military laws until 1966, and have continued to face further land confiscations and general discriminatory policies over the years.

Today, for example, all the Palestinian citizens of Israel are living on only 2.5 per cent of the land in Israel, a result of ongoing land confiscations over the last fifty-three years. We receive only 4 per cent of the development budget, though 95 per cent of us live in the poorest villages and cities and in the areas of highest unemployment.

Over the years we have had to struggle to maintain our existence as a national minority. Faced with an official education system controlled by the state and insensitive to our culture, we had to learn to commemorate and honour our own history and identity, language, culture, etc. We had to learn to accept our new status as citizens of a state built on the ruins of our people. We had to learn to defend our rights as citizens without giving up our rights as a national minority in our own homeland. We had to witness the Israeli military subjugation of all Palestinians in the rest of Palestine. We had to witness the ways in which this history of domination has repeated itself, albeit with cosmetic changes.

Through all of this, we have learnt to struggle for our rights within the framework of the state, and to search, constantly, for new alliances within the Jewish population. We have had to struggle under existing laws that are, for the most part, designated through 'democratic' means to serve the interests of the Jewish majority. We have had to use all the means available to struggle for our people's right to self determination. We were the first to suggest a peaceful solution to the Israeli-Palestinian conflict. As an integral part of the Palestinian people, we find ourselves in a unique situation as citizens of a state which refuses to accept our people's right to self-determination.

We have had to continually strive as human beings to look for ways to improve the quality of our very existence. We continue to love, live, enjoy our lives and our environment, make music, dance, write books, marry, divorce, and raise families.

Throughout all these years since the founding of the Israeli state, we have learnt to struggle using different means such as being, living, developing, and learning, as well as striking, demonstrating, lobbying in the parliament, and advocating for our rights on the national and international levels.

The Events of October 2000

The first general strike by Palestinian citizens of Israel was organised on 30 March 1976, which has since come to be known as Land Day. On that day, six Palestinian citizens of Israel were killed just for participating in the demonstration that accompanied the strike. Since then the Palestinian citizens of Israel have organised different strikes and demonstrations. People were sometimes injured and jailed in these days, but never again were they killed … until October 2000, when thirteen Palestinians citizens of Israel were killed and hundreds were injured and jailed. It is important to mention that the Israeli police responds to demonstrations among the Jewish population differently, never using live ammunition, rubber bullets, or tear gas. As a participant in these demonstrations, I can attest to the extreme brutality of the Israeli police.

When the Follow-up Committee for Arab Affairs (a body of all mayors and elected representatives of the Palestinians in Israel) decided to call for a one-day strike to protest Sharon's visit to al-Aqsa, and the killing of Palestinians in the occupied territories and the areas under the PA, no one imagined that the Israeli police would react with such brutality. As citizens of the state, we perceive the right to protest as a basic right, one we are due as human beings and as citizens. The first protester was killed in Um El Fahim. Then another, and another. In the end, there were thirteen fatalities over the six days of protest. This was the first time that an Israeli Palestinian protest activity lasted more than one day. For several days, in the confrontation between protesters and police, the streets leading to the villages were closed. Still, the protesters continued their activities.

In the first two weeks of the October events, the reaction of the Israelis was very alarming. It seemed that the entire 'democratic structure' of the state was collapsing. Normally, democratic societies are protected by separation between different forms of authority (the army, the police, the government, the courts, the media) and by the presence of independent critical voices. In times of crisis, truly independent and critical media play an especially important role. But, in these first weeks, everything in Israel, including the media, collapsed. Most journalists (with the notable exception of two print journalists, Amira Hass and Gideon Levy of *Ha'aretz*) immediately sided with the police and the government and even used racist statements in speaking about the Palestinian citizens of Israel.

The Reaction of the Peace Movement in Israel

To understand the reaction of the peace movement in Israel in the first weeks after the events of October 2000, it is important to have a little background. The peace movement in Israel is divided into several groups. The biggest peace movement in Israel is 'Peace Now', which was founded by several army generals and traditionally has drawn its members from two political parties, Meretz and Labour. After the Oslo agreement and during Rabin's government, this peace movement became part of the government. Peace Now, reflecting its military and hierarchical roots, was never willing to work together with Palestinian citizens of Israel. It defined itself strictly as a Jewish and Zionist movement.

Other groups include Rabbis for Human Rights, Stop the Occupation, Women's Coalition for Just Peace, Physicians for Human Rights, New Profile (a group working against the militarisation of Israeli society). They are generally small groups, and some of them are feminist and left-orientated, struggling not only against the occupation but also for social justice. They raise issues of ways in which the occupation is damaging the fabric of Israeli society. For instance, they speak out against the prioritising of building more settlements instead of developing poor neighbourhoods inside Israel and show how the militarisation of Israeli society harms the society as a whole and women in particular. They also protest against the discrimination which exists inside Israeli society. They analyse the effect of militarisation from a feminist perspective, demonstrating, for example, the connection between militarisation, chauvinist and racist attitudes, and violence against women.

In the days and weeks following the events of October, most of the mainstream 'peace forces' expressed their 'disappointment' with the Palestinian citizens of Israel, in a way that reminded me of a father or mother who is disappointed when a daughter or son don't behave according to the parents' expectations. I would characterise this reaction as paternalistic, condescending, and insulting. The majority of Israelis, including the mainstream peace movement, clearly took a side: they were part of the governing system.

Months after the events, Palestinian cities and villages in Israel continue to suffer from the unofficial boycott imposed by the Jewish majority against these villages and cities. As a result many workers have lost their jobs, which in turn has contributed to the near-collapse of many families.

The only groups that acted immediately to voice opposition to the policies of the government and to the growing racist attitudes and policies against Palestinians inside Israel and in the territories were some of the women's peace groups and other small peace groups. This was especially true in the first weeks. Later, as the Intifada continued in the West Bank and Gaza, we witnessed new activism from the larger groups. This activism has increased, especially in response to the election of Ariel Sharon and Sharon's siege of Palestinian villages, towns, and cities in the territories.

The Women's Peace Movement and Jewish and Palestinian Women Citizens of Israel Working Together

Personally, as an activist in the peace movement in Israel, I have been a member of the left-orientated feminist peace movement for what seems like forever. Although over the years I have taken part in different coalitions which were not entirely leftist, my commitment has always been to those who have striven to create an alternative society which would enable Palestinians to actualise their dream of self-determination in their own land, in a state alongside Israel. This would mean the withdrawal of the Israeli forces to the 1967 borders and the creation of a Palestinian state with East Jerusalem as its capital. It would also mean granting the right of return to Palestinian refugees and the withdrawal of all the settlers from the occupied territories.

I deeply believe that although having a Palestinian state or having, in Israel, a state for all of its citizens will not solve all my problems, especially as a woman, it will create changes for a better society. My long-term vision is to be able to live in a state for all of its citizens, based not on national identity but rather on a humanist identity, a society which respects human rights and women's rights and provides better living conditions for *all*, free of discrimination based on differences in race, colour, sex, religion, and the rights of people living in special circumstances. This vision demands change throughout Israeli society, among both Jews and Palestinians, and a movement towards a clear preference for a more democratic society for all citizens, redefining Israel as not a Jewish state, but a state of all its citizens.

Therefore I belong to a minority inside a minority inside a minority. We are few.

The first day after Sharon's visit to al-Aqsa, some of the women from the women's peace movement called to ask 'What should we do'? I have to admit I myself did not know what we could do. Nor did I expect that that event would lead so soon to a 'shoot to kill' policy of the police in our cities and villages inside Israel.

When the first people were killed in the West Bank and Gaza, one woman peace activist from Haifa was able to mobilise three other Jewish women to demonstrate against the army's conduct; another small group of Democratic Front activists was able to organise a small demonstration in Tel-Aviv.

When the first Palestinian citizen of Israel was killed, the women from Haifa, who now numbered seven, went to demonstrate near Um El Fahim. The police prohibited them from reaching the town, and the television crews just ignored them.

Four days later, when the Jewish citizens of Nazareth Illith were attacking one neighbourhood in my town, Nazareth (the biggest Palestinian Arab city inside Israel), I called upon my friends in Haifa: 'Do something! We called the police to protect us but instead they shot at the Palestinian demonstrators and protected the Jewish attackers'. The women activated their network and reached the minister responsible for the policy, Professor Shlomo Ben-Ami. He promised that he would order the police not to use weapons. The outcome was another two Arabs killed and dozens of others wounded.

After these events, this part of the peace movement participated in various new activities. The Coalition of Women for Just Peace, formed jointly by Jewish women and Palestinian women citizens of Israel, raised the following demands:

- An end to the occupation
- The full involvement of women in negotiations for peace
- Establishment of the state of Palestine side by side with the state of Israel based on the 1967 borders
- Recognition of Jerusalem as capital of two states
- Israeli recognition of its historical responsibility for the events of 1948
- A just solution for the Palestinian refugees
- Opposition to the militarism that permeates Israeli society
- Equality, inclusion, and justice for Palestinian citizens of Israel
- Equal rights for women and for all residents of Israel
- Social and economic justice for Israel's citizens, and integration in the region

The Coalition of Women for a Just Peace is a major player in the peace activities now taking place all around the country and influencing other sections of the peace movement. For example, in 2001, for the first time, the Peace Now movement took part in the Land Day activities alongside other peace groups, as well as all the different parties acting within the population of the Palestinian citizens of Israel.

Racism in Israeli Society

Racism does not grow on trees. It does not appear suddenly. You don't wake up one day to find racism around you. It is a process that is created, supported, and legitimised by society through official and unofficial structures and systems.

Racist ideas which attribute specific characteristics to a group based on 'race/ethnicity' are very common in Israeli society. They find expression and legitimisation in different aspects of Israeli society; even religion is used to justify racist attitudes, such as the misuse of the notion of Jews as 'God's chosen people'.

There have been various studies analysing children's books and textbooks and the Israeli media which demonstrate the existence of racism in Israeli society, but here I want to focus on my personal impressions.

I don't exaggerate when I say here that I am confronted with some forms of racist attitudes, behaviour, or statements almost every day, on the street, in the media, everywhere. Racism is manifested not only against Palestinians but also against different segments of Jewish society, such as Ethiopian and Mizrahi Jews, women, and ultra-orthodox religious groups.

These racist attitudes towards Palestinians are created and strengthened by demonisation and dehumanisation of the Palestinians. This process makes people insensitive and accepting of racist ideas which they would not accept if the same was applied to their own group.

When a Jewish child from the settlements is shown demonstrating, no one refers to the fact that he is a child and that children are not supposed to be put in dangerous situations by their parents. Yet, when Palestinian children take part in the Intifada, on the very television programme, the announcer would comment: 'The Palestinian mothers send their children to be killed'. When a Jewish child acts out his fear and insecurity by wanting to be a hero and dress like a hero, it is accepted as a 'normal psychological response to a stressful situation'. But when the a Palestinian child does something similar and runs away from home to take part in the cat-and-mouse' show at the *mahsom* (army checkpoint) and play the hero, then he is a 'terrorist'. The killing of two Israeli soldiers by Palestinians in Ramallah is a 'brutal lynching'. The beating almost to death of a Palestinian worker by Jews in Netanya is a 'reaction of revenge from an angry public'. And so it goes.

This process of demonising and dehumanising Palestinians gives legitimacy to the Israeli government brutality and terror and creates and supports its picture of the 'enemy'. Since 'they' (the Palestinians) 'understand only the language of power', Israel has to bomb Ramallah. After all, they say, 'we are not living in peaceful Switzerland'. Incidents of Palestinians killing Israeli Jews are 'terrorist attacks' and 'murders'. When Israeli soldiers kill Palestinians, bomb Palestinian homes, and destroy acres of Palestinian agricultural land and olive groves, they are simply doing this in the name of 'security'.

These are only some examples of an ongoing process. Almost every day I watch the morning programme on Israeli television (a bad habit which I can't stop since the October events, although the morning sleep is the dearest part of the night for me), and I can't control my anger.

Internal Conservative Forces in Palestinian Society in Israel

Palestinian women living and struggling within this context must face not only government discrimination but also the conservative and fundamentalist forces in Palestinian society, that are trying to control and reverse women's achievements. Palestinian women have demonstrated, over more than a century of activism, that they play an active and important role in the national struggle. Having participated in all areas of political activity, women have gained power. Their role in society has begun to change. Even the most conservative forces need women's votes to win elections, and therefore they must try to reach women.

In the history of the Palestinian struggle, we have witnessed women's participation in every sphere, but whenever they seemed to gain enough power to become a force for real social change, they were forced to face the opposition of conservatives and fundamentalists. This happened in the first Intifada and it is happening now. In recent years it has been happening within Palestinian society inside Israel as well. It began when the fundamentalists tried to stop us, women, from taking part in demonstrations. This attempt was blocked by the 'progressive' leftist forces in our society, who introduced the famous slogan: 'United struggle. Men and women': '*Wihda wihda wotania alshab behad alsabia*' (national unity is possible only through men and women). But the fundamentalists and the conservatives don't give up. In recent years we have struggled harder to maintain the gains we have made, especially in the public sphere.

Conclusion

The complexity of the situation demands complex strategies for struggle. It is crucial not to leave out any important element of this struggle. Many people think that you must struggle step by step and prioritise your issues. According to this view, only after we have won the struggle against discrimination, or for national rights, or for peace can we struggle for social justice or women's rights. These people are asking us to put our lives on hold. In fact, if the issues were important to them, they would not for a moment consider ignoring them. When people ask you to prioritise, they are actually setting priorities based on their own interests; they are imposing their priorities on you.

Those national liberation movements that followed a two-stage model – first national liberation, then women's liberation – proved to be a myth, developed, legitimised, and implemented by patriarchal forces. At the end of these movements there was no women's liberation.

And in Israeli society, when government policy places 'national security' above everything, we see the other side of the same coin. The dominant patriarchal forces in Israeli society which use military might to maintain power over another people forget that a nation that occupies another nation can itself never be free.

Whether it is the Israeli government placing militarisation for the sake of 'national security' above all other interests, or conservative forces in Palestinian society placing the struggle for national liberation above women's rights, both of these approaches reflect the same patriarchal interests.

For me, life is holistic and indivisible. Either you live it in all its aspects, positive and negative, or you're not living. Therefore the struggle cannot be divided or prioritised. Acting out of one's deepest beliefs against racism of all kinds, whether it comes from Jews, Arabs, Palestinians, Germans, or anyone else, and acting against sexism in all its manifestations, and at the same time keeping track of all of that, is one of the most difficult jobs for anyone who is struggling to transform society into a better place for all to live in.

Badea Warwar

Beyond the Boundaries

Teta and the Moon

My step-grandmother was regarded by those who knew her as one of the most powerful women in town. I came to know her when she was in her nineties and even then, her uniqueness and power were obvious to me. Despite her deteriorating state of health, her strength and youth were all I could see. She was very different from my maternal grandmother, who was always too worried about doing the 'right thing' in life and mostly teaching us, the girls in the family, how to behave 'in the right way'. Since none of my maternal grandmother's ideas were publicly heard in our household, because of her soft voice, and the fact that she did not dare to discuss her views in front of my step-grandma, who lived with us, her distress was always discreetly expressed and understood. I loved both of them very dearly, even though I have spent all my childhood having very little interaction with my maternal grandmother. The difference in their personalities never escaped me, but it never bothered me either. I have never questioned my indifference to their profound differences. Later I came to realise that my indifference was not a personal matter. I lived in a place that treated the world with the same kind of indifference. Or so it seemed.

Unlike all the other women in my life, my step-grandmother (or Teta, as I used to call her) allowed herself to be angry and express that anger with no apprehension. Her language, behaviour, and manners were, according to everyone, 'inappropriate for women', but she never seemed to care. Later, I learnt from my mother, who always felt obliged to rationalise my Teta's inappropriate behaviour (perhaps because she feared the impact such an early exposure to the world of disobedience might have on my life), that my grandmother lived her life in a non-traditional way. All the stories that I heard about my grandmother spoke about a woman who crossed all gender boundaries with no fear.

She feared nothing except the moon. The moon itself did not scare her. It was the satellite moon that worried her whenever we left Nazareth. During these trips Teta would become a different woman. She would hardly speak, occupied with her search for the moon. 'Hush! Do not say anything! The moon is following us; they can hear everything we say', she would say to my parents in an effort to stop them from continuing their 'political conversation'. Her warnings were never taken seriously by my parents. My dad would laughingly try to explain to her that there is no moon that records people's conversation, but she was neither convinced nor amused by his smile. She was wholeheartedly convinced that outside Nazareth, the satellite moon was a great risk to all of us because it could record our talks and send them to the *Mossad* (Israeli intelligence).

For my grandmother, anything that contained the word Jew or Jewish constituted a political conversation that needed to end right there. I did not understand, as I was not even eight at the time, how these words 'Jewish' and 'Palestinian' are political or why they scared her so much, but I was not concerned or worried. What worried me the most was her warning to my dad following his dismissive remarks: 'you know what they can do to us'. She never cared to elaborate, and I never dared to ask what she meant by 'what they can do to us'. It was obvious to me that this was one of the adult conversations that I was not to interrupt. Intuitively, or perhaps sensing Teta's great distress and genuine fear, I knew that silence was my best choice. I kept quiet but I was genuinely scared without knowing why or of what. Just looking at her fearful eyes as they searched the sky for the moon was enough to scare me for a long time. I restrained myself from asking her any questions about the identity of those people whom she referred to as 'they' or about 'what they can do to us'. I knew that questions of this nature would have intensified her distress, fear, and search for the moon. Between watching the moon and censoring my parents' conversation, she was never conscious of my existence in the car. When I finally decided to break my silence and ask her to explain, she panicked. Noticing that I too existed made her realise that the stakes were higher than she had anticipated. I do not recall seeing her sadder than on that day. With the look of someone who has just realised the meaninglessness of everything around her, she looked at me and said, 'You are too young to understand these things but one day you will understand, you will, you will see'. She had nothing more to say, and the despair in her voice made me realise that there was no point in asking further questions.

After her death no one spoke of the moon.

My Parents

My parents' generation, born during the first years of the Zionist occupation, or what we call 'al-Nakba', marked a major break with my grandmother's generation in terms of their thoughts and lifestyle. Their generation was more interested, more willing to speak about issues such as the occupation, the Arab defeat, and Jamal Abdel-Nasser's nationalism. Sometimes they were even willing to criticise Israel's discriminatory policies and express their dissatisfaction over being treated as third-class citizens. Inside our home and over a cup of coffee, I heard many passing conversations about the confiscation of Palestinian lands, the fact that the majority of Palestinians residing in Israel ('Arab Israelis', as they call us/them) live under the poverty line, the limited opportunities their sons and daughters have in the job market, and the ongoing struggle that our municipality has to go through in order to get funding. Occasionally, these local conversations of anger and dissatisfaction would transcend the walls of our homes and take the form of public demonstrations.

Public demonstrations were unusual times in Nazareth, not only because they did not happen so often, but mainly because they went against rooted societal notions of obedience and discipline. Since these demonstrations often became very violent, with the police shooting and throwing tear gas and people throwing stones and hiding in the back alleys, our disobedience became more physical and in a sense more obvious. Since my home was located in the middle of downtown Nazareth, I literally witnessed all the demonstrations and violence that took place. From the window of my room and later when I joined these demonstrations, I saw Nazareth and its people transformed from passive observants into active participants.

Despite the immense power that we felt during these times, I always felt that in fact we remained powerless. We managed to publicly express our anger for a few hours, but we did not learn how to channel our rage, frustration, and legitimate quest for equality and justice into a meaningful and continuous struggle: thus we remained inactive.

We remained inactive despite the fact that, like all people living under racist regimes, we have always struggled to make ends meet, to live a dignified life, or simply to dream of a better future. However, the struggle which living in a racist regime entails and the struggle to end oppression, even in their connectedness, remain two different projects. The former is essentially an experience of endurance and acceptance, while the latter is a conscious resentment of the status quo. It is misleading to suggest that we have only endured oppression, but it is equally incorrect to suggest that we resisted our oppression, even though I believe we did. The question in the case of Palestinian citizens of Israel is not whether or not they resisted their oppression, but rather, why, even when they resisted their oppression, they remained silent and inactive. How is it possible to be conscious of your oppression, to ensure that you never forget the history of your occupation, and yet to act in the absence of this consciousness and memory?

We have always, I believe, tried to remember what the Western and Zionist propaganda wants to erase from the memory of the world: how, through the occupation of Palestine, Israel came into existence. It is difficult to maintain your experience of history, your memory of what happened, when everything around you insists on stripping you of the right to remember. During my high school years, through various artistic, political and social events, our memories and experiences of oppression were relayed. Every year my school would commemorate the late Jamal Abdel-Nasser. I still can vividly remember the teachers coming one by one to the podium facing the long line-up of students ordered to stand still while they spoke about Nasser's life and legacy. During these hours we were repeatedly and endlessly told about the important role Nasser played in restituting Arab rights and dignity. For them, Nasser was a nationalist hero whom they, as well as we, should never forget. Moreover, during the first Intifada our school refrained from participating in any non-political event or celebration. Even major events like Christmas and *al-Adha* were cancelled and the money that we would usually spend on these events was sent to the people in the West Bank and Gaza. These religious events were substituted with what our school called 'Palestinian Heritage Week', during which we would be participants in, as well an audience for a variety of politically committed artistic and educational programmes. Such attempts at politicising the young generation were carried out not only by my school, but also by other schools, the municipality of Nazareth, political parties, and various other social organisations.

Our Generation

While we remembered and worked on remembering, we acted in the absence of our memory and the knowledge it brings. We knew about the past but lived as if the past has no presence or is not present. In some ways, the Intifada of 1987 altered old perceptions of the pastness of the past. The Intifada made it impossible for Palestinians in Israel to carry on with their normal lives or to retain that sense of security and fulfilment they have always longed and worked for. During the Intifada, all the efforts that we made to accept and rationalise our subordinate position as third-class citizens became questionable. Even the ghettoised life that we were forced into and eventually accepted in exchange for 'peace' could not prevent us from hearing and seeing the cruelty and the brutality of the so-called 'democratic' regime that we lived under. After the Intifada, it was hard for me to look at the Jewish faces around me without feeling angry, without remembering. The same faces that I had learnt to treat with indifference frightened me once again. The Intifada was our first and main opportunity to potentially overcome this incredible state of powerlessness. But this opportunity never really materialised. Instead of seeing the Intifada as an ongoing struggle, we sliced it into images and moments. The images were horrible and the moments intense; nevertheless, they remained brief images and moments that we would momentarily respond to whenever the brutality of Israel exceeded its 'proper limits'.

The brutality and violence that Israel displayed in its attempt to control the Palestinian uprising were a great source of pain and anger for its Palestinian citizens. Yet life inside Israel did carry on as if nothing had happened (with the exception of a few days of demonstrations once in while). The grief that I felt was happening everywhere was great and genuine but brief and contained. It never got 'out of hand', and even if it did – as during October 2000 – in the Second Intifada, when the Israeli police killed thirteen Palestinian citizens of Israel who were demonstrating against the state's brutality in the West Bank and Gaza – was never enough to create any fundamental change or to indicate a commitment on our part to change. Religious segregation and hostility remained intact, despite the solidarity. Moreover, the need to resist Israeli oppression, while endorsed by the majority of Palestinians, nevertheless continued to be seen as the work of politicians and not the duty of the citizens. Our dreams and aspirations continued to revolve around material acquisitions and the betterment of our individual lives. In that sense I felt that their/our dreams and aspirations did not differ much from the dreams and aspirations of the average European or American citizen, even though we were marginalised by, and lived at the margins of, their worlds. In other words, we continued to live and act not as a marginalised group, in total contradiction to the reality of our situation.

Refraining from submitting to the reality of our oppression, even as we live it and even though we can clearly remember, reflects a basic need underlying the experience of all marginalised groups: the need to forget. Oppression is an experience of violence and dehumanisation that we must resist but must also forget. It strips from us the illusion of stability and continuity of life, even as it constantly reminds us of and confronts us with death. And as such it must be forgotten. Still, that need to forget cannot fully or adequately comprehend the complexity of the Palestinian Israeli experience of oppression.

Questions regarding the Palestinian citizens of Israel are centred around issues of their economic and racial subordination, and the need to struggle towards achieving equal rights and representation within Israel. This collectivity's struggle is looked upon as the struggle of a minority group to gain equal rights and representations in all areas. While there is no doubt that the struggle of this group of people is similar to the struggle of any minority group, such an understanding can only undermine the complexity of the experience and the identity of these Palestinians and their struggle.

To be a Palestinian in Israel is to be neither the self nor the other; rather you are the self and simultaneously its other. Legally we are part of the Jewish state. We carry Israeli passports and we supposedly have the same rights and duties as any other Jewish citizen. And yet, Israel is a Zionist country established on the basis of excluding all non-Jewish people. It is no secret to anyone, and definitely not to us or to the government of Israel, that Palestinian citizens are treated in their 'own country' as disposable human beings. The fact that Nazareth, the largest Palestinian city within Israel, with a population of almost 80,000, has no recreational facilities or centres, no theatres, no gardens, no parks, one main street, and ancient infrastructure that is supposed to accommodate our changing needs, has never once led the government of Israel to question its policies or admit its own racism. It never seemed important enough to the government of Israel that a simple walk through Nazareth Illith (a Jewish settlement built around Nazareth on confiscated Palestinian lands) speaks loudly of Israeli racism. Nazareth Illith is a modern city with all the educational and cultural facilities and features of the first world. The differences in terms of infrastructure and facilities between Nazareth and Nazareth Illith which, literally exist side by side, or rather one beneath the other, are indeed profound and speak loudly of racism, and of our exclusion from the country we supposedly belong to. However, the fact that we carry Israeli passports, speak Hebrew, and live with virtually no connection to the Arab countries around us has made our Arab identity questionable.

Thus, one cannot discuss the experiences of the Palestinian citizens of Israel as simply one of exclusion. Rather, it is an experience of inclusion that creates our exclusion. It is by belonging to a specific place (Israel) that we live in exile, and through identifying with a specific national group (Palestinians) that we become orphans. The ambiguity of our position stems from the fact that we never fully belong to the Palestinians/Arabs, nor can we ever be Israelis. And yet, we belong to both camps. Our land, houses, and most of our belongings are the inheritance of our past, and yet we are viewed and treated as intruders living on someone else's land. *We are always in exile while we are home* and we can never find home while we are in exile. This ambiguous subject position has pathologised our relation to space and perception of time (past/history), and determines how we narrate/articulate our selves within the context of place and history.

In a normal world, a citizen exists within three spaces: household, city, and country. Each of these places has its own dynamics, purposes, and functions in the formation of one's subjectivity and political identity. The

Palestinians in Israel have no country in the sense that their/our needs and interests as citizens are not, and cannot be, represented through a Zionist framework. What we are left with is a ghetto-like existence that we call a city. This ghetto (city) substitutes the absence of the country, as the neighbourhood comes to substitute the city. These processes of erasure, exaggeration, and substitution force us to narrow our perception of the world as it imposes its boundaries on us. In other words, for Palestinian citizens, the Israeli occupation did not dislocate us, since we are still living on the same land, but it severed our ability to forge any meaningful relation of affiliation/belonging to the world. The world, for us, becomes the self in its immediate surrounding (neighbourhood/city).

This limited perception of the world renders any dialogue we might have with the world into at best a monologue. Propaganda, power, politics, and interest all play a major role in continuing the Palestinian tragedy. However, one must also recognise that these factors not only determine, but are also determined by the oppositional forces and voices they encounter. In the Palestinians' case, due to the pathological experience of space, these voices remain monological, autobiographical, and, hence, ineffective.

I have met many secular Jewish people who have never been to Israel. I am always amazed to hear them speak about their 'home' with longing, conviction, and passion, even though they have never once visited this 'home'. They speak with eloquence and articulation not just of their 'homeland' but of the concentration camps and the anti-Semitism they face in Canada and elsewhere, and above all, about their right to end their historical suffering by establishing the state of Israel on the land that God has given them. I heard the same stories and arguments many times over the years, and never once argued back. I had nothing to say. Even though I have witnessed day by day what it means to be a disposable human being, to be in a space that refuses to recognise your basic right of existence, with people for whom your very presence is a threat to their security, and in a regime that confiscates your land, destroys your home, and deprives you of any chance of living as a respectable human being, I had nothing to say.

I had a lot to say, but all my arguments seemed to me to be personal, autobiographical, even when they were not. By autobiographical I mean that our stories of occupation did not transcend their focus on the self, and as such, failed to locate, translate, or communicate with the rest of the world. This interiority with which we think and narrate has led us to focus on the individual as we narrate our story of occupation, rather than on occupation as it is experienced by the individual. A non-autobiographical mode of expression discusses the autobiographical experiences of occupation only to emphasise its non-autobiographical nature. It reads the violence of occupation even when the story is not about the occupation as such. If we are to successfully challenge our oppression, this non-autobio-graphical mode of expression must be the collective experience of the people, not of only a few politicians and intellectuals. Otherwise, I believe, we will remain silent even as we speak, and paralysed even as we act.

I always remember the stories my parents told me about their child-hood. I always remember how sad I felt every time I listened to their sto-ries. There was always an underlying background of misery, poverty, sickness, and violence caused by the occupation, which set the tone for all their stories. But neither they nor I ever seemed to realise how everything they told me was a story about the violence that the Israeli occupation in 1947 brought to their lives. My dad started his stories by telling me how he lost his mother when he was three years old, to explain why he ran away several times, or to tell me about the different tricks he and his sib-lings played on their stepmother. Only when I asked was I told that his mother died because she could not resume her medical treatment in Lebanon after the Israeli invasion of Palestine. To him, the focal point was always his mother's death, which we can blame no one but God for – that is, of course, if one dares to believe that God can be unjust. It was bad luck which made the seven of them orphans at such a young age.

My mother was adopted by an elderly lady when she was five years old because her father lost his job after the Israeli occupation and could not feed his five children. She – and later we, her children – lived with her step-mother all of our lives, even though my maternal grandfather and grand-mother were alive, without wondering why, or questioning the cruelty of such reality. Like my dad's case, hers was also a personal story of bad luck.

Today I have two children who live many thousand miles away from home. Their lives have not been touched by the reality of occupation. They know nothing about, and perhaps they will never know or experience, the violence of colonisation. And yet, I wonder sometimes if their lives, just like mine, have not also been shaped by the Israeli occupation? Is the fact that they were born in Canada not a testimony to the ongoing occupation and violence that my grandparents, parents, and my generation have experienced? How can I tell them the story of Palestine in such a way that they will realise that the Israeli occupation is violence not simply against Palestinians but against the very principles of humanity and justice? Such violence leaves its marks everywhere, even where it is not present.

Nahla Abdo

Dislocating Self, Relocating 'Other':
A Palestinian Experience

—ᶯᶯ—

For many, if not most Palestinians, the term 'dislocation' acquires a very special meaning, as it appears to be synonymous with the very identity they have acquired or have been forced to adopt. Dislocation has histori-cally been perhaps the single most important marker in the socio-economic and political culture and identity of Palestinians. Whether Palestinians are positioned as 'self' or as 'other', this reality is often unchanged. Speak-ing from the vantage point of being Palestinians, they see themselves as being the rightful inhabitants, the indigenous people of Palestine who were dislocated from their own homes by the 'other', who therefore, were searching for a new location. Viewed from the lenses of the dislocator, i.e. the Zionists (and later, Israelis), Palestinians, or the indigenous people of that very location, were turned into the 'other', into an invisible entity. At this juncture of the encounter, the foreign settler emerged as the legiti-mate 'self' who, as the myth goes, 'finally found its place of relocation', while the natives of the country lost their rightful and legitimate claim to their own land. Over the past fifty-three years, indigenous Palestinians have turned into a dispossessed entity with life in exile, in diaspora, mostly taking refugee camps as their 'homes'.

The Palestinian experience of dislocation may not necessarily be unique. After all, many peoples and collectivities, both in the past and the present, have undergone experiences of dislocation, including forced expulsion; territorial, emotional, and psychological negation; and even physical killing and extermination. For some, the act was done in the con-text of 'ethnic cleansing', such as the cases of Kosovo and Rwanda; for others, it was committed during the Holocaust, as in the cases of the Slavs, Jews and Romany Gypsies under Nazi Germany. Yet, as Ward Churchill has rightly observed, the largest mass of people to undergo genocide in history was the natives of the Americas (Churchill, 1998).

Having said that, however, it remains true that Palestinian experiences of dispossession and uprooting are a powerful human tragedy rooted in the complexities of late twentieth-century global politics. The Palestinian lived history of dislocation appears to be just one episode in a successive wave of uprooting, dispossession, and constant denial of who they are and what is rightfully theirs. Both dislocation and refugeeism have become integral to their epistemological and ontological psyche. Whereas dislocation has become an important marker in their collective memory, consequently acquiring an ontological status, refugeeism had come to occupy a central place in the episteme of the individual Palestinian.

Where Are My People?

As the twenty-first century is ushered in, Palestinians continue to find themselves under Israeli military occupation, the longest occupation in modern history! One can hardly find a Palestinian without an immediate or closely related family member who is not a refugee. It is this ontological state of identity which led the famous poet Mahmoud Darwish to refer to Palestinians as *haqeebat safar* (travel suitcase). What is most poignant about this identity is that wherever this 'suitcase' goes, it is always reminded of its invisibility and non-material existence. In other words, as a Palestinian, one does not have to be in the Middle East or in the middle of the conflict to be part of the conflict or even to feel that her presence or existence is unwelcome. Thousands of miles away from the Middle East, in a country that is not even directly involved and has a general reputation of being somewhat neutral, my national, cultural, and historical identities have been challenged and even denied more than once. Some of this denial comes out of genuine ignorance, such as when your Canadian fellow, the phone operator or the officer at the post office, mistakes Palestine for Pakistan and, when you try to explain the difference between the two, they respond they never heard of Palestine. This type of denial comes as no surprise, despite the fact that Palestine, the Middle Eastern conflict, and for many months the Intifada have occurred almost daily in Canadian news broadcasts. Still, the form of 'denial' to which I refer as a product of 'genuine ignorance', or political illiteracy, does not hurt as much as the other type which comes out of a conscious act of denial. To illustrate this I will quote a recent incident, something that happened to me while I was writing this essay. On 23 January 2001, I received a four-page letter, partly typed and partly hand-written, in which the author decided to inform me that Palestinians are neither a people nor a nation. 'Palestinians', the author wrote, 'are either Arabs or Jews'. Otto

Bleuer – the name signed on the letter – wrote the letter in response to an interview I gave on a CBC prime-time show called Counter Spin, where I articulated my position on the conflict in general, and the issues of Palestinian refugees in particular. While the letter was full of historical distortions, contortion, and mutilations, one line in particular struck me: 'There is no Palestinian nation, history, language or culture'.[1] The irony here is that I received this letter on my way to a seminar I was teaching entitled 'Women, Politics and Everyday Life in the Middle East: Palestinian Experiences'.

My experience of dislocation as a Palestinian Canadian, one of the issues to be dealt with in this essay, has come to constitute a major part of my identity as a mature feminist, anti-racist activist. In this essay I will reflect on the experiences of Palestinians in Israel, using my own life story as an illustration. The concept of 'dislocation' in this essay will be used beyond its limited territoriality to denote as wide a space as life itself; it involves the social, economic, political, cultural, gendered and sexualised dislocation of Palestinians.

This essay is divided into three parts; 'Nazareth: Childhood Identity' speaks of the experiences of inclusion/exclusion and identity confusion I had as a Palestinian Arab growing up in Israel. The second part entitled, 'Haifa: The reaffirmation of national identity', speaks of the conditions that strengthen national identity and prioritise it over other forms of identities and belonging. The third and final part, entitled 'Toronto: Challenging Exile and Essentialism', discusses the surge and complexities of multiple identities and the feminist activist challenge to these.

Why Nazareth?

At the outset, it is important to note that I have chosen Nazareth as the starting point not just because Nazareth is my birthplace and the place in which I spent the better part of my life. This choice, in fact, was made to articulate the experiences of a section of the Palestinian population, which is often ignored by Palestinian scholars. Existing literature on Palestinian experiences of dislocation has covered most areas of alienation, dispossession, and estrangement undergone by Palestinians, whether at the geographical/physical level or the socio-economic and cultural levels. This literature has also covered the major historical moments in the lives of Palestinians, including the 'Nakba' (catastrophe) in 1948, which resulted in the uprooting of the Palestinians and their consequent re-emergence as refugees, exiles, and diasporic communities in their homeland as well as abroad (Said, 1979; Gilmore, 1983; Hadawi, 1988).[2] It has also covered the second major exodus of 1967, resulting from the Israeli occupation, and colonisation of the West Bank and Gaza Strip (Hilal, 1974; Zureik, 1979; Metzger, et al., 1983; Roy, 1995).[3]

As important and indispensable as this burgeoning 'canon' on the Palestinian diaspora has been, accounts and analyses in most of this literature have basically sidestepped two very important issues. On the one hand, the overwhelming majority of the literature has focused on Palestinians under the Israeli-occupied territories of the West Bank and Gaza Strip, as well as the refugees in the Arab world and the diaspora, ignoring, in the process, Palestinians who remained in Israel after 1948. On the other hand, most, if not all of this literature has been male-stream, and as such, oblivious to the gender specificity of dislocation and dispossession.

Finally, my choice of this section of the Palestinians, also known as the Palestinians within the Green Line, is because their experiences are doubly silenced. Largely due to racism, power relations, and a relationship of subjugation and subordination, Palestinian citizens are silenced by their citizen neighbours Israeli Jews. They have been, until recently, also ignored – albeit for different reasons – by other Palestinian nationals, as will be demonstrated in the following pages. For this reason, this essay is about giving voice to this section of the Palestinian population.

Nazareth: Childhood Identity

As was mentioned above, Palestinians in Israel have historically been cast outside the national plan and configuration of both Palestinians and Israelis alike. They exist in a precarious position, where their legal presence has overshadowed their actual or real existence as a nation or national collectivity. The official Palestinian Liberation Organisation view, until the past decade or so, has seen this collectivity as Israeli, and as such has played a minor role in Palestinian plans for sovereignty, independence, or national self-determination. On the other hand, Israel, as the state in which they find themselves citizens, has excluded them from its national politics and policies, and on many occasions has constituted them as 'enemies' or inauthentic Israelis. This collectivity, in other words, has been excluded from the national plan of both Palestinians and Israelis, a reality which has had a grave impact on its national identity.

Before I discuss this issue further, there is another factor to consider that has made Nazareth a historically specific case for Palestinians: Nazareth remained the sole Palestinian town with an overwhelmingly – and perhaps exclusively – Arab population. Every other Palestinian town or city has been either partially destroyed and a new Jewish settlement erected on its ruins, or vacated by its indigenous residents and repopulated with European (Jewish) settlers. For example, the cities of Yaffa (Jaffa), Acca (Acre), Ledd (Lod), and Ramleh were partially destroyed during the 1920s and 1930s and on their ruins new Jewish settlements were erected. For example, the city of Tel-Aviv was built on lands confiscated from Jaffa, while Acre and Haifa were turned into the so-called 'mixed' cities. In other cases, such as that of the city of Safad (Tsfat), an almost total destruction of the Arab character of the city, along with a wide-scale expulsion of its Palestinian inhabitant, was effected during the 1947–8 Nakba, resulting in the total Judaisation of the city.

It is not surprising, therefore, that Nazareth became the only refuge for Palestinians who were internally dislocated, or 'Present Absentees', as they were legally defined by the Israeli state for purposes of robbery and land confiscation. As a large town, Nazareth also became the only commercial centre for the surrounding Palestinian villages. This process of internal dislocation, alienation, and exclusion has obstructed the development of national identity of Palestinian citizens of Israel, at least until the late 1970s and early 1980s.

I was not born a refugee, nor was I sufficiently aware of my national identity or the refugee problem until much later in my teens. This, however, does not mean that phrases like 'we had to leave our house in Haifa' or 'They took our big house in Acre,' were not voiced in my family house constantly by both parents. It does not mean that Nazareth itself did not have to accommodate a large number of 'internal refugees'. In fact, I remember vividly that until my early teens I used to have close friends who were refugees living in 'zinc camps' on the main road leading to the only governmental secondary school, an area called at the time 'R.E'. The place was literally a dump for spare parts of old cars. I always found it difficult to differentiate the parts of the zinc or steel belonging to my friend's 'house' from those belonging to the garbage dump!

This notwithstanding, and perhaps not unlike other Palestinians who were dislocated and relocated within historic Palestine (which became Israel), my parents did not see their dislocation and relocation as an act of uprooting, as an act of refugeeism. They did not consider themselves 'refugees', as did the overwhelming majority of the Palestinians who were uprooted and forced out of Palestine. For example, although my mother would use the term 'refugee' to refer to most of her close family members (aunts, uncles, cousins), she never equated her status with theirs. The fact that she stayed in Palestine and kept a close form of physical and cultural attachment to it probably made it difficult for her to see a change in her identity. Like my mother, I believe, some Palestinians, particularly those who left or were forced to leave their homes and move to another place, had a sense of 'being lucky' or 'advantaged' for having not been totally uprooted and thrown out of their country. The identity of 'internal refugee' which currently enlists over 300,000 people, some of whom live just a few kilometres from their original villages (e.g. the villages of Iqrith and Kufur Bire'm), while materially real, was not consciously translated into an equal plight.

The sense of 'luck' mentioned above, fostered by the alienation and exclusion imposed on us by the Israeli military rule until 1966, was not to last long. Palestinians in Israel soon realised that they were not welcome on their land. Soon after the Israeli state was established, it expropriated and annexed much of the remaining Palestinian land – by hook or by crook! It did not take native Palestinians long to realise that they were unwelcome and in fact excluded from the Israeli society and economy, nor did it take them long to be made to feel that they were enemies of the state to which they now allege official belonging, as citizens.[4] If anything, this reality suggests that there must have been other reasons behind Palestinians not identifying themselves as refugees like the rest of their people. These were psycho-political factors affecting their public behaviour: fear of the mighty state which allegedly 'defeated all Arab armies combined'; fear of more massacres, à la Deir Yasin, Kufur Qasem, Tantura, etc.; fear of being forced out, expelled, or uprooted again like the rest of their people. In other words, fear of dispossession, expulsion and facing the unknown if they adopted a national identity; of being branded the 'enemy' by Israel, has been a primary reason for the Palestinian national identity crisis in the first decades of Palestinians living under Israel.

Although during the 1950s there was a small, yet strong resistance movement, known as *Harakat al-Ard* (the Land movement), it was forced underground when some of its members were jailed and others sent into exile. During the years up to 1966, all Palestinians were placed under Israeli military rule, prevented from moving between villages without a permit from the military commander, also known as the 'Qayemqam' (Abdo, 1987: 34). It is not surprising, therefore, that my parents' generation, known in my generation's public psyche as *Jeel al-Nakba* (the generation of the catastrophe), were often described as politically reserved, fearful, submissive, and even complacent. I experienced this through my relationship with my father, especially in my early days of political activism.

I grew up in a poor working class neighbourhood in the old quarter of Nazareth with no paved streets, no playgrounds, no public library, no cultural or other form of entertainment, and not a single government hospital anywhere in the Palestinian area or 'Arab sector'. As was true for most children I knew, my house was always clean because we female children had to help with chores, but it was old, very small and often crowded with people. It consisted of three big rooms, which housed three families (ours and my two paternal uncles with their families) totalling about twenty members. Each family had basically one room, which was divided into a bedroom and a kitchen. My three siblings and I shared two beds in the kitchen, while the bedroom was used as a living room during the day and as my parents' bedroom at night. Although I never had a manufactured toy (doll or otherwise), we children constructed our own toys: for example, we made dolls from popsicle sticks and cloth covered round bottle caps. Despite this, I never thought of myself as poor. I did not think I was deprived, either, even though new shoes and clothes were never bought according to need or want, but only during Eid.

In fact, I remember many times thinking that I was luckier than many of my friends. At the time, I even thought that because my father had a store we were wealthier than others. Little did I know that my father's meagre income was spent on a family of six! Relatively speaking, we were a small family in the neighbourhood. Other families, including my two paternal uncles', had an average of six to eight children each. The feeling of advantage I sensed then also came from the fact that we were more mobile than others. We were able to go beyond Nazareth and visit places like Haifa and Tiberias, especially during summer. A visit to any of these places, especially Haifa, which is no more than a thirty-minute bus ride, was seen as major travel, requiring days of preparation and organisation. Going to Haifa, which was always an emotional trip, especially for my mother, who would be reunited with some of her family, used to take several days of preparation and prayers that we would not be denied a permit from the military commander. Until 1966, under military confinement, these permits were necessary for Palestinians to travel. They were not guaranteed: the military commander could deny you such a permit, dashing your hopes and emotions! Acquiring such a permit was not an easy, straightforward procedure, but rather a humiliating and demeaning process in which you basically begged your military occupier-cum-ruler for your basic human right of movement.[5]

My childhood years were spent between school, home, and the streets as the only playgrounds. Like most, if not all female children in my neighbourhood, I had many domestic chores to do: buying the block of ice from the market every morning before school; buying vegetables (and not the best, so I could scrape together some pennies to spend at school); making dough at least once a week for my mother to bake bread. But unlike most of my friends, I also had to carry lunch to my father and help him in his small store whenever he asked for help. The remaining time I used to spend playing in the streets with my male and female friends. As a child I didn't have difficulty doing schoolwork per se; the difficulty was, rather, in finding time during our busy days to do homework. For as far as I remember, electricity, not unlike running water, was always in short supply. I still remember as a little child having to walk for several kilometres to fetch water from Mary's Well. I also remember the oil lamps we had in several corners of my house, not for decoration but for use when electricity became scarce!

Having said that, I continue to think of my early childhood years as pleasant, enjoyable, and largely peaceful. Most pleasant was the social and cultural environment which stamped my national identity as what appeared to be 'naturally' Arab. I was never identified as non-Muslim-cum-non-Arab, as I was defined later. My neighbourhood had a mixture of kids from Muslim and Christian backgrounds. There was a certain 'oneness' or commonality among us, which was strong enough to cancel even some of the simplest religious differences. For example, both Christmas and Fitr (Ramadan) were referred to as Eid Kabir (the Big Eid), while Easter and Adha were known as Eid Saghir (the Small Eid) for both communities. Characteristic of Eid Saghir was the common tradition of making date cakes. Like most women in the neighbourhood, my mother would make time to go and help neighbours prepare the cakes, expecting reciprocity on their part. Neither the church nor the mosque played an important part in our childhood life. Late in my teens, when playing with boys became restricted I began to develop an interest in going to church, not to pray or hear any priest, but rather to be able to mix again with the other sex.

However, and in keeping with its Jewish (religious) character, the Israeli state was obsessed with identifying or separating us as Muslims and Christians. Through its educational institutions, and without consulting kids or parents, it would send those of Muslim background to special 'Islamic religion' sessions, while Christian kids would be sent to study 'Christianity'. Still, religious identity would never develop into any significant factor in identity difference or identity politics. At no time during my teen years or even in my early twenties, did I meet, for example, a veiled woman. Only once, as a young child, do I remember seeing a woman wearing all black, including a big black scarf covering her head and face. This woman, who taught Islamic religion in my school, was seen by most of us children as a 'sad case', and we never thought of her in religious terms.[6]

The Search for National Identity

It was not until my teens that I began to develop my Palestinian identity as a political form of self-assertion. Unlike 'normal' citizens or nationals, who tend to develop national identity by being a citizen of a nation-state, and by relating to the presence of factors such as the national anthem, independence day, the flag, and other forms of events or occurrences where 'national pride' is voiced (for example in 'national sports', 'national day', 'the national drink', and so on), I developed my national identity as an outsider, by being without or outside the nation-state. My national identity grew out of lacks, absences, suppressions, and denials. For me, as for most Palestinian citizens, national identity came to challenge our exclusion from, rather than express our inclusion within, the nation-state! *Palestinians remain undesired subjects for the state of Israel, despite the fact that it was not we who came or immigrated to the state, but the state that itself forced itself on us!* This irony is felt and lived by most Palestinians. These processes of exclusion, as will be further discussed in this essay, have dominated Israel's attempt at including or, rather, assimilating citizen Palestinians, particularly through its system of education.

I was fourteen when Israel waged its first aggressive war of colonial expansion against four neighbouring Arab countries, consequently occupying the West Bank, Sinai, the Gaza Strip, and the Golan Heights. On a hot June day, we suddenly heard jet fighters screaming in the skies over our school, while our teachers ran from one classroom to the next, shouting at us children to run home. Unlike Jewish kids, who had shelters at school, at home, and in their parents' workplace, we had no shelters. Not at school, nor at home, nor anywhere in our living quarters. In order to run faster, I and my schoolmates carried our shoes in our hands and ran at a speed that would be expected only from those terrified for their lives. Yet, little did we know that this war would mark a significant turning point, not just for Palestinians in Israel, but for all Arabs as well, especially considering the manner in which the war started and ended. In fact, it was hardly a war: Israel launched a preemptive strike that knocked out almost all of the Egyptian, Jordanian, and Syrian air forces before they could even get off the ground, forcing the humiliating retreat and defeat of all Arab armies. The revelations of Benny Morris on this era in the Arab-Zionist conflict are of particular import (Morris, 1999).

There was little doubt that this war marked a new era of confrontation between the wider nation I belong to and the state to which I was supposed to owe citizenship rights and responsibilities. Also significant were the internal dynamics of national debate and discourse that the war generated among citizen Palestinians. Stringent military rule over indigenous Palestinians was lifted, allowing Israeli military personnel to effect better control over the newly occupied territories. For citizen Palestinians, this meant more mobility and the freedom to communicate with their fellow Palestinians, both in Israel and later in the occupied territories.

More crucial to the development of my political identity as Palestinian, though, were incidents with perhaps less general significance than the 1967 war, incidents that were more direct and personal. The first took place in 1970, when along with a large crowd of women, men, and children, I took part in a demonstration expressing anger, sadness, and frustration at the death of Jamal Abdel-Nasser. For many Arabs, and perhaps most if not all citizen Palestinians, Abdel-Nasser was a national symbol, figure, and leader whose death, it was felt, would threaten Arab national aspirations for many years to come. I could not have predicted that affirming my Arab nationality through such an event would be considered a threat to Israel's state security, and that we would therefore be removed from the site by military force. But this is exactly what happened; a large police force marched into the demonstration and started pushing us in all directions forcing us to leave the site. It is interesting to note that no Palestinian flag, national poem, or other 'Palestinian' national marker was used or displayed during this event. Yet we were prevented from expressing our sadness at the time.

The second, even more personal, incident took place while I was in the eleventh grade, just one year before we were to start our adult life at the university, in the public sphere, or in the labour force. Incidentally, Nazareth, then as now, had only one government secondary school, serving not only Nazarenes but also all Arab villages in the Galilee. Its overcrowdedness made me go to a private school. There, in Arabic grammar class one day, as the teacher was returning our exams, he ordered one student to stand up and began to insult him about his work in front of all of us: 'Aren't you ashamed of yourself? Don't you care about the reputation of the school or of your family? Don't you care about your father and his career in the government? What if they kick your father out of his job?' and on and on. These words, used by the teacher, caused all of us great embarrassment as we witnessed the humiliation of one of our best classmates. I took this event more personally, as the student in question was a close friend of mine.

It was not the attitude of the teacher that troubled me here. Throughout my twelve years of schooling, I saw boys and girls humiliated, cursed, pushed, shoved, kicked, and beaten by teachers. Our education system in the so-called Arab sector in Israel was no more than a system of control and policing of children by teachers. Teachers' lack of respect for students was the norm, not an aberration. But most such actions were taken against students classified as 'no good', 'don't do their homework', 'don't obey orders', and so on. At no time before had I witnessed such rage and humiliation directed at a student for actually doing homework, and giving what the teacher himself confessed was a correct answer!

Outraged by the behaviour of the teacher, I began to question my very existence and the existence of many things around me. The first question I asked myself was, Why would a sentence like *'Bi'sa Dawlatan Israeel'* (literally translated, 'Damn a state called Israel') threaten the reputation of our school? Why would it threaten the life and survival of the student's family? Why would the Israeli government expel someone from his job if his child used a 'political' statement to demonstrate his knowledge of the Arabic language and his ability to use a verb like 'damn' in a meaningful sentence? Was the teacher himself afraid of losing his job if the incident was reported to the authorities? Would he really lose his job for this reason? What was it about my friend – who incidentally was not a big guy – that threatened a state like Israel, when the armies of all Arab countries combined could not? This host of perplexing questions began gradually, albeit intensively, to find its way to a more complex reality: that of being Palestinian in Israel.

As an 'insider', I had to participate in the school curriculum. Like all citizen Palestinians, I had little to no say about what I was taught. It was relatively late in my schooling when I realised that the curriculum was a system of imposed ignorance rather than an educational tool, and that Palestinians like myself were to be made invisible victims of this curriculum. The curricula used in the Israeli boards of education were a Zionist-based set of programmes and subjects aimed at raising a new Israeli 'Zionist' generation. It employed the catch phrase of the Zionist constructed mythology: 'Palestine was a land without people for people without land', 'sparsely or hardly populated country'; that the Zionist (European Jewish) settlers had 'turned the desert into green', 'planted eucalyptus trees in the valleys to dry a land full of swamps', and so on. Reflecting on all these myths, I began to wonder: What about me? What about my parents and everybody else I knew? Where did we come from? That we were here before the European settlers and before the 'Jewish' state, I always knew. I also knew that my parents were originally urban, but most of my neighbours were peasants and had been active in the tilling, planting, and farming of the land. They had lived off the land for hundreds of years. How had they been left out of the curricula? Why were we forgotten? Where was the Palestinian flag, whose colours I have always known, but never seen outside of children's drawings? Why had our teachers never taught us anything about our families, our ancestors, or ourselves? Why were we never allowed to study Arabic national literature and especially not Palestinian literature, poetry, or short stories, despite the fact that some of the best Palestinian poets and novelists were also citizens of the state?

These and many other questions sparked my interest in Palestinian national identity. I began to realise that the Arab school curriculum in Israel was largely an attempt at distorting Palestinian history and national identity, obliterating our cultural identity, and denying our very existence and replacing it with a newly created 'Israeli history' and identity. The Eurocentric and Orientalist bases of Zionism made it possible for Israeli officials to rewrite the history of the East, and of Palestine in particular, by either totally ignoring it, or, if confronted with its existence, by reconstructing it as a history of lacks, absences, and inferiority. In the same process, they also constructed a new history, culture, and identity and presented it as Western (read, superior).

The above events along with various other experiences I encountered as a citizen Palestinian were crucial in the development of my national identity. The full realisation of my national identity began when I began to see our 'otherness', or when I began to experience the 'othering' process that most of us Palestinians were subjected to. In other words, I can say that my everyday life experience as a Palestinian 'national/other' of Israeli citizenship was the primary force behind the crystallisation of my identity. As soon as I completed the twelfth grade, I applied for a teaching position. This, I believed, was almost immediately guaranteed provided my name was not on the 'black list'. Little did I know how unique this was: it was true that only you could get a teaching position without experience, or teaching skills, or even university education, as long as you were a member of the Palestinian community! After all, we were the 'other'; the Israeli government did not care about our education. Thus, a conditional job was promised to me, without going through a formal application process. In fact, at the time and as an Arab, you did not have to apply; you just needed to know someone who knew an Israeli official, and you were set! My father, who at the time knew an Israeli official, was specifically asked to give me this message: 'As long as your name is not on the black list you will have a job'. Later I realised that virtually all Palestinian Arabs who did not collaborate with the state, or were seen as troublemakers, were placed on the 'black list'. I became one of those 'troublemakers' only later in my career as a teacher.

The 'othering' process can be experienced individually, as in the above case, or as a collective experience, as the following example will demonstrate. As a child, I loved the Eid (Christian or Muslim, it did not matter; schools would be closed on both occasions) because I would gather enough Eidiyyeh (gift money) for a bus ride from Nazareth to the new settlement known as Natzeret Illith (Upper Nazareth). For most of us kids in the bus, the new settlement looked like a place from heaven, and nothing like our Nazareth. We admired the place and wished we could live there! This settlement, built about forty years ago on land confiscated from Nazareth and the surrounding villages, had all that Nazareth (established over 2000 years ago) never had. It had big green parks; wide, paved, clean roads; water sprinklers; lights (electricity) everywhere; playgrounds; public places; and many nice government buildings. Even the board of education that served the Arab sector was there. In contrast, our Nazareth suffered from a shortage of drinking water and electricity; had no parks, hardly any green spots, and no paved streets except for the one main street connecting Nazareth with neighbouring Jewish cities and settlements; lacked all cultural facilities; had as its only government buildings (1) the infamous police station, used to torture Arab political activists, and (2) the Maskoubiyyeh prison (a remnant of the eighteenth-century Russian colonial/missionary presence in Palestine).

Nazareth was debilitated to the extent that it could no longer fulfil its most important cultural function as a Palestinian city or village, namely, providing the necessary infrastructure for weddings and death ceremonies, as the popular saying goes: *La lil-afraah wa la lil-atraah* (Neither for happiness nor for sadness). The overall Zionist policy of national and cultural genocide practised against Palestinians was and continues to be implemented by the Israeli state, through policies of land confiscation and lack of financial support and infrastructural attention to the Arab cities and villages. This situation has made it almost impossible for new-lyweds to rent an apartment or find land to build on, and made it equally difficult for the inhabitants to find a spot in the graveyard to bury their loved and lost ones. Living as an Arab in Nazareth made it easy for me to feel not only my 'otherness' but also that my very presence is undesired, regardless of my strong sense of natural belonging to the land.

Reconstructing Palestinian citizens as 'others' in our own country seemed to the Israelis to be a working process during the 1950s and 1960s. Israel was relatively successful in alienating, subordinating, and some-what silencing a generation of Palestinians, as was noted earlier in the experiences of my parents' generation. Such a process was made possible due largely to the excessive force and power exhibited by the Israeli state, including the destruction of about 500 Palestinian villages, several mas-sacres, and massive expulsions. Added to this is the forced confinement of all remaining Palestinians under military curfew for about two decades. In contrast, my generation, who had benefited from the lifting of the military curfew, the unintentional advantages brought about by the Israeli occupation of the West Bank and Gaza Strip, and the trickle of democracy left for us after serving its intended subjects (Israeli Jews), turned out to be qualitatively different. This generation, as will be shown later, became the mouthpiece for and advocate of Palestinian nationalism, democracy, and citizenship rights.

Haifa: The Reaffirmation of National Identity

Haifa is chosen as a title for this section because of the special meaning this city has for me. I lived in Haifa for several years while I did my under-graduate and graduate education at the university there. As this section demonstrates, Haifa, which was my mother's hometown and the town she was forced out of, played an important role in the development of my national/political consciousness in general and my identity in particular.

A Nation Fragmented

Despite concerted efforts on the part of the Israeli academic establishment to treat Palestinian citizens as an ethnic or visible minority, in the process obfuscating our national identity and concealing the racist character of the state, we Palestinian citizens, especially since the 1976 Land Day have begun to insist on the indigenous character of our national identity as Palestinians and demand citizenship rights equal to the other Israelis. Our demands presented the state with a major challenge: to choose between a true democracy, as it claims to be, or to maintain its basically theocratic character as a 'Jewish' exclusivist, and consequently racist, state. This challenge, which occupied Israeli official and public attention throughout the 1990s – and continues to be widely debated in Israel – is the result of major changes in the political and economic dynamics of citizens' relations, particularly those of Palestinian Arabs. Most important among these are the strong forms of resistance waged by Palestinian citizens on different fronts of their social life. I shall now turn to these aspects of alienation, forms of resistance, and the implications they have had on developing further Palestinian 'self' or identity as an alternative.

For the past three decades, Palestinian citizens have been involved in major political and cultural struggles, trying to reclaim their national identity while simultaneously attempting to resist the systemic policies and practices of estrangement by the state and society within which we live. For political and ideological reasons which befit the settler-colonial nature of the state, Israel invented a new identity, or rather, identities, and imposed them on indigenous Palestinians. These identities ranged between the very general and dehistoricised definition of 'Arab Israeli' or 'Israeli Arab', to the more specific ethnicised or religious identities of 'Christian', 'Muslim', 'Bedouin', and 'Druze'. In the first category, 'Arabs', the Zionist project or Israeli establishment aimed at obliterating Palestinian identity, which historicises our specific roots and contextualises us in place and time. Moreover, turning us into 'Arabs' became a useful political tool, enabling the Israelis to justify the exclusivist existence of Jews in an area surrounded by Arab countries. Not once, but many times we were told: 'you Arabs have twenty-two countries, but we Jews only one', or 'Why don't you go to live in other Arab countries?' In fact, this line of thought is not unique to Israelis but has also been exported as a working ideological line to Jews and other Euro-American supporters of Israel. On a February 2001 national CBC show, while commenting on the proposal Clinton made just a few days before leaving office, one Canadian Jew, resenting my insistence on the Refugees' right of return, announced: 'But Israel is such a small country, and you have twenty-two countries to choose from!'

It is here, in reference to the Palestinian refugees and their right to return to the land, homes, and villages they were uprooted from or forced out of, that such utterances acquire particular importance. For this logic does not stop at the discursive level, hurting the individual involved only. Based on this logic of power and might, Israel has been able to ignore every international law which speaks to people's right of return, undermining every UN Security Council and General Assembly resolution speaking to the right of return of Palestinian refugees.

Reducing Palestinians into mere religious fractions was another policy well calculated by the Israeli state. Following the traditional colonial policy of divide and rule, Israel tried to fragment us into 'Muslims', 'Christians',

'Druze', and 'Bedouins'. This division, which suited the Orientalist/ racist character of the state, aimed at reconstructing Palestinians into fragments with little if any relation between them/us. Thus, only 'Muslims' were considered Arabs. 'Christians' were distinguished as being a non-Arab 'higher species', albeit they were met with the same inferior treatment, as were their Muslim fellows. The 'Druze' and 'Bedouins' as a whole were portrayed as totally out of the picture. Whereas the Druze were considered non-Arab altogether, Bedouins were seen as Arabs but not Palestinians! Elsewhere, I have elaborated extensively on the history and experiences of the Palestinian Arab Druze and Bedouins in Israel.[7] For now it is sufficient to mention that the Druze as a sect within Palestinian Muslims have been isolated from their Arab Palestinian roots since the beginning of the state. Israeli officials, through bribe and/or force, were able to convince Druze elders (*Mashaiekh*) to enlist the young males in the Israeli army. By doing this, Israel hoped to isolate the Druze from their national context. Such plans, similar to others aimed at removing the Bedouins from the Arab national scene have, as most know, failed miserably. Since the 1970s, the voices of younger male Druze have been made loud enough for all to hear. Through refusing conscription into the Israeli army – despite tremendous pressure placed on them by the state – and participating in other national forms of resistance, the new generation of Druze began to take matters into their own hands, reaffirming their Palestinian national roots and pride. Nonetheless, the contradictions between loyalty to the Israeli state and loyalty to Palestinian nationalism remain. This state of confusion is particularly acute for those who find themselves forced against their will to serve in the army.

The irony and absurdity in Israel's policies and practices are most glaring when we consider Israel's attempt at reproducing 'Jews' or 'Jewishness' as one homogeneous entity or 'nationality'. Thus, the Israeli Jewish population, who come from Europe, the Arab countries, the former Soviet Union, North America, and other Asian and African countries, are somehow made into one 'Jewish nation', while Palestinians, who used to share the same history, language, territory, economic continuum, and cultural traditions as one national collectivity – real or imagined – were denied their national identity. Instead, we were divided into fragments of disconnected and unrelated groups of individuals. The practice of alienating and estranging the indigenous population by turning them into marginalised fragments of groups rotating at the periphery of a white European core is a well-known colonial strategy. The only way Israel can succeed in neutralising, absorbing, or getting rid of the 'other' in the new entity it wants to claim as 'its own' is to reduce indigenous Palestinians into a nonentity, by a process of their assimilation and 'Israelisation' – a process, as we shall see shortly, that has also failed miserably.

Fighting Back

Working at the level of culture and ideology while emphasising the discursive level, as shown above, was only one aspect of the process of denial and negation imposed on citizen Palestinians. Along with this, Palestinians have been subjected to different policies of subordination affecting all aspects of their daily lives, from restrictions on their access to employment, to poor infrastructural services provided to their cities or villages, to restricted educational opportunities, and so on. However, perhaps the most important form of oppression was the expropriation of their remaining land. Israel expropriated the overwhelming majority of Palestinian land either through its racist law known as the 'Absentee Property Law' or through a set of colonial regulations borrowed from British colonial war measures. This law legitimates the expropriation of Palestinian land under the pretext of 'security reasons'. Israel's 'security', like its 'borders', is the most elastic concept one can encounter in any modern state. These two concepts are constructed and reconstructed by the state to maintain, reproduce, and constantly serve its settler expansionist aims.

Indigenous Palestinians, in different forms and at both the individual and collective levels, have expressed resistance to these measures of oppression and subordination. During the 1970s, I personally took part in several collective forms of resistance, the most important of which was the student movement that began in the early 1970s and reached its peak after the 1976 Land Day, which was followed by annual commemorations and subsequent killings of citizen civilians by the state's army. My participation in these events was crucial for asserting my national identity *not as 'Arab' or as 'Israeli' as the state and its official document intended to make me*, but as *Palestinian or what I felt I should be*. There was little doubt in my mind then, as now, that my struggle was a political struggle par excellence, and that my need for asserting my national identity was not a 'natural' phenomenon, but rather a political statement, a challenge and resistance to the oppressor!

Immediately after the 1973 war in which Syria and Egypt returned small tracts of the territories occupied in 1967, Israel began to introduce special security measures against what it perceived to be potential 'Palestinian terrorist acts'. One such measure involved beefing up the security measures in all government offices and buildings, including university campuses; hence the introduction of a new system of campus security. This new system entailed the organisation of student groups to take turns 'guarding' all entrances to the campus. Palestinian students were also required to do this service. Partly because Palestinians did not serve in the Israeli army and therefore did not carry weapons, and partly because they were not 'trusted' – as we were often told – Palestinians would sit at campus entrances under the command of armed

Jewish students. Both Jewish and Palestinian students were supposed to safeguard campuses from potential 'Palestinian terrorists' by searching the bags of all incoming people.

Whereas Jewish students performed such tasks with 'national pride', Palestinian students considered the act as betrayal of their national identity and were humiliated: they felt they and their people were the target of this task. This resulted in an almost unanimous decision by Arab Palestinian students to refuse such duties. Despite threats by the university administration to penalise us by forcing us to pay for the service or even kicking us off campus, our voices of resistance were loud enough to force the administration to cave in and the rule was rescinded. The cancellation of this ordinance, however, came only after repeated and ugly clashes between Palestinian and Jewish students, resulting at times in swearing and the exchange of racist labelling, as well as physical fights using any object found, including large steel garbage cans! The situation undoubtedly led to an intensification of tensions and even hatred between students who shared the same campus. This reflects my own experience at Haifa University; similar situations were also reported on other campuses, such as the Hebrew University in Jerusalem, Bar Ilan University, and the Technion.

It is worth mentioning that the imposition of 'security duties' on Palestinian students may not necessarily have been the only reason for the eruption of clashes and enmity. Analysing it retrospectively, one can see it as the 'straw that broke the camel's back'. Becoming a university student when you are a Palestinian Arab was – and still is – not easy. As university students, we had no right to choose the topic we studied. Even a masters degree in geography, for example, was not possible for us. Like many government jobs which we were not accepted for, several academic topics, including geography, were considered 'army or security related' fields, so entrance to such fields by non-Jews was restricted or prohibited altogether. It was not incidental that most Arab students ended up being slotted in academic topics that were less challenging, but more politically 'safe' for the state – or at least, they were thought so. We could become schoolteachers and community or social workers. In my case, for example, I was neither interested in Hebrew literature (or any other language) nor in philosophy, but these were the topics I found myself studying. Another important thing to mention here is that like many Palestinian students, I did not come from a well-to-do family and was in need of a scholarship or other financial support – something denied to Arab students under the excuse that all scholarships were provided by the Jewish Agency (*Sokhnoot*). It was not surprising, therefore, that many of us students worked full time jobs while studying.[8]

Incidentally, the issue of national service by non-national Palestinian citizens was reintroduced in the late 1990s. During the Barak government, the debate on the legalisation of national service, and its imposition on citizen Palestinians, was heightened. Without going into this complex debate situated within the context of Israeli citizenship, it is important to note that Palestinians strongly resent this new demand, arguing that it is yet another humiliating and subjugating state policy, intending to obliterate Palestinian national identity. Drawing on the experience of their Druze brethren, who serve in the Israeli army yet live under the same, if not worse, socio-economic conditions, Palestinians argue that neither army service nor any other form of national service will improve the socio-economic and political status of the Palestinian Arabs.

My Haifa University experience, which involved living and interacting with the Jewish community for several years, had little effect on my feelings of isolation and alienation. In fact, this experience, as rich as it was, did not leave very positive marks in my memory. In almost nine years there, I was able to make only three Jewish friends from the university, all 'kibbutznik' teachers. One of these three happened to live just ten minutes from where I live in Nazareth: Dr Barzell from Kfar Ha-Horesh kibbutz, which is built on land confiscated from Nazareth. Still, he became a very close friend for many years. Other than these people within my immediate circle, Palestinians in this 'mixed' city were not mixed at all. Most Arab residents of Haifa, both original inhabitants and others who settled there after 1948, basically lived in the known Arab quarter of Wadi el-Nisnas, or in more recently built apartment buildings, most of which are occupied by Arabs. There are hardly any 'mixed' cultural, political, or social activities. Yet there was a peaceful co-existence between the two communities, or at least it seemed so in that there was little or no formal contact. Changes in intercommunity relations have occurred since, partly as a result of population growth and the generally increasing activism and visibility of Palestinians in mixed cities. But discrimination against Palestinian citizens, including those living in mixed cities, is still visible. Arab quarters in Jaffa, Acre, and Haifa are still distinguishable from the rest of the city by their underdeveloped state, overcrowdedness, and lack of adequate infrastructural services. Poverty, underdevelopment, and living inside the contradictions have also had their social and cultural costs. It is no surprise that among Palestinian citizens, the highest rates of social problems such as crime, substance abuse and drug trade, and prostitution are found among Arabs in mixed cities.

The Prison Experience

The height of student activism in the 1970s came in 1979, through the widespread Arab student protests and marches against Anwar El-Sadat's visit to Jerusalem as part of the Camp David Agreement. Student protests opposing this political visit, deeming it against the national (Arab and

Palestinian) consensus, consisted of peaceful assemblies of citizens prac-tising their civil rights. These were disrupted violently by the police and army, leading to the arrest and detention of almost fifty students from dif-ferent campuses. I was among those detained and underwent twelve days of inhuman interrogation, which included physical, sexual and moral abuse. My detention experience was – and still is – too painful to relate in this forum. What needs to be stressed here is that Israel's ugly face of state racism, sexism, and terrorism is not a sporadic thing, nor a mistake committed by a handful if 'crazy' or 'power maniac' army gen-erals. Israeli state terrorism was and continues to be systematically used against citizen Palestinians and especially political activists. Physical, sexual, and moral abuse and torture are the norm, and not aberrations in the Israeli prison system, particularly insofar as citizen Palestinians are concerned. In my case and the case of the other students detained then, the treatment was extremely cruel, despite the fact that all were released without any specific charge.

In prison I witnessed one case of extreme torture and humiliation. Despite the passage of over twenty years, the scene remains vivid in my memory. One afternoon, I was taken from my urine-spattered cell to the interrogation room, to be interrogated not directly but 'indirectly', through witnessing their treatment of another prisoner. When I arrived, two prison officers showed up holding a young Arab fellow, whom they insisted I knew. How I wished, later, that I had known him, or anyone close to him! They had the chap's hands tied behind his back and placed five cigarettes at once, in his mouth. They lit them all at once and the young man had to take the torture of inhaling all the smoke. I felt the smoke was coming out of my eyes, ears, and nose and not those of the chap himself. He had to smoke all the cigarettes until they were gone.

During the whole episode, the only thing I could think of was whether the officers in front of me were from the human species or from a different planet, for they were treating the scene as an entertainment, smiling all the time and occasionally looking towards me. I felt the need to scream; 'Fas-cists! Racists! Inhumane Bastards!' ... but I couldn't! When the cigarettes were gone, they untied the chap's hands and forced him to get down on all fours. They then told him to crawl on all fours, which he painfully did. They asked him his name; he did not answer. They kicked him in the back and buttocks with their big ugly boots. Once again he was asked his name ... again no answer ... another kick in the butt. The third time he was asked his name, he answered in a low, humiliated voice: 'Poodle!'

This was only one of the various 'lessons' prison interrogators wanted to teach me on what happens if 'you do not confess' or 'if you do not co-operate'. Incidentally, to date, I still am unable to understand just why I was dragged in the middle of the night, under the most frightening cir-cumstances, to that infamous jail!

Alongside the many dark faces of the prison, there still was a bright side, which I discovered many years after stepping out of the time and space that served as the context of that event. This is the sense of solidarity and support that develops at the site of a justified struggle. Only one lawyer, Leah Tsemel, was able to visit me. It was not unusual for most Israeli Jews to consider any Jew who supports Palestinians, a 'Jewish traitor'. The term 'bat zonah' (whore) was often used by my interrogator to describe my lawyer, Tsemel.[9] I realised later that many Palestinian lawyers had volunteered their services without knowing me, but were refused entry. I also realised later that the few Jewish friends I had at the university were dismayed enough to write letters to both media and prison authorities ridiculing the alleged 'security reasons' used as a pretext for my incarceration. These gestures on the part of my Jewish friends were important in that they laid the groundwork for future solidarity work between us, which I began to be involved in very early in my new host country, Canada. The presence of mounting support by lawyers, who volunteered to represent me without being asked to, was another positive indication of the rise in Palestinian national consciousness and commitment. These were daring acts by young professionals just graduated from Israeli law schools who were willing to confront the Israeli legal system on political grounds.

The prison experience of Palestinian women has always been a complex issue with contradictory implications. On the one hand, it is important to stress here that prison experiences by Palestinian female political activists are not a new phenomenon; they go back to the 1967 Israeli occupation of the West Bank and Gaza Strip. However, despite the passage of much time and the fact that a large number of women have gone through the experience, most women continue to face contradictions between their political and social lives. On the political level, these women are revered as 'heroines', women who have sacrificed themselves for the 'nation'; at this level they are seen as equal to male nationals. On the other hand, upon their release and after the initial happy hour, day, or week, they begin to feel the social pressure. The woman political prisoner is seen as strong, perhaps too strong and independent for a traditional marriage, which is the future most Palestinian mothers expect for their daughters. The women must be remoulded back into the domestic sphere, reshaped in the old traditional way of 'women belong at home and not in the streets'.

This is perhaps the predominant experience of imprisoned Palestinian women, though it is not the only one. Educated, independent women who are already 'out' in the public have a different experience. Upon my release, I did not feel any pressure from my family, friends, or neighbours. In fact, when I arrived home accompanied by my father and brother, who had attended the court session, the house was full of 'congratulators' who brought sweets to celebrate the occasion. Despite the fact that I was the first Arab woman citizen of Israel to be detained for political reasons, excluding hundreds of sisters from the occupied territories, I did not have to face any immediate social pressure. But this reprieve did not last long. For psychological, emotional, and personal reasons, I left the country just a few months after my release. I never knew – nor did I seem to have cared at the time – whether I would have been accepted back in my job as a teacher, or whether I would have found any decent job had I stayed at home (in Israel).

In retrospect, analysis of the reasons for the clampdown on Palestinian students suggests that it was not only student activism that concerned Israeli police and security forces: all forms of Palestinian political activism came under close scrutiny. This is particularly true for activism around the 1976 Land Day and the consequent 'Days'. Unlike the students' political activism, which remained largely confined to the campus and had limited effect on the community at large, activities which preceded and occurred during the 'Day' itself impacted the whole community, reaching almost every city, village, and quarter where Palestinians lived. The 30 March 1976 saw massive street demonstrations by Palestinians throughout Israel, from the Galilee, to the Triangle, to the Negev. Citizen Palestinians of all ages, men and women from all walks of life, poured into the streets to show their frustration and express opposition to the government policies of land confiscation and general discrimination against them. Fearing the widespread frustration and resentment of its Palestinian citizens, the government declared all demonstrations illegal and threatened to fire 'agitators' from their jobs. Particularly threatened were schoolteachers, whom the government warned would be dismissed if they incited students to participate or to take the day off. The fact is that not many teachers paid attention to the warnings: they and their students left the classrooms and joined the demonstrations. This day, though not the first on which official army or government personnel killed non-Jewish citizens of Israel, was unprecedented. Six Palestinian citizens – three men and three women – were killed by police, and the army was allowed to drive armoured vehicles and tanks along the unpaved roads of various villages in the Galilee.

On 30 March 1976, the veil of Israel's democracy was removed and the myth of equal citizenship rights exploded, bringing down with it the existing beliefs and remaining hopes some citizen Palestinians still held. What was remarkable was that almost all important acts of aggression and Zionist expansionism happened not under the so-called right-wing or revisionist Zionism of the Likud party, but rather under the Labour, or so-called Socialist Zionist Party, during the war of 1967 and the ensuing building and expansion of illegal settlements in the occupied lands of the West Bank, Gaza Strip, and Golan Heights. The campaign was conducted under the consecutive governments of Levi Eshkol, Golda Meir, and Yitzhak Rabin, who, incidentally, was the one who gave the order to crush Land Day, resulting in the killing of six innocent civilians. Under the same prime minister, hundreds of Palestinians were killed and tens of thousands injured and imprisoned during the first Intifada. Today, as I write these reflections, I am also reminded of the current Intifada, in which, for the first time ever, the Israeli Labour Party leader, Ehud Barak, used tanks, gun ships, snipers, armoured vehicles, and helicopters to bomb, shoot, and fire on the overwhelmingly civilian residents of the occupied territories, territories recognised, even by Israel, as being under the 'Palestinian Authority'! This point is made not in order to exempt the right-wing Likud leadership from its role in suppressing Palestinians, but to serve as a reminder to those who see Labour Zionism as 'progressive' or 'leftist'. For, despite its liberal ideology towards the Jews, Labour Zionism pays no attention, nor does it care about indigenous Palestinians. Throughout its history, it has followed one strict policy: the Judaisation of Palestine, a policy aimed at confiscating Palestinian land; labour on the land and the produce of the land into the 'inalienable property of the Jewish people' – an essentially racist policy, as various Israeli authors have pointed out. For more on this debate, see Shafir (1989), Mark Marshall (1995), and Peled and Shafir (1996).

The intensity of the political struggle has made it difficult for me, and for other women activists, to spend any time on the social and gender concerns of Palestinian citizens of Israel. It was not surprising, at the time, to see how the political/national was prioritised over other forms of oppression and struggle. The only women's organisation we had until the late 1970s was the Democratic Women's Movement, an arm of the Communist Party. The term 'democracy' was restricted to the political/national struggle, and the movement, which, similarly to other traditional or male offshoot organisations, espoused national concerns and considered 'feminist' or 'women's' issues secondary or even trivial compared to the national struggle. The general environment of the 1970s, in other words, was conducive to enhancing the collective national/political consciousness, but not gender or social awareness. The absence of collective consciousness on social/gender issues, however, did not mean that women were not making individual decisions and fighting their own gender/social battles. In fact, at the individual level, an increasing number of women began to join the ranks of those ready to defy social traditions within their village or city. Instead of succumbing to early marriage, more women chose to go to university, succeeding in the process in delaying marriage; others began to insist on choosing their own partners, or even engaged in socially taboo 'love relationships' outside of marriage. The 1970s undoubtedly ushered in a new form of social and gender change and activism, albeit in a non-organised, unstructured manner. This process, as we shall see later, was crucial to the emergence and solidification of the collective or organised form of gender and even feminist consciousness and organisation in the early 1990s.

Toronto: Challenging Exile and Essentialism

Life under conditions of alienation, dislocation, and disenfranchisement in my homeland was partly responsible for my own exile in 1979. The political repression I lived under during the seventies exacerbated the already difficult social and gender constraints under which I was living; this combination made me choose exile over my 'home'. In fact, during the late 1970s I began to question the extent to which my home was truly 'mine' and not a temporary or transitory one. 'Home' and 'homeland' began to assume meanings in contradistinction to what humans usually associate the terms with. My 'homeland' had turned into a most generous home for so many outsiders – but not for its native insiders! It became the most friendly space and host to the 'other', yet hostile to and intolerant of 'its own'. My objectification as a Palestinian by the Israeli state and society, combined with my objectification or 'thingness' within my own traditional patriarchal society, made the idea of diaspora and exile seem more comforting.

At the outset of this section, I would like to emphasise that exile is a form of dislocation and an expression of uprootedness. It is true that exile encompasses the notion of refugees and that all refugees are persons exiled by force; still, not all exiles are refugees. Common to all exiled persons and peoples are socio-cultural and national uprootedness and estrangement. The former carries a significant meaning in host countries with their own histories of settler colonialism, whose present is characterised by a hierarchy of racial and ethnic collectivities, such as Canada, the US and Australia. Nevertheless, unlike refugees (particularly those forced to live in camps), exiles in the West have the ability to forge a positive and constructive experience by opening up space for improvement in their social, economic, and sometimes even political lives and circumstances. My experience of exile is undoubtedly a case in point.

The very first years of my immigration to Canada proved to be a great disappointment. My schooling in Israel had provided me with little information about the West. Outside of the wars, themselves taught in the most superficial ways, Canada had occupied a very minimal place in my education. All I knew about Canada was that it was 'democratic', 'very large', a place of 'equal opportunities', where 'everybody is rich', and a land of 'milk and honey' in the true sense, not in the sense applied to Israel. Unfortunately, it did not take long for these beliefs to crumble.

I immigrated to Canada under the category known as 'dependent' or 'sponsored' class. My fiancé was my sponsor. One month after my arrival

I received a notice from the Department of Immigration presenting me with the alternative of either marrying my sponsor or facing deportation! As much I loved my sponsor, I was just not ready to get married then. At the risk of our union potentially developing into an unwise partnership and in order to avoid being deported back to Israel, I found myself committing to marriage quite unwillingly. Although I remain with the same man, twenty-three years later, my initial hope for the freedom of choice in my new country was dashed quite rapidly. This disturbing experience was followed by another, in the labour market: despite my academic background, I found myself unable to assume any job because I did not have 'Canadian experience'.

The concept of 'Canadian experience' is still in use, as an ideological tool used by the state to control its labour market, keeping immigrants, especially those of non-European descent, in an inferior position. The term 'Canadian experience' represents a discriminatory practice quite similar to that underlying the term 'security reasons' used by the Israeli state to discriminate against citizen Palestinians, keeping them outside of the labour market reserved for 'Jewish citizens'.

Recognising the impossibility of gaining 'Canadian experience' without physically engaging in the labour market, most immigrants, particularly Third World immigrants, tend to accept any job offer, no matter how overqualified they are. For the first two years in Canada I did manual labour in a grocery shop, accepting less than minimum wage. Unhappy with my position, I began to explore graduate school again. Here too I found myself struggling to engage in a third language. The English taught at school and at the university level in the 1970s in Israel could barely prepare one to communicate in the language at the level of daily encounters, let alone at the level of academia. While trying to overcome difficulties associated with the English language, immigrant students also find themselves under pressure to choose an area of speciality or expertise for which proper guidance or supervision can be available at their academic institutions. This choice proved particularly difficult for me, as I had decided to research and rewrite Palestinian history and re-examine the historical reasons for our eventual dislocation or, more precisely, dissemination. The difficulty lay largely in my eventual recognition of the power of the Zionist or Jewish lobby in North America, including Canada. This realisation was made more acute after I learnt that my department had received a letter (or letters) of dissatisfaction in which the sender(s) expressed concern about the 'lack of scientific account and objectivity' in a Ph.D. thesis submitted earlier by the first Palestinian student in the history of the department. I felt I had to work over and above the efforts of any other student to prove to my supervisors, department, and the whole university that Palestinians are not only capable of scientific research, but also are true victims of Zionist settler colonialism.

Being an immigrant in North American academic institutions with English as a third language was difficult enough, but being all of this and Palestinian to boot was insurmountable. The presence of a relatively large contingent of pro-Israel Jewish scholars and professors made it difficult to engage in any constructive or progressive debate on the Palestinian-Israeli or Arab-Zionist debate. Graduate and undergraduate courses in social sciences, particularly sociology, anthropology, and political science, provided ample examples of cases of underdevelopment, colonialism, settler regimes, and so on. The only example often skipped or intentionally downplayed was the Palestinians. In fact, on more than one occasion I found myself arguing very passionately with one of my professors, trying to convince him that similar to Algerians and South Africans, Palestinians were also victims of British colonialism and the Zionist settler project. Using his position of power, he would brush my argument aside by asking me to get over my 'naïveté' and think more 'realistically' about the Jews who were 'pioneers' motivated by 'socialist' principles.

My experience with some professors was quite unpleasant. I still remember an encounter I had with one professor in the summer of 1982. Furious, frustrated, and very frightened, I ran into him in the lobby of the sociology department, and in the spirit of a student searching for some support from her professor, I asked him, 'Can you believe what the Israelis are doing to the Palestinians?' He looked at me and, unsurprised, asked in a nonchalant manner, 'What are they doing?' Almost certain he was honest and, did not know what happened, I answered, 'The massacres in Sabra and Shatila.' Totally ignoring my state of anger, tears, and emotional distress, he replied, 'What's the big deal? History is replete with massacres and genocides!' At this moment I wished I hadn't seen him or even spoken with him. I realised then how powerful the victimisers and their supporters were, and how fragile the victims, not only in their own land, but even in 'advanced', 'developed', 'free' countries. These experiences undoubtedly strengthened my determination to take up the case of the Palestinian people as one deserving the utmost attention as a legitimate and just cause of international proportions. Academically, despite these experiences, I insisted on having Jewish (albeit non-Zionist) faculty as members of my supervisory team and completed a Ph.D. The thesis was on the very premise I had adopted earlier, namely, proving that while Zionism was historically specific, it was never unique nor markedly different from other projects of settler colonialism. Like apartheid in South Africa and French Algeria, Zionism had as its premise a racist structure and institutions, as well as the policies and principles of 'othering', exploitation, and exclusion.

Diaspora: New Challenges and Changed Identities

Life in diaspora, particularly for Third World immigrants 'of colour', is often complex. The difficulties engulf most spheres of life, including employment, education, and housing, as well as other legal aspects of life. These issues have been widely debated, particularly within the Canadian context (Abdo, 1993b; Bannerji, 1999; Stevenson, 1999; Leah, 1999; Das Gupta, 1999). What is quite specific, if not perhaps unique, about the Palestinian experience in the North American diaspora is the very identity, or multiple identities, they are expected to assume. As a graduate student specialising in the general category of Third World underdevelopment, I often wondered what would it take to convince Canadian authorities that I qualified for the travel funds given to other Third World students. More than once, I entertained the idea of changing my identity in a manner that would allow me to get such funds. For them I was 'Israeli', and as such I belonged to 'Europe', not the Third World or Middle East. Being Palestinian and living as what amounted to a third-class citizen in Israel did not seem to matter. It was frustrating to realise that the very conditions I had hoped to escape or avoid were to follow me into the new 'host' country. Neither in Israel, nor in Canada was I able to enjoy 'student life' with grants or funds, despite my very good academic record. In Canada, I often found myself having to work at more than one job while accumulating student loans in order to survive. Having experienced such pressure and endured the onslaught on my 'nationality', it is no surprise that I took refuge in cultural nationalism as a source of pride and belonging as well as a political means for survival, particularly during the first years of diaspora.

In some respects, the experience in the host country felt more rewarding than life in my 'own' country. Despite the many challenges I faced as a Palestinian feminist and later academic, Canada gave me a degree of freedom I had never enjoyed before. In the early 1980s, I began to associate with various women's organisations, taking a visible role on International Women's Day, for instance. It was not surprising that the organisations I found myself closest to were the Jewish women's organisations, particularly the progressive Women Against Israeli Occupation and Women in Black. The anti-Zionist and non-Zionist stances of these organisations made it possible for me to not only 'recover' my identity as Palestinian but also develop it in such a way as to go beyond its limited nationalistic boundaries. The repeated collaborative work we, Jewish and Palestinian women, engaged in – vigils against the occupation; massive demonstrations against Israel's invasion of Lebanon and against Sharon's fascist policies, which had resulted in the massacres in Sabra and Shatila; massive street demonstrations we organised against the Iron Fist policies used to suppress the first Intifada in 1987; and so on

– undoubtedly fostered a relationship of trust among us. This relationship, strengthened by various social gatherings, had a major impact on the development of my national identity, bringing the theoretical and abstract down to the practical and empirical levels.

Before further elaborating, I would like to mention that unlike life in Israel, where one lives under constant tension, often in a state of war, life in the Canadian diaspora provided a more relaxed environment, one more conducive to the development of a form of objectivity otherwise unavailable or difficult to attain. Being the bearers of Zionist/Israeli uprootedness, and physically close to the site of oppression, most Palestinian refugees are unable or perhaps unwilling to differentiate between the state of Israel and the individual Israelis, or between Zionists and Jews in general. For most refugees, the direct enemy who forced them out of their homes and villages is the Jewish soldier who speaks Hebrew. Moreover, it should be stressed that Israel has not helped to enable this differentiation. If anything, it has laboriously tried to equate the notion of Jew with that of Zionist to legitimise its ideological stance of colonialism and racism. It is against all these odds that I have tried to develop the difference, at least academically, in my writings, and personally/socially, through my friends.[10]

Building solidarity with these organisations undoubtedly helped crystallise the difference between the Zionists, for whom Israel, wrong or right, is sacred and untouchable, and the progressive Jews, for whom Israel is but another colonial settler and racist state, and for whom the dismantling of this racist oppressive structure is of no offence or consequence to Jewish progressive identity. This experience made it possible for me to imagine a future state of Israel which would relinquish its Jewish (read, racist and exclusivist) ethno-theocratic character, to become a truly democratic entity with Jews and Palestinians living in full peace and equality. It is telling that such a position is more accepted and in fact finds more support among the very victims of Zionism and the Israeli state, namely, Palestinians, yet is confined to a small group, if not totally rejected – by North American Jewish academics, most of whom are liberals with Zionist leanings.

My diasporic experience taught me a rich lesson about the special dynamics that govern the Israeli-Palestinian or Arab-Zionist conflict in the West. In the Middle East, including Israel, the struggle is straightforwardly lying between the occupier and the occupied, the coloniser and the colonised. In the West and North America in particular, other dimensions, i.e. the Eurocentric and Orientalist frame of thought within which Muslims or Arabs in general and Palestinians in particular are often boxed, are brought to the equation, making it more complicated and difficult to disentangle.

A detailed critique of Eurocentrism and Orientalism has been provided elsewhere (Abdo, 1993a; 1996), what is important to emphasise
here is that among the characteristic images of oil, desert, richness, and
terrorism presented in juxtaposition to the notions of Islam and Arabs is
a highly masculinist, stereotyped vision of the diverse domain known as
the Arab world. Within this masculinist onslaught, Arab and Muslim
women are depicted as passive, silent, veiled, and secluded. They are
seen as subjugated and over-oppressed by their own men, religion, and
culture. Orientalism does not recognise differences; instead, it homog-
enises Arabs, Middle Easterners, and Muslims, presenting them as an
undifferentiated, homogeneous entity. The facts that not all Arabs are
Muslims; that not all Muslims are Arabs; and that the overwhelming
majority of Muslims reside outside of the Middle East appear to be of little or no import to Orientalists.

Orientalism, or the specific ideological frame within which Arab
women have generally been constructed and reconstructed, complicates
the struggle of Arab women in general and Palestinians in particular. As
an Arab, Palestinian feminist who is not from a Muslim background, nor
religious altogether, I find myself having to de-homogenise and de-objec-
tify the Arab identity before I can take part in any meaningful political
discussion. My physical appearance, activist background, and academic
training have never been significant enough to (re)present in me the heterogeneity of the Arab culture. What seems more important for many in
official and non-official meetings, both academic and non-academic, is
the a priori perception they have already constructed about Arab women.
Yet more complex are the encounters I have had with male and female
Jewish academics. No matter how scientific your data, how precise and
to the point your argument, and how articulate and well argued your
presentation, the second your talk seems a damnation of Israel and its
racist policies, you are almost immediately challenged, disputed, and
even discredited. All this, one might add, occurs irrespective of whether
or not your (Jewish) challenger is familiar with the data or has ever visited or been to Israel!

I was, and still am, struck by this phenomenon. You always find a
quite impressive core group of Jewish scholars and academics fully committed to issues of human rights and questions of justice in Latin and
South America, South Africa, and many other parts of the world. Yet,
when it comes to Israel's constant violations of international conventions,
UN resolutions, and other laws regarding Palestinians, one is faced with
a situation in which either those 'progressive' Jews do not show up altogether, or the ones who do show up; for one reason or another, tend to be
on the defensive, as if they were personally under criticism.

This situation is not confined to male Jewish liberal academics. Feminist Jewish academics are not much different. In fact, I find them more

perplexing. I could never comprehend how a Jewish feminist, whether Israeli or Canadian, could separate between being feminist and being non-racist, let alone anti-racist. The introduction to this book deals more elaborately with these issues, particularly within the Israeli context. For the sake of this essay, it suffices to mention that Israeli feminism, like much of Canadian academic Jewish feminism, remains entrapped in the conventional Weberian paradigm, which can conveniently depoliticise feminism and separate it from its political context. This liberal type of feminism can be as damaging to the feminist movement as the colonial state is, because it serves as an ally to capitalism, colonialism, and imperialism. For more on the collusion between racism (including Zionist feminism) and colonialism (see Lazreg, 1988, 1993; Gottlieb, 1993; Mohanty, 1995; and Bannerji, 1999). In a 2000 address I gave at Beit Berl College to a group of Israeli academic feminists, my critique of Zionism as a racist colonialist movement was faced with extreme resistance and dismay by most Israeli feminists present, some of whom angrily interrupted my talk, 'accusing' me of being 'political' rather than a feminist. Like other Eurocentric middle-class white feminists who are still silent about their states' atrocities towards native women and women of colour, Israeli feminists, I believe, are guilty of the same dishonesty. In addition to turning a deaf ear towards the atrocities and crimes their state commits against the Palestinian people, Israeli feminists also try to silence the voices that try to speak against state crimes, and in defence of human rights.

It is not surprising to note that Western feminists in general and Israeli feminists in particular identify more with discourses, presentations, and public talks by Arab feminists who decry their oppression in their own land, be it under patriarchy, their men, culture, religion, or Muslim laws. This is partly the reason that issues like honour killing, veiling, domestic (not state) violence against women, and so forth, are particularly attractive to the North American and Israeli media and public alike. The attraction of such phenomena, it must be added, is not a result of interest on the part of North American or Israeli feminists aimed at gaining some understanding of the causes and objective conditions which give rise to these issues, but rather because of the 'different' and perhaps exotic or violent images which veiling and honour killing, for example, conjure. The attraction of such phenomena also lies in that they provide some further validation or justification to the Orientalist and racist feminist approaches to Arab patriarchy, Islam, and traditional culture.

This position taken by Western/Israeli liberal and radical feminists leaves a negative, if not destructive, impact on any attempt at developing feminism in general or widening its scope outside of the Western sphere. In such a position, these feminists place themselves in the same camp as the oppressive racist state, causing Arab/Palestinian feminists, in turn, to doubt their sincerity. One of the main victims of the attitude of these

Western/Israeli feminists is the issue of sexuality or more precisely, sexual violence against Palestinian women, which, as a result of fear of being misused or abused by the 'enemy', is often underplayed and even suppressed by Arab/Palestinian feminists. This, I believe, is one reason that many Arab and Palestinian feminists tend to cling to nationalism, even in its essentialist character, when discussing feminist or womanist concerns. However, as will be shown shortly, experiences learnt and challenges faced in the diaspora can also contribute positively and constructively to identity formation, either by solidifying already existing identities, or by engendering new ones, albeit, this time by choice and not by force.

The Changed and the Changer: Bridging Diaspora with Homeland

The challenges faced by people in their own 'homes', especially if the latter are characterised by wars and strife, do not disappear in exile. Diaspora, it must be remembered, is not a neutral space or a challenge-free place. Immigrants and refugees who turn to the West for social, economic, or political reasons are overwhelmed by the challenges. Some often encounter new realities, difficulties, and challenges and decide to respond with a degree of withdrawal by leading a basically domestic or private life, with little interest in engaging in public or political life. Others, like myself, do not find the private or domestic life sufficiently appealing, and as a result opt for an activist role. In my case, I developed a strong resolve to confront the various injustices, mistreatments, and challenges in an attempt to minimise their impact, leading in the process to some change.

As elaborated earlier, the major challenge I faced in Canada was orientated towards my strong national identity, which I made public. I often have conversations and debates with Arab and Palestinian friends who exhibit signs of discomfort at hearing me constantly speak about the need to confront racism, Orientalism, and the anti-Arab sentiments that exist institutionally and structurally in Canada. Yet, it is crystal clear to many immigrants, particularly activist feminists, that confronting discrimination in all forms must be part and parcel of one's own identity affirmation and development. Facing and confronting the wrongs, rather than responding with silence or indifference, provides more chances for correcting or righting them. As the Arabic saying goes *'el Saket a'la el Haqq kal-mujaher fil-Batel'* (Those who are silent on what is right are equally guilty of wrongdoing).

One day in the fall of 1991, I received a phone call in my office from the principal of my children's elementary school informing me that my children 'were placed in seclusion from other children for their safety'. Uncomprehending, I called the principal back, asking for details. In a confused tone, she said that she had had to place my children (one was five and the other eight) in a separate room away from the rest of the kids who were in recess, for their own protection'. In utter shock, I asked 'But why my children only? Why not protect all other children?' 'Because', she answered, 'your children are Iranian.' Hearing me humming over the phone, she added, 'I assumed your children were Iranian or Iraqi!' Trying very hard to keep my calm, realising the unequal treatment of my children, I replied, 'Neither this nor that'. 'But aren't you Arabs?' she asked. 'Yes we are Arabs, Palestinians', I answered. 'Oh, these are not the same? I am sorry'. At this point I was not sure what to do. Should I educate the school principal? Or launch a formal complaint to the Board of Education? More immediately, however, I felt the need to go and check out my children and ensure they were not psychologically affected by her thoughtless, ignorant act of discrimination! This type of racial discrimination, while it might not be conscious or intended, is known as ignorant-based forms of ethnic or racial discrimination.

As bitter and difficult as such encounters have been, the fact remains that they have further consolidated my Palestinian 'national' identity and opened up more space to develop strategies for survival. Nonetheless, national identity did not remain the only, or even the most important, identity in my life. In the process I became more aware of the danger of 'essentialism', particularly nationalist essentialism, which can turn into ethnicism, or even exclusivism. Along with embracing what I believed to be a progressive national identity, I also started, in the Canadian environment of academia, activism, and a degree of political democracy and tolerance unfound before, to develop my feminist identity as an activist feminist. Without going into the debate of whether feminism is 'naturally' born into every female, or is similar to 'womanism', or to 'women's awareness of their subordination', I can say that feminism for me is a learnt and experiential phenomenon. Yes, I felt discrimination on a gender or sex basis at home. I felt it from my father's treatment of my mother and my mother's treatment of my brother, which was different from her treatment of us daughters. I also felt it in the streets, at school, at work, and in higher education. I felt sex discrimination and oppression most of all as a mature woman who was prevented from choosing her partner or her relationships. Finally, sexual assault and humiliation were daily occurrences during my prison incarceration. Nonetheless, these experiences did not turn me to feminism at the time. In other words, although objective conditions for feminist identity were present, subjective conditions, or self-readiness and awareness, were still underdeveloped.

For feminism to emerge as a phenomenon and a movement, both objective and subjective conditions must demonstrate sufficient ripeness. As I stated earlier, the overwhelming occupation of citizen Palestinians with their very national and daily survival in Israel makes it difficult for objective conditions to open up to other phenomena or movements. Similarly, living in a traditional patriarchal system whose control over its female members has been reinforced by Israeli state policies makes it very difficult for most women to find a space to move in. The few activist women during the 1970s and 1980s were themselves overwhelmed by the political/national, which they found to be more important than any 'side' struggle, a situation that has markedly changed since the late 1980s and the early 1990s (Kuttab, 1990; Abdo, 1999). In fact, today one cannot fail to see the diverse strands of feminisms that have developed with the strong gender and sex-related agendas placed in the forefront of the small but growing citizen Palestinian feminist movement.

Feminism for me is not just about my individual development and freedom. Informed by a strong anti-racist, anti-classist, anti-sexist principles, feminism for me has developed into an objective, alternative means to fight all forms of oppression, in the Canadian context as well as internationally. The very fact of being 'outside' of the social, cultural, economic, and political contradictions which characterise Palestinian society, be it in the West Bank, Gaza, or Israel, make it possible for me to provide an 'objective' assessment of these contradictions. The most important area that this 'objective positionality' contributes to is that of sexuality. Exposure to a wider base of resources and knowledge about issues of sexuality give it more prominence and begin to free it from its traditionally constraining social and cultural taboos. With this degree of 'mental' or 'conscious' freedom I was able to do extensive research on Palestinian women's sexuality, not here in Canada, but there, in Palestine and Israel. According this area special attention has also resulted in a much clearer and more critical perspective on all forms of ideologies, most importantly, that of my own nationalism, as will be seen shortly. In addition to my academic and discursive contributions to the spread of the feminist movement, whether through my students or through my publications, I have been involved in practical field visits, which include training, research, networking, and other forms of activism among Palestinian women in both the Gaza Strip and the West Bank. While in the latter, I was involved in the establishment of the Women's Studies Programme/Women's Institute at Bir Zeit University. In Gaza I established a nucleus for gender/women research by training women on feminist research methodologies. Bridging my 'home' with its Canadian diaspora, I must confess, was the most positive and constructive experience I have gained in exile.

While developing my feminist identity I have struggled with the question of how to reconcile feminism with nationalism. Despite the tremendous amount of ink spilled over the issue, feminists, I believe, are still debating it. It is true that most feminists recognise the powerful role nationalism plays as an 'imagined community', to use Benedict Anderson's words.[11] They also realise that nationalism is able, particularly in the form of the movement, to subsume all forms of contradictions: gender, class, ethnicity, religion, and so on. Most feminists also keenly insist on keeping the gender or womanist agenda alive, even during periods of national struggle.[12] Still, as a feminist who has witnessed and, albeit indirectly, participated in the recent Palestinian national struggle, expressed as the 1987–92 Intifada and the current Intifada, which began in September 2000, I find the balance, or rather, imbalance, of feminism and nationalism to be of primary concern to most Palestinian women activists. The major concern is the future of the many changes and promised changes that the women's movement has achieved, but now sees as dwindling, if not totally submerged, under Israel's constant aggression and Palestinian national response. The situation poses the question of whether it is possible to maintain a balance between national demands and women's demands. Is it possible, in warlike situations, to open different fronts including the social and gender agendas? Finally, is it possible at all to solve the issue of prioritisation – for example, nationalism over feminism and vice versa – solely at the academic or intellectual level?

Despite my strong commitment to feminism and unwavering support for women's liberation, considering it a top priority in any attempt at building a democratic civil society, the reality practised on the ground during the Second Intifada suggests a different scenario. Most women's organisations, who until September 2000 were busy dealing with issues concerning gender and sexuality, such as violence against women, honour killing, shelters, and hotlines, are currently working as messengers, communicating to the world the atrocities and aggression of the Israelis against Palestinian women and children. Documenting the lives of Palestinian women under Israeli bombardment has become a priority for most feminist organisations. Women of the Second Intifada live under constant attack, enduring house demolitions, deforestation and the uprooting of groves and fruit trees, continuous siege, and closures resulting in impoverishment and high rates of unemployment, and cutoffs in electricity and running water. Finally, one needs to remember here that it is the middle-class, academics, and intellectuals who are the disseminators of the concerns of women or feminists. In Palestine, most official research on women has traditionally come out of the Bir Zeit University Women's Studies programme. Today, the whole of Bir Zeit, like the whole of the Palestinian territories, is brutalised by the Israeli siege, which prevents any movement from or to the university.

I have often been asked about where I stand on the question of prioritising one form of identity or struggle over another. Recently, in a nation-wide televised debate among Palestinians, a young, enthusiastic woman challenged the panel on which I was a speaker to speak out more strongly about what she referred to as 'cleaning house', suggesting that airing our own dirty laundry in public must be priority to Palestinians. While in principle I could not disagree with her, I found myself struggling as I tried to answer her concerns. Yes, I resent nepotism, and the lack of transparency and corruption which enriches a very small number of Palestinians and impoverishes many. Most of all I resent the twisted and hypocritical ways in which Palestinian women have been treated by the Palestinian Authority, and the stick-and-carrot policies used by the latter whenever the former ask for legal changes. (For an updated account on Palestinian women under the Palestinian authority, see Abdo, 1999). However, working and living with these women for prolonged periods of time, during the first Intifada and afterwards, has brought me much closer to their day-to-day experiences, and to the realisation of the degree of complexity of these questions. The question of prioritisation of one struggle over another, I have learnt, is not a subjective decision we make as individuals, at our leisure in Canada, the US, or elsewhere, enjoying a life of relative peace and tranquillity. The reality, sad as it may be, is that life is mostly dictated by the objective conditions most people find themselves forced to succumb to while trying to maintain and reproduce themselves.

I would argue, by way of conclusion, that the oppression and victimisation often brought on by experiences of exile and refugeeism have a dual impact on Palestinian subjectivity. On the one hand, through racism, sexism, Orientalism, and other forms of discrimination and humiliation, the self or the person has largely been objectified. Thus, Palestinians in general have been used as instruments to affirm the power of the colonial 'other', while women are placed in double jeopardy, having to face both the patriarchal-national 'self' and the foreign oppressive 'other'. Yet, on the other hand, we find that for others, especially those who have had some choice over where they live, the experience of diaspora and exile can turn into a force for recapturing the very subjective self or identity, turning it into an agent of change. This, I strongly believe, is the best way to experience diaspora-of-choice: the self becomes the changed and the changer at the same time.

Notes

1. Although my first reaction to the letter was to forget all about it, three days later, as I discovered that I was not over it yet, I decided to call the number in the letter. I reached the owner of the letter, an older Jewish man, originally from Hungary. He had immigrated to Palestine in 1945, lived there for four years, and then left again for Canada. Mr Bleuer insisted on sending me the letter because I 'should remember the Holocaust and the suffering of the Jews'. But why did you not stay there, I asked. No answer. After a long discussion I was forced to have with him about his experience, although I was the one who made the long-distance call, I thought talking to him was not so bad after all! The man was less threatening than I originally thought. Yes he was Zionist and a defender of Zionism, but he was not sure or clear as to why he held that position. despite his strong paternal attitudes, his stories about visiting the West Bank thirty years ago, speaking to 'Arab' children and giving them candy, made me forget my initial anger and adopt a new tolerance level for an older orientalist, paternalist guy who meant little, if any, harm at all. This was especially true when I repeatedly asked him to let me off the phone, while he insisted I listen to his stories of children and the candies and food he shared with them.

2. It is important to note that the overwhelming literature on Palestinian refugees has concentrated on those who were forced out during the establishment of the state of Israel. The term refugee, as will be seen in this essay, was until recently removed from implicating internal refugees, or those who lost their homes and land and were forcefully relocated, but within historic Palestine.

3. An important analysis of the 1967 Israeli occupation of the West Bank, Gaza Strip and Golan Heights and the consequences thereof for the Palestinians is found in Jamil Hilal, *The West Bank: Socio-economic Structure, 1948–1974* (Beirut: Markaz al-Abhath, 1974). For a brief account of the different periods of history undergone by Palestinians, see Nahla Abdo, *Family, Women and Social Change in the Middle East: The Palestinian Case* (Toronto: Canadian Scholars' Press, 1987).

4. For a detailed analysis of land confiscation which began with the Zionist project in Palestine; the exclusion of Palestinians from land, labour and the 'Jewish' market; turning the expropriated land into the 'inalienable right of the Jews'; and other racist/exclusivist policies practised against Palestinians, see my 'Colonial Capitalism and Agrarian Structure: A Case Study', *Economic and Political Weekly (EPW)* 26 (30): 73–85. It is interesting to point out here that according to Don Peretz, 'more than 80 per cent of Israel's total area belongs to Arab refugees. Thus abandoned property was one of the greatest contributions towards making Israel a viable state.' Commenting further on the meaning and implications of the 'Absentee Property' law, Peretz adds: 'Every Arab in Palestine who had left his town or village after 29 November 1947, was liable to be classified as an absentee according to the regulations. All Arabs who held property in the new city of Acre, regardless of the fact that they may have never travelled farther than the few metres to the old City, were classified as absentees. The 30,000 Arabs who fled from one place to another within Israel, but who never left the country were also liable to have their property declared absentee. Any individual who may have gone to Beirut or Bethlehem for a one day visit during the latter days of the British Mandate was automatically an absentee'. Don Peretz, cited in Elia Zureik, *The Palestinians in Israel: A Study in Internal Colonialism.* London: Routledge, 1979: 116.

5. Having witnessed more than one such event, I must stress that the experience of acquiring a permit from the Israeli military ruler (*Qayemqam*) was humiliating. I used to accompany my father on his 'trips' to get a permit. We would leave early in the morning and take our place in a very long line on the main street (while the military

commander had his offices indoors, the public was largely served outside the office, literally on the street). Most people lining up were men asking for permits allowing them to leave their village to look for work, or older women wanting to either visit relatives or do other chores. In addition to the pushing and shoving, the commander was very rude to people; he would shout, scream, and even scold them.

6. Wearing black in my culture is a sign of mourning. Upon the death of a family member, Arab women don black clothes, an often conservative type of attire which is not expected to show parts of the body. The period for wearing it varies according to the closeness and age of the deceased. Based on these customs, we thought that this teacher has lost a dear family member.

7. The uniqueness of the Israeli state's relationship to the Bedouins is a striking example of how laws can invent culture rather than reflect a reality. Unlike the 'security' justification used as Israel's basis for confiscating Palestinian peasant lands, Bedouins' lands were confiscated on 'cultural' grounds. Perceived by the state as 'rootless nomads' and not communities who have moved on these lands for centuries, the Bedouins were used by the state as a tail to its own image. Thus, in order to assert its own power and domination over this population, Israel constructed the Bedouins as 'backward and incapable', while the Zionist project was 'modern' and 'Western'. For more on the Bedouins and Druze in Israel, see Ronen Shimmer, in Nahla Abdo (forthcoming), *Sexuality, Citizenship and the Nation State: Palestinian Experiences*. Syracuse: (Syracuse University Press), Chapter 3.

8. The Jewish Agency was known prior to 1920 as the Zionist Agency. Before the establishment of the state of Israel, it had followed strict policies preventing Palestinians from working, leasing, or buying back land they had lost, mostly by force. These policies and practices remained intact many years after the lifting of military rule. In the mid-seventies, in a speech given to the settlers, the Israeli minister of agriculture was reported to have complained about the presence of Arab labourers in Jewish settlements, considering them a 'cancer which needs to be uprooted'. The same policies have been pursued after the establishment of the state of Israel. For more on this, see Abdo. *Sexuality, Citizenship and the Nation State.*

9. Lawyer Leah Tsemel is a leftist, activist, anti-Zionist Jew. She took up the task of defending Palestinian political prisoners on principle and as a political cause she believed in. She has also written on the ordeal of Palestinian political prisoners and their torture and illegal incarceration by the Israeli authorities. Her public support of the Palestinians and political stance against Israeli aggression and racism marked her as a 'Jew hater' and a 'traitor' to Israeli officials. 'Bat zonah' (whore) was the only way prison officers would identify her when she used to come and visit me in prison.

10. The difference between Zionism and Jewishness, or who is a Zionist and who is a Jew, is a matter of political position and social consciousness. As was stated earlier, this question is of no importance or consequence to an ordinary Palestinian, for whom both are equally oppressors. I must admit that it took me a lot of reading and hard work to develop a position on this issue and feel satisfied with it. The first articulation of this difference is found in my 'Nationalism and feminism in the Palestinian women's movement', in Valentine Moghadam (ed.), *Gender and National Identity: Women and Politics in Muslim Societies*, London: Zed Books, 1994: 148–70. Another articulation of this difference is found in an article co-authored with Nira Yuval-Davis, 'Palestine, Israel and the Zionist settler project', in Daiva Stasiulis and Nira Yuval-Davis (eds.), *Unsettling Settler Societies: Articulations of Gender, Race, Ethnicity and Class*, London: Sage, 1995: 291–322.

11. For Benedict Anderson (1991), the concept 'nationalism' assumes a special role and importance in the life of communities in general because of the power it commands as a 'unifying force' people can depend on, take pride in, and develop a sense of belonging to. What is peculiar about this concept is that it can be used for all sorts of purposes, for the purpose, including 'love, unity, togetherness and group solidarity'.

Yet, when stretched to its logical extension it can lead to oppression, exclusion, and even racism.

12. This was true for most academic and activist feminists I met during the first Intifada. The slogan 'No going back' was a credo of most feminists at the time. In fact, this slogan inspired my earlier articles on the Intifada (1991; 1993).

References

'Gendered Politics of Location'

Abdo, Nahla. 1994. 'Nationalism and feminism: Palestinian women and the Intifada – no going back?' In Valentine M. Moghadam (ed.), *Gender and National Identity: Women and Politics in Muslim Societies*. London: Zed Books.
Moghadam, Valentine. 1994. 'Introduction and Overview'. In Valentine M. Moghadam (ed.), *Gender and National Identity: Women and Politics in Muslim Societies*. London: Zed Books.
Sizoo, Edith. 1997. 'A polylogue'. In Edith Sizoo (ed.), *Women's Lifeworlds: Women's Narratives on Shaping their Realities*. London: Routledge.

'Dislocating Self, Relocating "Other"'

Abdo, Nahla. 1987. *Family, Women and Social Change in the Middle East: The Palestinian Case.* Toronto: Canadian Scholars' Press.
——. 1991. 'Women of the Intifada: Gender, class and national liberation'. *Race and Class* 32 (4): 19–35.
——. 1993a. 'Middle East politics through feminist lenses: Dialoguing the terms of solidarity'. *Alternatives* 18 (1): 29–41.
——. 1993b. 'Race, gender and politics: The struggle of Arab women in Canada'. In Linda Carty (ed.), *And Still We Rise*. Toronto: Women's Press.
——. 1994. 'Nationalism and feminism in the Palestinian women's movement'. In Valentine Moghadam (ed.), *Gender and National Identity: Women and Politics in Muslim Societies*. London: Zed Books.
——. 1996. 'Orientalism, Eurocentrism and the making of theory'. In Nahla Abdo (ed.), *Sociological Theory: Beyond Eurocentric Thought*. Toronto: Canadian Scholars Press.
——. 1997. 'Family law: Articulating gender, state and Islam'. *International Review of Comparative Public Policy* 9: 169–93.
——. 1999. 'Gender and politics under the Palestinian Authority'. *Journal of Palestine Studies* 28 (2): 38–51.
Abdo, Nahla, and Nira Yuval-Davis. 1995. 'Palestine, Israel and the Zionist settler project'. In Daiva Stasiulis and Nira Yuval-Davis (eds.), *Unsettling Settler Societies: Articulations of Gender, Race, Ethnicity and Class*. London: Sage.
Anderson, Benedict. 1991. *Imagined Communities: Reflections on the Origin and Spread of Nationalism*. London: Verso.
Bannerji, Himani. 1999. 'A question of silence: Reflections on violence against women in communities of colour'. In Enakshi Dua and Angela Robertson (eds.), *Scratching the Surface: Canadian Anti-racist Feminist Thought*. Toronto: Women's Press.
Churchill, Ward. 1998. *A Little Matter of Genocide: Holocaust and Denial in the Americas, 1492 to the Present*. Winnipeg: Arbeiter Ring Publishing.
Dajani, Souad. 1994. *Eyes Without Country: Searching for a Palestinian Strategy of Liberation*. Philadelphia: Temple University Press.

Das Gupta, Tania. 1999. 'The politics of multiculturalism: Immigrant women and the Canadian state'. In Enakshi Dua and Angela Robertson (eds.), *Scratching the Surface: Canadian Anti-racist Feminist Thought*. Toronto: Women's Press.

Flapan, Simha. 1987. *The Birth of Israel: Myths and Realities*. New York: Pantheon.

Giacamman, Rita, and Penny Johnson. 1989. 'Palestinian women: Building barricades and breaking barriers'. In Zachary Lockman and Joel Beinin (eds.), *Intifada: The Palestinian Uprising Against Israeli Occupation*. Boston: South End Press.

Gilmore, David. 1983. *Dispossessed: The Ordeal of the Palestinians*. Spheres Books Ltd: London.

Gottlieb, Amy. 1993. 'Not in my name: A Jewish feminist challenges loyalty to Israel'. In Linda Carty (ed.), *And Still We Rise*. Toronto: Women's Press.

Hadawi, Sami. 1988. *Palestinian Rights and Losses in 1948*. London: Saqi Books.

Hilal, Jamil. 1975. *The West Bank: Economic and Social Structure, 1948–1974*. Beirut: Palestine Research Centre.

Kuttab, Eileen. 1990. 'Al-Intifada wa Ba'd Qadaya al-Mara' al-Ijtimaiyyah'. In *The Intifada and Some Women's Social Issues*. Beisan Centre: Ramallah.

Lazreg, Marnia. 1995. *The Eloquence of Silence: Algerian Women in Question*. New York: Routledge.

———. 1988. 'Feminism and difference: The perils of writing as a woman on women in Algeria'. *Feminist Studies* 14 (1): 81–107.

Leah, Ronnie Joy. 1999. 'Do you call me sister?: Women of colour and the Canadian labor movement'. In Enakshi Dua and Angela Robertson (eds.), *Scratching the Surface: Canadian Anti-racist Feminist Thought*. Toronto: Women's Press.

Marshall, Mark. 1995 'Rethinking the Palestine question: The apartheid paradigm'. *Journal of Palestine Studies* 25 (1): 15–22.

Metzger, Jan, Martin Orth, and Christian Sterzing. 1983. *This Land is Our Land: The West Bank under Israeli Occupation*. London: Zed Books.

Mohanty, Chandra. 1995. 'Under Western eyes: Feminist scholarship and colonial discourses'. In Bill Ashcroft, Gareth Griffiths, and Helen Tiffin (eds.), *The Postcolonial Studies Reader*. London: Routledge.

Morris, Benny. 1999. *Righteous Victims: A History of the Zionist-Arab Conflict, 1881–1999*. New York: Alfred A. Knopf.

Roy, Sara. 1995. *The Gaza Strip: The Political Economy of De-development*. Washington: Institute of Palestine Studies.

Peled, Yoav, and Gershon Shafir. 1996. 'The roots of peacemaking: The dynamic of citizenship in Israel, 1948–1993. *International Journal of Middle East Studies* 28: 391–413.

Said, Edward. 1979. *The Question of Palestine*. New York: Times Books.

Shafir, Gershon. 1989. *Land, Labour and the Origins of the Israeli-Palestinian Conflict, 1882–1914*. Cambridge: Cambridge University Press.

Sharoni, Simona. 1993. 'Middle Eastern politics through feminist lenses: Toward theorising international relations from women's struggle'. *Alternative* 18 (winter): 5–28.

Stevenson, Winnona. 1999. 'Colonialism and First Nation women in Canada'. In Enakshi Dua and Angela Robertson (eds.), *Scratching the Surface: Canadian Anti-racist Feminist Thought*. Toronto: Women's Press.

Zureik, Elia. 1979. *The Palestinians in Israel: A Study in Internal Colonialism*. London: Routledge.

THREE

Life under Occupation

Mona El Farra

Diary of the Dispossessed: Women's Misery and Suffering under Israeli Occupation

—m—

At the beginning of al-Aqsa Intifada I invited my mother, a seventy-nine-year-old widow and retired head teacher, to stay at my place so I can look after her during this state of national emergency. Her house is near settlement areas in Khan Younis, south of Gaza city, and the situation is very unsafe, with daily violent confrontations between protesters and the Israeli army. Everywhere in the Gaza Strip and the West Bank, Palestinian stone throwers face an army shielded from any serious threat to its safety by armoured vehicles, tanks, and highly protected barracks.

Since my mother came to my place, her only contact with our neighbours has been by telephone. The news about house demolitions, land levelling and tree uprooting reached her only gradually. Sensing unexpected events, she could not sleep for many nights, and worried about her house, unable to reach it or send anybody to get her special belongings.

On 22 November 2000 we heard about our next-door neighbours, a very poor widow and her two children. The bulldozers started their work at eleven o'clock at night. In great shock, and unaware of the danger, our neighbour threw herself against the bulldozer. She hoped to save her house, her only shelter, but she could not. She collapsed in agony, pain, and hatred. The Israelis had given no notice prior to the demolition. All the houses on their street were demolished, with the furniture inside. In some cases, the Israeli bulldozers started their job while families indoors. To this very minute, families have not been allowed to return to their houses, or their levelled land.

The Israelis continue their inhuman actions. The amount of damage is far beyond any warranted by the security measures they claim were necessary. It is simply collective punishment, humiliation, and harassment.

On 26 November 2000 I received the shocking news of my mother's house demolition; I expressed my feelings in the following letter, which was distributed worldwide.

Best Wishes from Gaza

I woke up this morning to hear the shocking news of my mother's house demolition. The Israeli bulldozers demolished the well adjacent to the house, as well as dozens of houses in the area. They also uprooted vast areas of bountiful agricultural land that includes orange, olive, and guava groves. Many families in the area are homeless, with the Red Cross just recently supplying them with tents. I cannot explain to you how bad I feel. All my childhood memories.... I still remember my late father's rare photos, the minute I first drank that water from our well out of his hands. I still remember the joy of the relatives, friends, and neighbours coming to celebrate this moment with us. The olive, orange, and guava trees, and many other trees, do not carry symbolic value only; they also have great economic value. They are lifelines for many families in the area. Agriculture is these people's only income. The Israelis aim to decimate our already annihilated economy, to uproot us, to destroy our culture and to deny our very existence on this land for thousands of years.

It is worth telling you that the Israeli army did not give any warning. The houses were demolished with the furniture inside. As you know, my mother lives in that house, but recently I invited her to stay with me because of the difficult times. My mother feels so bad about what happened. Our thoughts are with our neighbours, who are very poor and have no alternative homes.

Besides everything else I have mentioned, these demolitions are a huge blow to the environment. Some of the trees, especially the tall beautiful trees we call *Jumaiz*, are very rare species. What is happening is a major violation of human rights, a blow to the economy, environment, and peace. I feel angry, helpless, devastated, abandoned. The sad fact is that despite all these crimes against humanity, most Israelis do not care.

During these difficult moments, I remember a very touching poem, by the most gifted Palestinian poet, Mahmoud Darwish:

> I came back from the dead,
> To live
> I represent an uncompromising wound,
> The brutality of my executor has taught me,
> To bite the bullet,
> And carry on,
> And sing,
> I will sing,

I will resist,
I will resist.

I can assure you that one day, we will replant these trees and rebuild our houses, and water will flow again, even stronger than before, hopefully washing away the horrific memories of the decades-long Israeli aggression. We may be weak, but justice is on our side and one day it will prevail.

I suffered from a sleeping disorder. My mother did as well. I am still experiencing different sorts of nightmares, up to this very minute.

I felt strongly that I must go to the area, to see what is going on, to meet with the families, to express solidarity and to find out if they need any help. I had personal feelings. I felt as if I had lost one of my children, and could not grieve before holding it in my arms.

The main road leading to Khan Younis, where my family lives, was closed. It was diverted to a country lane under the supervision of army tanks, and is open, theoretically, for only two hours a day, though most of the time it is not. I am talking about the only connection between Gaza city and the southern part of the Strip. Medical supplies were delayed in reaching hospitals, and medical teams faced many serious effects, especially when the Khan Younis hospitals lacked oxygen cylinder supplies. This siege continues on and off. Still, I insisted on going. With the help of a friend, using side roads, we walked for one hour. I was greatly shocked to see the extent of the damage, the uprooted trees, the ruins of houses, the uprooted plant nurseries, the destroyed wells and poultry farms. I could not recognise my very dear place. My God! I could not recognise the area; it had lost its identity completely. I could not but burst into tears, crying loudly, as did my companion.

I was fifty metres away from my parents' place. An Israeli jeep stopped us. The soldiers pointed at me and threatened to open fire if I did not leave the place. Still in tears, I tried to talk to them. I hated myself later on for showing them my weakness and misery. They ordered me to leave at once. I felt abandoned, devastated, helpless. This is inhuman, I thought to myself! The anger and determination to resist increased inside me.

The Israelis will not succeeded in demoralising us, I swore to myself. It is not only my personal pain, but other people's pain too. Twenty-five families are living in tents. These people are not just numbers. They are real people with stories to tell.

A week later I went to visit the families in these tents. What I found was shocking. These women refused to leave the sites of their houses, despite daily shooting intended to force them to leave. I met children who go to school while Israeli soldiers shoot above their heads to terrify them. I felt empowered by meeting these women. I felt it is my national duty to work hard to tell the entire world about the Israeli soldiers through real human acts.

While I was writing these words, I received a phone call from one of the families I had visited. A woman had given birth to a baby – another addition to the twenty-first century refugees. I received another call from a member of the UHWC (Union of Health Workers Committee), a doctor, who shared her ordeal with me. 'I was stopped at the checkpoint, asked to leave my car and stand by the army tank', she said. 'When I refused, I was threatened with being shot. Still I insisted on refusing to obey their orders. They stopped my car for one whole hour, then let me go home'. 'I admire your attitude very much', I said. But the fact is that my doctor friend went home completely distressed and psychologically shocked.

One only needs to go to al-Qarara village to realise that what has been done goes far beyond anything warranted by security, it is simply occupation, collective punishment.

On 27 January 2001 I revisited al-Qarara and met with the dispossessed families again. Every time I go there, feelings of anger and pain boil inside me. What I see is real: one of the houses was occupied by the Israeli Defence Forces while the family that lived there was relegated to the ground floor. Living with your killer under the same roof, and by force, is unbearable. And this is not the only house where this is happening, I was informed.

Walking through the Night in Labour

I met a woman who had just given birth to a little baby boy. While in labour, and with strong contractions, she had to walk for one hour to reach the nearest available transportation. Cars are not allowed to enter that road area after 8 P.M. and the Israelis open fire without prior warning if any car passes by. An uneasy delivery followed. The baby is fine, but his mother was distressed.

I still cannot overcome that painful experience. I saw another baby who was malnourished. I arranged immediate medical help. I asked the women, 'Do you believe in peace?' and they all answered strongly, and without hesitation, 'We pray for fair peace, not humiliating peace'. I say with them, 'We do not want peace that will divide us into pieces'.

I met with farmers in a protest tent near their levelled land. The destroyed land needs a lot of work to be planted again in time for the harvest. The farmers feel strong pain, watching the rain but not being allowed to reach their land. They feel helpless and isolated.

I am describing just some of what I met in al-Qarara village near Khan Younis. But this is the case in all agricultural areas of the Gaza Strip. All people of destroyed land, including myself, will sue the IDF in the high court. But who will return the environment to its original state? Old trees, landmarks on the road for decades, have been destroyed; rare species of trees have been uprooted. They are very old and real witnesses to the barbaric Israeli acts.

The Israeli practices are inhuman and out of control. Serious action must be taken by the international community to stop the Israeli destruction, the uprooting of our trees, culture, and history!

1 February 2001

I have just arrived from al-Qarara, the destroyed village. Here are some new stories.

The night the bulldozers started was so dark and frightening; children were crying. One seven-year-old girl escaped the terrifying scene, walking alone in the dark, unaware of time or space. All she wanted was to be away from the soldiers and the bulldozers. It was not until the next day that her parents found her in a terrifying state. The girl still suffers from psychological distress and learning difficulties, according to the family.

The women of al-Qarara insisted on not letting the Israeli soldiers demolish their houses and made a human shield with their bodies to stop the bulldozers. In response, the Israelis called further military forces who shot at the women and threw tear gas bombs until they surrendered. The bulldozers carried on with their destruction.

On her wedding night, Mrs Algebra's house was demolished with all the furniture and *Gehaz* (bride gifts she had brought with her) inside it. The newlyweds are still unable to overcome the trauma and the psychological effects it had upon them. The husband told me he would never forget or forgive the Israelis for what they did to his new home and his hopes.

To date, the Israelis are still occupying four houses in the area. The irony is that they are living with their victims under the same roof. As armed soldiers, the Israeli occupiers feel safe; meanwhile, the owners of these houses are being terrorised and feel unsafe. They undergo systematic harassment, and they are placed under curfew from 6:00 P.M. until 6:00 A.M. the next morning.

I have to say here that I cannot describe the real suffering, distress, and agony which the people in al-Qarara have experienced in the several months that have passed since the beginning of the Intifada. There are no words that can express these people's lives.

Every time I go there, the women in particular are happy to see me. I have the feeling that my presence empowers the women, but this is not enough. Serious actions must be taken. These people have to be reached and visited regularly by other humanitarian organisations and political solidarity groups. They need medical and especially psychological care and attention. They need the solidarity and support of all concerned humanitarian bodies and political groups.

Hala Mannaa

Between Dispossession and Undying Hope: The Refugees' Eternal Agony

—⟋⟍—

The following is a brief account of the lives, dreams, struggles, and hopes of four refugee women. The women vary in age, social status, and in education. They also carry with them different experiences of diaspora and exile. Although each case is unique, all women share some common baggage that seems to characterise life in exile for most refugee women; this is the articulation of gender oppression and national oppression, or the accumulation of social and cultural contradictions and their exposure during political strife. The first three stories emphasise the national/ political concern of women's identity, while the fourth story exposes a refugee woman's gender identity within the patriarchal traditional culture of Palestinian refugees.

My Life

I am a twenty-two-year-old Palestinian girl living in Gaza, where I was raised and have lived all of my life. I have never known anything other than Gaza, as I have left only it once, to travel to Cairo with my father. How painful it is for human beings to live under oppression, stripped of their human rights and dignity, denied the essential means of survival, knowing that their rights of securing their daily life existence are embedded in land and national resources that have been siphoned from them. Placed under these conditions makes us feel that the only thing we, the dispossessed, can resort to is one thing, namely, to pray to God to deliver us from our oppressor's wrath. And this is what my mother, and my grandmother before her and other women in Gaza have been saying. My grandmother used to tell us the story of al-Nakba (the catastrophe) and the exodus from her home-town, Jaffa, to Gaza in 1948. She used to describe to us their house and the beautiful belongings and furniture they had. She loved her house. When-ever her misfortune and agony got the better of her, my grandmother would escape her fate by sharing with her children – including my father – the beautiful memories of her home before 1948. After al-Nakba my grandparents became refugees in Gaza, where my father's family lived in a refugee camp with neither a home to live in nor a piece of land to live from. They got by on minimal means, suffering sickness, sadness, and poverty. How painful it was to listen to my father tell me about his child-hood days, when his home was a small tent that didn't protect him from neither the cold weather of the Gaza winter nor the heat of the long sum-mers. He remembers spending most of his childhood in only one pair of pants, a single shirt, and no shoes. Although he lived amongst his family, none of his eleven brothers and sisters was adequately nurtured, as his family was only able to provide them with basic foods. This little was the maximum that he could wish for under the circumstances in those days.

While I admit that my position today is much improved since the gru-elling and arduous days of my fathers' time, despair and suffering in Gaza continues.

I am a refugee, daughter of a refugee, despite the fact that I have lived in Gaza city since I was born. That Gaza was my birthplace did not free me from the label of Refugee! We refugees are dispersed and rejected by everyone, including the local Gazans. In Gaza, there is a difference between *Laji* (refugee) and *Muwaten* (resident). While many Gazans are landowners, and most have priority in employment and education, refugees have no such rights. Refugees have no right to own land: there are even separate schools for refugees and the locals: refugees go to the United Nations Relief and Works Agency (UNRWA) schools, while resi-dents go to government-sponsored schools. The two schooling systems differ widely in terms of curricula, the education and skills of the teach-ers, and the standards of students. These differences are also manifested at graduation when it is made known which university kids get accepted to. This situation, along with the fact that we have a different lifestyle, affects our employment opportunities.

For Gaza locals – *Muwatenoun* (plural of *Muwaten*) – we refugees are seen as 'outsiders' who have come and taken their land; we have there-fore become a nuisance for them. They look at us with disdain and always remind us that we are refugees. We feel out of place, outsiders even amongst our own people. Everywhere that I am, I am asked the same question: refugee or local? And the treatment that I receive depends on my answer.

I often feel the need to raise my arms and do as my mother used to do – to pray to God for deliverance from this feeling of inferiority, especially when I compare myself with someone my age somewhere else in the world. Why do we refugees feel unsafe and unstable, with compromised rights? Why can't we live like other human beings, with our basic rights secured? Does this feeling, my need to raise of arms in prayer, make me look like Mother? Do I want to become like Mother? My mother, incidentally, is not a refugee; she is a Gazan and belongs to a landowning family. Although lately, since the first Intifada, and especially now, during the Second Intifada, she has been feeling most insecure, my mother finds a certain pride in her background. She sometimes, albeit jokingly, used to tease my father about his refugee status, and would remind him that her family ceded its status by allowing her to marry him. My father would take my mother's words lightly because he loved her dearly.

This notwithstanding, I often find myself perplexed at hearing this type of exchange. I wonder, had I married a local Gazan, would he reproach me the way my mother reproaches my father? And would I feel that I am lesser than he? I notice how in Gaza, refugee women married to local men tend to accept their differential treatment because of their refugee status, which renders them weaker and lesser. Yet, I always take solace in my origin: I am, after all, from Jaffa, the great Palestinian city. I feel a deep sense of pride because of my belonging to this city, and I always dream of returning to it one day.

Maryam and the Legend of Challenge

My friend and I stood by a three-story house with shattered windows. Its locked doors seemed like metal gates that had been locked for thousands of years, except for a child's head that appeared on the upper floor for a few seconds, as if scared to look outside its window for any longer.

My friend and I wondered if the shattered windows were caused by the brutal Israeli shelling that had hit the Beit Lahya police station, near Maryam's house. I gathered enough courage to climb the stairs leading to the interior doors. When I knocked on the door, a smiling woman in her thirties answered. She asked us to wait while she opened the metal doors leading to the reception area. She wanted to receive us in the guest room because we were visiting her for the first time. Without us even asking her about Maryam, whom we wanted to see, she excused herself and left to inform Maryam of our visit. With slow and cautious steps, and leaning against the wall for support, Maryam entered the room and joined us. Without asking about the reason for our visit, she inquired about our well-being. Maryam is fifty-four years old. She lives with her four daughters and three sons in this three-story building. She ensured her children's (daughters' and sons') education, despite the fact that she herself was deprived of education. She then married her daughters to their cousins

(*Ibn el-Amma* – the father's sister's son – and *Ibn el-Amm* – the father's brother's son). Her two sons work in trade. In accordance with traditional Palestinian familial norms, her eldest son has looked after the family since his father's death. Maryam lives on the first floor with her eldest son and his wife and children, while the other brothers live on the other floors. Despite the relative independence of the younger sons, their income is given monthly to the oldest brother who, as noted above, ensures the well-being of the whole family. In addition to ensuring that the needs of the family are met, the eldest brother is also the decision maker in the family. He has literally replaced the absent father.

Prior to becoming a refugee in Gaza, Maryam lived a serene life on her father's land in Majdal. She still carries with her the memory of those beautiful days, when all she knew was how to work the land and assist her mother in household chores. In those days, the options available to girls her age were quite limited, despite the fact that they worked the land and even interacted, when necessary, with the men in their village. Interaction with the other sex, again, occurred out of necessity, not out of choice. In fact, sexual relations, love relations, and gender mixing in public and outside of the immediate family remained a taboo subject that was never discussed. No man was even allowed to address her, and she was also forbidden to speak to men, whether they were relatives or strangers. Despite this, she was happy and serene, and she never thought of or longed for a different life – until she became old enough for marriage. Without consulting any other member of the family, Maryam's father decided to marry her off to her cousin whom she had barely seen. Thus, following his decision, she married her cousin, who was a few years younger than her. Maryam had only one option: to surrender to her family's decision and marry her cousin. Otherwise, she would have been subjected to unbearable consequences by all her relatives, without exception.

Maryam found herself digging deep in her memory in order to remember the fateful day when she awakened from her calm, routine life. She could only recall her mother holding her hand and pulling her behind her with the rest of her siblings, as her father led the way. They 'left', leaving everything behind: their homes, their land, their rightful belongings, their mill. Escaping the bullets and cannons, they ran amongst a crowd of people yelling and crying for help. Those were the days of involuntary dispossession, the days of the forced expulsion that Maryam and other Palestinian families went through. They were forced to leave their land, homes, peace, stability, and contentment, even as the enemy spoiled their existence.

Those moments will never fade from Maryam's memory. They have accompanied her ever since she left Majdal, even though she now lives in her own home. Dreams of returning to her calm and beautiful home, land, and life in Majdal are still alive. And she has never for a moment failed to share those images with her children and grandchildren, in order to keep the dream of return alive for generations to come.

But on the day of severe bombing in Gaza city, the sad old days of dispossession and al-Nakba returned to her in a single second, bringing back the sorrow and agony of exile. One of her sons was late returning from work that day. She decided, after much anguish and indecision over whether to leave the house, to go out and check on him.

In the midst of the heavy shelling and air bombardment which was aimed at Gaza during that night, Maryam suddenly jumped and screamed as her left eye was hit. This is Maryam, who still considers herself one of the millions of refugee women who have suffered past dispossession and dislocation and continue to undergo present hardships, uprooting, and refugee status. Maryam's dream, like mine, is to regain her humanity and security by returning to her rightful home.

The Mother of a Martyr and Her Dream of Return

If you follow her silences, her movements, and her disrupted and disturbed words, you immediately realise where she comes from. Her experience is undoubtedly that of someone who has suffered hardships, exile, diaspora and the richness of living in various societies. She is not your ordinary refugee: Umm Luayy is educated and has spent most of her life schoolteaching.

Umm Luayy who is fifty years old, has been teaching for over twenty years. Although such a profession imposes limitations on social relations, her acquaintances did not go beyond students and teachers, and sometimes parents – Umm Luayy was still able to cultivate a great deal of social consciousness.

Umm Luayy has experienced multiple exiles. After al-Nakba she had to move from one place to another, until finally, she moved to Kuwait, where she was married and had three boys and five girls. Yet, nowhere has she been able to forget her origin and the dream of return she has always kept alive, despite her many responsibilities as a mother of eight and a teacher. Umm Luayy was always keen on playing her motherhood role as a cultural transmitter of national dreams and aspirations. Her and her people's story of exile, dispossession, fears, dreams, and hope were always kept alive, and like their mother, her children are eager to work for the materialisation of the 'Dream of Return'.

Umm Luayy knows the meaning of the dream of return, she knows that it entails freedom, independence, a sovereign state, and return. She also knows, however, that this dream cannot materialise while in exile. Life in exile is very hard, she insists. 'You spend most of your days and nights working to secure a decent life for your children, and being who you are makes it worse.... As a Palestinian', Umm Luayy continues, 'you are always made to feel a stranger.... We were unwelcome guests, made to feel guilty for upholding our Palestinian nationality'.

In 1997 the first sign of a possible return to Palestine emerged. Umm Luayy took all the money they had saved in exile, and together with her children went to Gaza. The family's return, however, was not complete; the father was prevented from joining the family by order of the Israelis.

In the 'home' country, Umm Luayy found herself having to work hard in order to shelter, feed, and educate her eight children, of whom the eldest – Luayy – had just finished twelfth grade and decided against continuing his education in favour of helping his mother. In his search for a job, Luayy looked everywhere, from a small workshop, to construction, to sales, with little success. Employment in Gaza is very hard to get, as Umm Luayy has come to understand. Nonetheless, the strong relationship between Umm Luayy and Luayy remains unaffected; after all, he is the 'man' of the family, her *sanad* (social-psychological resource base). He was the core of her family even when she was the only breadwinner and he was unemployed.

The mother's relationship to Luayy was further solidified when the father was unable to join the family for many months after their arrival to Gaza. Luayy was her solace during hard times. He supported her when she was frustrated, comforted her when she ran out of the money she had brought from exile and had to beg for work, was the source of consolation she often looked for in her isolation. Described as a man with a great and loving heart, he loved all people young and old, and was loved by all who knew him or dealt with him. Through hard work and a lot of patience, worry, and repeated visits to different government offices, including the Ministry of Internal Affairs, passport offices and so on, Luayy was instrumental in effecting a policy of *'Lam Shaml'* – family reunification – bringing the father back from exile to rejoin the family. With the father's arrival, Umm Luayy decided to take time off work, be with the children, and depend financially on the meagre income her husband made as a member of the police force. Her relationship to Luayy remained as strong as ever. Umm Luayy could never imagine a day would come when Luayy would not be there!

During the al-Aqsa Intifada, Umm Luayy's apartment has become an observation tower used by her children and herself to watch the events. Her feelings and position in these days are similar to the feelings and position of other Palestinian mothers: she weeps and cries at the scene of martyred children, gets furious at the fascist acts of the Israelis, and is pained every time she sees a civilian hit or injured. Despite all the pain she feels and the cruelty she has witnessed, Umm Luayy never changed her position: There is no balance between the stone and the tank. There is no escape from fighting occupation, attaining freedom, and implementing independence and sovereignty – but not through this asymmetrical relationship between the occupier and the occupied.

As the Intifada progressed and more martyrs and injured fell, the struggle began to escalate and take different political and diplomatic forms. After the loss of her son, Umm Luayy began to take interest in news, political analysis, and other discourses on the struggle. On the one hand, she became more confident that the imbalance of power between Palestinian civilians (stone throwers) and Israeli soldiers (with armoured vehicles, tanks, helicopter gunships, marine guns and so on) would not bring an end to the struggle. On the other hand, she strongly believed in the logic which insists that the Intifada should continue and grow as a popular form of resistance. Her belief in the importance of the popularity of resistance, she later learnt, was simultaneously shared by her children and especially her Luayy, who ended up giving his life for the Intifada. Luayy's martyrdom was a 'fatal loss' for Umm Luayy, thus despite the presence of her husband – Luayy's father – she has not yet been able to free herself from the emotional and psychological dependence she had on him. In the absence of her husband, Luayy was for her the security every woman looks for in a patriarchal society such as that of Palestinians.

After Luayy's martyrdom, Umm Luayy began to take a more active role in the Intifada, attending meetings and other activities organised by various women's associations. Between her belief in the imbalance of power, noted earlier, and her commitment to contribute to change, Umm Luayy began to explore a new position for herself. As the following example demonstrates, this new position was not easy to articulate: Umm Luayy is still stuck between the need and drive to speak and the inability to act.

In a press conference for the 'Mothers of the Martyrs' organised by some women's organisations in Gaza city, Umm Luayy showed up accompanying another woman. Although uninvited, Umm Luayy impressed the organisers and most women participants with her strong personality, specificity, and prominence among her peers. When all the women invited had had the chance to speak about their experience as mothers who had lost their sons, Umm Luayy took the podium to tell her story. She was unstable and had not prepared for her speech, but spoke elegantly and with confidence. She talked at length about the pain and grief that have engulfed her since losing 'the first one who called me mama', who became a 'man' at a very young age, who as a teenager carried the responsibility of a family of eight. Umm Luayy went on to talk about the need for the 'mothers of martyrs' to take a more active role and suggested that these mothers establish a special organisation, something similar to the Israeli organisation 'Four Mothers', a body responsible for safeguarding the rights of the martyrs, so their sacrifices would not be in vain.

There is no doubt that Umm Luayy has a strong character which expresses an acute social and political consciousness and a desire for activism which contributes to nation-building. In fact, during the press conference, Umm Luayy did not shy away from expressing her disappointment at not having more effective weapons than stones to struggle against Israeli aggression. Umm Luayy made her wishes and thoughts about the different means of resistance clear during the press conference. One such thought was her deep faith in the strength of the Palestinian woman, who, according to her 'is also brave and can prove to the Israelis her bravery, if she is given proper training and proper weapons.... Stones are not the answer; they miss more than they reach!' Umm Luayy made a passionate appeal for the adoption of a policy of boycotting all foreign products including Israeli, American and British goods. Boycotts, she argues, are another effective form of national resistance.

As impressed as all participants were by the charismatic character of Umm Luayy, most women were also disappointed that she did not take the initiative to form the 'mother's organisation' that she herself had suggested. Umm Luayy is an example of the typical Palestinian female nationalist, whose fight and struggle take place through her motherhood role, as the 'mother of', and not through her role as a woman. In fact, when pressed, Umm Luayy told the women that she prefers to go home and fight through her children, the children of the Intifada. It is important to note that Umm Luayy's name was never revealed throughout my acquaintance with her.

Agony for Ibtissam: Between the Political and the Cultural

Her dreams were simple: a husband, a home, and children. Her education was limited to elementary school, so she spent the rest of her days 'waiting' at home. When she got bored by housework and tired of waiting, she decided to take up the profession of beautician for a short period of time.

She did not regret her choice, for it helped her fill the time during her long waiting journey, and was the most convenient way for her to fulfil her simple dreams of joy. Besides, she thought, her profession will always be in demand among women of all classes, in good times as well as bad.

After only a few months that felt like an eternity a man proposed to her and was approved by her family., Thinking she had finally found the happiness that she had been seeking for all of those years, she felt her problems disappearing. Yet, had Ibtissam known that her happiness would turn into grief upon her becoming the widow of martyred Omar Abed, she would not have been capable of a modicum of joy; nor would she have allowed herself to feel calm and content, had she known the future was to bring such a shock.

Nonetheless, Ibtissam's biggest dream had materialised; she got married ... and awaiting of the other dreams, especially forming a family. But she was caught by surprise as her mysterious fate began to assail her with one tragedy after another. She never thought any of these tragedies could be part of being married. She had only simple impressions of marriage; mainly, that it would be better than her life in her paternal home. But within five months after her marriage, still in her early twenties, Ibtissam was undergoing unexpected humiliation and striking shocks, starting with the secret world that marriage holds for a sheltered 'Eastern' girl. She also found herself subjected to many problems arising from her new married life among her husband's extended family.

It was not easy for a young woman whose life experience had been modest and selfless. She was now required to accommodate the demands and expectations of her husband's extended family, such as doing their housework, which prompted her to lose her patience and endurance. Moreover, her personal life and needs were neglected by all the family members in an attempt to diminish, disregard, and disrespect her.

Meanwhile, her first pregnancy brought an added layer of pressure, worries, and concerns. She was overwhelmed by stress resulting from the endless household chores she had to perform for the extended family, as well as her husband's constant complaints about his job requirements. Her husband worked on a heavy truck that was owned by his father. His job demanded a lot of time and energy, but provided him with substantial earnings that benefited his entire family.

It became clear to her, through her daily rows with various members of his family, that she could always depend on her husband for love and support. He always supported her, standing by her side during the daily family arguments. His support saved and inspired her, and was crucial in enabling her to be patient and tolerate her situation, thereby steering her away from feelings of anger and revenge she otherwise would have held against his family. What also partially helped her were her separate living arrangements, as she lived in a room on the upper floor of the family house with her husband, his brother, and his brother's wife and children.

Her husband never ceased to show his hatred and disdain for the nature of his job. At every chance he had, he would express his wish to leave his line of work. His father's control over the business, however, forced him to work and inhibited him from sharing his dislike of his job with his father. Ibtissam was always supportive of him, most likely because of his undying support for her. She would beg her father-in-law to agree to her husband's wishes and to stop pressuring him to keep his job. This is where Ibtissam's new life as a married woman begins, a repetition, or rather, reproduction, of the lives of the women in the Jabayla camp, where she lives: a life whose sequences are disturbed only by family disagreements, whose roots can be shaken only by the births and deaths of loved ones.

As for Ibtissam, her fate was to suffer an agonising loss that changed her life and transformed her routine for a while. One day, it occurred to her to tread in isolation and break free from her role as a wife, if only in her private thoughts. She was drawn closer to the true nature of the woman living within the depth of her soul. Surely, this need to be alone overtook her one day and blurred the memory of her loving and warm husband. Yet, this means of solace turned out to be of tragic consequence, for in the end, the hero of her thoughts was none other than her beloved husband. How else would she have been able to explain the dispiritedness and grim sorrow that overcame her during the few days preceding her martyred husband's death?

Ibtissam recalls that her husband had constantly been talking about his wish to die a martyr, both jokingly and in serious conversations she had with him. His constant talk of martyrdom and sacrifice for the nation and freedom fuelled similar feelings inside of her and kindled her fire. She hid her deep feelings of anxiety as much as possible. She was unable to understand the reasons for her emotions at the time. Moreover, she was terrified to closely follow the news of the Intifada, out of fear that a tragedy might strike her personally. Her fears materialised with the loss of her husband. Her vivid memory of these thoughts was no less clear than her recall of all the intricate details of the circumstances surrounding her husband's martyrdom, despite the fact that she feels very sick every time she remembers the event.

She clearly remembers how distinguished and fashionable he looked that day, carrying all his identification papers with him. The look in his eyes was markedly different that day. Thought she could not say exactly why, she felt something fatal was going to happen that day ... and it did. Her husband never came home again ... he was killed. 'Martyred'.

Despite her utter devastation, Ibtissam refuses to blame her husband for what he did, nor does she hold any grudges against him, despite what he has brought on her. She fully realises that he was not forced into this act, that he did not have to die, that he walked to death with his own feet, fully conscious and willing. What is more important, not for one moment has Ibtissam felt that her husband has victimised her, despite her deep conviction that 'martyrdom' is a senseless act. 'Martyrdom is a futile and pointless way of ending one's life', she insists.

Ibtissam was never ready for her widowhood, nor was she able to envision the kinds of troubles that she was to face after her husband's death. In less than three months – with the congratulatory wedding graffiti found in refugee camps still visible on the walls – Ibtissam had turned from a joyously married woman into a widow, the wife of a martyr. Now, instead of receiving congratulations for their marriage, she had to accommodate visitors coming to mourn the martyr and to offer their condolences.

Shortly after the official mourning period was over, Ibtissam decided to keep her grief inside her and begin to take constructive, positive action towards her future, especially now that she knew she was pregnant. She decided to live for her child, the child of the only man she knew and loved for three months.

Unfortunately, life for a woman like Ibtissam is not simple or easy – how little she knows about this new life of hers! Soon after the death of her husband, she discovered that her child was not hers, and that her marriage home – her only room – was not hers either. She was told by her in-laws that 'this child, after the death of its father will not be yours ... nor is this room yours after the loss of 'its' man!' Totally startled by this revelation, Ibtissam could not believe her situation: Was it possible that after all those years of waiting and yearning for a family life, she had lived with her husband for only a few days? Was it possible that the 'house' she had always dreamt of building would only last for such a short period of time? Was it possible that even her own child, whom she had not even seen, would be also taken away from her?

'I asked, What is the solution? What can I do? They answered: you must marry one of your husband's brothers or you lose everything!' Ibtissam felt like exploding, staring at the family members who were nodding in approval of the demand of the 'Father'. She burst into tears. She felt like screaming aloud: Do you know what you are talking about? Do you know that you are treating your children like objects; substituting one son for his missing brother and giving him everything the latter had, including his wife? How awful! How inhuman!

No one in her in-laws' family cared about her objections or heeded her appeal. She begged the family not to force her to marry her husband's brother and to let her keep her baby; she begged to stay in her 'home' and take care of the baby when it was born. But their firm answer came loud and clear: 'These are our norms and traditions and they must be followed. Anyone who disobeyed these norms would not be part of our society, would be ostracised, and would lose everything'.

Afraid of losing everything, Ibtissam was forced into silence. She hid her emotions and thoughts from everybody around her. She kept her worries, fears, and anguish to herself. Even her own mother was against her; she too supported the idea that her daughter marry her brother-in-law, according to the wishes and dictates of her in-laws! Ibtissam's pleas for understanding and support were all quashed!

Her love for her child, and her insistence on keeping it beside her, pushed Ibtissam to live in denial of her emotions and her feelings of objectification. 'I felt I had to choose between my baby and my humanity ... I chose the former'. After this, anything began to appear as possible for Ibtissam. 'This is what everybody thinks, and this is what I should think as well, especially if I want to stay with the baby'. In an effort to stay sane,

Ibtissam gave in and accepted the dictates of people around her. By doing this, she felt she made a choice to stay in her in-laws' home, instead of packing and returning to her maternal home, the practice in Palestinian culture. This choice was also calculated against the difficult economic conditions of her maternal home, where her mother and several siblings live in difficult economic straits, especially after the death of her father.

Three months after the interview I revisited Ibtissam and found that as much as she was looking forward to the birth of her baby, she was terrified of what the future will bring, namely, having to marry 'the shadow of her husband', as she says. At that moment all Ibtissam possessed was no more than the waiting game – with a heart and mind that have lost their enthusiasm for life.

Nadera Shalhoub-Kevorkian

Growing from Within:
The Decolonisation of the Mind

—ᴍᴍ—

Being Palestinian means to me being intimately connected to intense personal and emotional upheavals regarding place, location, identity, and desire. It means living – mostly in silence – the personal/political struggle of an oppressed people, working diligently to mend the broken voice inside and between us that carries within its cracks the agony and sufferings of my people. It reflects a discourse of imposed and unheard anguish expressed in the unheard voice of Palestinian refugees scattered throughout the globe. The voice of Palestinians is growing louder, however, and makes claim to our location, place, rights, and desires. We may be unable to control the new image colonisation has constructed for us in the world and in our own country (Israel) to suit its purpose of objectification. The process of decolonisation means that Palestinians must confront a hegemonic system of oppression with political vision and critical thinking on the road to liberation. Perhaps we were deprived of our place and location, but our past and present sense of self and place is part of our current voice and the motive behind our will to decolonise the self. This essay aims to uncover some of my inner thoughts, locations, and voices, a few of which are surfacing to consciousness for the first time.

The essay takes the reader on a journey of a Palestinian woman. For me, discussing self, people, space and location within a framework of human justice is a painful process. This essay is meant to uncover the struggle of deconstructing the hegemonic system of the oppressor while renaming the experiences and pains in our lives and language. I also hope to reconstruct our history, legacy, identity and lives through the personal stories of my family's and my own experiences.

My point of departure for this essay is based on others' denial of our existence, and my life struggle to prove not only that I exist, but that I have a voice. The first part of the essay will focus on voices of resistance, followed by a focus on how the constructed identity of resistance has affected my work of fighting gender oppression. The third part will discuss the method used by the colonisers to rename pains and nullify their abuses. In the forth part I show how, despite such renaming strategies, I keep searching for hope, and how such hope is believed to be the only empowerment strategy. The last part emphasises my refusal to remain hostage to oppression and objectification, despite the continued massacres and the killing of my people (most recently in October 2000, inside and by the Jewish state), to conclude with an affirmation of my drive to stop racism, ethnicism, and gender blindness and carry out my liberating mission to stop oppression and decolonise the mind.

Voices of Resistance

The denial of our pain and voice was the motivational power behind my resistance. I have confronted the silence because, at times, there are no words capable of reflecting reality. Talking back and voicing the unspeakable were part of my identity and struggle, even though it was difficult to hear the muted voices of my people. One example is Marwan. Marwan's broken voice was too strong to be heard; he was more than a voice. His voice not only reflected the struggle between the will to preserve memories and the onslaught to erase them, as well as the concomitant struggle to preserve one's identity, entity, place, location, and survival. Language is one arena of struggle, and we need to know the language of the oppressor in order to resist. The language Marwan used as an oppressed person will reverberate throughout this essay, and I hope that the reader will not only read it, but also hear it.

Marwan was a twelve-year-old boy who lived in one of the refugee camps in Nablus, where I was working on a project. I met him during one of my field visits to traumatised families at the beginning of November 2000 (one month after the onset of the Second Intifada). When Marwan noticed our car, he ran towards me and the foreign psychologist I was with, spurting words loudly and rapidly; he wanted to explain to us that his house had been demolished by the Israeli troops three days earlier. He asked me to go with him to see the demolished house. My psychologist friend looked at me and asked: 'Nadera, how do you explain the way the boy is behaving? His house was just demolished and he is so eager to show us around, trying to proudly explain that the house is gone. You know, to me he seems a happy child; he doesn't look like a traumatised kid'. My visiting colleague's comment made me wonder: how does a traumatised child look? Is he relying on his 'professional cookbook'?

I followed Marwan to the demolished house. He showed me his geography notebook, a leg of their dinner table, and some kitchen utensils. He dug with vigour and energy, trying to tell me more about what remained of his house. I looked at him with tears in my eyes; I did not know what to say. I needed to react to the power of pain, the power Marwan displayed despite his loss, and the manner in which he expressed it. I asked the only question that came to mind at that moment of pain: 'Marwan, what do you want to be when you grow up?' He stood up, shook the soil from his hands, and said with much pride: 'My math teacher told me that I will be a clever person in the future, so I decided I want to be an engineer ... the one who will rebuild all the houses and places that were destroyed'. I then replied, 'You know, Marwan, I think that I could help you in becoming an engineer if you do well in school'. He answered promptly, 'So many people come here, look at the house, and then leave. If you really want to help me, write it down and give me your name and telephone number. Only then will I be able to tell my mom that I found someone who will help me'. He found a pen and a piece of paper and started writing his name and age. I then wrote: 'I, Nadera Shalhoub-Kevorkian, pledge to do all I can to help Marwan to become an engineer if he works hard in school and gets good grades'. Marwan was delighted to have both our signatures on the same piece of paper. I took the number of the closest telephone to keep in touch. He talked to me twice after my visit to tell me about his school; he told me that they were staying with relatives and that he missed the house. On one occasion he said, 'I wish we still had the house because all my things are there – even my favourite pillow'.

I was proud of my 'engineer' and talked about him to everyone I met. The workers at the Family Defence Society (FDS) where I worked as a consultant felt that I exaggerated in relaying Marwan's voice and story to everybody. However, I felt that despite the pain, I had one more opportunity to empower myself. Many people lost their lives in the Second Intifada, and we were overwhelmed by pain and mourning, but Marwan had brought some hope and life to my broken heart. Two weeks later, I received a call from one of my colleagues in Nablus. I was expecting to hear that the new hotline we initiated for distressed families was operable. Instead, I learnt that Marwan had become a *Shahid* (martyr) the night before.

This is our – my – broken voice, but no longer Marwan's voice. How can I transform and voice the struggle of the oppressed when this voice (hope) was murdered? What words can articulate this pain? I am not sure. I do know, however, that I have heard Marwan's voice. Is this sufficient for us as Palestinians and members of the human race? For me, coming to voice started in Haifa, when I first learnt that muted voices are preferred; otherwise, one runs the risk of not surviving.

To remain a Palestinian in the state of Israel, to survive the oppression of the Jewish state, meant that we needed to preserve our history by embedding it in our songs, dances, and rituals. It meant hiding it in the manner in which we dress and walk, for this, our tortured history, is unspeakable and prohibited. Making sense of the non-sense of oppression and occupation was the only way for us to survive. When I look at my mother, I see the pride, beauty, and assertiveness of Palestinian women's survival. She kept contact with the earth, not only as a witness, but also as the custodian of our memory. My mother was the one who spoke the unspeakable while my father tried all he could to hide the horror, perhaps out of shame, perhaps out of fear of losing more – losing us – or perhaps out of the power of the powerless. What made it terrible was that my father spoke about the struggle to survive only on rare occasions. He would always say that everyone was trapped, that the Arab world turned a blind eye to Palestinian suffering and dissemination. He often repeated the poet Wadi'a Al Bustani's reply, who said to his daughter, who left Palestine to study and was unable to return, but who asked her father to water the jasmine plant. The poet wrote, 'Your father waters its soil with tears and blood, not with water. He chanted Arab nationalism throughout his life but lived to mourn it the day after'.

My mother held on to the memories of her own experience, stories, proverbs, and love, lest others erase them. She refused to glorify the madness we, as children, lived in, but she also refused to succumb to amnesia. Her own personal story attests to courageous acts by a young female child. Her immense power in remaining close to her inner world and memories may have been born out of her limited contact with the outside world. My life was energised by her memories, and by the wisdom and courage she and my father imparted to me. The manner in which my parents spoke to us was unique: their language was not only decoratively expressive of feelings – fears, love, happiness, and anxiety – but also reflected a political formula for dealing with the madness and pain imposed on the Palestinian minority by the Zionist invasion of their homeland.

For my family, remaining in Palestine was a duty – the duty of a mother to a child who was ravaged and abandoned by her collective (regional and international) community. My family's involvement stemmed from their belief that it was their responsibility not to propagate our *Shatat* (diaspora), as not to do so was considered madness. Moments of madness came very fast, especially when my parents needed to answer my questions. One question plagued me yearly, on the occasion of their 'independence' and our 'Nakba'. I always wanted to carry my flag high and sing my national song. I asked whether the white and blue flag was my flag but I never received an answer, despite the pain and agony in my parents' faces. I wished to hoist my flag like my neighbours, who flew their flag on their houses and cars, but we never did. There must have been a reason. I later learnt that living in madness has its advantages. The iron walls constructed between the 'you' and 'you' helps the 'me' to survive in the 'theirs'. The question remains, however, are there alternatives to living in madness?

Israeli policy forced us to reconstruct the meaning of al-Nakba to connote a joyful meaning of independence. To bury pain and reconstruct it as the bearer of the essence of joy was a deliberate Israeli policy based on a clear ideological vision that targeted the dislocation and scattering of the Palestinian nation. It was a policy that attempted to superimpose a semblance of order on the chaos of emotions, motivations, and outcomes of those in the *Shatat*. It was based on the construction of a new abstraction of 'Palestinian', a label that now was burdened with a connotation of being a terrorist. Hence, we were given the amorphous label of 'Israeli Arabs', or as many Jews called us, 'dirty Arabs'. They employed linguistic manipulations in order to establish a new language – a language in which the meaning of *nakba* was transformed from 'calamity' to 'joyous celebration of independence'. We were faced with the choice of being active, creative, and surviving, or of remaining passive and mad, and suffering. They utilised al-Nakba's stories of pain and *a`rd* (shame) to change interpretations. They put forward the fabrication that there was no such thing as a Palestinian. Although I rejected their naming, I failed as a child to find proper alternatives, because I studied under a system that was structured on, and orchestrated by their fabrications. Our colonisation and occupation went beyond the realm of land and property, extending to our minds, memories, and for some of us, even our feelings.

One day in Haifa, as I was riding in the car with my father, he said: 'Do you see this building? Your grandmother is buried beneath it'. I remember asking, 'How can someone build on the graves of those we love?' He answered: 'They did more than this, building on our loved ones' graves was very minor, Baba.... But as sad as it is, we need to keep on going, for this is the only way to live'.

I was very fortunate to be a child who belonged to a family that strived to live. My mother is a very strong woman who worked endlessly as a seamstress. She was considered the best in Haifa, and planned together with my father to build a strong and large family. My father studied law with her help and support; she believed he would become the best, because he was her first lawyer. My mother believed that my father was her lawyer long before he had earned a law degree; he had helped her to return to her homeland when she escaped to Lebanon. My mother's ordeal was similar to that of so many Palestinians who suffered horror and pain in the face of others' unwillingness to acknowledge it. She was first married to a man in the Palestinian resistance movement in the early 1940s. He escaped with her and my two brothers and sister to Lebanon in 1948 when he learnt that the *Haganah* (Israeli pre-state paramilitary forces) was planning to kill him. Poverty and dispossession turned him into a very violent man, especially towards my mother. His mother, however, helped my mother to leave him and flee to Beirut. My mother recounts the ordeal of a frightened fifteen-year-old trying to find the home of her uncle in Beirut:

> I was scared and did not know what would happen to me. My mother-in-law told me to keep on walking until I reached Beirut; there I was to ask about my uncle, who was a diplomat working for Palestine. I remember walking all night, praying and asking God to help me find my way ... help me run away from the abuse and suffering I had encountered since we moved to Lebanon. I got very tired walking, and by sunrise I was exhausted. I stopped and started looking at the streets of Beirut. I suddenly felt that I couldn't keep on walking and decided to knock on one of the doors. I did, and a man opened the door and looked at me. I said, 'I am Evelyne, and I am looking for my uncle'. It was my uncle who had opened the door, and I stayed with them for a while until my parents got the help of your father who helped me to escape and return to Haifa. I lived the harshest years of my life following my return to Haifa – a mother who had lost her children and family, and who was imprisoned in a house where I was badly treated by my father, who refused to accept that I had become a divorced woman, and punished me continuously. Although I earned my livelihood as a dressmaker, I was made to feel that I was a burden on my father and brothers. This suffering and pain, however, was gone after I met your father. Together we tried to get over our past lives – he as an orphan, and I as a divorcée. We promised each other to work hand in hand to build a home filled with children, and here the six of you are.

A retrospective review of Palestinian history reveals the hardships Palestinians endured when they were forced to leave their land and learn to survive under the most difficult of circumstances. I feel pain each time I am reminded that I was deprived of seeing my brothers and sister who remained in Lebanon. This pain constructed my vision of the geopolitical dimension of my history, and consequently became a vital factor in my definition of self.

The story of my father's life is similar in some respects to the one recounted by my mother. He was also active in the 1947–8 struggle and was evicted by the Zionists to Lebanon. He suffered gunshot wounds twice and spent forty days in a Tyre hospital before he was able to infiltrate the borders. Although he was limping, he managed to return to his family and home.

My family's ordeals were instrumental in constructing the links between my political and personal selfhood, on the one hand, and the meaningful and dynamic belonging I felt on the other. This construction was not based on feelings of anger, hatred, or domination, but on the search for love, care, and preservation of one's history through the power of love and not the love of power. As Mahmoud Darwish stated in one of his poems:

Ye whose eyes and palms are bloodied;
Night will end.
Neither the interrogation room nor the chains will remain.
Nero died, but Rome remained to struggle –
Struggled with her eyes.
And as one wheat grain falls and dies,
It fills the whole valley with wheat stalks.

My long silence and fear of facing my parents regarding what I considered their escape from confronting our horrible history was not a form of passivity. Instead, I described my feelings in poetry that I shared with my loved ones. My silence was a deliberate choice not to speak in order not to offend. Still, it did not last forever, for I feared that my actions would be considered a form of complicity with a system that values the silencing of women. Some people claimed that I should have remained silent regarding matters I have not experienced personally. According to these people, as a post-Nakba Palestinian, I am not qualified to delve into such matters. The 'qualified' ones, however, failed to see that I lived that experience through the pain of my parents and my people, and through perpetual fear and worry for our future.

I felt that the Israeli system under which I was educated was suffocating me. My grandparents insisted that the past had held a better, simpler, and purer way of life than the one we were raised under. Hence, my grandmother served as a reference for the collective memory of my society. She felt obliged to educate me, my sisters, and my brother on the virtues of the solid values and good sense of the past in order to combat the deleterious effects of the occupation. The school curriculum, however, never reflected grandmother's stories or values. As an educated adult, I know the role education plays in constructing thinking citizens. I am also cognizant of Paolo Freire's ideas about education as a practice of freedom. In contrast, education under the Israeli system was a front the oppressor used to further the oppression of the oppressed. It neither promoted critical enquiry nor helped the student to develop tools for personal and social transformation. Thus, the political abuse by the educational system in colonising the mind remained intact. The textbooks we used in schools were basically descriptive, based either on past generations or on the lessons of Jewish history. School texts were devoid of political, economic, or social issues. Consequently, as a child I felt the tension between what was taught in school and what was carried in the hearts and minds of those I loved and trusted. Geography and history were distorted to such a degree that even those who were entrusted to teach us these subjects could not tolerate the hypocrisy of 'objectively' explaining the material imposed by the Israeli Ministry of Education. I recall many times when my teacher, Mr Simaan, found himself unable to respond to the question of why we should study Jewish history when no textbook dealt with our history. His refusal to address our questions stemmed not from sentimental or ideological factors, but rather from confusion. It was Mr Simaan's confused state that prompted me to search for the meaning underlying it, ultimately leading me to the painful recognition of our reality as Palestinians.

I was once told by my aunt (Umm Samir) from Shafa Amr: 'You know, there is a big difference between what they teach you and what is very well known to us. They teach you what they have in mind for you ... what they want you to be and believe in. But what exists differs in more ways than you could ever comprehend. The village's elderly women could tell you the truth because the new generation wants to live ... they forget their past and live in the present'. It was my aunt, Umm Samir, and other relatives, such as my cousin Nabiha, who introduced me to my favourite collection of manadeel (scarves) as a means of our refusal to accept the colonisation of our minds. The manadeel carried much meaning for me and my female friends. Not only did we enjoy adorning our heads with them, we were also able to express in a non-incriminating voice, our belief that they serve as a documentation of our people, our land, our pain. Hence, our songs, dances, poetry, art, and attire expressed what our hearts felt. The manadeel were the thread that connected the joy I saw in my father's eyes when I wore them and the pain I observed in my aunt's eyes when I asked her to make me a new mandeel with new oyya (decorative embroidery circumscribing the mandeel). I felt that making, wearing, and adorning the manadeel were my aunt's sole way of preserving her legacy. Numerous stories reflecting thoughts, meanings, and feelings were associated with the manadeels' oyya – apparent to many, but voiced by few.

The fact that we dealt with our folklore with so much pride and love led to the emergence of a new culture. It reinforced positive feelings of oneness and solidarity, and functioned as silent, colourful, and beautiful national memories carrying embedded meanings and concerns. The power and impact of my aunt, childhood friends, and manadeel exhumed the buried history of my nation and culture. My national consciousness was formulated by the unspoken colours, shapes, and embroidery of the manadeels.

A retrospective view of my childhood reveals I possessed a strength that enabled me to be different from my sisters and brother, although I lived in a world of pain, oppression, and silencing. My drive to be different at home was transmitted to my school environment. I was considered too rebellious and daring, especially by my mother, who feared my behaviour would impede my success. Political oppression and discrimination are omnipresent in my childhood memories; they were the rule rather than the exception. It was not sufficient to struggle against the haunting phantoms of history, domination, oppression, and gender injustice; we also needed to combat the machinery that preserved, activated, and nourished them.

Gender, Oppression and Resistance

The agony of oppression, occupation, discrimination, and pain continues, and the savage struggle over identity and hegemony has not yet been erased. I continue to observe Palestinian compatriots who prefer to live in historical amnesia as a means of coping with and surviving their suffering and pain.

Living in Amnesia

In a recent research project I conducted on female child sexual abuse amongst Palestinians living in Israel, a Palestinian Nazarene female social worker said, 'I was born in 1948, and my father was killed by the Zionists. I was raped viciously in the womb of my mother because they deprived me of a father and caused me so much pain and suffering throughout my life. Coming to the world as a fatherless female made everything harsh and painful. Therefore, I work today to help and protect these children from abuse; I do not want anyone to suffer and go through the fear, abuse, and pain I have experienced. Maybe I was not aware of why or what I was doing, but if I need to use the oppressor's legal system to prevent abuses inflicted on Palestinian females, this is what I will do'.

It seems that our history, legacy, and location have afforded me a vantage point from which to observe the multiple strands that compose the narratives of women. These narratives and their interpretations within the women's life experiences are instrumental in maintaining (consciously or unconsciously) their spirit of resistance and survival, as shown in the above case and in my mother's narrative.

In my work and study I have always attempted to examine the ways women combat silences imposed on them by tradition and politics. I have searched for a potentially feminist agenda grounded in cultural, social, and political premises predicated on our refusal to be oppressed. The gender plight of oppression, however, is stronger than our defiance. Thus feminist issues were associated with a socio-political context that made the orchestrated undermining of the oppressive political reality an almost impossible mission for my oppressors. Living in a post-colonial period strengthened my opposition to domination.

I was introduced to a new form of suffering when Bethlehem University employed me in 1985 as a lecturer in social work. My students had lived under Israeli military occupation since birth. Each student brought personal stories and experiences to recount. One female student, living in the nearby Dhaisheh refugee camp, was apprehensive about bearing her first child in the absence of her husband, who was imprisoned by the Israelis for political reasons.

The ordeals experienced by wives of political prisoners were accentuated at a later juncture in my experience, when another student shared her pain and suffering with me. This sharing of experiences led us to form group discussions in the hope of helping young women face their suffering, anger, pain, and fear. I learnt from my work with these young women that vulnerable groups, mainly women and children, suffer the most. I learnt that although their husbands and loved ones were imprisoned, they too were prisoners of their patriarchal culture and masculine tradition. The young women shared with me their apprehension about dressing elegantly, using cosmetics, leaving the house, or visiting friends, fearful that others would circulate rumours and gossip about them. I learnt that irrespective of all the oppression and pain these women were experiencing, they were compelled to face the various stereotypical beliefs regarding women's purity and sexuality. The social imprisonment to which these women were subjected is articulated succinctly in the following statement: 'My husband is imprisoned in an Israeli prison. He knows who his enemy is and is there fighting for a clear cause. I am imprisoned in my own house amongst my family. I do not know who my enemy is or what my cause is'.

My experience with student wives of imprisoned men propelled me to work on issues related to gender oppression. I helped female students who were forbidden by their families from continuing their education due to the political conditions prevailing at that time. My newly found direction found expression in my doctoral research in which I focused on the reaction by victims and society to abuses inflicted upon women, especially within the domestic sphere.

I discovered, however, that I could not be effective in my quest of helping abused women if my efforts remained solitary. Hence, in 1993, as a member of the board of trustees of the Women's Centre for Legal Aid and Counselling, I proposed to establish a hotline service to aid females in distress. The idea came to fruition when the al-Aman hotline was established in a small kitchenette in the old city of Jerusalem, and I was able to dialogue with my coworkers, friends, and students about gender oppressive practices. The purpose of the dialogues was to create a cultural climate where we could challenge biases, cross borders, and question the unquestionable. Crossing the border of the powerful in order to enter the domain of the powerless was not easy, even for those who considered themselves feminist scholars and were eager to cross borders and challenge existing structures. My personal history and individual life experience made it difficult for me to accept existing systems of domination, even from sisters in the struggle who believed that knowledge and acknowledgement of social reality is liberating.

I believe my daring attitude enabled me to gather the silenced and scattered parts of myself and my history, and to construct my personal formula. Oppression, humiliation, and agony were the elements that I read and observed in this formula. I discovered, as bell hooks did before me, that theory, as a liberating practice, stems from pain (hooks, 1994: 59). Hooks explains that she came to theory 'desperate, wanting to comprehend, to grasp what was happening around and within me. I wanted to make the hurt go away. I saw in theory then a location for healing'. Similarly, I formulated my theory on gathering the collective but unspoken history. This was linked to the process of self-recovery, of liberating myself from the various boundaries surrounding me. Resisting the coloniser's construction of rules, laws, and boundaries made me resist the segregation of females from males, even when my teachers insisted on it. It made me refuse the institutionalisation of women's roles in the private sphere, and led me spontaneously to challenge and deconstruct women's socially accepted roles. Later in my life it pushed me to question and delegitimise the existing relationship between women and the law. It made me resist the hegemonic masculine culture and sexism, and engage in oppositional political dialogue and critical theories. Thus, questioning the politics of domination and of marginalisation became the focus of my clinical practice and research endeavour.

Renaming Pain

I discovered that not only was my history distorted, but also that some mysterious hand had altered my map and the names of my streets. Our street in Haifa, which was called al-Mukhallis for generations, became Y. L. Perez Street (after a famous Jewish writer in Yiddish). This illusionary distortion of names also haunted me when I moved to Jerusalem. My home is situated on a street known as Suq al-Husur because it was the place where people bought their straw rugs (*husur*). Renaming it Habad Street (Habad being the initials of the Jewish religious Hasidic movement) after Israel occupied and annexed Jerusalem excised the tethers binding us to our identity and history, just as the transformation of my grandmother's grave into a building had done. Places and events lose their identity and permanence when their names are altered.

The tale of my mother and my father's limp was retired to a closet of forgotten memories. Denial was the best tool the oppressor employed to conceal ethnic marginalisation and oppression. I lived in a reality that had changed the map of our roads, places, and homes, a reality where the mere mention of my name spelt 'an enemy' for the other side. I was engaged in resistance without having a political language to articulate it. I was born in Haifa, where my Jewish neighbours called me a 'dirty Arab' countless times. I studied in the Italian Carmelite School where they taught us to sing in Italian songs that were approved by the colonisers, but we were not allowed to sing our own songs. I remember being taught to sing the following song on Independence Day: 'The birds were singing on the day of my country's independence'. I did not comprehend why this was considered either a celebration or independence. Am I independent? Whose country is it, after all? If it is my country, why am I treated like this? I was born in a state that continually reminded me that 'they' permitted us to study and reach university level, 'they' offered us medical, educational, economic and social services. We were made to feel like the benefactors of 'their' benevolent generosity!

Although I was born in an atmosphere of resistance, I also lived a life of oppression. The identity of my birth, however, was one of resistance and struggle. Thus, the process of decolonising the land, mind, body, even my feelings, became part of my identity in resistance. Even today, the struggle for liberation flows in my blood and occupies my mind. I attempted continuously to engage myself with meaningful praxis.

I constructed a new mode of intervention for women threatened with death on the basis of what is termed 'family honour', believing that one does not need to stifle a woman's breath in order to kill her. I believed that an individual could be imprisoned without the confines of iron bars and concrete walls. Imprisonment of the mind and spirit is far more ominous than imprisonment of the body, as Woodson states in his book *The Mis-education of the Negro*: 'When you control a man's thinking, you do not have to worry about his actions. You do not have to tell him not to stand here or go yonder. He will find his 'proper place' and stay in it. You do not need to send him to the back door, he will cut one for his special benefit' (Woodson, 1990).

The first step I took when dealing with femicide cases was to redefine the construct of femicide to incorporate the victim's voice. I challenged the existing definitions of homicide and femicide to claim that females who live within a zone of perpetual death threats become victims of femicide. As one victim told me, 'Do you know what it means to be a living death?... This is how I feel'. The issue of femicide also means the forced marriage of sexually abused females to their rapists in order to preserve the family honour. Only through the process of crossing borders are we able to construct a new discourse and begin to decolonise the past. My construction of a new model (Shalhoub-Kevorkian, 2000) to deal with female sexual abuse was predicated on the belief that advancing a dialogue of liberation with the victims is contingent on decolonising their minds. I also kept up a continuous and painful dialogue with myself, as well as with my family, teachers and loved ones, and even with the oppressor. In my professional work I advocated dialoguing with various systems of oppression. Advancing a dialogue between the traditional hegemonic patriarchal system and the collective familial caring system in cases of female victims of abuse encouraged family members to help and support the women. This dialogue showed family members that killing females on the basis of 'family honour' is not an acceptable alternative to dealing with (sexual) abuse inflicted upon women. Such crimes of femicide strip us of both family and honour.

The knowledge and ability to institute change that I had gained from my clinical practice and field work encouraged me to offer another model (Shalhoub-Kevorkian, 2001) meant to resist domination and engage women in a dialogue aimed at breaking the mental chains imposed by an oppressive socio-political context.

I learnt, however, that engaging in a politically progressive movement entailed not only being part of an existing political movement, but also building a personal praxis. As Antonio Faudez states in *Learning to Question* (cited in hooks, 1994: 48):

> One of the things we learnt in Chile in our early reflection on everyday life was that abstract political, religious or moral statements did not take concrete shape in acts by individuals. We were revolutionary in the abstract, not in our daily lives. It seems to me essential that in our individual lives, we should day to day live out what we affirm.

In Search of Hope

As a child living in Haifa, I was cognizant of the discriminatory atmosphere surrounding me; my continuous self-dialogue helped me to find a friendly way of interacting with the 'other'. This chosen policy remained intact, even as we suffered derogatory name calling, had rocks thrown at us, and desecration of our religious sites. My mother constantly feared that we would be harmed simply because we were Arabs. I, however, interpreted the insults and ridicule levelled at us as fear that I could detect in the eyes of the abusers. We survived living in that neighbourhood because of our oppositional mode of thinking and determination to live. I became convinced that Palestinians in general, and my family in particular, survived atrocities, massacres, and the Nakba because of our oppositional mode of perception. I managed to read reality with all its concomitant pain, but I continued to invest in myself. I chose to become friendly with some Jewish children in the neighbourhood in order to assure them that they need not fear me, and also in the other to hope that the gesture would open new avenues with our 'enemy', despite their behaviour towards us. My faith in my fellow human beings remained intact during my childhood, as did my hope that the situation would change at some future time. My childhood convictions were the primary impetus for the close friendships I developed with our Jewish neighbour's son, Doron, and many other Jews, such as my professors at the University of Haifa and the Hebrew University, who seemed to accept me and showed a willingness to acknowledge our history as Palestinians. Reality, however, always managed to deal me hard blows, as is demonstrated in the following incident.

I was a very active university professor at Bethlehem University during the first Intifada (1987–93). The Israeli occupation authorities imposed closure of all educational institutions in the West Bank and Gaza Strip. Refusing to allow them to deprive my students of their education, I set up makeshift classroom in my small apartment in the old city of Jerusalem for my social work students, whom I promised to help to graduate on time despite the hardships we were facing. One winter day in 1990 I was rushing home in order to prepare the apartment for my students, I was stopped by an Israeli soldier near Jaffa Gate. Although I was pregnant with my youngest daughter, Salpy, he shouted, 'Come here whore!' I choked with anger at this humiliation, but decided to ignore the insulting remark. He approached me menacingly, brandishing a baton in his hand. I stopped and looked around for someone who could protect me from the wrath of his baton, but then looked him in the face, shouting not to hurt me. My attempt to be heard was futile. He continued to spew a stream of uninterrupted expletives. He appeared to be bereft of all intelligible civil terms to convey his order prohibiting me from entering the Old City. Gazing into his face, I nearly suffocated at the realisation that the face bombarding me with humiliating and insulting remarks, and the hand brandishing the menacing club, belonged to none other than my childhood friend Doron. That was the moment I came to traumatic discovery: The theory on which I had based my care, love, and hope was faulty. Doron, part of a structure that constructs not only its members' minds but also their hearts, could not perceive me as anything other than his enemy.

Despite this hurtful event, I came to realise that I was a much freer person and thinker than Doron. Like many Israeli Jews, he developed an oppressor's self and identity. His desire to be part of the fabrications, the injustice, and the abuse of power served to delete his humanity, replacing it with superficial weakness dressed up in the powerful uniform of the Israeli state army. My critique of oppression was crucial to preserving my dignity in the wake of rapidly developing Israeli objectification policies. I felt that Doron was imprisoned by his own oppression. I was angry, not only with Doron, but also with myself for believing that I was not an enemy, at least for all my other Dorons. This anger stemmed from my belief that the machinery of oppression oppresses its own practitioners. Such oppression threatens Palestinians who believe in hope, dialogue, peace, and restoration of justice. But I also believe it could threaten the Jewish state by serving as a counterproductive force in the Jewish community. Doron's longing for power, wealth, and control over the other rendered him a symbol of dangerous and vicious Jews such as Baruch Goldstein (the Israeli settler who committed the Hebron massacre).

The Doron incident had a profound effect on how I planned my life: I began to need to construct barricades around me to preempt any humiliation that threatened to obstruct my path of resistance and struggle. I decided that not only would I teach my students despite the restrictions, but I would also keep in touch with the field to support those who suffered humiliations and abuse. The encounter with Doron remains etched in my memory and mental map, alarmingly reminding me that the Dorons surrounding us aim to objectify us.

I was struck by this objectification when one of my students from Dura, a village near Hebron, requested my help to support a forty-three year-old father of eleven children who became isolated, fearful, and depressed. The man, Khalil, was barred from entering Israel – such is the fate of countless Palestinians every time violence erupts in the area (even if it is perpetrated by the Israelis). Khalil, who was mired deep in desperation as a result of being unemployed, risked taking a communal taxi to find work in Israel in the hope that the sentry at the checkpoint would turn a blind eye. At the crossing point, Khalil, his son, and his fellow work-seeking companions pleaded with the soldier to allow them entry into Israel in order to pursue their employment. The soldier, however, made fulfiling of the request conditional on Khalil's willingness to bark like a dog in view of other soldiers and his travel companions (including his own son). In desperation, Khalil barked, which only spurred the soldier to order him to bark longer and louder. Although Khalil was permitted to enter after fifteen minutes of barking and howling, the humiliating experience caused him severe psychological maladjustment.

Khalil's ordeal is but one example of the many incidents that demonstrate how oppression and colonisation manage to paralyse the power inside us. Their image of us (dirty Arabs, whores, dogs) increases their need to further objectify and humiliate us, and to reinforce their feelings of supremacy over other beings. These constructed images function to internalise racism and ethnicism within their ranks. As an individual who is committed to the Palestinian struggle for liberation, freedom, and self-determination, I must confront the daily reality of these objectifying images. Our lives as Palestinians living in Israel are very complex and worthy of sophisticated critical thinking. Even though I think we have decolonised our minds, I have difficulty in validating this perception with our experiences. No dictionary could describe the horrors Palestinians underwent and continue to experience. Samia Mehrez elaborates the necessity of bilateral enlightenment:

> Decolonisation continues to be an act of confrontation with a hegemonic system of thought; it is hence a process of considerable historical and cultural liberation. As such, decolonisation becomes the contestation of all-dominant forms and structures, whether they are linguistic, discursive, or ideological.

Moreover, decolonisation comes to be understood as an act of exorcism for both the colonised and the coloniser. For both parties it must be a process of liberation: from dependency, in the case of the colonised, and from imperialist, racist perceptions, representations, and institutions which, unfortunately, remain with us to this very day, in the case of the coloniser.... Decolonisation can only be completed when it is understood as a complex process that involves both the coloniser and the colonised. (hooks, 1992: 1)

Over time I have experienced the Israelis continuing to build a mechanism designed to maintain their 'supremacy', oppression, and power, on the one hand, and institutionalise our images as Palestinians through various methods of objectification, on the other. Objectifying the Palestinians reinforces and maintains oppression, exploitation, and domination. I was painfully reminded of this recently when during the Second Intifada I saw soldiers stopping a middle-aged Palestinian man as he trekked home toting bags in both hands in preparation for breaking the fast during Ramadan. The soldiers ordered him to approach, deliberately pulled down his pants, and brought his naked buttocks to view for all to see. The shocking scene and my rage and humiliation prompted me to stop my car and confront the soldiers. I tried to appeal to the young soldiers' sense of logic and conscience, but to no avail. Such objectification has deeply affected me, my beliefs, and my power to keep faith in the goodness of human beings.

Dialogue with the Muted

I recently started work on a project in the Galilee (Dialoguing with the Muted), aiming to study girls' perceptions on how society can assist them, mainly through systems of social control, in coping with sexual abuse. Given that women's purity and sexuality are sensitive issues in Middle Eastern society, I felt a need to examine the subject in depth, to listen precisely to the voices of those who fear to disclose their abuse because of the dire social repercussions it might generate. School was chosen as the setting for opening such a dialogue with the girls, in an attempt to reach them before it was too late, and learn how we could help victims of abuse and build social policy to address their needs. Many girls approached me during our encounters, expressing their willingness to share painful experiences, but I was precluded by law from providing assistance to the girls without the official consent of the criminal justice system.

This experience reaffirmed my belief that to Palestinian girls in Israel the Israeli legal system is not only alien (as the coloniser's legal system); it is also a contextually insensitive system that fails to provide help for victims of abuse. No officials, not even the Palestinian helpers, were willing to listen to the voice or needs of the girl victim. Rather, they all were serving their own needs; they were all serving a system that is based on a culture of power. This culture of power is ill-suited to deal with abuse inflicted upon powerless groups within an ethnic minority. The legal system serves the formal official colonising system; the helpers serve both the system and their own interest in perpetuating the system. The girl victim is denied a voice, and an opportunity to be heard. The politics of sexism, gender blindness, and ethnicism further empower the powerful, but fail to address the needs of the vulnerable and powerless.

How can you progress within a system that not only dominates you, your history, and lifestyle, but also your voice and will? How can I struggle against the domination over girls? How can I increase their knowledge on how to cope with abuse if I am blocked by the same system of domination? Bell hooks, quotes Freire on the nature of help:

> Authentic help means that all who are involved help each other mutually, growing together in the common effort to understand the reality which they seek to transform. Only through such praxis – in which those who help and those who are being helped help each other simultaneously – can the act of helping become free from the distortion in which the helpers dominate the helped. (hooks, 1994: 54)

I continue to look for methods to combat such silencing and intervention/ movement paralyses.

The Refusal to Remain Hostage

Although I was aware of the Israeli state's existing potential to commit atrocities against Palestinians, as evidenced by massacres, such as Deir Yassin in 1948, Kufur Qasim in 1956, and Hebron in 1994, I did not anticipate it would turn its weapons collectively upon its own Palestinian citizens. The events that took place inside Israel in October 2000 shattered this certainty. In one of the incidents Jewish settlers, armed to the teeth, descended on the eastern neighbourhoods of Nazareth to terrorise their Palestinian inhabitants. My youngest sister, Yasmin, who lives in Nazareth, called me, very fearful. She explained, 'The Israeli police and a group of Jewish settlers attacked the eastern part of Nazareth, I could hear the shooting. The local Palestinian radio stated that people are killed and injured, and the police are not allowing the ambulances to reach the area. The whole family is in such a shock … although it is good that we are all together [she lives in one building with four brothers in-laws and their families], we are scared that they are heading towards us. It seems that they are attacking poor and packed neighbourhoods; I really hope we are not next'. While Yasmin was talking to me, her husband painfully explained that ambulances were not allowed to reach the area. 'People are being killed like animals', he stated.

The local radio, at that time the only trustworthy source of information for Palestinians living in Nazareth, was calling for help, and asking inhabitants of the attacked area to call the radio station with information. It appeared that the Jewish settlers desired to silence the demonstrations of solidarity the inhabitants of Nazareth were showing towards their brethren during the Second Intifada. When the Nazarenes tried to defend themselves from the mob attacking them, the Israeli police intervened on the settlers' behalf. Thirteen Palestinians (from Nazareth, Umm El Fahim and other locations) lost their lives, and scores suffered serious injury. None of the settlers sustained serious injury. While Israeli gunfire had previously killed numerous Palestinians who were Israeli citizens (e.g. on Land Day protests in 1976), Israel can take pride in never having killed a protesting Jewish citizen, even when the protest was of a violent nature.

Fear of the coming massacre, threatened lives, and people who were injured or shot to death were again our reality, but this is the year 2000. Until that day I thought, or at least my hopes and love made me think, that I could rest assured that no more massacres would happen to my people, at least not inside the borders of the Jewish state. No more Deir Yasin, Kufur Qasim, Tantura, Safsaf, or any of the other massacres that took place during the 1948 Nakba. No more Sabra and Shatila, no more Goldsteins. Unfortunately, I was mistaken.

Conclusion

As a child, I often felt I had no words, no language, and no voice. My memories were shattered and replaced with ones forged by the coloniser, memories which I disliked. My wish for change endured through the passing years, with their massacres and the Intifadas of my people, but the change I hoped for never materialised. Instead, the other side improved its sophistication and fabrications to the point where they became 'believable' for many of us. The stagnation I experienced became heavy and oppressive – even threatening and negating. I refuse to be a hostage to the artificial world that was woven around me, and which started to collapse when I first learnt about my mother's ordeal.

I realise today that nothing exists which is not planted in our minds, knowledge, and writings. When I started voicing my opposition to the prevailing violence. I grew in maturity and independence. Only then did I affirm my need to be heard and to be an active member of my society.

I learnt that we might fail to control our image in the world and in our own country, because colonisation has constructed new images that serve its own purpose of objectification. But decolonisation means facing the hegemonic system of oppression, it needs political vision and critical thinking. Despite all the agonies and atrocities, I hope that we are in the process of liberation.

My life reflects my moral position, and my living reflects my politics and my vision. The politics of daily life was and continues to be extremely difficult for Palestinians. Since childhood I have maintained the need to liberate myself from oppression through education and social and political involvement. My story and history affirm the difficulties I will face, but they will not dissuade me. As my late father kept repeating, 'Rocks stop only the weak, but they are a source of support to the powerful in order to reach the peak'.

References

'Growing from Within'

Freire, Paolo. 1972. *The Pedagogy of the Oppressed*. Harmondsworth: Penguin.
hooks, bell. 1992. *black looks: race and representation*. Boston: South End.
———. 1994. *teaching to transgress: education as the practice of freedom*. New York: Routledge.
Shalhoub-Kevorkian, Nadera. 2000. 'Blocking her exclusion: A contextually sensitive model of intervention for handling female abuse'. *Social Service Review* 74 (4): 620–34.
———. 2001. 'Using the dialogue tent to break mental chains: Listening and being heard'. *Social Service Review* 75 (1): 135–50.
Woodson, C. 1990. *The Mis-education of the Negro*. Trenton: African World Press.

PART II

ISRAELI JEWISH WOMEN

FOUR

Exile as Home

Alice Shalvi

Transformed by Joy

—〰—

As I write this, I am preparing myself, mentally and emotionally, for a return to my birthplace, where I have not been for sixty-five years. I already know that none of the three houses in which we lived during the first six years of my life is still standing. As the city where the Krupp munitions factory was located, Essen's wartime role ensured its massive devastation by Allied bombing. And although I have vivid memories of childhood expeditions to the Stadtwald, the municipally owned forest-park on the city's outskirts, and of shopping with my mother in the Marktplatz, where we bought live chickens to be taken to the ritual slaughterer, of seeing some performing 'little people' on a balcony above a theatre in the Kopstadtplatz, and of the cinema façade across the road from our last place of residence, where I spent hours gazing at stills of the films that were being screened there, Essen is not a place for which I have nostalgic longings.

Quite the contrary. Some even more vivid memories arouse anger and a reluctance to return: shots ringing out in the night, bloodstains in the snow when, the following morning, I joined my father at the window overlooking the backyard and heard him tell my mother, 'They got the Communists'. Coming home one day soon after I started school to find all my toys and books scattered on the kitchen floor as a result of a Nazi search – a search which led to my father's prompt departure to join his younger brother in England. My brother returning from high school bruised and bleeding from a beating by Hitler Youth.

The last eight months of my life in Germany were not even spent in Essen, but in Mannheim, at the home of my oldest aunt, a widow who none too graciously provided accommodation for my mother, my maternal grandmother, my brother and myself as we waited – for longer than antici-pated – for the entry visas that would enable us to join my father in London.

We left Mannheim by train at 1:32 A.M. on Sunday 13 May 1934. My beloved father came to meet us in Ostend, but at first I was uncertain that it indeed was my father: he no longer had the dapper Spitzbart, the little pointed beard he'd had in Germany; his clothes, his hat, were different, no longer – I realised much later – Continental. This was the first visible indication of the major change that all of us were about to undergo. We had to learn a new language, literally and metaphorically. We were out of place; we were refugees.

Lack of language. Could there have been a more painful condition for someone who had been reading avidly since the age of three, who was extremely verbal, extremely sociable, and had been greatly admired for her rich High German vocabulary? Among the few books – all in English – which I found in the bookcase of our new home was one intriguingly entitled *Alice in Wonderland*, with delightful, though somewhat incomprehensible, illustrations that failed to elucidate the unintelligible text. My own name on the spine – and yet I could go no further in understanding what the contents were all about.

And there were other frustrations. Three children played in the next-door garden, one of them a girl clearly about my own age. I hid behind the portière curtains of our first-floor dining room to watch them, believing myself invisible. But they caught sight of me, beckoned me to join them. Opening the window, I enquired, 'Sprechen Sie Deutsch?' and was overjoyed by comprehending nods of assurance. Yet once next door I discovered that in fact none of them understood me, and not all their good will nor that of their hospitable Scottish-born mother could compensate for my disappointment. Only when their father, a Polish-born doctor, returned home was there finally someone with whom I could communicate in more than sign language and gestures.

My first day at school was equally frustrating and profoundly humiliating. When my father introduced me to the headmaster I was told that if I wanted to say anything in class I should put up my hand and say, 'Please, teacher!' Extraordinary as it may seem, nobody bothered to tell me the meaning of the phrase. So when, seated in the front row of the classroom into which I was ushered, I rapidly calculated the answer to the sum which the teacher chalked up on the blackboard, I did as I'd been told – put up my hand and, in response to her inviting gesture, uttered the apparently magical words – 'Please, teacher!' With words and more gestures, she attempted to elicit a further response, but I knew nothing else. Repeating the phrase, I began to hear titters behind me, which rapidly turned to laughter as my uncomprehending classmates, unaccustomed to foreigners, enjoyed the spectacle of my embarrassment, which finally gave way to tears.

Apparently they were later subjected to the kind of explanation of my status which should have preceded or at least accompanied my introduction into the class, for soon I found myself surrounded by children demanding that I say something in German and being introduced to other staff members by Miss Armstrong, my homeroom teacher, as 'our little refugee girl'. It was with considerable pride and no little amusement that, by the end of the school year, I found myself second in class for composition and, in 1936, the winner of a school prize for an essay on – of all subjects – the British Empire!

English became my 'mother' tongue, English literature my passion. It was what I studied when I went to university. And yet I did not *feel* English. It was clear to me that I was an alien and, moreover, that I was perceived as such by the English people around me. Not because I spoke with an accent (I didn't), not because I had a Polish passport or had to report at the Cambridge police station so long as the war continued (none of my acquaintances knew either of these details), but because I was Jewish and made no secret of either my religious affiliation or my political Zionist proclivities.

I first encountered overt anti-Semitism at Aylesbury Grammar School, which – as an evacuee from London during the blitz, once again a 'refugee' – I attended from late 1941 until the end of the 1944 school year. Crude generalisations such as 'Jews are black-marketeers'; hissed insults – 'Dirty Jew!'; aggressive actions – the books on my personal shelf in the classroom tossed onto the floor (reminiscent of what had occurred in Essen in 1933) – all these led me vainly to attempt a hopeless appeal to intellect and reason. I brought a copy of Cecil Roth's *The Jewish Contribution to Civilization* to school and left it on the table in our classroom – where it was promptly vandalised. Undeterred, I brought little booklets published by the Board of Deputies of British Jews, a series apparently designed precisely to counter the phenomenon I was experiencing. Nothing helped. The provincial residents of this bucolic market town, in which no Jews had lived before the London evacuees arrived, had their minds firmly made up. The Jews killed Christ, the Jews were devils incarnate. (I was once even naïvely asked by a neighbour my own age, who every morning travelled to school on the same bus as myself, where Jews kept their horns and whether I could one day show her my cloven hooves!)

Evacuees were, in any case, 'foreigners', transients. Jewish evacuees were doubly alien. Though we spent four or five years at the school (some had arrived at the very outset of the war; others – like myself – only when the Blitz drove us from London), our names were not inscribed on the Honours Board when we won state scholarships or – an unprecedented achievement so far as the school was concerned – scholarships and exhibitions to the Oxbridge universities. Since it was the Jewish pupils who thus distinguished themselves it surely indicated a great deal of animus on the part of the authorities to deny themselves the renown we were bestowing on the institution.

Anti-Semitism at my Cambridge college was more subtle and at first took the form of questions about my 'un-English' name, the pronunciation of which (*Marg*ulies? Marg*ew*lies? Margoolies?) appeared to cause problems. But as the Zionist struggle against British Mandatory rule in Palestine grew fiercer and the 'terrorist' activities of the Irgun Zeva'i Leumi (National Military Organisation) and the so-called 'Stern Gang' (LEHI: Lohamei Herut Israel, Fighters for the Freedom of Israel) took a greater toll of British lives, the fact that I was the official, acknowledged representative of the Cambridge University Jewish Society made me an object of open anathema. My non-Jewish peers may have been too educated and sophisticated to regard me as a Christ-killer, but many of them had no hesitation in considering me an ally of those 'Zionist thugs' (as the British tabloids called them) who were fighting and killing British soldiers, civil servants, and members of the Palestine Police in the Holy Land.

Growing awareness of the fate of European Jews at the hands of the Nazis and their willing collaborators in Eastern Europe further strengthened my Jewish identity ('There but for the grace of God ...'), and not even the far more cosmopolitan, left-wing, and less traditionally upper-middle-class atmosphere of the London School of Economics, where I studied after I left Cambridge, could dispel my sense of being an alien. On the contrary, my first encounter with what were then called Palestinian students – Jews who came to study in Europe after World War II – intensified my perception of my 'otherness'. Here at last were people with whom I could closely identify and even emulate.

Already in 1946, at the end of my second year at Cambridge and following a first meeting with a group of teenage DPs – Displaced Persons, as we then termed what later came to be known as Holocaust survivors – I had decided that I would study social work and go to Palestine to help rehabilitate such wretched people. My resolve was irrevocably strengthened by my first visit to Palestine, during the Christmas holiday in 1947, less than a month after the astounding UN decision to establish a Jewish state there. Overwhelmed by the vitality and optimism of the population, their work ethic, their explosive ebullience, and captivated by the bright sunshine, the clear blue skies, the Mediterranean light, the orange groves, the pristine quality of the landscape – all so different from the predominant greyness of post-war Britain – I was also delighted to become reacquainted with my cousins, who had emigrated from Germany in the 1930s and some of whom – indeed, the ones I most admired – had been actively involved in establishing the kibbutzim where they now lived. I was overwhelmed by a desire to stay there, never to return to England. Finally, I felt really at home. I now understood, as never before, why immigration to the Land of Israel is termed *aliyah*, 'going up', 'ascending'.

It was primarily because the professionals to whom I was introduced advised me to complete my studies before immigrating that I did go back to London, but as soon as I had completed my studies I began my preparations for once again moving to a new country, an old-new culture, a language in which Jews had always prayed but in which they were only now conducting their everyday working lives, devising neologisms for objects and activities unknown in earlier times.

* * *

The Israel in which I arrived in November 1949 was in many ways very different from what had so enthused me two years earlier. Food was scarce and rationed; in Jerusalem, water was pumped up only once a week and used sparingly, recycled from laundry and dishwashing to flush toilets and scrub floors. Many families were bereaved, including that of my oldest aunt, the one with whom we had lived in Mannheim, whose youngest son, though lame in one leg, had insisted on joining the battle to defend his kibbutz in the Galilee and had been killed on the Syrian border. The casualties numbered some 6,000, out of a then total Jewish population of 600,000. Israel's victory in the War of Independence was considered nothing less than a miracle, and though Jerusalem was divided, the Old City and Mount Scopus inaccessible to the Jewish population, nobody minded too much. We were content with our lot. We had, at last, a Jewish state. Within that state, working for my living – not, as I'd hoped, as a social worker but, to my own surprise, as a teacher of English at the newly reopened Hebrew University, now in exile from Mount Scopus – I felt at last completely at home.

* * *

It was not, however, until I returned to England the following summer to prepare for my wedding to a fellow immigrant that I realised how profound a psychological difference my aliyah had made. A mere 5 feet 1 inch in height, I had always (with justification) felt small in comparison with my English peers. Now, suddenly – thought needless to say unchanged in height – I *felt tall*. Furthermore, while throughout the fifteen years during which I lived in England I never unnecessarily referred to my non-Englishness when I was with strangers, I now (as I only gradually came to notice) went to considerable lengths to make it clear that I lived abroad, in Israel. Purchasing the clothing, household goods, furniture, linens, and carpets that constituted my trousseau, I found myself, often without need or provocation, mentioning that these items were to be shipped to a warmer climate. This inevitably led to a query as to their precise destination, providing me with the opportunity to answer, with pride, 'Israel'. It was an acceptance, an assertion, of my otherness. I was indeed 'not English', I was a foreigner, but I now had a distinct identity of my own. I was not a 'naturalised' Englishwoman. I was an Israeli, a Jew.

* * *

Sometimes our own experiences make us more sensitive to others who have endured similar situations; sometimes we are too concerned with, or too self-righteous about, our own sufferings. I confess that I gave little thought to the Arab refugees who had been forced to flee from their homes as a result of Israeli independence. Their condition was explained by the fact that they had attacked the Jewish population and, once the state of Israel had been declared in May 1948, had been joined by the surrounding Arab nations, determined to strangle this new nation at its very birth. If Israel was victorious in the ensuing conflict, despite the superior numbers and arms of the attackers, her foes clearly had no place among us. Though, as a liberal, I was disturbed by the restrictions placed upon those who remained and by their second-class status, the personal and private preoccupations of my life – marriage, family, academic interests – kept public issues in the remote recesses of my mind.

Only after the Six-Day War and, more forcibly, with the outbreak of the Intifada in December 1987, did the 'Palestinian Problem' become of greater concern to me, as I grew increasingly aware of the injustices of occupation and, above all, of the inevitable coarsening of the moral fibre of the occupiers. My own sons' military service, their reports of brutality and crude insensitivity which they could not and would not condone, made it no longer possible to hide my head, ostrich-like, in the sand of either nationalism or privacy.

In 1987 I first encountered a Palestinian woman with a background comparable to my own – married, the mother of grown-up children, an academic educated (of all places!) in Germany. We were introduced to each other by Father Emmanuel, a philo-Semitic priest at the Dormitian church, who left us alone in his study. The dialogue that ensued established for both of us the similarities that bound us. We expressed no hostility, because we felt none.

Following this one-on-one encounter, I began to attend women's dialogue groups, where we listened as much as we spoke. I confess that I always emerged from these encounters with a strong impression that, like trains passing each other in the night, we had caught glimpses of each other, but had failed to fully comprehend each other's experiences, mindset, and intentions.

Most specifically – and understandably, given our relative status vis-à-vis each other – the Palestinians simply could not grasp that we – the victors, the occupiers, the colonialists – were afraid of them. No explication, no amount of reference to terrorist attacks on innocent citizens, could persuade our interlocutors that we, too, had suffered. In Hebrew we have a term for uncomprehending 'dialogue'. We call it 'conversation of the deaf'.

Why is it so difficult to accept that others have experienced, are experiencing suffering like our own? In the spring of 1989 I attended a meeting of Jewish and Arab women – Israelis and diaspora Jews, Palestinians living in the occupied territories and abroad – that took place on neutral ground in Brussels. We took turns in speaking, seeking from a feminist viewpoint to find solutions to the deadlock which no one on either side had been able to resolve. There was considerable anger and far too many mutual recriminations. Holocaust survivors, in particular, sought to draw attention to the annihilation of European Jewry – an undoubted, incontestable justification for a Jewish national home. 'My suffering's greater than yours' – that was the game we were playing.

Finally, this clearly futile exercise was interrupted. Suad Amery – tall, stately, beautiful and eloquent – addressed not us, the Jews, but her fellow Palestinians: 'We *have* to realise what the Jewish people experienced. We *have* to understand the Holocaust, not only because then we will understand why the Jews need a country of their own, but because it will help them realise that we, too, deserve such a country'.

That was the turning point in the discourse. From then on, for the remaining half day of the meeting, we worked together, collaborating on producing a statement that would give expression to the equally just claims of both sides and to the modus vivendi of compromise that needed to be achieved.

And yet ... On the closing evening, at dinner at the home of the (Jewish) couple who had been the prime sponsors of the dialogue, I found myself next to a distinguished Palestinian spokeswoman. As at my first encounter with a Palestinian in Father Emannuel's study, we exchanged personal information – where we came from, what we did. We were both professors of English literature; we both taught and loved Chaucer. On learning that I was a graduate of Cambridge, my companion exclaimed, 'Oh, so you're English!' 'No, not really', I responded. 'I came to England as a refugee'. 'A refugee?' She repeated the word in a tone of surprise, of puzzlement, with clear lack of comprehension. 'A refugee?' I explained that we'd been forced to flee from Germany after Hitler's rise to power. Still the lack of comprehension registered on her face. She was clearly mulling over my words, trying to come to terms with the fact that 'refugee' could apply even to an Israeli Jew. And suddenly I realised how blinkered our views are, how blunted our perceptions, by the solipsism of our self-centredness. 'Fellow-feeling': the capacity to put ourselves in the other's shoes, to empathise – this alone may one day bring peace, or at least peaceful co-existence, to this troubled land to which two peoples lay justified claim.

Postscript: Did Sarah ever wonder what had become of Hagar and her son after Abraham had, at her behest, cast them out into the wilderness? The Midrash relates that when, after Sarah's death, Abraham took a second wife, Keturah, she was in fact none other than Hagar, whom Isaac had gone to seek out at Be'er Le-Hai Roi – Isaac, for whose sake the expulsion had been carried out. Can we, dare we, emulate that gesture of compensation and bring the outcast back in order to live together in peace, to start a new life?

Rela Mazali

In Tow: A Mother's and Daughter's Gendered Departures and Returns

—ɯɯ—

Militarised Grave Sites and Nationalised Children

I never met Eiga Shapiro. I'm positive Fagale Sevin never met her either. 'I'm taking the liberty of expressing my condolences', Eiga Shapiro wrote Fagale Sevin, whose first name – pronounced faygeleh – meant 'little bird' in Yiddish, though in fact her friends and family mostly called her Fagie – pronounced faygee. Eiga Shapiro wouldn't have known that, of course. 'Though I don't know you personally', she wrote, 'I'm taking the liberty of expressing my condolences'.

Eiga Shapiro was working at the Foreign Ministry of the new state, just recently declared, when she wrote to Fagie Sevin on 2 July 1948. She was probably in charge of some kind of equipment for receiving and sending messages – maybe a telephone? More likely a radio. Possibly, she was in charge of more than machines. Eiga Shapiro might have been a senior official with a broad job definition incidentally including access to, and responsibility for, communications equipment. I doubt it. Most high level officials were not women in the new state of Israel in 1948. Most high level officials are not women even today, in Israel in 2000.

In addition, high level officials don't usually deal with receiving and forwarding personal messages. And the message that Eiga Shapiro sent to Fagie Sevin was unquestionably personal. Part of the letter she wrote to Fagale was a precisely quoted cable, sent from the United States of America and addressed to 'Fagale', who was living in the upper Galilee. The cable had been received, typed out, and forwarded by Eiga, whose office was in Tel-Aviv. Besides expressing her condolences, Eiga's letter, written in Hebrew, asked Fagie to confirm the letter's arrival, 'seeing as in times of war things go wrong with the roads and the mail doesn't always reach its destination'. Eiga ended her letter with an offer: 'If you have any answer, you can send it to me and I'll transmit it to America'.

The cable, typed out in English, word for word, in the middle of the Hebrew letter, says – with almost no punctuation and one misspelling, 'With all the fibres of our soul we are with you in the loss of Shrull however we are prepared to pay for your plan or ship fare to United States for you to have the baby here the family Sevin are asking the same plea. If you need anything wire collect Eli Gaba'.

Eli Gaba was Fagie Sevin's father. The family Sevin were her mother-in-law, brother-in-law, and sister-in-law. Shrull was her husband, killed early in June in a car crash on a Galilee road. I was the baby. Not, as it turned out, born in the United States. Fagie stayed in the Galilee to have me. Our trips to the States came later.

These trips – departures and returns – are among the dis- and re-locations which I'll be describing here, in a form of writing that crosses and recrosses the borderlines between storytelling and theorising. These hybrid observations, also moving between, and linking, personal and social-political existence, draw upon a collection of fifty-some-year-old letters preserved by my mother and father.

For the moment, then, I'll continue the storytelling. Eiga Shapiro, an apparently kind and conscientious civil servant at the Foreign Ministry in Tel-Aviv, wrote to my mother in a careful, studied Hebrew to explain that she had forwarded her Eli's message by three routes: regular mail, in cable form, by military mail, in some other form that she called a 'transmission', and finally also by post again, in the present letter form. Possibly, my mother, whom I can't ask in person because she died in 1995, ended up receiving the message in all three forms. 'We are with you,' 'We are with you', 'We are with you', underlining the extent to which they weren't. Her entire family a sea, an ocean, and half a continent away – in the American Midwest. And she was young, newly emigrated to Palestine-just turned-Israel, now widowed, and five months pregnant.

Multiplying the message through all possible channels to maximise its chances of arrival, Eiga Shapiro meanwhile took the liberty of condolences. Probably well meant, they were nevertheless a liberty. She deviated from the standard form of unavoidably eavesdropping without comment in the line of her duties. She commented. She felt free to do so. She was confident of the propriety of inserting her voice into the flow of personal information she was facilitating. Positioned by her public office, she felt it her prerogative to extend her semiofficial sympathy under the letterhead of The Temporary Government, The Foreign Ministry, Tel-Aviv, rather than respecting the illusion of privacy by effacing her role as message bearer.

A dead young man and a pregnant young woman were in fact not private matters in the newly declared state, in the times of war to which Eiga referred. Dead Jewish men and Jewish pregnancies were at least to some extent public concerns, part of the balance of national losses and potential gains, part of the demographic competition between Jews and indigenous Palestinians, anyone's and everyone's business in the Jewish community that was establishing the state.

Almost any parent who has taken a child for a walk down the street in Israel can testify that today, too, babies remain everyone's business in Jewish Israeli culture – community children, as it were. Anyone and everyone feels free to comment on how the baby is dressed (too warmly, not warmly enough), how sweet she looks, how much he resembles (or doesn't resemble) his mommy, how convenient those new bottles are, etc.

Some of this is well meaning, as I imagine Eiga Shapiro's comments were. She had no obligation to write in the first person. Even if it was her job to offer a means of return communication, she could simply have added an impersonal notice, 'Your answer may be sent via the following address', etc. So I can read a distinctly humane and indeed feminine impulse in her decision to introduce herself by name and to write directly to Fagale (or actually Fagie) as a visible, individual woman who cared. I attach a degree of humane-ness to the gossipy, unabashed interest in other people and other people's business, which seems to me characteristic of Jewish Israeli culture.

But the intervention impulse that parents meet with on the street is also, to some degree, proprietary; an expression of assumed partnership in every child's, all Jewish Israeli children's, custody. The comments, not usually framed in attentive, careful terms, are largely assuming, controlling in tone. And this tone, though maybe slight, is discernible in Eiga Shapiro's intervention. Her request to confirm the letter's arrival, in fact an official directive, had little if anything to do with caring about Fagie's needs or condition. Other message bearers and transmitters along the way could have been asked to confirm delivery. The directive seems to have stemmed from Eiga's needs and conditions; for instance, from a need to verify that people on the receiving end recognised the power of her official capacity and signalled this by following her politely phrased orders.

Eiga Shapiro's letter is assuming as well, mainly in the way it both implicitly and explicitly appropriates Fagie's mourning: 'I'm taking the liberty of expressing my condolences and my participation in your sorrow'. As if to say, 'It's not exclusively yours, this sorrow. It's a communal, community sorrow, of which all are free to partake, particularly institutions of the state. Make no mistake', it seems to say, 'the Temporary Government and the Foreign Ministry in Tel-Aviv stand bereaved beside you'.

The vehicle my father was killed in – called a 'tender' in Anglicised-Hebrew, a kind of hybrid pickup truck and tarp-covered personnel carrier which is now almost non-existent – had been carrying provisions to the besieged town of Tzfat. This fact earned him the epithet 'killed in the line of duty', though the cause of death was an accident, an unresponsive steering wheel or a turn taken too fast on a winding, potholed road. He had been sitting in the passenger seat. In extending her condolences, Eiga Shapiro was claiming him as one of the national dead, Israelis killed in some form of action for the sake of the state. The shared ownership of loss, his loss and that of many others, was – and still is – exercised routinely as a way of defining and constituting the national community. Eiga's decision to comment on the cable she was forwarding reflected his status as public emblem. His dead person, like Jewish Israeli children's living ones, was a piece of public property, one of the exhibits marking out the common sphere.

The site of his grave and the form of his gravestone strongly signify his placement in this sphere. He is buried on a hill commanding a beautiful view of the Chula Valley and the modest mountains that surround it. It is a militarised cemetery, maintained by military rather than civilian authorities, with rather uniform gravestones, similar in size and set 'in parade' at regular, repeated angles. His grave is just behind the grave of Joseph Trumpeldor, which is marked by the largish stone lion that overlooks, and can be seen from, many sites in the upper Galilee. Trumpeldor, of course, is one of the catchiest, best-known Israeli emblems of nation-constituting battle and death. In the past his alleged and possibly falsified coinage 'It's good to die for our country', was hallowed and passed on to cohort after cohort of young Israelis. By now it has been re-examined, subverted, criticised, and sharply satirised or alluded to in works of art, studies, and essays, that have themselves achieved the full-fledged, many-faceted scope of enduring national symbols.

Further back in the cemetery where Shrull Sevin is buried – a cemetery bearing the name of Tel-Chai (literally, 'living mound') the Jewish outpost or village where Trumpeldor died – there is an Israeli pantheon. A large rectangular arrangement converging on a central lawn, it assembles together all the graves of the members of Hashomer, a proto-militia active in the early days of pre-state Jewish settlement. The bodies of several Hashomer members were actually reburied at this state-conceived memorial site, moved here from the original burial places near their respective homes. Shrull's grave site, then, locates him firmly, physically. within a field of nationalised, mythologised memory.

He was placed in this field with my mother in tow. While she and he had freely chosen to immigrate to Palestine – voluntarily relocating themselves, rather than being dislocated by events beyond their control – and while both of them had undertaken a potentially life-changing commitment to the national movement known as Zionism, Shrull's death in the line of duty in 1948 tethered Fagie more distinctively to a nationalised symbol system. Months later, on 22 February 1949, she would write to the man she'd become involved with, 'I have to laugh when I see what respect I command just because my husband was killed'.

Widowhood, in many societies, is a heavily constrained status subject to detailed regulations. These can be magnified when the widowhood is directly linked to a national, militarised cause. 'It is precisely because sexuality, reproduction, and child-rearing acquire such strategic importance with the rise of nationalism that many nationalist men become newly aware of their need to exert control over women. Controlling girls and women becomes a man's way of protecting or reviving the nation', Cynthia Enloe (1993: 238–9) has written. Not only men but many women too take part in policing their own reproductive functions and sexuality, along with those of their daughters, sisters, and friends, as a manifestation of nation. National widowhood in the new Jewish state in some ways paralleled a burial site, a living mound (tel chai) perceived by the community as continuously signifying a death, which in turn staked out a tract of shared, identifiable community property. The widow's special trait of widowhood came to designate a collective experience. The child of a woman widowed 'in the line of duty', would then extend the mound, growing up as a genetically and culturally imprinted signifier of formative national meaning and memory.

Probably sensing the pressure to play a role, and attempting to reclaim for herself feelings which seemed 'real', rather than 'programmed' by social convention – emotions that seemed individual and in that sense true – my mother apparently struggled with her national widow's pose. She refused parts of it. She named me after my father, as was expected, playing on the then significant coincidence that his registered, though unused, Hebrew name was the same as that of the state. So I was saddled with the name Israela, simultaneously signifying a dead father and a resurrected nation. But then, within months, my mother abbreviated the name unrecognizably to Rela, a nickname virtually unknown in Hebrew, erasing my commemorative label and even obscuring its Hebrew origins. She proceeded to raise me until my teens as the unsuspecting daughter of another father, a step almost unheard-of for the child of a national casualty, one approaching sacrilege. Though my siblings and I eventually learnt she had had a former husband, no pictures of Shrull were hung up anywhere in our house. Transgressing the routine and implicitly mandatory rituals of national widowhood, my mother hardly ever visited the cemetery and definitely never attended official memorial ceremonies of any kind for the nation's dead. And she never applied for or received any of the state support extended to war widows or war orphans.

Her resistance to the duties of a war-widowed mother would probably have been much more difficult had I been born a boy. It is a gendered aspect of national identity building that the sons of young dead men, far more than their daughters, are cast as preservers of the nation-constituting deaths of their fathers. This is an extension of sons' roles in many societies as preservers of the patrimony, signified through inheritance of the fathers' names. For my part, I was largely freed – both by gender and by my mother – of the fearsome duty of being a walking memorial.

A reverse dynamic, equally gendered, seems to hold for widowers. It could easily have been my mother sitting beside the driver. Had my father been bereaved, I believe his loss would not have placed him to the same extent in a publicly orchestrated role. Men who are dead in the line of duty define living wives and living sons as national icons. Women, even when dead in similar circumstances, are not assigned comparable powers over their surviving husbands, sons, and daughters. Their bereaved families can remain relatively unbound by state roles and duties, and analogously unsupported by comparable status and respect. Eiga Shapiro probably wouldn't have sent her condolences to a widower, partly because she wouldn't have felt free to adopt such a patronising tone towards a man. Also, based on my father's gender, she could safely assume he'd been killed in the line of some kind of duty, whereas a similar assumption concerning a dead woman would have been much riskier.

One of the main points of my mother's discord with her state widow's role seems to have centred, predictably perhaps, on the fact that she felt love again 'too fast'. On 8 February 1949, she wrote Ronnie, who would be my adoptive father within the year, 'I'm so mixed up. And I feel so guilty. I feel so hard hearted. And so all on the surface. As if my emotions of the past were all gone, as if I had never felt them – for how could I have and feel the way I do now? I wish, I wish, I wish that I were young and without a past to think about....' She was only twenty-six. In this case, she didn't need regulative comments from civil servants, or friends, or family, to feel she had to control this development, this new love, or to feed her guilt at being able to feel it.

In fact, I'm not sure she encountered any marked disapproval or policing in her surroundings. I don't see disapproval of national widows' remarriage as consistently or clearly pronounced in the Jewish society of Israel. In most of this society, such widows are expected to live, love, and marry and, in many ways, go on as usual, or, as it is often put, to 'be strong', so that their normalised lives can demonstrate the productivity of their husbands' deaths. 'In their death they bequeathed us life', says the standard text at countless services and on numerous memorial walls throughout the country. As long as the mandatory commemorative rituals are solemnly observed by the widow, going ahead and getting a life is the prescribed, 'healthy' route. The normalcy of continued life is supposed to assign the death its deepest, most satisfying significance. The 'living mound' is felt not only to signify, but indeed to justify, the death.

This, however, doesn't mean a full, simple, social endorsement of state widows' remarriage. Or of any widows' remarriage, for that matter. Most women in Westernised societies both then, in 1948, and today, learn and expect, or at least hope, that love for a life partner will be basically exclusive. Modern, Western society has constructed this expected exclusive emotion as justification for the legal and structural exclusivity of the marriage contract. And the expectation that love for a partner will be overpowering to the exclusion of others turns into a measure of the supposed sincerity or 'truth' of what one is feeling. Thus, feeling love for another, when a partner has died, may seem to belie the validity of the widow's earlier 'true' love, with the result that her present feelings become suspect too. One major indication of validity, though, is thought to be time. The widow expects and is expected to need 'enough' time to make the transition to a new emotional attachment. And an appropriate temporal interval between loves can safely support another social construct, that of a different, unique, special feeling of love for each successive partner, in the event that exclusivity isn't a realistic possibility. So besides unhinging the conviction that her feelings are 'real', loving again 'too fast' can cast the widow as precisely that – 'fast', or loose, that is, immoral, unreliable, socially undesirable.

Respectability and desirability – by social standards and the widow's personal ones – would seem, then, to depend on the vaguely defined measure of what 'enough' time is. As the secular Jewish culture of Israel offers no clear, normative standard, and didn't do so in 1948, each widow has had to negotiate this measure individually with self and surroundings. As often as not, she has had to navigate the obstructing body of her own guilt as part of this. My mother apparently found the nationalised injunction to 'be strong', to make a home and a life, to justify and commemorate my father's death through her own vitality, very difficult to reconcile with socially sanctioned convictions about love, loyalty, and marriage. On 20 February she wrote to Ronnie: 'I found an Indian bracelet Shrull once bought for me and then all the doubts and the self-hatred and the feeling of cheating and being cheap and superficial came up again'. And in the letter of 22 February she mentioned a woman she knew of, 'whose husband was killed at about the same time as Shrull. She – well, she's lost about 25 or 30 pounds, she's still in a state of shock, etc., and she's supposed to be a very strong, controlled personality. And look at me. I feel ashamed when I think of that.... I have lost a great deal of my respect for myself....'

In the vein of much feminist writing, I am trying to put my finger on an evasive intersection between social, political processes and individual choices or unchosen actions. I am not presenting a psychological analysis of motives, whether conscious or not, or of the elements of personality or the type of predisposition that would explain my mother's decisions and moves. I am trying to look at her, and at myself, as autonomous but constrained agents, to view our movements within a matrix of social and political forces. While my materials are highly personal acts and texts, I am trying to trace their interaction with the power structures in which they occurred. I am placing and reinterpreting parts of my mother's life and mine within a system of critical, feminist concepts, in a manner not unlike – though much more accountable and conscious than – the location and construal of my father's death within a system of nationalised ones.

The relocation of my father's identity in death, his shift to a status of full membership in the nation, of being 'one of us' now definitely and deftly – which was, moreover, an important means of defining this 'us' – must have badly jarred my mother's sensibilities. While she came to Palestine moved (at least partly) by a passionate belief in Zionist ideas, once here she didn't easily 'belong'. She was a newcomer, made to feel distinctly inferior and excluded by the native-born Jews whose parents or grandparents had arrived here a few decades earlier. This was, and still is, standard practice in the immigrant state of Israel, which seems to be an arena of perpetual competition for the privileged status of 'native-ness'. Fagie wrote to Ronnie on 10 March 1949: 'I was quite shattered when I first came to the country and to [kibbutz] Ma'ayan Baruch. I was horrified and I held aloof from forming attachments. I never voted on any issue, I never took part in a discussion, I didn't want any responsibilities'. On 18 March she wrote: 'You know what irks me? Many of the *sabras* up until now have treated me (most of the time) as a mental inferior.... I'd like to spit in their faces sometimes'.

Proprietary condolences and expressions of grief, appropriating her husband's death as these people's loss, must have felt quite hypocritical to Fagie Sevin. From the little I know of her husband's short life in this country, he – no less than she – had felt unsure about 'belonging'. Had he lived, that might have changed gradually, or stayed an unchanging part of his immigrant's identity, or contributed to an eventual decision to leave. But the instantaneous membership solemnly bestowed on him by death must have felt to my mother like a glaring farce. At the same time, it gained her a kind of membership she hadn't enjoyed before, a place of visibility and possibly even worth in this new, difficult, exclusionary community. I can imagine, though I don't know for a fact, that this attracted and gratified her in spite of herself. She seemed to imply as much in her humorous quip about 'losing a great deal of respect'. And maybe her conflictual attraction to becoming a significant part of national events can also be surmised from the account of Shrull's death that I heard from her at age eleven. Placing rifle shots in the vicinity of the crash, though I later learnt there were none, she seemed drawn in spite of herself to enhance the nationalised, glorified meaning of this death-by-accident.

I can easily imagine her excruciating ambivalence. I sensed something similar forty-five years later, when my oldest son became a soldier. By then deeply critical of what I view as the militarised policies of the state of Israel, I had openly contested my son's enlistment (although it was mandatory by law), and his decision to volunteer for a top combat unit. But as he made his way through the arduous course of basic training, I was fascinated and troubled to find myself feeling pride at his success at the very same time I detested it. Part of it was a parent's pride in a child's healthy ability to meet challenges he'd set himself. But part of it was a sense of the status he was acquiring as a member of a glorified select group, and the consequent status this bestowed on me, his mother. I could fleetingly identify these feelings in myself, in spite of, and concurrent with, my strong, painful objection to the deeply discriminatory practices reflected so precisely by this emerging army-based status. Accepting Israeli mythology for so many years of my life, I had long equated this particular type of army service with the best of men – beautiful, decent, daring, and selfless – men who would not even speak of their feats due to security risks and secrecy, but due also to a deep, lovable, gentle modesty. I felt this image still present in my mind, strong and seductive, right there alongside my clear understanding of just how manipulative it was (and still is). And I felt the attraction of belonging – gaining a significant place through my son's militarised, national rite of passage – along with my rejection of the social stratification that created the group I would consequently join; with my anger at its militarised definition.

Imagined Geographies

Widowed and five months pregnant in June 1948, Fagie had to be fearing the future she faced as both a single, widowed woman and a single mother (which are two separate, though related matters). She probably keenly sensed what Susan Moller Okin calls the vulnerability of exit – that is, from a marriage, where 'custody of children', Okin says, 'is known to be a factor that discourages remarriage' (Okin, 1989: 166). In Israel in 1948 there was probably a relatively large number of widows and widowers – resulting from the Second World War, the ongoing war of 1948, the violence leading up to it, general hardships, poor sanitary conditions, lack of health professionals and medical equipment. I imagine that remarriages, and fairly fast ones at that, were more widespread then than in many other times and places. Regardless of statistics, though, my mother and the society she lived in clearly assumed that widowhood and motherhood made her less desirable. Both my mother and much of her social milieu considered her femininity to be somewhat 'second-hand', used and tarnished. On 8 February 1949 she wrote to her lover, Ronnie: 'You don't deserve to be saddled with me.... I tried to get up the courage to put a stop to this and I find I can't. But I'm ashamed of myself for not being able to. I told you I hate myself and I do. Didn't anyone ever tell you not to trust widows? Ladies with babies? Don't you know that they are conniving females who only want to get their hooks into you?' On 7 March she wrote: 'I guess I needn't tell you that it hasn't been an easy question for me. Who wants a lady with a baby? Can it be like 'your own'? Will I resent it if it is? Or if it isn't?'

And while Fagie's motherhood made her less desirable, less marriageable, it – I – was at the same time considerably deepening her need for the material and emotional support of a marriage. This added neediness imposed by a baby, coupled with her reduced desirability, was the crux of her vulnerability of exit. When I was born my mother had spent just over a year in the country. She was still very foreign to its society and culture, struggling with the language and only haltingly literate. She had a bachelor's degree from a Kansas University, where she had majored in psychology. She had never practised. Even then a BA probably wasn't qualification enough. In addition, she believed that the Zionist effort needed farmers and Jewish labourers rather than more Jewish intellectuals. Before marrying and immigrating, she had spent time on a training farm in New Jersey, practising for the communal farming life she'd decided to adopt. As far as I know, she had not lived on her own or supported herself before her marriage. And she didn't come from a family that could support her and her baby for very long.

She could, of course, have gone on living on the kibbutz, but her serious misgivings intensified after I was born. On 24 August 1949 she wrote to Ronnie: 'the idea of [a woman], whom I consider incompetent, raising my child until the age of two, while I (whom I consider very competent indeed!) raise hers used to eat and eat at me. It just didn't seem fair.... The work for women also bothers me. I was very lucky. I worked with the kids, but most girls are just plain drudges ... it's really a kind of slavery. And I see no hope for improvement'. Six months earlier, on 18 February she had written: 'What I would really like is work in the *refet* [cowshed], or *binyan* [construction] or *masgeria* [welding] but fat chance I or any woman has in this set-up! Do you know that for women the kibbutz is a retreat to the middle ages? Emancipation, my foot! I'll never be in the position I was in at *hachshara* [the training farm] where I knew all about the *meshek* [farm economy] and talked on a level with the guys about everything that went on. I loved it'.

Elaborating on the last point, she wrote, 'This kills me.... I must find a way out of this.... I'm beginning to get claustrophobia'. Claustrophobia, by various names, figured repeatedly in her letters. On 22 February she had written that she often felt the kibbutz 'hemming me in too closely'. On a later, undated page she said: 'I would love to get away from here for a little while. I'm more than slightly bored. I'm sick of looking at the same people's faces and hearing the same old complaints'. This sense of being shut up, shut in, bored, was, I believe, highly pertinent to my mother's thinking and feeling about how she was going to make it as a single parent. It lucidly reflected the mental construction placing women, then and still, in a sphere perceived as enclosed, domestic, private; and men – in opposition – in a sphere viewed as 'out there in the world'. Women, assigned the domestic sphere, ostensibly through the binding functions of mothering, were – and to a large extent still are – viewed as less able to engage the competitive reality of professional bread-winning. Men, who were – and again still are – navigating and managing the 'big, real world', make women's occupations seem insignificant and powerless by comparison. As Griselda Pollock (1994: 78) worded it, 'He is the privileged traveller through and occupant of public spaces of money, exchange, leisure and power'. This familiar construct has, of course, been analysed in depth in feminist theory. My interest here is in the extent to which it formed and determined the outlook and personal decisions of my mother and my adoptive father.

In a letter to Ronnie dated 18 February, Fagie wrote: 'Damn! I think I'll come in and take the job that you once offered me. Only, there's the baby and is she cute. I'm a little afraid to talk about her to you. I don't know why. But I am'. Most probably she could actually have done this job he had once offered her. Ronnie was officially on loan from the kibbutz, employed by the nascent Israeli air force to set up a battery of screening tests for pilot trainees. He too had a bachelor's degree in psychology, his from a university in Johannesburg, South Africa. He had also had some practical experience, gained during his service in a testing unit in the South African army. Fagie definitely had the background to do such work and could have learnt on the job, as his letters show others did. Yet the job offer, made 'once', was now past, and she framed it in the sentence between a 'Damn!' and an 'Only there's the baby', clearly reflecting her perception of motherhood and significant (demanding) work as opposite poles, and indicating that she wouldn't presume to take seriously her daydream of having such a job. I don't think she felt truly eligible for a position in the 'real world'. She could only gain one through a partner.

In the letter of 18 February Fagie rendered herself in the classic image of the waiting woman, weaving or wielding a broom while her man is out on an odyssey. 'Everything is upside down, on top of the beds and the chair, waiting for the floor to be washed.... You'll be on the way to Haifa now and me, I'm pining away.... I wish it were last Friday night instead because then I didn't expect you to come ... now altho' I know you're not, that you have more *important* things to do – I wish you would'. On 22 February she pressed for details of his 'real' work: 'You have to tell me more about what you're going to do, the work you're thinking of, etc. It sounds fascinating....' Meanwhile, where she was, 'The days roll by ...' in what she called (on 18 February) 'the cackling atmosphere of the *machsan* [communal clothing store] and the tense, catty air of the *Bet Tinokot* [communal nursery] (tense because everybody is fighting to work there, 'catty' because there are women, and where there are women ...)'. These characterisations of Ronnie's (men's) and her (women's) roles, did not stem from a singular, personal lack of confidence, or from idiosyncratic attitudes. They reflected what were, and to a large degree still are, the prevailing stereotypical gender roles to which men and women are socialised in Western societies. Through these deeply internalised stereo-types, Fagie sensed and represented herself as passive, waiting, doing nothing of consequence, and the women around her as practising petty intrigue and infighting.

Reflecting similar mindsets which placed him at the opposite pole, Ronnie wrote Fagie on 2 March 1949 that he wanted to spend time with me, her child, and that 'she and I one day will have a very serious father-daughter chat about the big wide world outside the four corners of her room'. The playful image draws upon, and in turn feeds, the assumption that he was both equipped and called upon to acquaint an uninitiated child with the 'big world outside'. By the opposition that structured both their worlds, then, he was 'out' in interesting, important, reality and she was 'shut in', confined to unimportant domesticity. He operated on an expansive scale, while she existed in diminutive, trivialised dimensions. And embedded in the opposition was his implied independence and ability to make a living, versus her dependence and at best precarious ability to provide.

Fagie's letters were dated and often noted the time underneath the date. I take this to imply a familiar, unchanging routine. The only way to characterise parts of her uniform, domesticated existence, it seems to say, are mechanical clock-readings. Most of Ronnie's letters were headed with the name of the department he worked for above the name of the air force in English in the earlier letters, and later, in Hebrew: 'Psychological Department, Camp "Ariel", Israel Air Force'. It wasn't that he used official air force stationery; the letterhead was penned in spontaneously by hand. As he wrote to his lover, he unthinkingly, very naturally, placed himself in a sphere of official positions and meaningful state institutions. He shifted to Hebrew letterheads as he mastered the lingua franca of this sphere and grew increasingly fluent in its protocol. Fagie, meanwhile 'shut in' on the kibbutz, felt left without language. She wrote on 13 March: 'My English is degenerating; unfortunately, my Hebrew is no better for it'.

In an undated letter under the letterhead, from late February or early March 1949, Ronnie wrote: 'Some of this work is fascinatingly interesting, and really worthwhile. I've learnt such a lot also that it amazes me ... [I] prefer the kibbutz. Only wish it could give me the same satisfaction that this work gives me.... Now I'm pretty proud of what I've done here and I don't want to see it break up'. And on 15 March 1949 he wrote: 'From all over the place people are coming to see our unit and going away excited or jealous according to whether they're in the business or not. Today was a conducted tour of 20 people'. On 3 March Fagie wrote to him: 'What are all the lectures about? Who can go to listen to them – anyone? What about the new work, you certainly keep mum!' On 10 March she wrote: 'Your work: Judy told me you told her that you might go to Europe or America … is it too nebulous to talk of?' She represented him as a man of the world, a member of a privileged circle, privy to confidential information from which she was excluded. From her perceived position of marginalisation, she wrote him, on 13 March: 'There's really no news. There's nothing actually to write you about'.

I think this pattern is particularly interesting in view of some of the environmental facts. The newly founded kibbutz my mother lived on was a frontier settlement. Since she'd arrived there in 1947, there had been sporadic fighting in the area. On 8 May, about a month before he was killed, Shrull had written to his mother about a trip that he and Fagie had made to the upper Galilee, starting from a point near Tel-Aviv. 'The trip, which takes about two days or less in peaceful days, took us almost a week. We had to wait for convoy and roads to be opened'. While Israel's borders are ill-defined, chronically disputed and shifting, the kibbutz of Ma'ayan Baruch has been situated just south of the dangerous, turbulent intersection of Lebanese and Syrian borders ever since the 1948 armistice agreements. Land mines have been repeatedly planted in its fields, and even today, in 2000, it is within range of katyusha rockets, and is sometimes their target. In addition, the kibbutz was out in what was then, and to some extent still is, 'nature'. And conditions were rugged in 1948. Far from the moderating influence of the Mediterranean, upper Galilee weather ranges from bitterly cold, rainy, and windy, to baking hot and dry. As a child, I heard my mother tell stories of freezing showers in winter in a tin-roofed communal shower shed, and of red clay mud, climbing to the tops of their knee-high boots whenever they went to the communal dining room or to feed their babies or take a shower. Ronnie was stationed in Jaffa, also a scene of concentrated fighting, and the expulsion and flight of about ninety thousand Palestinians. But while Ma'ayan Baruch remained a border zone, Jaffa and Tel-Aviv, by then predominantly Jewish with a mainly Jewish-settled hinterland, were no longer a frontier. The scene was that of a busy, lively town and many of Ronnie's letters report his going out to films and variety shows, or paying social visits.

In many ways, then, my mother was placed in the more adventurous setting. On one reading, living in Ma'ayan Baruch, as opposed to Jaffa, could have been construed as 'being out there', facing difficult realities, participating in a masculinised project. But superimposed on this were her gender and her consequent professional and social placement in the kibbutz, as opposed to Ronnie's gender and his employment by the national air force. Shrull's letter to my grandmother, dated 8 May 1948, aptly described Fagie's placement. 'Fagel is fine and by the time you receive this she'll be already four months pregnant. She looks wonderful and feels fine. She isn't working at anything too strenuous now and she gets some extra nourishment (milk, egg) as do all the pregnant girls'. The girls, especially pregnant ones, weren't slated for anything too strenuous or serious, it's implied. On 18 March, about a year later, Fagie wrote to Ronnie: 'I can't stand the work I have to do (*Machsan*, [the communal clothing store] which drives me batty). In fact, I'm sick of the kibbutz and all its problems and all it stands for and all my own failures'. Rather than adventure, she experienced a constrained, disempowering existence.

I propose an imaginary reversal of roles and a look at the hypothetical perceptions it entails. As I've mentioned, given her education and her background, Fagie could probably have done a job similar to Ronnie's, although, as I've mentioned, management jobs, particularly in the army, were not actually open to women at the time and are still largely staffed by men. As for Ronnie, it's notable how hard I find it to imagine circumstances in which he would have worked in the communal laundry or the nursery. It simply wasn't (and generally still isn't) done. Fagie's work was virtually untouchable for a man. This seems a revealing reflection on the severity of Jewish Israeli and/or kibbutz taboos against deviating from cultural norms of masculinity. Pointing out how fragile masculine gender identity seems to be, Sandra Harding has written, 'Central to the notion of masculinity, is its rejection of everything that is defined by a culture as feminine' (Harding, 1986: 54). In any case, had Ronnie been living on the kibbutz while Fagie lived in Jaffa, I believe 'the world out there' might have shifted location, projected by both of them onto the Galilee border zone, while Jaffa would have been construed as more domestic and unchallenging. Part of the gendered organisation of reality, then and now, assigns the places where men are the higher status of 'world', and the places where women are the inferior status of 'not-really-world'.

These were dominant parts of the social, mental infrastructure underpinnings the expectations of my mother and future father and affecting the decisions they were to make about issues such as their relationship, marriage, where each of them or both of them would live, what would happen to Fagie's child, how they would handle their respective educations and careers.

In June 1949 my mother left for America, taking her six-month-old baby with her. She wanted, and felt obligated, to show me to the two families in which I was the oldest grandchild. I doubt she'd have made a similar trip had my father been alive. Again, this absent man was a living force, obligating and motivating his widow, moving her and his daughter enormous distances. (At the time, the flight to the US took some 40–45 hours, stopovers included.)

Fagie's letters, both before and during the trip, state definite plans to return – to the kibbutz or at least to Israel. She wasn't harbouring serious thoughts of staying in America. The self-initiated relocation of her life seemed too important to her, too much a part of her identity, to be reversed. While the fact of her husband's death might impose a long trip, she resisted its potential for returning her to the US for good. And to some extent, his death probably deepened her commitment to the national project that produced its significance, and to the geographical territory on which its meaning was inscribed. Apparently confident in the conviction that she would return, she wrote Ronnie from her parents' home in Kansas City, on 28 June 1949: 'I can't say I miss anything. Not you or the country, or the kibbutz. That may come later when I've settled down a little. Right now I'm still drinking in all the beautiful green trees and grass, the comfortable living and the food. I had gotten so adjusted that I really had forgotten what all these things mean, what they were like. Sometimes, in an off moment, it seems to me that I'm pretty crazy to think of leaving it all again'.

But by 24 August Fagie would write: 'I'm so homesick! There is a pro-gramme called Town Hall which broadcast yesterday from Palestine – oops! Israel! – one girl (it's a forum) asked a question in Hebrew and I could have wept because it sounded so good. I hadn't realised how attached I was'. On 18 October, as she prepared to return, she wrote, 'I've never been so shut in, so cut off from activity in my life. I have an inkling now of what madness must be'. The feeling of insular domesticity, of bored, powerless inactivity, had intensified in America. She wasn't work-ing, or studying, or even looking for a job. The occupations, friends, and duties that would regularly take her out of the house were absent from her visitor's existence. Going out was hard in any case because her mother, Fagie reported, was afraid to stay with the baby, public trans-portation was quite limited in Kansas City, and Fagie didn't drive. Exam-ining the granted, very different existence of African nursemaids in South Africa, Griselda Pollock describes a process of infantalisation: 'What she does as an adult identifies her with the realm and status of her childish charge' (Pollock, 1994: 78). While the subaltern status of these nursemaids made theirs an extreme case, I think many mothers are rendered some-what infantile by the combination of financial dependence and physical constrictions often entailed by caring for children. My mother's confine-ment in and to a baby's world was further compounded by the fact that she herself had reverted to being a charge – back with her parents, finan-cially dependent for the duration, driven around by her mother in the family car, and physically distanced from the work, community, and choices that had briefly structured her adult life.

From this position, Ronnie, still at the air force base in Jaffa, must have represented even more of a link with activity, reality, meaning. Despite a phase of serious uncertainty in their relationship, Fagie wrote on 24 August: 'You want to stay in the psychological field. As for me, I go where you go, and I do so gladly because I like you and the work you like so well'. On 18 October she wrote: 'It's as if I had suddenly found that I was holding my breath and started to breathe normally again!... This last while I was sure that something had happened and that we would never get together. I was just about ready to come back as is. Your letters, I just can't tell you on paper what a difference it's made to me. For the first time in a long time I have a feeling of knowing where I'm going'. She might indeed have returned to Israel 'as is' – as a single mother, uncertain of job, partner, or home. But it was her prospective partner's decision that gave her a clear destination and sense of direction.

Meanwhile, her daughter who had lived in the US from age six to twelve months, had acquired a language. On 29 October, Fagie wrote about me: 'She talks a lot now. She understands almost everything. I'm sorry actually because now she'll have an adjustment to make in languages. Oh well, she's pretty pliable'. In fact, I wasn't.

Intrusions: Blind and Seeing

By early winter, we were in Jaffa. Fagie and Ronnie married in December 1949 and moved into an apartment on the air force base. Very soon after this I was officially adopted by Ronnie. While my mother at least partly resisted the role of nationalised widow, she actively chose to comply with the role of 'air force wife'. For a second time, then, her male partner – performing a military or militarised function, intentional or otherwise – became a link reinforcing her connection with the Zionist collective and the national project.

The apartment we lived in was property appropriated by the new Israeli government and allocated to the military. In all likelihood, the buildings that made up the air force base, 'Machaneh Ariel', had belonged to Palestinian families and organisations which were forced out of Jaffa. My parents undoubtedly believed with all their hearts that the takeover was justified and couldn't be helped. Nevertheless, they may have felt an unsettling sense of intrusion into someone else's home.

I felt it eighteen years later, when I hitchhiked onto to the Syrian Heights in 1967, three days after its takeover by Israel. At the time, I believed – as firmly as my parents did in 1948 – that Israel had had no choice, that it – we – were defending our lives. And also, that we didn't want or need or intend to keep the newly captured territories. I was a soldier, stationed in Tzfat, serving in military intelligence, privy to top-secret information and initiated into the special status achieved by having confidential knowledge. As part of my job, I had spent many months closely following every event along the Syrian-Israeli border. I knew for a fact that very little had been going on there. Since I'd been in this job, just under a year, there had been almost no shooting. When there was, we had usually been notified in advance that a tractor would be out that day, making good on Israeli claims to the disputed border zone. As Noam Chomsky (1983: 103) has written, summarising from an article by the late Israeli General Mattityahu Peled, 'Prior to 1967, Israel followed a "planned strategy" designed to impose its interpretation of the 1949 Armistice Agreements, including settlement in the demilitarised zones which infringed on the rights of the local inhabitants, leading to shelling in reprisal'. The stories of Syrians shooting down at peaceful farmers simply trying to cultivate their land were good publicity, but I already knew they were seriously slanted. At the time, however, that didn't shake my conviction that the practice was justified, as one of the ways that Israel necessarily defended itself.

On my summer visits to Ma'ayan Baruch in my teens, or at youth movement work camps in the Galilee, the Syrian Heights had long loomed above as a dark, fearsome entity. This template remained unbroken by my new crumbs of awareness that official and conventional images could be highly manipulative. Three days after the six named the 'Six-Day War' by Israel, a friend and I travelled up to face our nightmares, to slate our troubling curiosity. We were wandering. We didn't really care where we wound up. We just wanted to see, to gaze upon this forbidden, forbidding space – to try to turn it, under our gaze, from an ominous presence into just a place. We went wherever we could hitch rides in one or another military vehicle. I remember at some point catching half a glimpse, through the window, of a human form splayed out in the back of a Syrian pickup, one arm dangling. We weren't sure what we were seeing and at the same time we were: he – now become it – had yet to be brought to burial. It was the first time I had seen the wonderful, black-lace stone walls that marked off property in the fields of the Heights. Black basalt rocks of very irregular shapes, carefully fit, single file, into long, shoulder-high fences, netting between them intricate patterns of cracks, of air and light. These walls have all been toppled and scattered by now, erasing their visible claims to past ownership. At some point during the day we were in Kuneitra, the largest town on the Heights, wandering deserted streets. We walked through an unhinged door.

Breakfast was on the table. An outsize glass jar of sour cheese balls in olive oil. Home-baked pitta with a piece torn off to scoop up some cheese. A plate of olives. Tiny china coffee cups on the blue and white patterned oilcloth. One of the chairs was overturned. I could feel the people's urgency rushing out, their terror. I could see in front of me scattered pieces of their day, their life, their now crumbled habits. I was appalled at my intrusion. Physically sickened.

Two months later I felt sickened by every shower. Part of our unit had relocated to the top of a hill near Kuneitra. Heated arguments had accompanied the move – one of my colleagues and I had struggled to be part of it. Our male counterparts were being deployed there, taking the more sophisticated radio equipment. The meaning-generating aspects of our work would be physically shifted to that masculinised hilltop. What would there be left for us to do on the base in Tzfat? And should we two 'girls', as they called us, as we felt, be sent there too? Did they really need us? And could we really manage – in makeshift conditions, sharing living space with some twenty men? The two of us were adamant and persistent, determined to stay meaningful, and also attracted to what we saw as the adventure. We succeeded in convincing some commanders. And then, during the weeks we were there, with no showers on the hilltop and a dugout latrine, we regularly drove to nearby abandoned homes to shower, making my showers repeated, repulsive intrusions into interrupted lives. Showering, I used to feel filthy.

But in 1949, my parents had no direct contact with Palestinian Jaffa in its previous form. They were assigned their living quarters by a middleman – the state and its army. By the time they moved in, the original dishes and furniture were long gone. The uneasy sense of intrusion into someone's home, whether or not they believed it justified, was certainly muted by these buffers. At the other end of their move, their 'desertion' (as leaving a kibbutz was seen then, and for many years after) was also muted through the mediation of national-militarised institutions. My father was on a mission for the army, important and earnestly performed; my mother had lost a husband to the state, earning a right to find a new life, home, and means of livelihood. This was why in later years I was able to spend my holidays at Ma'ayan Baruch free of the animosity felt towards many ex-members and their children.

In 1950 we moved again. And again, the realtor was the army. A housing project for army officers was set up north of Tel-Aviv at what was then an inconvenient, rather isolated site. It only occurs to me as I write this that to this day, I have no idea why or how the location was chosen and which, if any, Palestinian habitats were there before army-commissioned contractors began building my childhood home. The results, freestanding or semidetached homes, were sold to officers on relatively comfortable terms, as part of the system of state incentives and benefits for long-term military service. Open only to officers, who in the formative years of the military were appointed based on recognised Western education and military experience, the neighbourhood was almost exclusively Ashkenazi. It was named 'Tzahala' after the Israel Defence Forces (*Tzahal*), and evolved in about a decade into an upper- and upper-middle-class neighbourhood, though the homes and salaries there at the time were modest by American or European standards. An adjacent project, 'Ramat Hachayal' (Soldier's Heights), where similar but smaller homes were sold a few years later to lower-ranking army personnel, was predominantly Mizrahi and became, over the same decade, an area associated with poverty and crime (by now it is largely gentrified). Stretched in between was the *ma'abara* or the new immigrants' transit camp, a roadless expanse of tin and wood sheds, with communal outdoor water taps, also predominantly Mizrahi and poorer than Ramat Hachayal.

By the time I was four and already fully fluent in the Hebrew spoken by the neighbours' kids in Tzahala, my parents, my then two-year-old sister, and I, left for the States; Fagie and I for the second time. Ronnie and Fagie had decided that he would go back to school to study for a Ph.D. in psychology, supported by scholarships and by my mother, who found a secretarial job at the university library. This time we were away for seven years, first in the Kansas university town where my father studied, and then in neighbouring Missouri, where my grandparents lived and my father interned at a city hospital. Not surprisingly, I forgot my Hebrew. Surprisingly, I retained a belief that I was 'really' Israeli and didn't belong in the States.

My sister and I were repeatedly told that we were in America temporarily, that before long we would go home – when we could, when my father finished his degree, when he finished his internship, when he had made enough money to finance the move. I can't reconstruct what kept intact my strong sense of non-membership in the community around me. I barely remembered Israel. I carried in my head one or two strong, split-second images: my baby sister and I on the veranda in our Jaffa apartment, the baby obnoxiously shouting down at passers-by, 'You go away!' But my mother told me the apartment had had no veranda and also that when we lived there my sister wasn't yet talking. Myself climbing to the top of a trellis in front of our Tzahala house and looking out at green grass-covered hills. My mother explained that there couldn't be grass covered hills near Tzahala, where everything was dry and brown and bare. Such sleight of memory notwithstanding, my sense of self, strongly nurtured by my parents, was distinctly labelled 'Israeli' and positioned me as alien to my immediate surroundings, the only surroundings I actually knew. While perhaps such persistent foreignness is the lot of many immigrants, it is often different for their children, who struggle and succeed at losing their foreign, immigrant identity. Besides, my mother wasn't an immigrant: she was back where she came from. And my father was at least back in the language he came from, though his accent was wrong. Still, after a brief, intense interval in their deeply foreign adopted country and language, they apparently felt, and made us feel, alienated from the country and language around us. This would turn out to be partly irreversible for me, my habitual state of being.

My first name was a conspicuous marker of my foreignness to American society. No one had ever heard of it before. Most people mispronounced it. Without even realising it, I mistakenly assumed that back in Israel it would be unremarkable and no longer single me out as different. I very much wanted to go 'home'. Meanwhile, I had no inkling of the dense materiality of language and culture. I was told that Hebrew was spoken in Israel, but had no grasp of what it meant to live in a language and not knowing it. I had no remembered experience of language as opaque. I knew it only as comfortable, taken for granted. I wasn't worried about not understanding because I truly didn't understand that I wouldn't understand. I took it on faith that eventually I would be going back where I belonged.

And, eventually, I did go, but of course I didn't belong.

Relocated Texts

In thinking about this volume and about dislocation, which I originally understood to mean *involuntary and imposed* relocation, my initial reaction was, 'But I've just written about that'. The passages I had in mind are sections of a chapter of *Maps of Women's Goings and Stayings* (Mazali, 2001), a book exploring women's physical movement through the world. In these passages I have examined the ordeal of unbelonging that I experienced when, at age eleven, I came back to – but for all practical purposes first arrived in – the country where I was born. Motivated by the idea of discussing dislocation, I began to recontextualise both the ordeal and my narration of it. Writing in *Maps* of my experience of moves and readjustments, I hadn't dealt with the chain of events or the reasons, with the development of my parents' choices. The narrative depicted the moves as arbitrary, external events to which I was subjected. And of course, for the most part, that was what they were to me. But the focus on dislocation needed chronologies and connections, a log book of comings and goings and processes. I was drawn back to the two thick folders of letters that my mother and father had exchanged in 1948 and 1949, lent me by my father soon after my mother died. Reading these, I gradually began to make out a backdrop of deeply gendered social constructs within which my parents' individual choices were embedded and enmeshed. I could follow, at least partly, how private emotions emanated from socially formed expectations or perceptions of self, and how these reflected the vital coping mechanism of clearly grasping, and acting on, the imperatives of social reality. I could also see, or remind myself, how these imperatives sometimes engendered strategies of personal resistance – piecemeal, perhaps, but doesn't all resistance have limits?

Myself a product of a deeply gendered culture, I find my mother's experience more accessible, more readily readable than that of my father.

The circumstances of her existence seem to me more immediately, intimately familiar. In addition, I believe my father experienced immigration in a way that was made very different by both his gender and his active, significant role in the military – the most unequivocal membership-defining institution of Israeli society. For my mother, although her many moves were mainly motivated by what seem like voluntary, fully autonomous decisions, the process of immigration was still, to a considerable degree, an experience of dislocation. Reading and rereading her letters and those of my father, I could hear my mother's ordeal of belonging resonating in my own. I could trace how parts of her alienation-of-choice from the place she came from fed into my propensity for margins, both chosen and unchosen. Reacquainting myself with the tone of her determined resistance to more than one socially required role, I also discovered part of what forged the space enabling my own stubbornly nonconformist politics and practices.

Studying my parents' fifty-year-old narrative of this experience, I could trace its echoes – though sometimes inverted – in my own experience and my own narrative. The following passages from *Maps* are some of the pertinent parts of this narrative:

> My mother's tongue was English, spoken at home, in Hebrew surroundings. And *my* tongue was probably first hers and then, pretty fast I guess multiplied – into hers and the surroundings'. But when I was four, the surroundings got changed and turned English. And my other tongue got lost. And then when I was eleven, the surroundings got changed back and turned Hebrew, and my mother's tongue was no use any more and my other tongue was gone.... Back in Israel at age eleven I learnt my other tongue. Again. Fairly fast in terms of calendar time, painstakingly humiliatingly slowly in terms of mine. But I never backtracked to read the books my old-new playmates had long been reading, in the florid syntax and vocabulary that mark literature as literature in Hebrew. Or to follow the radio serials they loved. Reading was too slow and too far from enjoyment in this re-acquired language. And the conjunctions and terms that made it literature, made it aloof, intimidating and sharply alienating to me... I could never un-have the organisation of reality that was already put in place in American English surroundings. I would never act or think, unquestioning, on their presuppositions. I could revise my own and consciously suppose, but never presuppose, theirs. So when I came back from the American fifties, still a child, and communist Russia was the terrifying conspirator of global evil and hideous oppression, it was mind-jarring that in the Hebrew of my suburbanite playmates, Russia was just one of two potential big brothers; not particularly fearful or hated, though perhaps by then slightly less likeable than the other. And America wasn't the baseline standard of liberty and good, but another country, grantedly more big and powerful than most. While justice, liberty and good were embodied in Zionism and the proud young Jewish state. A reality reorganised isn't as real as the original.... I could never turn back into a genuine, simple child of my, which?, culture. Or socialisation. I

couldn't completely lose the third dimension. I tried really hard. I didn't even realise I couldn't. I believed I could unlearn, as well as learn. I desperately wanted back in – to belong. I wanted to be as Israeli as humanly possible. A total, unsuspect and fully acknowledged member. I acted out my construct of Israeli-ness with all my teenage might.

Now, almost four decades later, I find it curious and unperturbing, maybe enriching, that I don't have a simple, secure, automatic 'mine' attached to a single language, a single culture. But then, me then, wanted to be a natural, organic part of the place where I was born, the place I was from. Mistakenly equating place with people. Unnoticing that the place had more, many more, than one body of community and custom to be from, to be part of.

Overlooking that I didn't actually issue from place, I wanted to know the land. The actual land, in detail. To know ahead every tricky turn-off on remote footpaths. To know the names of the brambles and the changing, seasonal flowers and the different kinds of trees, and the separate names of each of the low-altitude mountains in the Galilee and the southern desert. My American born mother … used to use Arabic place names, disdaining the newer Hebrew versions. (Her Hebrew wasn't very good anyway.) Nebi Yusha, Jermak, Jabalya she called them, where my school and schoolmates taught me Meiron, Givat Aliya. My mother shrugged them off, disdainful, 'Jermak, Jabalya', proud to be party to old-timers' intimacy, from before the overlay of invented Hebrew names or of re-imposed and covertly relocated biblical ones.

She was struggling to belong too. To her ideologically chosen, unnatural community. Our common struggle pitting us against each other. I needed to be unlike her and disown her American accent and habits and tastes. She needed to show herself and me that she was more in the know than I was, so she and I would have reason to keep her. I appropriated but aimed at more than her linguistic exhibit of old-timers' savvy. I wanted to walk away, to literally walk the land, to feel it all over and feel all over it.

My best girlhood friend had a big map hanging on the wall of her room. Taller than I was.… I had to face it standing, really close to it to read the names, for what I remember as really long stretches of time. Not hours but long pieces of time. I was looking at it. Recognising some of the sites and names, but mainly just looking. I think trying to have it, to take it in as part of me. To devour it. It was longed for, exotic, magnetic – this foreign From. Where I was from. Where I was foreign.… Conflating community with place, [I] felt a need to become so much at one with the space that it would become an extension of my self, totally comfortable. With native comfort irretrievable, to me total comfort had come to mean mastery through total mapping. (Mazali, 2001: 244–9)

Kathleen Kirby (1996: 48) has said, 'Part of the function of mapping … is to ensure that the relationship between knower and known remains unidirectional. The mapper should be able to "master" his environment, occupy a secure and superior position in relation to it, without it affecting him in return'. I muse over this analysis in *Maps*, asking:

Is it a paradox of belonging to a home site, that members acquire a mastery *over*, rather than being *in* and fully part of it? That belonging entails a mental distance from a land flattened by long repetitive acquaintance? … habitual, long erasure…. [B]elonging seems to include the kind of mental distance needed for viewing location as a finitely known, permanent underpinning, which I can travel unstartled and confidently manipulate…. [T]rying to be part of a people I was in fact struggling to distance myself slightly but crucially from the land…. Now distanced from my need for distance, for mapping, I can see in it clearly my need for over view. For oversight. That belittles or disappears a lot of things from sight. Particularly people. Not only people but particularly people. In a need for mapping I can see a need for overlooking. And for overseeing. Managing. (Mazali, 2001: 253–4)

Later this description goes on to say:

There is a store of places in this country where I still live, which is still only partly my homeland (although I don't have any other any more) … put there courtesy of the youth movement. From age thirteen to eighteen, a tight-knit bickering intense group, we hiked the land for days and weeks on school holidays, carrying backpacks with all our food and water and sleeping bags and towels and extra socks and underpants and shirts and pants. A lot of the time I felt top-heavy and wobbly on my feet, which were supposed to firmly tread the land. But I loved being cut off from family and neighbourhood and town, isolated on this moving island peopled with the best of my friends and the worst of my enemies. And I loved the expanse and the unartificial space, the rocks and sheer bluffs and trees and brush and scrub and stars. And for all my persistent, slightly shameful clumsiness, I loved my intense physicality and my activated senses. Arriving back at my mother's house was always painful, a severance.

Out of all proportion with practical constraints, we moved through the landscape as a self-sufficient unit. We could have been met by pick-up trucks with food and equipment, or detoured into villages to buy fresh bread and cheese and houmous (chick pea spread). But we even carried cartons of eggs and little kerosene stoves and big tin containers of kerosene that banged against my shins as I hauled it up a steep path in front of me. Only half-realising it, we were a quasi-military bivouac, marking out proprietary. The choice to hike through them, implied the zones around our routes to be unspoiled nature. And we actively unsaw, or saw as quaintly picturesque and part of nature, the stone houses of Arab communities we never thought of then as Palestinian. And we actively overlooked, or saw as out-of-place and marring nature, the concrete houses of communities of Arab Jews come from the towns or grazing lands of the Levant, and positioned by the state at isolated sites. Our youth movement marched out a practical concretisation of the Zionist delusion of virgin land to be possessed and gorgeously fertilised. Ideally, by beautiful, caucasian featured, male youths. We styled ourselves accordingly and suppressed conventional femininity. Our paces measured and mapped onto the ground our unfolding, forming beliefs. Our parents' firm convictions. And in a cyclic, self-perpetuating process, the sensual experience then powerfully reaffirmed our unseeing perceptions. (Mazali, 2001: 253–4)

Alison Blunt and Gillian Rose (1994: 9) have written, 'Maps were graphic tools of colonisation, themselves colonising spaces perceived as empty and uninscribed'. I have elaborated on this in *Maps*, saying:

> true to the maps, I didn't know I was a coloniser. Embedded in me by my old-new community, was a mindset I could presuppose – that is suppose without knowing I was doing so – because it lay outside the interrupted presuppositions of my half an American childhood. It wasn't my unbelonging that made me unsee the suppressed Palestinian presence in Palestine. Or the suppressed heritage of Arab-Jews. On the contrary. It was a symptom of my developing belonging. To the Zionist ethos and maps that drew an empty unsettled land to be lovingly settled – by the likes of the us I wanted for mine. And by coincidence, or none, this was a mindset well tuned to my TV training, in the American settlers' state, to love the land and its objectified, picturesqued, lore. So practising a settlers' religion, I felt deep love for the land.... [T]he new nation state, born the same year I was, with its slightly older myths of heroes scouting out the land, figured large in my teenage needs for belonging and self. And our youth movement, like others, also simulated the paramilitary operations of the years before we were born, before the Israeli state. Which operations needed, and also acted out, detailed knowledge of terrain. (Mazali, 2001: 253–4)

'Geography', Michel Foucault has written, quoting the editors of *Herodote* (cited in Colin, 1980: 69) 'grew up in the shadow of the military'. My above description goes on to sum up our quasi-bivouac youth movement treks: 'We were revelling in the titillating tradition of adorable fighters whose names or stories we pronounced in special, reverent voices. And I, all that much more than the others, for being unsure of my rightful, justified claim to them. I deeply identified with the rough repossessiveness, with the trail-blazing, claim-staking romance' (Mazali, 2001).

Redefining the Sidelines

Like the full community membership my mother was barred from and could only begin to achieve through her partners, the membership I craved as a teenager clearly 'gendered me out'. As documented by several writers (e.g. Ben-Yehuda, 1981; Mazali, 1993; Gluzman, 1997; Kosh-Zohar, forthcoming), it was a membership open to men only, more specifically to fighters – military men, heterosexuals of Jewish Ashkenazi descent. The people in Israeli Jewish society who didn't fit those specifications could only aspire to do so, to emulate the real thing, while muting their own distinctive features – feminine, Mizrahi, homosexual or otherwise. Or they could rebelliously ignore the social exclusion to which they were subjected and face the difficult consequences. So my friends, no less than I, needed to become 'ungirls' if they wanted to earn the sense of full Israeli-ness that many of them coveted. My mother used to recount how, in the space of a year, she watched several of us learn to use the same sloppy walk and adopt the same slouch to hide our embarrassing new breasts. Throughout our teens, we all bought the same clumsy, unfashionable cotton pants at a particular store in Tel-Aviv and wouldn't wear any other kind. We all observed a strict dress code regarding colours and the cuts of blouses, which were usually big, loose, and as masculine as possible. We all wore heavy high-topped shoes that by now have become high fashion, but were then a blatant anachronism. For me, though, a long American interlude, my English-speaking parents, and the resulting irreparable holes in my nativeness compounded the need to 'ungirl' myself with a need to un-Americanise myself.

This dual undertaking, it seemed, should have come closest to gaining me community membership, when I served in the army, particularly in the summer of 1967, when it was fighting a war and I was part of it. In the breaks between long work shifts, I would stand at the edge of the bluff and watch fires in the fields below. It looked to me like the whole Galilee was burning. It would be many years yet before kibbutz homes had phones in them, and I had no way of contacting people I loved in Ma'ayan Baruch, or close friends I had in several other kibbutzim. The thuds of falling shells, muffled, like slamming heavy doors, were an almost constant background theme. After working straight through the night in one gruelling two-day shift, the structure of my routine task, continual surveillance of events in the border zone, began to disintegrate. The type of information I could collect and provide became non-existent or irrelevant when people in tanks, on foot, and in helicopters and troop carriers were actually moving en masse inside and through the zone. For want of ways to be useful and needed, I think, we stayed glued to the receivers and our habitual workshifts. At some point in midmorning a day or two later – and I'm purposely citing not the historical date (which I could verify from official records) but rather my foggy, confused mental, and emotional record – I heard shouts from the cabins around me. People were running out into the lane that cut through the middle of the eight or nine wood cabins and prefabricated concrete cubicles that constituted the camp. Six months before, in midwinter, we had all run out into the lane the same way when it started to snow – laughing, opening arms, turning faces up, opening mouths to the magic flakes. Now, in June 1967, one of my close friends, the one with whom I would hitchhike up to the Syrian Heights in less than a week, was the first to hear the announcement: 'We have taken the Old City!' (*Ha'ir ha'atika beyadeynu* – literally, 'the old city is in our hands').

There's a great deal that I don't remember now about those two months thirty-three years ago. First I was confined to the base on alert, waiting … then six days of shelling and listening and smoke and watching flames and planes like a silent film, doing aerobatics over the Syrian Heights ... and then three weeks more before I went home on leave. Most of it is a haze. But these few minutes are very clear in my memory. I stood slightly off to one side, watching over my friend's shoulder as he shouted, excited, over and over 'We have taken the old city!' – precisely quoting the sentence coined and broadcast by state radio, preserving its formal, literary structure, rather than using his own spoken Hebrew, unthinkingly paying his respects to the occasion, acknowledging its solemn importance. I listened to the strange words, listened and found them strange. Alien. Right then, in the middle of it all, I distinctly remember incomprehension. People. People – were killing people. Mechanically. Brutally. This old city – who cared? What difference did it make? I believed the systematic, premeditated, mass killing was supposed to be self-defence, not a means of 'taking' places. What difference did places make? What was making them happy? What could they be so happy, so excited, about? Visibly joyous? They – not 'we'. Looking on from the sidelines of the war, I knew I didn't understand. I knew I wasn't one of that 'we'.

This wasn't a uniform, overriding conclusion. It was a powerful sensation which I would forget and remember, intermittently, even simultaneously, rejecting and yet holding onto it. The emotional habit of longing for belonging was – still is I suppose – very strong. As part of my ongoing belonging project, I would struggle two months later, to be included in my unit's move to the Syrian Heights. Eight years later I would be one of the founders of an innovative communal settlement in the western Galilee. I wouldn't see or take much interest in the implications and mechanics of the state programme settling Jews throughout the rural, largely Palestinian parts of Israel. I was well into my thirties, back in Tel-Aviv, before I began knitting together a coherent dissenting consciousness. And well into my forties before I started allowing myself the use of my American English to write parts of my prose.

By now my belonging project, though still intact, has turned into something else. It has fed the active search for, and formation of, an alternative feminist community. Composed of mostly women and some men, who share various versions of the type of hybrid consciousness this essay has tried to describe, the community is highly politicised and dissenting, but it is also a group of caring and mutually supportive individuals. I'm referring to New Profile, a movement working for the demilitarisation and, as we call it, the civil-isation of Israeli society. Together, we continually study the society around us and take action based on our analyses, moving back and forth between critical discussion, practical actions, and symbolic protest.

This isn't a happy end. The circumstances I live in, we live in, I and we are part of, are deeply problematic. Our constantly increasing awareness makes them all the more painful. Each of us sometimes asks herself,

'What am I doing here?' Recognising our complicity in what goes on around us, perhaps inescapable despite the awareness, is unending and morally charged work.

It isn't a sad end, either. We're putting a lot of joint creative energy into changing the terms of membership in Israeli society. Echoing the silenced impulses of individuals, in some cases lending them form and words, theorising our criticism and anger, accessing the media, catching public interest, creating an organisation that struggles to avoid conventional patterns of power-hierarchy – all of these are hopeful, empowering endeavours. And for me, looking on from the sidelines of the war, has become a point of strength.

Gila Svirsky

Feminist Peace Activism during
the al-Aqsa Intifada

—ᶆ—

My journey into the radical left began in the non-Zionist right. 'Non-Zionist right' may seem like an oxymoron at first blush, but that's because most people who know me today can't picture me coming from the ultra-Orthodox schools of the diaspora, where Zionism was ignored in favour of *Yiddishkeit* (Jewishness). I am, in fact, a product of this very conservative schooling, which emphasised religious observance in the rigid Lithuanian tradition and was devoid of Zionism, not to mention devoid of relevance to my life, as I understood it. My early forms of defiance focused on religious observance.

But while my school and synagogue ignored Israel, my mother was a passionate *Betar* Zionist, a follower of Jabotinsky, who saw the Jewish state as extending to 'both sides of the Jordan', and refused to settle for less. I did not understand the relevance of this in my own life when I moved to Israel in 1966 – under the influence of my mother's fervour – until the war one year later brought about the occupied territories and the rise of the settler movement. I briefly flirted with the idea of moving with my friends to a settlement near Jerusalem (Gush Etzion), but something stopped me. To this day, I don't know what that 'something' was, or I would bottle it for inoculating others against joining the settlement movement. But some general lack of political self-awareness during my twenties and early thirties obscures my memory of why I left the movement. Perhaps the preoccupation of being a mother with young children crowded out any other matters.

My political education began at the New Israel Fund, where I served as director from 1985, and learnt the basics about the injustices and inequalities at the heart of Israeli society. The more thoroughgoing radicalisation and feminisation of my politics began with Women in Black in Jerusalem, which I joined on its third vigil. Standing week after week with those women and listening to anti-female invective – it didn't take long to sign up for feminism. And a progressive politics of peace was not far behind, as the Intifada made explicit the misery of the Palestinians under occupation. Feminism and peace were perfectly meshed in the Women in Black movement.

Women as women – in groups separate from men – began to take an active role in the Israeli peace movement in January 1988, one month after the outbreak of the 'first' Palestinian Intifada, with the formation of the first Women in Black vigils. In this essay, I look at women's peace activism through excerpts from a journal that I have kept over the years. Why did women need 'a peace movement of their own'? I think this first excerpt – although it happened after we women had already been organising on our own – may help explain.

3 January 1999

Subject: Rifle Grenade #400

A group of about a hundred of us from Jerusalem and Tel-Aviv – men and women – travelled to Kifl Hares, a village where two Palestinian homes had been intentionally demolished by the army. When we arrived, we gathered at an access point leading into the village and demanded entry. The soldiers blocked our way and demanded that we leave. Our large group began to walk along the main road towards another access point, knowing full well that we would be blocked. Suddenly, Gail, a woman from Jerusalem, broke ranks and began to walk across the field towards the village. It seemed so simple, and a group of us followed her, spreading out to make it harder for the soldiers to stop us.

The soldiers came at us quickly, grabbing us to prevent our progress. I made a quick head count of them and climbed on a mound to call out, 'There are many more of us than soldiers, just walk through peacefully, no violence'. A few more broke ranks, but soon the soldiers were running back and forth to stop more of us from walking through the field. Against some, the soldiers were more violent than others. Gail was forcefully thrown to the ground. My arm was well twisted. Although the soldiers were blocking us only with their bodies – twisting arms, pushing, grabbing – I guess it was the M16s slung across their backs that prevented more of the larger group from following us. In the melée, seven of us made it past the soldiers and walked the five minutes through the fields into the village.

Inside the village, we walked to the site of one demolition, now a mass of ruins, and found the family and neighbours in the nearby tent where the family of four now lived. Husam, the father, a slight, soft-spoken man, spoke to us as his four-year-old son maintained a tight clutch on his pants. He described how five tear gas canisters (labelled 'Rifle Grenade #400') were lobbed into the home to evict them and their neighbours, who had hunkered down inside. In the ensuing chaos and escape from the fumes, the two-year-old was left behind until the father had raced back in to emerge with his child unconscious from smoke inhalation. Was this the only way to remove unarmed adults and infants from their home?

As he showed us the ruins of his home, I had a call on my cell phone from someone in the group outside, who told us that, following negotiations with the army, an official delegation of the peace activists who had remained behind would be allowed through. Within an hour, we saw a group walking towards us along the access road: Jeff Halper and Amos Gveertz of the Committee Against Home Demolitions, Uri Avnery of Gush Shalom, Ya'akov Manor of Peace Now, and others.

It was at this moment that we looked around at ourselves and were struck by something: Those of us who had taken the risk of breaking through the soldiers to reach the village were all women. All those in the self-appointed 'official delegation' were men. It was food for thought as we moved with them through the village, repeating the 'official tour' of the demolished homes and promising the families that we would return to help in the reconstruction of their homes....

Women have consistently been a large part, if not the majority, of the rank-and-file peace activists in Israel, and have often led the pack in out-of-the-box thinking, as epitomised by Gail's breaking of rank in the above story. In fact, I think even more can be said. Ever since Women in Black began its first vigil in January 1988, women's peace activism in Israel has consistently been more varied, more progressive, and more courageous than the peace activism of the mixed-gender peace groups. It was more varied, because we didn't just hold the occasional rally (the speciality of Peace Now, the largest movement), but also engaged in a wide variety of activities – conferences, lectures, marches, bringing food and medicine to refugee camps, street theatre, dialogue groups, and a seemingly endless series of vigils. It was more progressive because we took radical positions well before the mixed-gender groups did, from 'the PLO is the legitimate representative of the Palestinian people' to 'Jerusalem must be a shared capital'. And it was more courageous because ... well, I have no idea why, but we were. Evidence follows.

It took the women's movement only one month to get together and gear up after the start of the 'al-Aqsa Intifada', currently being waged. We called an emergency meeting and representatives of eight women's peace organisations showed up. We named ourselves the Coalition of Women for a Just Peace, and agreed to work together to support each other's peace work, to avoid scheduling activities that would conflict with each other, and to plan major actions that would include everybody. Here are the names and basic aims of each member of the Coalition:

Bat Shalom is the Israeli side of The Jerusalem Link, an Israeli-Palestinian partnership for peace.

Neled: Women for Co-existence promotes Palestinian-Jewish co-existence.

New Profile: Movement for the Civil-isation of Israeli Society addresses issues of militarism and gives support to conscientious objectors to military service in Israel.

TANDI: The Movement of Democratic Women for Israel is a mass movement of mostly Palestinian women from the north of Israel.

WILPF refers to the Israel chapter of the Women's International League for Peace and Freedom.

Women and Mothers for Peace is the re-grouped Four Mothers movement, which was instrumental in bringing an end to the Israeli occupation of Lebanon.

Women Engendering Peace seeks to promote a culture of peace in Israel.

Women in Black – women dressed in black have stood in vigils throughout Israel for one hour every week for thirteen years calling for an end to the occupation.

At the second meeting of the Coalition, although we were a broad coalition – from Zionist to anti-Zionist and all points in between – we nevertheless managed to hammer out a set of principles that was acceptable to all eight organisations. Here are the principles we approved:

- An end to the occupation.
- The full involvement of women in negotiations for peace.
- Establishment of the state of Palestine side by side with the state of Israel based on the 1967 borders.
- Recognition of Jerusalem as the shared capital of two states.
- Israel must recognise its share of responsibility for the results of the 1948 war, and find a just solution for the Palestinian refugees.
- Opposition to the militarism that permeates Israeli society.
- Equality, inclusion and justice for Palestinian citizens of Israel.
- Equal rights for women and all residents of Israel.
- Social and economic justice for Israel's citizens, and integration in the region.

This co-operative spirit was a direct product of the sense of urgency we each felt about *doing* things, and not just talking. We were determined to use our combined strength to make a powerful statement.

Our first mass event, held at the tail-end of the year 2000, was an unprecedented statement during days that were otherwise filled with violence and horror.

30 December 2000

Subject: On the Way to Crowning Jerusalem with Peace

Yesterday, Israel saw the largest rally for a just peace that has been held since the outbreak of the Intifada three months ago … and it was a joint Israeli-Palestinian event.

Women came in droves from all over Israel – Jewish, Muslim, Christian, and Druze. And despite the 'closure' that Israel had imposed on the occupied territories, Palestinian women and men also managed, by means known only to them, to cross the Green Line and reach us.

The day began in the Notre Dame conference centre located symbolically on the border of Jewish and Palestinian Jerusalem. The walls displayed two huge banners in Hebrew and Arabic: *Women Demand: No to occupation – Yes to a just peace!* We opened with greetings from three international women peace leaders who flew in especially for the occasion: Luisa Morgantini from Italy, Simone Susskind from Belgium, and June Jacobs from the UK. The co-moderators, Hannah Safran from Women in Black and Nabeha Murkus from TANDI, reported to the crowd about solidarity demonstrations being held throughout the world, and relayed greetings from organisations and individuals in a long list of countries.

Women then took the podium one by one, Palestinian and Israeli alternately, to speak movingly and passionately of the suffering as well as the determination to end the bloodshed between our peoples. This was a conference 'of the people', but we were glad to see in the audience three Israeli Members of Knesset (Tamar Gozansky representing the Communist faction in the Hadash party, Naomi Chazan representing the left of centre party Meretz, and Muhammad Barake, also of Hadash) expressing their support for the grassroots work. The simultaneous translations into Hebrew, Arabic, and English allowed each woman to speak in her own language. Particularly noteworthy were the speeches of Michal Pundak-Sagie, an activist from New Profile, who called upon soldiers to refuse orders that their conscience does not allow. and Zahira Kamal, a leading grass-roots spokesperson for Palestinian women in the occupied territories, who declared that the principles of the Coalition of Women for a Just Peace provide a sound basis for peace between our peoples.

From the conference centre, waiting buses moved the entire crowd to Hagar Plaza, the location of Jerusalem's Women in Black vigil, and an estimated 2,000 women filled the entire plaza and spilled over onto the side streets carrying the traditional black hand signs with 'End the Occupation' painted in Hebrew, Arabic, and English. This silent one-hour vigil was an even more dramatic sight than usual, and TV crews from all over the world – even from Israel – were there to capture it. The extreme right wing did their best to infiltrate the ranks, to provoke us and draw attention to themselves. They finally ended up exchanging blows with the police, but were overcome and moved behind barriers – out of sight, mind, and media.

At 2 P.M., the crowd poured out of the plaza and from every corner and side street, and we began our march towards East Jerusalem. Men and women who had joined us from other organisations – Gush Shalom brought its own busload of activists – held aloft their own collection of banners and signs for peace. The sight of the street filled with marchers and voices was overwhelming. Nabila Espanioly from Nazareth grabbed a megaphone and led responsive chanting: 'Peace?' 'YES!' – 'Occupation?' 'NO!' doing renditions in Hebrew, Arabic, English, and even Italian for the delegation of thirty-five who had flown in for the action. Flying high were signs and banners saying 'Palestine side by side with Israel – On the '67 Borders', 'Jerusalem – two capitals for two states', 'The age of generals is over', 'Fund the poor, not settlers', and 'We refuse to be enemies'.

It was breathtaking to be part of that march. But the moment that brought tears to my eyes was when I greeted a man being pushed in a wheelchair beside me and asked if he wanted to hold a sign. In response, he unbuttoned his collar and pointed to a deep scar just below his neck. The man pushing the wheelchair explained: 'We're from Hebron. This is one of the victims of the massacre by Baruch Goldstein. He wanted to join you today'. A victim of the violence who harbours no hatred in his heart. I shook his hand wordlessly.

As we finally all assembled in the park beside the ancient walls of the Old City of Jerusalem, people spread out on the grass, exhilarated, and await the closing ceremony on this unusually warm and sunny winter day. Because of the traffic jams we had caused, the sound system had not yet arrived, but the crowd waited patiently. Meanwhile, four brave young women took banners and actually managed to climb to the top of the wall from inside the Old City – some took the stairs, but one also took quite a daring leap – and made their way to the top of the wall just over our gathering, beside two armed soldiers 'protecting' us. From here, they unfurled four banners down the height of the wall reading 'Shalom', 'Salaam', 'Peace', and 'End the Occupation' in the three languages. The crowd roared its approval and the Old City was crowned the City of Peace for one brief moment – until the soldiers assaulted two of the women and their banners. The women wisely threw the other two banners down to the crowd – to save them, and probably themselves, too. Their bold act was a great moment in modern history. Thank you Naama, Tali, Moran, and Micheline.

Finally, the sound system was set up, and Halla Espanioly spoke movingly of our longing for peace. When Nabila called for a minute of silence in memory of all those who had been killed in recent months, the stillness in the crowd was palpable. Following this, I made a slightly modified Jewish prayer: 'May the Divine Presence give strength to all her peoples, and may she bless all her peoples with peace'. And we all ended by singing 'We Shall Overcome'.

This demonstration was moving and empowering to those who participated, and the Coalition followed it up with less uplifting, but no less dramatic events: a series of actions to protest the so-called 'closure'. Although we invited men and mixed-gender organisations to join us, at this stage, they formed a small minority of those in attendance.

Here's what happened at the 4 February 2001 civil disobedience action that we had the chutzpah to hold in front of Israel's Defence Ministry in Tel-Aviv (written in the wee hours of the next morning):

5 February 2001

Subject: Putting a Closure on Tel-Aviv Tonight

It's 1:30 in the morning, and seventeen of us just returned from the Tel-Aviv lockup, where we had been under arrest since six in the evening, when the police decided they had had enough of women taking control of the streets away from them. It was our demonstration against the cruel 'closure' that Israel has imposed on the occupied territories.

The demonstration was brilliantly conceived by a mostly Tel-Aviv group of the Coalition of Women for a Just Peace. About 500 women were there from all over Israel. We dressed in black and donned black 'sandwich boards' with the word 'Closure' painted in white in three languages (Hebrew, Arabic, and English). We massed outside the entrance gate to Israel's 'pentagon', its 'Defence' Ministry in Tel-Aviv. At the signal, a group of women started to cross the street very slowly, with the intention of slowing traffic through this busy artery. But when the spirit moves you, you respond: A group of women suddenly sat down on the road in a line clear across the street and completely blocked all passage of cars. Within moments, a larger group of women thickened the line, standing with their placards facing the cars – a solid block of 'Closure' signs preventing the drivers from advancing. For us, this was a small representation of what the Palestinians experience every day – being blocked entry and exit from their towns and villages.

The sight was dramatic – some women sitting in a line across the road, others standing behind them with arms linked, and the Closure signs forming a solid black message clear across the road. We started to chant a very powerful set of slogans. Here's the literal translation, though in Hebrew it rhymes and is very strong:

> End the closure in the territories –
> Get out of their bloodstream.
> End the closure in the territories –
> Give jobs to the workers.
> End the closure in the territories –
> Give food to the children.

It was amazing to be part of this powerful line, and to have brought this busy road to a complete standstill.

Then the police drove up, sirens shrieking. They didn't waste time asking for co-operation – they just ploughed in and grabbed, dragging women to the sides and wading in for more. Some women returned to the road as soon as the police let them go, but there were car drivers who took their cues from the police, and tried to use their cars to plough us off the road. I stood facing a car with my sign, and the driver first hit me (gently), then kept moving forward on me. I was not violent, but I wouldn't step to the side. The police dragged some of us off the street many times, but we returned again and again until they suddenly realised what we were doing and began to throw us into paddy wagons. All this was done with, shall I say, excessive force. My body feels bruised all over, and I'm not the only one.

After the police had taken away two carloads, women returned to the road and again sat down and blocked traffic. It was wonderful how they were not intimidated by the previous brutality. They continued for quite a long time, until an hour or so had been spent illustrating for Tel-Aviv drivers the tip of the iceberg of what it means to have a closure imposed on you. We did not, of course, demonstrate how it feels to be cut off from access to medical care, jobs, schools, and family. That they will have to imagine.

At the police station, we were first twelve women and four men who had come to the demonstration. Then they arrested the lawyer who showed up to represent us! The interrogations were civil, though they charged us with everything they could think of: participating in an illegal demonstration, disturbing the peace, blocking traffic, resisting arrest, attacking a police officer, and even (in my case) attacking a car (poor car!). Two of us (including me) admitted to acts of civil disobedience – though not to the accusations of violence – and the rest took advantage of their right to remain silent. Gradually, until about 1 A.M., they released everybody after bail was posted. Many, many thanks to our sister demonstrators, who waited for us the whole time at the station, drove to the airport to find an open post office to post bail, and met us with food and soft drinks when we came out. And thanks to tireless Knesset Member Tamar Gozansky, who came to the station for a solidarity visit. And big, big thanks to Leah Tsemel, human rights lawyer extraordinaire, who stayed with us to the bitter end negotiating with the police for our release, brought enough cash to front bail for everyone, and gave her professional services completely pro bono as her contribution to the cause.

I'm not sure how much will be in the media tomorrow. There were TV cameras from French and Belgian stations, and lots of still photographers. We had excellent coverage on the radio, with an accurate explanation of who we were and why we were doing it. We think the Israeli newspapers tomorrow will have some coverage. I hope so. The Israeli media have a terrible track record of covering women's peace actions, even though the women's actions are much more dramatic, progressive, and even larger than the mixed-gender demonstrations. Could it have something to do with the fact that we are, after all, only women?

I don't think we stopped the closure tonight, but we did let Tel-Aviv know what we think about it. The only way to maintain a brutal occupation is by brutally suppressing awareness of it, and criticism. We must not let that succeed.

Rather than put off the women, this confrontation seemed to energise and further empower Coalition members. And, mind you, I am talking about hundreds of women, not just a handful. For our next event, we decided to draw attention to the blockade of Bethlehem, which prevents Palestinians from entering Israel for jobs, school, medical attention, among other things. Although no one was arrested this time, more men did join us and actually got credit in the media for organising it!

25 February 2001

Subject: Protesting the Closure Today

Today felt like another good demonstration against the 'closure' of the occupied territories.

About 300 Israelis, mostly women but with a growing contingent of men, showed up at the Jerusalem-Bethlehem border crossing to protest the so-called 'closure'.

'Closure' is sometimes called 'blockade' or 'siege', because the Israeli army actually encircles Palestinian towns and prevents residents from freely leaving or entering. Imagine how frustrating it must feel to have your freedom of movement obstructed – picture yourself prevented from leaving your own city because foreign soldiers have bulldozed the roads and set down concrete slabs. But beyond the insult, there are serious problems: access to medical care, food and supplies, education, and jobs. Several sick Palestinians who were held up at these barriers pending a decision by the young Israeli soldiers on duty on whether to let them through, actually died as a result of the delay, including a baby. It is also shocking for me as an Israeli to realise that the closure provides virtually no security dividend to Israel; it is simply a deliberate act of intimidation.

The Coalition of Women for a Just Peace held its first 'closure' protest opposite the Defence Ministry in Tel-Aviv three weeks ago (ending in police violence, seventeen arrests, and practically no media exposure). Today's event was fairly quiet; no one was arrested, but the Israeli media announced that we 'tried to force our way through the barriers'. Well, not quite.

It was a sunny day, and many Israelis had come from Tel-Aviv and other cities. Soon after the demonstration began, both sides of the road were already lined with demonstrators carrying or wearing signs 'Closure kills', 'Closure starves', 'Closure creates enemies', and the usual 'Stop the Occupation'. Our presence, of course, caused the quick mobilisation of a larger contingent of soldiers, who now manned the barrier. At the signal, the protesters stepped off the sidewalk and filled the road, marching quietly towards the checkpoint. We walked slowly, in a dignified manner. The soldiers began to scramble to prevent our getting through. At the checkpoint, they formed a cordon across the road, and our forward movement was stopped. We stood there facing them and began to chant our powerful, rhythmic slogans.

During the chanting, journalists from Israel, Europe, and the United States had some good opportunities to photograph this confrontation. One young man in our group was forcefully shoved to the ground by a soldier, but after we pointed out to the soldier that he was on candid camera, he controlled himself much better. Other than that, it was a completely non-violent action, and therefore powerful. From there, the entire group walked 100 metres back to hold up our signs to the drivers headed to the 'bypass roads', which lead to the settlements.

On the way to the event today, a friend of mine complained that no one had called her about the demonstration, but she had fortunately read about it in the newspaper ad. 'You're making a revolution', she said, 'and I don't want to be left out'.

The news this evening had good shots of the confrontation. The soldiers were armed with their M 16s and we were armed with our signs and determination. In the long run, it's not much of a contest. The subjugation of a people is always doomed to failure – *sic transit tyrannis*. Ultimately the closure and all the apparatus of occupation will be dismantled. It's only a matter of time … and of how many more people will have to suffer first.

After this demonstration, we decided we would definitely cross the line into defiance of the occupation – what the literature calls 'resistance'. This first action was now done in full co-operation with several mixed-gender organisations.

23 March 2001

Subject: Not Co-operating with Evil

I wish I had not just gotten the phone call I did – this story would have had a better ending.

As you probably know, the Israeli army has laid siege to many cities, towns, and villages in the occupied territories. One way they do this is by digging trenches across the roads leading in or out, making them impassable by cars. Where once soldiers merely patrolled these exits and granted permission to enter or leave, today the trenches prevent all access by vehicle. This serves no security function whatsoever – it prevents Palestinians from having access to each other, not to Israel. It is but a cruel and arbitrary way to assert power and control.

Today's action was the next level of resistance, and the Coalition of Women worked hand in hand with three other organisations: Rabbis for Human Rights, Gush Shalom, and the Committee Against House Demolitions. The idea was to come to a village under siege and physically fill in the trench, thereby making the road passable. The army was clearly intent on preventing that from happening.

We chose to lift the siege on Rantis, a peaceful town of 3,000. Rantis has no doctor and no employment opportunities; under siege, there is no access to medical care and almost total unemployment. One woman gave birth at the trench when she was unable to get out for medical attention, and seven students have lost a semester of university studies.

Together we were about 300 activists who set out on buses this morning. Most of us were Israelis, but there was a significant presence of internationals, too, including the undauntable CPT-ers (Christian Peacemakers Team) who work in Hebron. On each bus, one person led a discussion about the strategy of non-violent direct action, the importance of not provoking soldiers, and the commitment to breaking the law openly and non-violently. We talked about rights under arrest and interrogation, and our responsibility for one another's safety and well-being. On our bus, I shared the words of Gandhi, 'Non-cooperation with evil is a sacred duty'.

When we reached the perimeter of the village, we began to march with our shovels and hoes towards the trench, which was being blocked by a line of soldiers. But we were many more activists than the soldiers; they didn't open fire, and we easily passed through. As soon as we reached the trench, we swarmed all over, shovelling rocks and dirt into it, trying to fill it up. It seemed an impossible task, as we had few tools and the trench was gouged quite deeply from one side to the other. What's worse, the ground was very hard, studded with rocks; it was very difficult to loosen earth for use as fill.

Soon after we began work, someone found a second trench about fifty metres (roughly 160 feet) further along. Half the group broke away to work on filling up that trench, and we realised it would be twice the work to break the siege on Rantis. But then, suddenly, soldiers swooped down on those of us holding tools and grabbed them out of our hands. We began to chant 'Dai LaKibbush', which means 'End the Occupation'. Some struggled not to release their shovels, others put up less resistance. Soon, the soldiers had confiscated every single tool we had brought and arrested four of us.

In my recollection, there was no pause at that point and no discussion about what to do. We just all got down and with our bare hands began to scratch out handfuls of dirt and rocks, throwing them into the trenches. Some of us used rocks to loosen the ground, others tried sticks. Some held posters (reading 'Dismantle the Settlements') on the ground like big dustpans, and others pushed pebbles and dirt onto them, for transfer into the trench. Some of the children from Rantis came out and joined us, and we worked together like that in the hot sun for over two hours. When it was over, everyone was amazed to see that we had actually filled in both trenches, and made the road passable.

We did a little speechmaking on top of what had once been a trench, vowing to continue to subvert the mechanisms of occupation. We admired our persistence and co-operative spirit. We laughed at how covered with dirt and mud we were. And just as we started to plan the release of our partners sitting in the army van nearby, just as the army actually let them go, seeing we were finished with our work and on our way out. They even returned our tools when we boarded the buses.

And now at home, freshly showered and sitting down to tell you about this small victory, I get a call from Dina, who had made friends with one of the villagers. The army had returned, the Palestinian told her, and used their heavy machinery to dig out fresh trenches. We expected that. And now, he said, they had also placed large concrete slabs in front of the trenches, which could never be moved by bare hands and grit alone. The truck that had brought these slabs had driven off the road, deliberately destroying crops in the fields. And one villager had been beaten and his car window smashed.

These are more than just reprisals against the Palestinians. They are a message from the army to us: This will happen every time you do something like this.

Tomorrow, five of us will go to Rantis to document the new damage and talk to the villagers. We'll also be thinking about how to continue to subvert the oppression without jeopardising the Palestinians themselves. It won't be easy or simple but, as Israelis, we've got to figure out a way to stop co-operating with evil.

This action was followed by a series of really dangerous events in which two or three women participated each time, with Neta Golan, a member of the Coalition, at the heart of it all. Neta is an Israeli woman who, at the invitation of some Palestinians, virtually moved to a village in the occupied territories, where she works as a one-woman human rights defender. Here are two stories of the bravery of this small group of women.

2 April 2001

Subject: Protecting the Olive Trees

A short story that is not over yet:

Yesterday two massive bulldozers arrived at the Palestinian village of Dir Istya to knock down 1500 olive trees that provide a livelihood for many of these villagers. The army used the excuse of 'security' – preventing stone throwing from the cover of the trees – although these were young trees and could hardly provide cover. Court appeals had been filed in previous weeks to prevent this destruction, but all appeals were dismissed and the villagers knew their orchard was threatened. When a settler was recently injured badly by a rock thrown nearby, a decision was made to demolish the trees at once, as a kind of collective retribution against the whole village. Yesterday the bulldozers came and began their work.

Not far from here, however, is another Palestinian village where Neta Golan, 29, spends considerable energy monitoring army and settler abuse of the local Palestinian villages, and intervening whenever possible. Neta is often a one-woman show, calling out to the Israeli soldiers from inside the Palestinian village to stop them from shooting in. This has worked a couple of times, perhaps because the soldiers were shocked to hear a fellow-Israeli speaking Hebrew to them from inside the firing zone.

When Neta heard that the bulldozers had arrived, she ran to the site together with two other young women – Zipporah Ryter, 28, an American, and Yasmin Khayal, 22, a German Palestinian. The villagers were already there, and together they all walked in front of one bulldozer and sat down. It stopped in its tracks. After some negotiations, threats, and determined responses by those resisting, one of the soldiers approached the Palestinians and explained that the army would not bulldoze any more, but the Palestinians had to move so the bulldozer could turn around. As soon as the Palestinians gave the bulldozer room to manoeuvre, it promptly drove through and mauled another tree. The Palestinians and the women returned to block the bulldozers.

Soon army reinforcements arrived and outnumbered the Palestinians and women. They forcibly arrested the three women, who refused to move of their own accord, and also one Palestinian man who had been photographing them. As a result of their action, 'only' 150 trees had been bulldozed. And meanwhile, the legal department of the local Quaker centre managed to get a temporary injunction to prevent the further destruction of the orchard, pending more legal activity.

Late last night, the three women were released on bail. Now the legal work has to run its course. The resistance is prepared in case that fails.

6 April 2001

Subject: Four Arrests and a Tree

Update:

At about noon today, the bulldozers returned. Neta Golan and Yasmin Khayal were waiting for them. Neta and Yasmin had wrapped chains around their necks and bodies, and chained themselves to olive trees in the path of the bulldozer. The soldiers demanded that they leave, but the women refused. The soldiers went off to find tools to break the chains. Villagers watching the confrontation knelt down in prayer. Upon their return, the soldiers managed fairly quickly to break through the chains, 'liberate' the trees, and arrest both Neta and Yasmin. Two other young Israeli peace activists who had just arrived on the scene, Shelly Nativ and Eyal Oron, were arrested with them.

After fairly brief interrogations, Shelly and Eyal were released, but they remained on site to support Neta and Yasmin. Neta and Yasmin refused to sign the terms of release – that they would not enter any 'closed military zones'. So now, twelve hours later, they remain under arrest and are currently being moved to the Kishon jail near Haifa, where there are 'cells for women'.

If you live near Kishon, you will be performing a patriotic deed by going to Kishon right now and welcoming Neta and Yasmin with a voice of solidarity. They will undoubtedly be spending the Passover Seder in jail.

P.S. After all that, a loss of only one tree was reported – the army bulldozer backed into it while trying to turn around. But it's not over yet.

Well, Neta and Yasmin were released from jail, though none of these stories are yet 'over', as long as the Israeli occupation is not over.

In this essay I have tried to give a sense of how the Israeli women's peace movement – united as the Coalition of Women for a Just Peace – has been the most vibrant and daring part of peace action in Israel since the al-Aqsa Intifada broke out at the end of September 2000. In addition to the growing subversiveness of Coalition actions, we have also taken the lead in 'the usual' types of demonstrations:

- A mass rally on the main road through the Palestinian region called Wadi Ara on 21 November 2000, demanding equality for Israel's Palestinian citizens after thirteen were killed by the Israeli police in October 2000;
- Marking International Women's Day on 8 March 2001 with a march through Jaffa demanding women's rights and explaining the connection between the oppression of women and the occupation; and
- Showing solidarity for Palestinian Land Day on 30 March 2001 by participating in the large rally in the Palestinian town of Sakhnin in the north.

In addition, the Coalition has 'spun off' a new group that calls itself *Machsom* (checkpoint) Watch, in which thirty women monitor at the checkpoints to reduce the abuse and humiliation to which some Palestinians are subject by some Israeli soldiers as the Palestinians try to enter Israel for work, school, medical treatment, or other reasons.

And yet despite this impressive collection of activities, and our best efforts notwithstanding, the media have ignored our activities or ascribed them to the other, 'mixed' movements. This has been frustrating and sometimes even infuriating. We are left trying to get our message out primarily by e-mail and independent media web sites (such as indymedia http://www.indymedia.org.il/), but we remain largely invisible to the Israeli public. Some of this 'ignoring' us has to do with the unwillingness of the Israeli media to portray activity that falls outside the consensus, and some of it – especially when an action does get coverage, but someone else gets credit for it – has to do with how women continue to be silenced or regarded as marginal to the main business of civil society.

The Coalition has pushed many women past their inhibitions of just half a year ago. Participating in non-violent civil disobedience has been tremendously empowering to all of us, I think. We seem to get a tremendous surge of energy from defying a brutal authority in the name of morality and justice, thereby placing ourselves squarely in the noble tradition of Gandhi, Martin Luther King, and Nelson Mandela. We end up being women who are not only bold and vibrant, but are actually starting a revolution.

I don't know what the coming actions will look like, but we have clearly moved beyond polite society. The story has yet to be fully told.

Note

'In Tow: A Mother's and Daughter's Gendered Departures and Returns'

Excerpts from *Maps of Women's Goings and Stayings* by Rela Mazali, © 2001 by the Board of Trustees of the Leland Stanford Jr. University, by permission of Stanford University Press, www.sup.org.

References

'In Tow: A Mother's and Daughter's Gendered Departures and Returns'

Ben-Yehuda, Netiva. 1981. *1948: Between Counts*. Jerusalem: Keter.
Blunt, Alison, and Gillian Rose. 1994. 'Introduction: Women's colonial and postcolonial geographies'. In Alison Blunt and Gillian Rose (eds.), *Writing Women and Space: Colonial and Postcolonial Geographies*. New York and London: The Guilford Press.
Chomsky, Noam. 1983. *The Fateful Triangle: The United Stated, Israel and the Palestinians*. Boston: South End Press.
Enloe, Cynthia. 1993. *The Morning After: Sexual Politics at the End of the Cold War*. Berkeley and London: California University Press.
Gluzman, Michael. 1997. 'The longing for heterosexuality: Zionism and sexuality in *Altneuland*'. *Theory and Criticism* 11 (winter): 145–62.
Gordon, Colin (ed.). 1980. *Michel Foucault: Power/Knowledge – Selected Interviews and Other Writings, 1972–1977*. Brighton: Harvester.
Harding, Sandra. 1986. *The Science Question in Feminism*. Ithaca and London: Cornell University Press.
Kirby, Kathleen M. 1996. 'Re-mapping subjectivity: Cartographic vision and the limits of politics'. In Nancy Duncan (ed.), *BodySpace: Destabilising Geographies of Gender and Sexuality*. London and New York: Routledge
Kosh-Zohar, Talila. [Forthcoming]. 'She walked no fields: Women's representation in texts of the founding generation'. In Dov Sadan (ed.), *Studies in Hebrew Literature*. Vol. 5: *Representations of the War of Independence in Israeli Culture and Literature*. Tel-Aviv: Katz Institute, Tel-Aviv University. [Hebrew]
Mazali, Rela. 1993. 'Military service as initiation rite'. *Challenge* 4 (4): 36–7.
———. 2001. 'Ninth visit: Bookmaps and housebooks'. In Rela Mazali, *Maps of Women's Goings and Stayings*. Stanford: Stanford University Press.
Okin, Susan Moller. 1989. *Justice, Gender and the Family*. New York: Basic Books.
Pollock, Griselda. 1994. 'Territories of desire: Reconsiderations of an African childhood'. In G. Robertson, M. Mash, L. Tickner, J. Bird, B. Curtis, and T. Putnam (eds.), *Travelers' Tales: Narratives of Home and Displacement*. London and New York: Routledge.

FIVE

Exile as an Oppositional Locus

Nira Yuval-Davis

The Contaminated Paradise

—ᘯ—

'Daddy, look there, there stands *an Arab!*' My small hand tightened con-
vulsively onto my father's big one. There the man stood, wearing a white
gallabiyya, his head covered with a kafiyyeh.

An Arab. And the 1948 war just recently finished, a period of sirens,
and fear, and sleeping at night in the shelter which functioned during the
day also as my nursery school. I 'knew' that the seven armies of the Arabs
had invaded our Land of Israel and wanted to throw us all to the sea, but
our small but brave army had defeated them all and now we have our
own state. We all sat around the radio listening to the votes of the UN
Assembly, and when the required two-thirds of the votes supported us
my parents started to laugh and hug each other and me and my sister and
shout 'We have a state! We have a state!' and everybody went out to the
streets and laughed and danced. I remember finally lying in my bed in
the dark, in the co-operative housing estate where we had our apartment
behind Dizengoff street, the main focus of Tel-Aviv's night life at the time,
listening to all the shouts and singing of the celebrating people.

Then came the war, with very little laughing and dancing, But now it's
over. And yet – there stood *an Arab!*

And then my father told me something that calmed all my fears, and
my hand relaxed its desperate grip.

'Don't worry, Nira'le. During the war all the bad Arabs ran away. The
Arabs that are still here in Israel are the good Arabs'.

'The good Arabs'. If so, wondered my sixteen-year-old self, twelve
years later, why is my mother hysterical because I have an Arab Druze
boyfriend, a law student whom I met when we visited the Druze village
Rama in the Galilee with the 'Youth for Youth' organisation? The relationship broke up shortly afterwards because I was too emotionally young to
handle the intense declarations of love that Essam kept on directing my

way. When I heard that his cousin, a poet, had refused to serve in the Israeli army, unlike most Druze men at the time, I used this information as a lever to end our relationship. Shortly after that, a friend showed me a small news item about Essam having disappeared, suspected of having run away to a kibbutz with his Jewish girlfriend (me?). Ironically, years later, friends from Rama told me that he actually went to Lebanon as a secret Israeli agent and was eventually killed by Palestinian guerrillas.

'The good Arabs'. If so, wondered my eighteen-year-old self, why am I the subject of a special security investigation in the army? After finishing the basic training of my national draft, I was sent to work in the offices of the Military Government Headquarters while waiting for the officers' course I was to be sent on, to start. It was considered a wonderful job – I would not even have to wear military uniform. However, at the end of my first day there, my new boss struck up some supposedly casual small talk with me. Among other questions, he asked me what I thought about the Military Government system. My innocent eighteen-year-old self answered him casually that I didn't think the military government and the travel restrictions applied to the whole Israeli Palestinian population were just, as it was collective punishment. Let them follow or even restrict those they suspected of being a 'fifth column' – but why restrict them all? As a result of this answer I spent a month subjected to further security investigations and attempts to convince me I was wrong. Now that I had to start thinking about it, I became really convinced I was right! They gave me a low security ranking, which doomed me never to attain a higher rank than 'private' in the military. Instead of attending the officers training course, I had to spend the rest of my time in the army (until I escaped to alternative service in a farm near the Dead Sea) as a typist in the central army garage in Tel-Aviv. I typed letters summoning different generals' cars for the weekly maintenance day and was alternatively petted or bullied by my boss. He used to cry on my shoulder about his wife, and then send me to polish the glass on the top of his desk after he put his greasy hands on it. That's when I developed my extreme aversion to arbitrary power – and to football games, the analysis of which constituted the exclusive topic of discussion (except for flirtations and sexual harassment, of course) of the military chauffeurs who were always gathered in our office.

'The good Arabs'. So why had Levi Eshkol, the prime minister of Israel (and the father of my best friend in nursery school) formally declared the initiation of a programme for the 'Judaisation' of the Galilee and approved of massive confiscations of Palestinian lands in order to establish the Jewish city of Karmiel amidst them?

As a student at the Hebrew University in Jerusalem I joined the movement against the military government and the land dispossession of Palestinian citizens of Israel. I was persuaded to become active instead of just hating what was happening by Uri Davis, whom I was later married to for a period of about ten years. Karmiel was established, but the military government was cancelled in 1966 and no more land confiscations took place during the following two years. We thought we were the winners.

And then the 1967 war took place, followed by the massive occupation and collective victory euphoria of a large majority of the Israelis.

It seemed that what we had fought against in the Galilee was just a dress rehearsal for what was to happen in the occupied territories.

I grew up in a co-operative housing estate at the heart of Tel-Aviv where only members of the Histadrut (the Zionist labour union) were allowed to live. Every Independence Day my father would put out the Israeli flag, and on May Day we had both the red flag and the Israeli flag waving in the wind. When the state of Israel celebrated its tenth anniversary we, the children of the housing estate, decorated the building with little flags and brightly coloured paper chains. I remember a passerby asking us what public authority was organising the decorations, and the contempt we felt for his question. *We* were the public, *we* were the state, *we* were the nation. Our parents, who had participated in the struggle against the British and the Arabs and for the establishment of the Israeli state, had no hobbies – the state was their hobby, the primary signifier of their lives.

The political differences among the people I knew when growing up spanned between centre-labour and left-centre labour Zionism. My questioning, as a teenager, first took me out of the labour youth movement when I decided I was not going to join a kibbutz when I 'grew up'. I felt then that life in the kibbutz would be too tame, too conformist and consisted too much of being part of the herd. The understanding of the national, ethnic, and class role of the kibbutz in the Zionist project came much later. Questioning, as mentioned above, made me a low security army typist instead of the officer I was going to be, like my older sister. And there were more shocks on the way as I became, for many years, the 'black sheep' of my family and my peer group.

It was shocking to discover that I had more in common with the non-Jewish hippies (the first non-Jews I had ever met in my life, except for Israeli Palestinians) that I met while serving the second year of my national service in a farm near the Dead Sea, than with all the people I grew up with and went to school with.

The process of demystification of all the naturalised nationalist history and perceptions took years to unravel. I remember hearing Professor Yeshayahu Leibowitz, who was teaching us a course on 'mind and body' as part of my psychology degree, state assertively that it was impossible for Joseph Trumpeldor, the one-armed folk hero of the Zionist settlement, to have actually said 'It's good to die for our country' as his last words before he died. People don't say such things just before they die, Leibowitz argued. And I, with all the supposed political and intellectual sophistication of my early twenties' self, felt a shock when another myth I was brought up with was exploded.

The place where most of these myths were attacked was a historical series of seminars organised by Matzpen, the Israeli Socialist organisation, which I chose to study for my MA dissertation. It was there that I heard for the first time an analysis of Zionism as a colonial settler movement. And it was there that I heard for the first time details of what Israeli scholars called many years later the revisionist history of what actually happened during the settlement period and the establishment of the Israeli state.

It took me years, however, to 'translate' this intellectual and historical body of knowledge into an emotional one. By necessity, this journey from being brought up at the heart of the Zionist establishment to the anti-Zionist left, involved my leaving the country. Only by being exposed to life in different, more pluralist societies, with different naturalised assumptions about human relations (although with their own forms of racialisations), could I really transcend the parameters of the social reality in which I grew up.

However, two emotional encounters, with two Palestinian friends, played crucial roles in this process.

The first encounter took place a couple of years after Uri and I had moved to Boston in the early seventies. Fouzi, an Israeli poet and journalist friend whom we befriended at the Nina Di-Nur forum (the first Jewish-Palestinian dialogue forum in the sixties), came to stay with us for a while after leaving Israel. He accompanied us to a meeting of the Israeli Students Association, to which we were invited to discuss the political situation. After a long and heated debate concerning the realities of the Israeli occupation and the need for full Israeli withdrawal, we went to a café in Harvard Square. I was feeling high, as I felt I had managed to argue my position successfully. So was Uri. Fouzi, however, was much quieter than usual and sipped his coffee with a sober face.

I asked him what was the matter. He looked at me for a long time and then said quietly that until that evening he had thought we were good and close friends. 'Of course we are', I protested. (Later on when our son Gul was born, we chose Fouzi as his godfather.) 'If this is so', answered Fouzi, 'why don't you want to live in the same state, let alone the same neighbourhood as me, just because I am Palestinian and you're Jewish? I have just heard you this evening explain to the Israeli students that the solution to the Israeli-Palestinian conflict is a partition of the land and the population into two states – Israeli and Palestinian'.

I was silent. I looked around us in the café, with its usual ethnic and racial mixture of Harvard Square, and suddenly something shifted in my guts. He was right. While protesting against the Israeli occupation, I still naturalised my position as a member of the hegemonic national collectivity in Israel and Fouzi's as a minority one. According to such a construction, he was right – in order for his positioning to be of equal to mine, he would have to move to the Palestinian state. Otherwise he would have to accept his position as an outsider in his own country.

Never again did I take my hegemonic membership of Israeli society for granted. Never again did I collude in the grand delusion of overlapping boundaries implied by the hyphen in the term 'nation-state'. And in terms of the Israeli-Palestinian conflict, I would later not necessarily object to the two-states solution – under certain historical conditions there may not be a better short-term solution. However, never again did I have any illusion that such a state division could solve the Israeli-Palestinian national question (especially in relation to the Israeli Palestinians), nor was I 'naturally' part of the 'common destiny' of the Israeli Jewish community. With all their faults and their various racialisations, I have come to appreciate living in pluralist societies such as the US and Britain (or, at least, in some enclaves in these societies).

The second shift I made in this direction was more complex, less intellectual, and more painful, penetrating deeper childhood strata in my psyche.

Rafiq (not his real name) and I met in London, at a political meeting on the Israeli occupation. He said such wise things. He sat a couple of rows behind me – I looked back – tall, handsome, with a high forehead, shining eyes, a lovely smile. I felt the joy of meeting him, a kindred spirit, an attractive man. We met for dinner, we ended up in bed – his bed – that evening. We talked. We made love. I don't remember how much we laughed.

What is clear is that when we met a few more times, we laughed less and less. There was a growing sense of unease between us. It was focused on the fact that I was a single mother, and that he didn't seem to like my son. I didn't like this at all.

And I didn't want my son to find him in my bed. At the time we were living in a shared collective household – an old, drafty, unheated large space above an optician in Hackney. I sent Rafiq out of my bed at three o'clock in the morning, to sleep on the sofa downstairs in the living room. He didn't like this at all.

We finally talked about it. He told me that he found children a problem and did not intend to ever have children of his own. Indeed, a couple of years later, when another anti-Zionist Israeli Jewish woman he befriended became pregnant with his child without his consent, he tried to persuade her not to have the child; having failed, he refused to recognise or meet the child. Nor did he ever have children with the Palestinian woman he eventually married.

He told me that this was connected with him being abandoned by his own mother as a child, and that he had never forgiven her for that, although he had met her – once – as an adult.

And then it came out. His mother had abandoned him during the 1948 war. She ran away when the Jewish forces advanced towards the village, and left him, a four-year-old child, behind. He was rescued by other members of the family and grew up in a different Arab country than the one she fled to.

'Which village was it', I asked, unsuspectingly.

'Oh, you might not know it, it doesn't exist anymore. A fishing village on the Mediterranean coast – Tantura'.

Tantura. Tantura? My magical childhood paradise?!

Tantura.

On one side lay the prosperous veteran kibbutz Nakhsholim, on the other, the new moshav, Dor, populated mostly by Greek Jewish fishermen, and behind there were some remnants of a glass factory built by Baron D. E. Rothschild at the beginning of the century.

And on the beach, overlooking the bay, the inlets, the islets, were the abandoned, half-ruined houses of the ghost village of Tantura.

A good friend of my parents worked in the municipality of Ramat Gan. For some reason this municipality had some property rights over the abandoned houses of Tantura. So it was that our families were able to rent one of these houses for the summer.

Not many people stayed there. I remember an opera singer who occupied a room on the roof in one of the only buildings that still had a second floor, one or two other families, and then us. We were three families occupying a big building with a big yard, a bustan, a walled garden. We, the children and our mothers, stayed there for about a month in the summer, and our fathers joined us for long weekends.

Tantura – where I learnt to swim in the sea, learnt the joy of empowerment and freedom, swimming in the deep, but calm waters towards the Seagull Islet; where I watched beautiful sunsets and starry skies, with the sun and the moon at different times of day and night projecting magic pathways across the water in which I could swim. Tantura, where I experienced a sense of adventure of exploring all the ruins – Palestinian and Roman (there was an ancient port there) – in and outside the water, accepting them both unquestioningly as naturalised relics of the past; where I escaped to a shady corner in the bustan, eating grapes and reading a favourite book; where my parents stopped being harassed, stressed city people and became fun people. I shall never forget the evening when we all lit a fire and sang and danced around it *'Yesh Lanu Taish'* ('We have a he-goat') and my mother laughed so much that – as she confessed to me – she peed in her pants!

Tantura – my childhood paradise.

I could never again meet my Palestinian lover after that night. The child in me hated him. He invaded, dispossessed, tainted Tantura. He took away my childhood haven, the sheltered, protected corner of Paradise. He took away the last vestige of my innocence, the innocence of the child of the colonial settler society.

Years later, I decided I must visit Tantura again. How would it look to me as an adult, no longer innocent, after all these years?

The sea, the sand, the little islets still seemed beautiful. The seagulls I had named my son after still circled over the water, defending their islet nesting areas from possible invaders. The remnants of the Roman port were still there, some of them reconstructed by archaeologists who had worked there over the years.

Unlike during the time of my childhood paradise, Palestinian fishermen were again working on the beach. They came from the one Palestinian village that did survive in the area – on the Carmel hillside – El Fridees. The origin of the name El Fridees in Arabic is Firdaus, which means Paradise – a coincidence? I found out later that those inhabitants of Tantura who survived and did not escape to Arab countries moved to El Fridees.

The local kibbutz and moshav did not engage in sea fishing anymore – too much hard work, too little profit. Tourism has become one of their main sources of income. Where the ruins of Tantura once stood, where the bustan used to grow, now stood prefab beach chalets inhabited by holiday makers. One could never guess that this was once the fishing village where the boy who became the man I knew was first born and then abandoned. Nor could one guess that this was the romantic ruinous paradise where I once spent some magical summers with my family and friends.

Except for one thing: the mosque still stood there among the prefabs – full of rubbish and smelling of urine.

Apparently there is a law forbidding the destruction of 'holy places'.

And Israel is a state of law...

With my narcissist innocence taken away, I was ready to view Israel and the Israeli-Palestinian conflict with somewhat more detached eyes. Things fell into place when I, almost accidentally, went on a lecture tour to visit Australia (following my then lover Stephen and meeting my present – for the last fifteen years – partner, Alain). The water in the bathtub swirled down the plughole in the other direction, and cute koala bears swung on the top branches of the trees near Hanging Rock, but the territory was familiar, and not just because of the scorching sun. This was another settler society, with dominant settlers, indigenous aborigines, and racialised ethnic minorities of later immigrants. Situating the historical case of Israel and Palestine alongside other settler societies – as I eventually did in the book I edited on the subject with my friend Daiva Stasiulis who grappled with similar issues in Canada – made it easier to understand the issues involved in a more comparative way, from the contested claims on the country between natives and settlers to the complex and racialised hierarchies among the settlers themselves.[1] It also helped me to start the process of healing in my relationship to the society I grew up in. I suppose this has been a process of maturation similar to that of adults forgiving their parents for not being as perfect as they would have liked them to be. It did not make me oppose less what was going on, but my opposition had a little less zeal of 'exceptionalism'. Being involved in global networks of women in militarised conflict zones (such as Sri Lanka and the former Yugoslavia), and with more general anti-racist and anti-fundamentalist movements, had its impact.

Of course, it was not only I who changed. The overall collectivist ideology started to weaken in Israel, and Israeli society became more fragmented ethnically, religiously, politically. While there were probably more fascist and fundamentalist groupings in the population than ever before, there were also processes of opening up and liberalisation. The 'other' Israeli history that I first heard of in Matzpen seminars has become part of mainstream 'revisionist' Israeli history and sociology. Among the many revelations was the story of the massacre the Israeli army committed in Tantura during the 1948 war. Most importantly, after the 1991 Gulf War, the mainstream establishment in Israel started to understand that it could never win by military means alone. If war is diplomacy by other means, Rabin, Peres, and others have come to look at peace as an alternative means of gaining and consolidating Israel's security and domination.

Things were developing also on the Palestinian side. The Intifada consolidated processes of nation-building and of civil and political empowerment. Then, after the fall of the Soviet Union and the ensuing US domination in the region, more and more Palestinians came to the conclusion that they would need to follow the Zionist movement's example by accepting historical compromises in order to consolidate their state apparatus. When the 'peace process' was started by negotiations in Washington D.C., I asked Laila Shahid, then the PLO representative in the Netherlands (where I was staying at the time as a visiting research fellow at the Institute for Social Studies in the Hague), why the PLO had agreed to take part in discussions under such disadvantaged conditions. 'This is post-modern politics', answered Laila. 'We talk, therefore we exist'. Indeed, after the Gulf War, with the stoppage of funding from the Arab states and the political credibility of the PLO seriously damaged because of its support for Iraq, this seemed to be the way forward.

This is not the place to analyse the ins and outs of the 'peace process'. It is important to point out, however, that when the dialogue shifted from the open space of the formal dialogue in Washington into the behind-closed-doors Oslo process, its character changed and its ability to contribute to a wide transformative social movement on both sides was seriously hampered. Instead, it became an instrument, on the one hand, for Israel to impose and consolidate the benefits of occupation without some of its most expensive military and political costs. On the other hand, it helped to consolidate a corrupt and undemocratic regime on the Palestinian side. It established an atmosphere of complacency in Israel, as if the peace had already arrived and Israel did not have to pay any significant price for it. It also fostered a higher and bitterer level of frustration among the Palestinians who had gone along with the beginning of the process with growing expectations for the end of the occupation.

When I first visited Israel after the Oslo agreement, people were 'drunk' with peace victory similar to their war victory drunkenness after the 1967 war. I was astounded to hear some respectable sociology professors argue at a sociological conference that Israel's relations with its near neighbours – from Palestine to Syria – have been solved and that the real problem for Israel would be Arab countries further afield, such as Iraq and Libya. I discovered that I could still get angry more easily in Israel than anywhere else.

However, the changes in the Israeli political climate were generally kind to me personally. People like me gradually stopped being treated as traitors and outcasts, and I was even invited as a keynote speaker to one of the annual conferences of the Israeli Sociological Association. Moreover, I also gradually discovered an academic community, mostly of younger scholars, who have been working within a paradigm similar to mine of Israel as a settler society, and who have been allowed to develop their analysis and discourse within the Israeli academia.

As a result, I found myself last year, for the first time in twenty-nine years, teaching a mini-course in Hebrew, at Ben-Gurion University, which, being the youngest of Israel's main universities, has a high concentration of such scholars. I did not feel exactly like 'a prodigal daughter', but for the first time since the last member of my close family died more than a decade before, I felt that I might establish again a 'home' in the 'homeland'. We agreed that I would return the following January with a view of establishing a permanent link with the department, coming each year to teach a course.

And then the al-Aqsa Intifada broke out, pulling the carpet from under the feet of the complacent and exposing the basic issues that needed to be confronted before any historical settlement of the conflict could be reached.

The Israeli government authorities responded with growing brutality, the establishment 'peaceniks' spoke about the Palestinians letting them down, and the majority of the Israeli population voted for Ariel Sharon, the extreme right ex-general, as the next prime minister, with most of the Labour party amenable to joining him in a national unity government. And yet even now, according to an editorial in *Yediot Aharonot*, the most popular Israeli daily newspaper, there is a widespread recognition that there is no military solution to the conflict. A relative who used to belong to the 'Greater Israel' movement and who had denounced me as 'a lover of Arafat' at every family opportunity, re-established contact after twenty years and wrote to me that Israel was now back in the 1948 situation except that it could do less now, because the world media were against it and constantly watching. But even he, who never considered the Palestinians as more than part of the biblical landscape and/or terrorists, ended his letter by saying: 'But we don't have any other choice. We have to find a way to live peacefully side by side with them'. The combination of the Intifada and the peace process has made the Palestinians permanent and autonomous historical agents even for my relative and his like.

And indeed, in spite of Israel being a powerful nuclear military force, a high-tech society with a population many times larger than in 1948, and despite the fact that my relative's existential anxiety has nothing to do with the immediate reality but with collective memories (and in his case also with personal memories – he is a Holocaust survivor), in some ways the situation has gone back to the 1948 state of affairs. The point is not just a question of whether there can be a Palestinian state alongside an Israeli one that would be more than a Bantustan, and of what would happen in Jerusalem and to the Palestinian refugees. It is not even the fact that for the first time the Palestinian citizens of Israel within the 1948 borders have become directly involved, and that any future solution, unlike the Oslo Accords, would have to consider them as another collective historical agent. The point is that the false foundation of the 1967 borders, in which the various imagined solutions of the conflict were anchored, has been broken. The reality of the history and the effects of a hundred years of the Zionist settlement project need to be looked at afresh, before any sustainable solution can be found. Meanwhile, the Palestinians suffer more than ever before, and their resistance is more violent than ever before.

I write this essay after yet another visit to Israel. In the first shock of the al-Aqsa Intifada, my visit back to the department was cancelled. But although the gap between the Zionist and anti-Zionist left in Israel has deepened again, I am still invited to come back next year to teach.

In the meantime I joined in one of the many resistance and solidarity activities of the Israeli left – both Jewish and Palestinian – organised with the Palestinians under siege in the occupied territories. It was called *Ta-ayush*, an Arabic term which means 'living together'. We went together, Jews and Palestinians, in a convoy of cars accompanying lorries loaded with food to distribute in a couple of Palestinian villages on the West Bank. We were accepted warmly and both sides talked about living together peacefully. Then the Israeli army used our presence there as a pretext to enter the village after seven months of absence. The soldiers claimed they came to 'protect' us, 'proving' it by trying forcefully to stop the unloading and prevent the food from reaching the local inhabitants. When we resisted non-violently, they beat some of us up, causing one of us, an Israeli Palestinian, to lose consciousness. He had to spend a night in hospital. Eight others were arrested by the police who were waiting for us at the village exit. Only the presence of CNN reporters, who accompanied us and took pictures of the soldiers' attacks, prevented the soldiers from taking any further action. The twist in the tale is that the reason we agreed to leave the village, although it became clear the police were waiting at the exit to make arrests, was to protect in the first instance the Israeli soldiers who were following us. It was made clear to us by the villagers that if we were not there, and if they did not appreciate the solidarity we showed to their plight, they would have started to shoot at the Israeli soldiers. This Intifada is a low-intensity war, no more just a civil uprising.

There is no end to this tale, but for now this is where I pause. Except to mention that in the car in which I rode in the Ta-ayush convoy, sat Tisam, an Israeli Palestinian living in El Fridees – a daughter of a refugee from Tantura.

Ella Habiba Shohat

A Reluctant Eulogy: Fragments from the Memories of an Arab-Jew

—ɯ—

Was it inevitable that I, an Arab-Jew, should end up writing in English about my lived linguistic schism between Hebrew and Arabic? As an Iraqi-Jew who grew up in the Israel of the 1960s, I did not enter the three languages in which I have conducted most of my life with the ease with which privileged children slide into cosmopolitanism. Only a decade had passed since my parents' hasty exodus from Iraq. The word 'Baghdad' did not evoke fantastic tales of Ali Baba, Aladdin, or Scheherazade. Although we could not jump on the next train to Baghdad, it seemed that many of the adults lived longing for a one-way ticket, somehow not exactly to a place but for a time that shall never return. For us, the younger generation who did not set foot there, Baghdad was the home, the neighbourhood, the faces, the Iraqi dialect, the music, the food, the grief and festivities shared in the small town of Petah Tiqva (the Gate of Hope), blithely unaware of how and when this first Zionist settlement submerged the Palestinian village of Mlabes (sweet candy). And yet, that Baghdad was a secretive one, existing on the 'margins' of the 'Israeli Nation' and often, incredible as it may seem, with our own fragile and disorientated participation. The airplanes that were arranged to transport Jews from Iraq to Israel uprooted millennia of life in Babylon, leading into a new diasporic existence. Overnight we were no longer Iraqis but Israelis.

In this essay I will piece together a few analytical passages with reflective fragments evoking my Iraqi childhood within Israel. A hybrid essay, the text partakes of diverse genres and forms to evoke a political autobiography and an emotional cartography of dislocation. I hope to offer a disjointed map for a journey across several places, largely my family odyssey as refugees from Iraq to Israel – a geographical and cultural displacement that in many ways prepared the way for my own decision to move to the US. Dominant cartographies draw clear boundaries between Israel and the Arab world, as well as between West and East. Here, in contrast, I want to reveal glimpses of the vital possibilities of a dialogical imagination that juxtaposes separate geographies and histories – in my case Iraq, Israel/Palestine, and the US. In interweaving these disparate narratives, I want to illuminate, through associative juxtapositions, the making of hyphenated identities – the pain and pleasure of hybridity.

Rupture and Return

Central to Zionist thinking was the concept of *Kibbutz Galuiot* – the 'in-gathering of the exiles'. Following two millennia of homelessness and living presumably 'outside of history', Jews could once again 'enter history' as subjects, as 'normal' actors on the world stage by returning to their ancient birthplace, Eretz Israel. In this way, Jews were thought to heal a deformative rupture produced by exilic existence. This transformation of *Migola le'Geula* – from Diaspora to redemption – offered a teleological reading of Jewish History (with a capital H) in which Zionism formed a redemptive vehicle for the renewal of Jewish life on a demarcated terrain, no longer simply spiritual and textual, but rather national and political. Concomitant with the notion of Jewish 'return' and continuity was the idea of rupture and discontinuity.

In order to be transformed into 'New Jews' (later Israelis), the 'diasporic Jews' had to abandon their diasporic – *galuti* – culture, which in the case of Arab-Jews meant abandoning Arabness and acquiescing in assimilationist modernisation, for 'their own good', of course. Within this Promethean rescue narrative, the concepts of 'in-gathering' and 'modernisation' naturalised and glossed over the epistemological violence generated by the Zionist vision of the New Jew. This rescue narrative also elided Zionism's own role in provoking ruptures, dislocations and fragmentation, not only for Palestinian lives but also – in a different way – for Middle Eastern and North African Jews. These ruptures were not only physical (the movement across borders) but also cultural (a rift in relation to previous cultural affiliations) as well as conceptual (in the very ways time and space, history and geography were conceived). The master-narrative of unique Jewish victimisation around the world has been crucial for legitimising an anomalous nationalist project of 'in-gathering of the exiles from the four corners of the globe'. Yet, this narrative has also legitimised the engendering of displacements of peoples from such diverse geographies, languages, cultures and histories – a project in which, in many ways, a state created a nation.

Physical dislocation from Arab and Muslim spaces was not adequate in the case of Arab-Jews, since the displaced Arab-Jews in Israel had to undergo a metamorphosis. The establishment, in a contemporary re-telling of the biblical exodus from Egypt, called for 'the death of the desert generation' (*moto shel dor hamidbar*), in order to facilitate their own birth as the 'New Jews'-Israelis, an ideal embodied by the sabra (native born) generation. Euro-Zionist discourse deployed opposing paradigms that often resulted in hysterical responses to any questioning of its pro-jected 'Western identity'. Zionism viewed Europe both as ideal ego and as the signifier of ghettos, persecutions, and the Holocaust. Within this perspective, the 'Diaspora Jew' was an extra-territorial rootless wanderer, someone living 'outside of history'. Posited in genderised language as the masculine redeemer of the passive Diaspora Jew, the mythologised sabra signified paradoxically the destruction of the Diasporic Jewish entity it claimed to rescue.

By provoking the geographical dispersal of Arab-Jews, by placing us in a new situation 'on the ground', by attempting to reshape our identity as simply 'Israeli', by disdaining and trying to uproot our Arabness, by racialising us and discriminating against us as a group – Israel itself pro-voked a series of traumatic ruptures. The Israeli establishment obliged Arab-Jews to redefine themselves in relation to new ideological para-digms and polarities, thus provoking the aporias of an identity consti-tuted out of its own ruins.

From the point of view of the Euro-Israeli establishment, our Baghdadi culture was perceived as the embodiment of Arab inferiority, backwardness, and savagery. To redeem us of our primal sins, we were subjected to an apparatus of erasure. Even the revival of the Hebrew language – a central Zionist project – formed part of this civilising mission. In this paradoxical national formation, the revival of an Eastern, Semitic language was sub-jected to Westernisation and de-Semitisation. In his influential 1930 essay, 'The Hebrew Accent', Ze'ev Jabotinsky, the Zionist leader of the Revisionist movement, wrote: 'There are experts who think that we ought to bring our accent closer to the Arabic accent. But this is a mistake. Although Hebrew and Arabic are Semitic languages, it does not mean that our Fathers spoke in "Arabic accent".… We are Europeans and our musical taste is European, the taste of Rubinstein, Mendelsshon, and Bizet' (Jabotinsky, 1930).[1]

Entering Language(s)

The Israeli-Arab conflict created a new situation for us. For the first time in our history we were placed on the horns of a terrible dilemma, having to choose between 'Arabness' and 'Jewishness' – the first associated with Islam, and the second with Europeaness. Upon their arrival in Israel, my grandparents did not speak Hebrew, and never learnt it. My parents, although basically fluent in Hebrew, spoke with a heavy Iraqi accent. On their first days as construction workers my father and his Arabic-speaking coworkers were disdainfully commanded by their Ashkenazi bosses in Israel: 'Stop speaking Arabic! We are not in an Arabic country!' Arabic, needless to say, was the language of 'the enemy'; a Jew could not speak it, and a Jew could certainly not claim it as an identity marker. 'In Iraq', my parents often lamented, 'we were Jews; in Israel we are Arabs'.

At home, as children, my siblings and I became the linguistic police, the secret agents, of Euro-Israeli hegemony. We came home voicing what was expected of us: 'stop speaking Arabic!' When my grandparents took the bus with us, we expected them to remain silent. My siblings and I virtually ordered our parents to forget that alien linguistic baggage of Iraqiness. The target of a colonisation of the mind, children like myself were expected to forget the transplanted Baghdads, Cairos, or Casablancas of our homes. Our bodies, language, and thought were regulated to a disciplining, corrective, normalising machine.

My first public performance of the Hebrew language was not a textbook example of the 'normal' linguistic development of a child. I vividly remember my first anxious days in kindergarten, when I was less terrified about the separation from my mother than about what Arabic words would slip into my Hebrew. Although no one had explicitly warned me, something in the social atmosphere made it clear even to a child like myself that Arabic was a taboo language. And soon I learnt to master Hebrew in the socially correct form, that is minus the Iraqi accent. Unlike my father and my mother, I was becoming free from the traces of the Iraqi shackles on my tongue. I was well on my way to assimilating, relegating the Iraqi accent in Hebrew as well as my Baghdadi Arabic dialect and culture to the private space of home and family. There we could not be observed, watched, gazed upon with scorn, or silenced.

Although we were on the margins of sabra-Ashkenazi culture, as a child I felt I had a central role in the space of my own family. I acquired the role of a translator, a mediator for my grandparents, who could not read the signs in the street, take care of bills, or even converse with non-Arabic speakers in the town. As a child, Hebrew gave me a sense of immense power over the adults in my community. My grandfather, despite his patriarchal status, actually lacked real power. He depended on a child like me to navigate the unfamiliar currents of Israeli society. And yet I soon learnt to be ashamed of that role. Not for the sake of my grandfather, but because my ability to translate was a mark of the Arab side of my identity. And, like so many Sephardi-Mizrahi children, I just wanted to be transparent, without that dark, opaque Arab history, unburdened by the Arabic culture. I soon learnt to pretend not to speak Arabic, and to speak a Europeanised Hebrew.

Standing in front of the mirror, I tried to put some order in the Babel of consonants and vowels. I learnt to push all these sounds to the front of the mouth as though there was a clear border dividing the deep throat where the guttural sounds of 'qa, 'ta, ha, 'aa were made. I was very good, an excellent self-colonised student. Gradually the sounds began crossing the interior cave of my throat and moved to the opening of the tunnel, liberated from the chains of Arabic consonants. Triumphant in the ease with which all the deep sounds became light, as though I was speaking French, and shifted into airy sounds of ka, ta, kha, a. After all, we were taught in so many ways at school to aspire to become sabras. 'This is it', I thought to myself, 'Hebrew is more like French', of which I had caught a first glimpse not from the French-speaking Moroccans in the neighbourhood but rather from my mother. She routinely and enthusiastically recited in French the same textbook dialogue, the beauty of which still escapes me, unless it had to do, perhaps, with her memories of her more glamourous childhood days at the Alliance School in Baghdad, prior to her eventual loss of her childhood French in Israel.

My bilingualism as a child, then, did not represent the harmonious co-existence of fluency in two languages. When the authorities entered our neighbourhoods and homes in their diverse incarnations as teachers, social workers, or police, my grandparents knew that the 'honour' of the visit was hardly a sign of some reward to be bestowed on the family. The anxiety level rose high, especially when their sons either defected for just a few weeks to take a break, or were trying to avoid serving in the army altogether.

'Ella! Tali hon! Shoofi ash qayirdun mena' (Ella, come here! See what they want from us), my grandmother, Nana Masouda, would call me from the backyard, begging me to abandon the hide-and-go-seek games I was playing with pigeons and chickens behind the guava tree in the back yard. My dress stained with mud, I ran to the house, only to find myself speaking with a military policeman searching for my shy and muscular uncle, Nachman. (His older sisters named him after Haim Nachman Bialik, the Hebrew national poet, who years later became known for saying he hated the Arabs because they reminded him of the Oriental Jews.)

The 'us' and 'them' was invariably clear to me. It didn't have to be spelled out. Yet I wanted to impress the blonde woman at the door whose proudly ironed khaki uniform made her look as though she had just stepped out of an ad in an Israeli magazine only to heroically land in our humble quarters. 'But why is Nana so worried?' Nana was far more breathless than I was after running all the way from the end of the back yard to the front door. Nana, who was always so slow, so lackadaisical, went through a metamorphosis, suddenly speaking fast, almost running in circles around herself like a headless chicken. 'Why does Nana want me to tell the khaki woman that she doesn't know where my uncle is? I know where he is'. But soon I uttered the words that I thought showed respect for my grandmother's education in hospitality: 'He is at Haskel's store. He left this morning', I said with the confidence of an insider. 'That will make Nana calmer', I thought as I received the warmest, shiniest smile I'd ever received from any khaki woman, who quickly turned away towards the central bus station, empowered by my urban topographical insights.

My act of hospitality was rejected by my tearful grandmother, who now froze in her spot at the entrance until my other uncle, Balfour, returned. (He was given a Zionist name after the English Lord Balfour who in 1917 declared his support for a Jewish homeland in Palestine. But Uncle Balfour also had an Arabic name, Naji.) Before he said anything, I found myself running for my life far ahead of the bottle of milk that followed in my wake and was smashed to smithereens of glass floating in a white puddle. I quickly reached the back yard frightening all the chickens and pigeons in my path, and climbed to my spot in the fig tree, which proved not to be the haven that I had imagined it to be. The burning memory taught me a clear lesson about the subtle but strategic difference between a translator and an informer.

By the Water: Remembering Babylon

My fluency in Hebrew and Arabic was experienced quite viscerally as a negative dialectic, except when my defences broke down, and when, on happy and sad occasions, I suddenly forgot that I was supposed to forget Arabic. My home was not easily seduced by linguistic assimilation. Arabic was the language in which all the emotions around me were expressed; it was the language of the music I heard, the songs we danced to, the prayers we chanted at the Babylonian Jewry synagogue; the language in which my father wiped away my tears with the by-now calloused hands of a man who had never known physical labour until he arrived in Israel; the language in which my mother got good deals at the market in Petah Tiqva, a market almost exclusively inhabited by Iraqi vendors; the language in which my parents heard news from Arabic-speaking radio and television; the language in which virtually everybody would tune to Umm Kulthoum's monthly song from Egypt; the language in which we watched hilarious Arabic films on television; the language in which my grandmother would put my hand on her lap and sing 'delelol delelol' to me when I, exhausted from climbing the fig tree on a hot summer day to build a nest, came back to her for a little siesta nap.

Arabic was the language of the thousand-and-one-nights stories our grandfather told us about 'antar, antar bint al-rih' after he brought us the Iraqi pita he baked with his own hands; it was the language he tuned in to on the big brown radio he was always reluctant to part with, even for meals, or even during war times, when piercing alarms made everyone run to the basement; and when transistors were introduced into our lives in the early seventies, he was greatly cheered by the new invention, for now he could be liberated from the confinement of the house, to walk freely, his head glued to the black transistor hiding his big ear, his eyes staring at an invisible space as he continued his routine of handing us *mlabes* (pastel coloured candies with peanut inside) or twisting the ears of my out-of-control young cousin.

Arabic was the language of the stories my mother told me at every lunch, often repeating the same magical story I knew by heart, 'ruman li-yehalher' and 'tufah li'yesafeq' (the pomegranate that yodelled and the apples that applauded), sounds without which I refused to chew on the tasteless *bamia* (okra). It was the language my mother spoke with the Palestinian Aamer, who carried a cloth bag full of oranges to sell in our town, a man whose age I couldn't tell, whose gentle smile seemed a perfect match to my mother's shyness – both, happy for a break from the harsh routines, talked about their lives: my mother, who in her virtuoso shape-shifting Arabic dialect began her voyage into his Palestinian dialect, found in him a perfect listener for her nostalgia for Baghdad, and he found in her a patient audience for his memories of a time before his village was disappeared by Israel.

Arabic was also the language in which I learnt to curse so well, much to the chagrin of the adults around me, who kept wondering how this little girl could know words that everyone seemed to deny they knew. What horror, *Eib* (shame)! my angry mother would repeatedly ask, 'Where did you learn that?' And without hesitation, I would grab this rare moment of revenge: 'From you!' only to almost hear her pulse rate dropping to a dead stop. Soon she caught her breath; her embarrassment only fuelled anger at the rude child who normally used to be polite and well behaved. Soon I was showered with fierce denials. 'Nehna min khosh beit' (We are a good family), my mother whispered, as though to demonstrate that she could never utter such unspeakable words. And soon I found myself a 'good girl' once again, as the blame fell on the temporary evil relative.

Perhaps I was not too bewildered at the denial – the lack of recollection of cursing. In fact, it became a point of debate for years to come. At the time, however, I did find solace with my girlfriend, Rachel, who faced a similar fate with her family. Just before graduating from elementary school, when we were gradually abandoning playing soccer with the boys, we spent a lazy summer day on a self-assigned research project. Sitting on the neighbourhood's half-broken pavement, we jotted down a co-authored informal anthology of almost one hundred curses. At the end of the day we had both enriched our lexicon, returning to our respective homes utterly equipped to further twist our tongues

Dreams of an Unpromised Land

Hebrew too was far from being a neutral language. To know Hebrew meant to be 'Hebrew', which by implication meant the erasure of anything Arabic. Thinking back to these years, it is no wonder that at a fairly young age, English became a language I fancied intensely. English also brought some affectionate childhood memories. My father was schooled in Baghdad in Shmash School, where English was an important language. (The school granted its matriculation according to the British educational system, his yellow-diploma still bearing the stamp of Oxford). While the Iraqiness of my father was, in the lexicon of my school, a sign of backwardness, his knowledge of English promoted him to the status of a kind of village scribe. Even our Ashkenazi neighbour, *Gveret* (Madam) Burshtein, a tall, gentle woman with shining green eyes which stood in contrast to the grey braids crowning her head, was forced to pay us a visit. She entered our modest living room whenever she received a letter from her relatives in the US, asking my father to translate the foreign words, and then to communicate hers to those people in the faraway place.

'America' was a far place, which came up in our games of 'enzap' (an Israeli distortion of 'hands-up'), in our cowboy-and-Indian games. Most kids wanted to be the cowboys, drawing their imaginary guns and provoking groans and moans of the dying 'reds', who fell to the hot asphalt holding their breath until the new round began. The universal desire to be the cowboy was not shared by my cousin, Eyal, who on Purim went against the grain: his love for the colourful feathers outshone his temptation to wear the plastic pistol even at the cost of forever losing to the cowboys. Were these Hollywood-style games already instilling in us a nationalistic paradigm? America was so far and yet so close: it even penetrated our everyday language, our smart mocking cliché 'gilita et America, ha ha ha' ('you've discovered America', i.e. belabouring the obvious.) And when we wanted to suggest that a place was far and inaccessible, we said it was in 'Honolulu'.

I remember that when we were growing up, we loved watching American television series. *Hawaii Five-O* was one of our favourites. The hula dancer in the opening credit sequence seemed far more exotic than our local belly dancers. Perhaps the hip movements of the hula dancer were familiar to us, but somehow we did not see this dance as part of the 'East', for we only learnt to recognise it as 'American' and therefore as 'Western'. We were dreaming about a new world, even as our old world of the Euphrates and Tigris was a forbidden memory in the state of Israel. Indeed, the global flow of American images and sounds gave the US the feeling of a *terra cognita*, even prior to my voyage to the island of Manhattan.

Our neighbour's monthly visit signified a momentary shift. My father's Iraqi accent in English suddenly mattered less, for we were full of pride

that Madam Burshtein, whose sabra daughter incarnated the true, legitimate Israeli (serving in the army), crossed the road and came all the way
to our house, just to hear my father reading the English she could not
understand. This monthly ritual brought larger audiences each time,
eager to hear my father, who usually performed for the family, playing
and singing Arabic music, now rolling the Iraqi melody of English from
his mouth. Could it be that for this moment we were no longer the 'stinky
Iraqis' the Ashkenazi neighbours talked about? Suddenly our Iraqi history came to our rescue; a social advantage brought from no other place
than Baghdad.

We all gathered to hear my father translating from English into
Hebrew, and then again translating Hebrew into English as he wrote
Gveret Burshtein's answer to her relatives. It was then that I first came
across the English script in its magnificent, imperious signs. My father's
confident drawing of the English letters was like magic, and I tried hard
to imitate him, transforming his elegant script into doodles. Full of pride,
I showed my father, asking him, 'Aba, ma katavti beAnglit?' (Daddy,
what did I write in English?), hoping that one of the doodles would
somehow reveal a hidden meaning beyond my limited understanding.
Each time, after Gveret Burshtein left, I jumped at my exhausted father,
who after a long day of work and good neighbour policy was forced to
admit that, although two months had passed since the last time I asked,
the answer remained the same.

But English soon also came in the form of television sounds. It was as
far from the Arabic of the children TV programme *Sami U-Susu* as it was
from the Hebrew TV programme *Hedva Ve Ani*. It belonged to a seemingly third space presumably untouched by the conflicts I was experiencing daily. A whole world drawn from the American TV series as well
as from the movies came to inhabit my young imagination. I have often
wondered about the infiltration of English into our world just as we were
all chanting Black Panther slogans about Ashkenazi discrimination. I
often think that English in this situation was a kind of a free zone that did
not involve that painful childhood conflict of Hebrew and Arabic. Yet,
English, obviously, was also not a neutral space. The United States'
post–World War II rise to global power, the 1970s Americanisation of
Israel, British colonial history in Iraq and Palestine: all contributed to the
English-language infiltration of my young mind, unsettling the presence
of Hebrew.

Dreams of America (or 'Amareeka', as we said in Arabic) were nourished by the travelling images and sounds. In addition, I managed to find
another escapist place where the Babel of languages produced a new
game of language guessing: the airport where my father worked. This in-
between space, not exactly belonging to Israel and yet not exactly belonging to another particular country, made my adult transition to New York

somehow natural. I loved to wander in the small airport, and looked forward to the day I would climb the stairs of an airplane. The small airport – the only international airport in Israel, known now as the Ben-Gurion/Tel-Aviv airport – was built on land that used to belong to the Palestinian town of Lydda. And while English, French, Italian, German and Spanish could all be welcomed and generously hosted, the mere presence of an Arabic sound – let alone an image, a human flesh – drew piercing looks. I wanted to fly away, anywhere out of the world where I lived seemed like a gate-of-hope. As I began my adult life, I realised that the closest I had ever felt towards the idea of 'home' was inside an airplane – right after taking off. When my body moved and careened in-between places, it seemed, for a moment, that I could exist ungrounded by geography, lifted above the shackles of identity.

I moved 'Ila Amareeka', as my family would say in Arabic, in 1981. Moving across the Mediterranean and the Atlantic Ocean to New York was for me, perhaps, the inevitable result of my parents' traumatic displacement from Iraq to Israel. That first displacement from Babylon and the arrival to an exile in the Promised Land, led me to find a more creative mode of exile, a displacement that allowed me to feel more empowered to reshape my life. Here I could begin my reflective voyage back into the first two decades of a childhood caught between two clashing worlds.

Processed Memories

After the establishment of Israel, Arab-Jews were caught in the vice of two bloody nationalisms: Arab and Jewish. While Euro-Israel, in its need to secure bodies to perform 'black labour', had an interest in creating the terrorising political climate that led to our mass exodus, Arab authorities added their own share of terror by suspecting us a priori of being traitors. At the same time, the two governments, under the orchestration of Britain, secretly collaborated in lifting us overnight from millennia in Mesopotamia. Although Arab-Jews were culturally closer to Muslim-Arabs than to the European Jews who founded the state of Israel, their identity was seen as being on trial by both national projects. Even anti-Zionist Arab-Jews ended up in Israel, for in the bloody context of a nationalist conflict, they could no longer enjoy the luxury of a hyphenated identity. My parents had to burn our photos, leaving little photographic inheritance from Iraq. As refugees, in the haste of the moment and under strict Iraqi government policing, my family left everything behind. My parents filled their suitcase with a few clothes, some jewellery, and a few photos. I cling to the handful of photos of my family in Baghdad, the city we still cannot go back to after four decades of traumatic rupture.

In my early twenties I used to pore over the few photos in a half-filled family album in order to discern the contours of a history, a lineage. I remember inverting the traditional biblical verse (taken up again in the Jimmie Cliff reggae song): instead of weeping by the waters of Babylon, it was by the waters of *Zion* that we lay down and wept when we remembered *Babylon*. Iraq, under Saddam Hussein, has continued to hold its annual Babylonian Festival, even as devastating sanctions continue to 'sanction' the death of many Iraqis. The staging of ancient 'Babylon' boosts Iraqi national morale, but it is yesterday's Iraq that we, displaced Iraqis, cry over when we see Iraqi images flicker over the television screen. In exile, Iraqi images, music, stories, and dishes are all digested in a kind of wake for what was lost. Wherever they go – Petah Tiqva, New York, or Rio de Janeiro – my parents immediately reproduce the aromas of Baghdad, in their pots and in their tears, as they listen to the sounds of old Iraqi and Egyptian music frozen in time: Nathum al-Ghazali, Salima Pasha, Umm Kulthoum, and Muhamad Abdul-Wahab. A few years after the Gulf War I gave my parents a tape of a young Iraqi singer, Qathum al-Sahir. They did not enjoy it. Perhaps it was too painful to admit that after their departure, life did not stop 'there'. And perhaps this feeling of still water in the rivers we could not see made me obsessed with taking photos. It is as if I wanted to fill out the half-empty albums.

Colonial images of 'natives' are often only distilled in the visual archives. I flip through British collections of photos of Baghdad in an attempt to visualise my grandmother in the streets, houses, markets, carrying her *beqcha* (bundle) on her head. These processed images have become processed memories. Could it be that my endlessly deconstructed colonial images are now invading my own familial memories? My work was an effort to bring to life a frozen past captured in the colonial visual archive. We kidnap Orientalist images of 'the exotic' and re-narrate them for our private/public memories.

A few years ago, around the quincentenary of the expulsion of Muslim and Jews from Spain, I was desperately looking for images of Jews in the Islamic world to accompany an essay I wrote for *Middle East Report* on the subject (Shohat, 1992). The editor and I approached the Yeshiva University Museum in New York (directed by Euro-American Jews), which was sponsoring a photographic exhibition on the subject. Aware of my critical stance, the museum refused to lend such images without first reviewing the political content of my essay, thereby barring access to my own community history. I have visited Jewish museums in the United States and Israel, only to see nightmarish reincarnations on display. Precious objects that belonged to our community or to its individual members, ranging from religious artefacts to 'Oriental' jewellery and dresses, are all exhibited within the framework of Jewish exotica. Fetishistically detached from their ambient culture and history within the worlds of Islam, they are appropriated into a universal Jewish narrative, often within the architectural confines of a triumphant European architecture, for example, the Gothic architecture of the Jewish Museum in New York. Jewish museums have become a collective burial site of our Arab past.

But that sense of the elusive homelands in Arab lands persists even after moving to a new continent. My grandfather, Ya'aqub abu-Sasson, was buried in the 1930s in the Baghdadi Jewish cemetery on Sheikh Omar Street, which in the 1960s was itself apparently buried under the new national television station: our millennial traces were thus erased. I have often thought it ironic, in light of this fact, that I became a professor of media studies, engaged in unearthing the deeper strata of the visual text.

The black-and-white photos taken on our roof in Baghdad gaze at me in my New York living room. My mother looks away. For me, the habit of looking at the photos has itself become part of a visual archive – an autobiography of looking at images; each time the look acquires a layer in an intricate palimpsestic narrative. Decades before these photos travelled with me to New York, they have experienced their first flight prior to my arrival in the world. They were packed in a suitcase that took them from Baghdad to Tel-Aviv via Cyprus, on my parents' first flight. As I gaze at them, I am overcome by the feeling that they are witnesses to a disjointed existence, and its survivors as well. Silent remnants, they give some coherence to a shattered world.

During my childhood, these few photos from Baghdad were kept in an envelope in the cramped closet, set apart from our photos taken in Israel, and placed in the cheap family album. It was never clear whether they were barred from co-existing with the recent photos, or deemed too important to be paraded for profane purposes. Did the photos occupy a subliminal spectre of disembodied existence in the wake of ghastly catastrophes? The sheltered Baghdadi photos only highlighted the potentially violent overtones of quotidian materials.

My mother wears my father's suit. ('Just for the photos', she tells me smiling, blithely unaware of recent performance theories about cross-dressing). Elegantly she projects authority as she stands there, her long, thick, curly black hair flowing gently. She lost much of that hair after they became refugees in an epoch of food rationing in the transit camps in Israel. She fell seriously ill, as the cold wind and rainy winter in the tent inflicted her with crippling rheumatoid arthritis. I often remember how I tried to reconcile these two mothers, the one in the photos from Baghdad, and the other one that I knew – the one courageously fighting economic and social degradation with a weakened, broken body.

In another photo my father, in dark pants, white shirt, and a tie, grinning below a heavy black moustache, lifts my mother in midair on a roof, enacting for the camera a romantic tale. Her long, black, curly hair stands in contrast to the featherweight woman floating between earth and sky.

The faces from Baghdad look at me, never knowing that these are going to be their last photos from a place they will be barred from. I am fixated; these photos from my parents' wedding in 1949, a year prior to their departure. They could not foresee what was yet to come – the disappearance of their Baghdadi lives, and the impossibility of return. Their first images in Israel were taken in the late 1950s after they had already survived the first displacements: my mother still wears her old chic suit from Baghdad, while her younger sister flaunts a fashionable 1950s dress that she stitched. Yet their pose of respectability for the camera cannot completely hide the melancholy in their eyes, the traces of their humiliated lives. My *seta* (Arabic for grandmother) Gurgeia, who left Baghdad as a widow and died in her mid-nineties a few years ago, enjoyed cursing back. She washed their dirty laundry as she joyfully rolled out her Arabic obscenities. She never learnt the language of *al-beitheen* (Arabic for 'the whites'). As she used several layers of *shaqsa* (Iraqi for female head covering) to wrap her dwindling greying braids, she was amused by my sister's efforts to bleach her hair, whose stubborn roots refused to fully erase their black past. And like many women of her class, my grandmother did not wash out of her dictionary the dirty words reserved for those whose houses emitted unpleasant smells in the absence of her ever-bleaching hand. In the Gramercy Park apartment I was cleaning, I could repeat *Seta*'s rate of production, fighting so that my life, too, wouldn't go down the drain.

Soap to wash the dirt off the shirt. To wash the dirt off your body. Cleaning for others while being called dirty yourself. My dark friend Na'eema used to frantically scrub her 'dirty skin' in a violent cleansing ritual that left her bleeding but never reached the promised hidden layer of white skin she so painfully desired. In Israel we were called 'dirty Iraqis'. I can still hear the Hebrew words '*Erakit Masriha!*' ('Stinky Iraqi'), shouted at me by a blond boy whose relatives in Europe were themselves said to have been turned into 'sabonim' – soaps – by the Nazis.

Euro-Israeli authorities, wrapped in the aura of science, marched on us to eradicate our Asian and African underdevelopment. Individual Ashkenazis were also full of confidence, seeing it as their national duty to carry out the civilising mission. My brother still speaks of a haunting memory from the mid-1950s – an Ashkenazi woman holding big scissors, running after a Yemeni child from our neighbourhood. She caught him, and although he was fearfully crying and resisting the strange woman's grip, he was forced to surrender. She cut his *peot* (side-locks) – for her, signs of traditional backwardness. On the yellow sand of the road lay two black curls – visual evidence of the work of an 'orderly regime'.

Iraqi, Yemeni, and Moroccan refugees in the 1950s were welcomed to Israel with white DDT dust, to cleanse them, as the official Euro-Israeli discourse suggested, of their 'tropical diseases'. In the transit camps, their hair was shaved off to rid them of lice. Children, some of them healthy, were suspected of ringworm, and 'treated' with massive doses of radiation. You could tell those who had been treated by the wraps covering their heads, covering the shame of hair loss. Decades later, as the treated children became adults, they again experienced hair loss. Now, though, they wore fashionable wigs or hats to cover a second hair loss, this time due to radiation treatment for cancerous brain tumours, caused initially by their early childhood 'treatment' for a simple skin disease that sometimes they did not actually have.

Can memory exist apart from the desire to memorialise? Perhaps my narratives of displacement are no more than a monument to our parents' and grandparents' generation, which performed hairy escapes across hostile borders. A fragmented testimony, not simply to the sheer 'facts' but to the intricacies of emotions, my essay speaks for a generation muted by the everyday burden of hyphenated realities, their dreams mutilated. Making the silences speak becomes for me an act of memorialising, a portable shrine for those taboo memories – a reluctant eulogy, lest they completely fade away.

Notes

'The Contaminated Paradise'

1. It is not that the Israeli settler society does not have its own specific characteristics. Nahla Abdo, one of the editors of this volume, and I wrote about it in one of the chapters of *Unsettling Settler Societies* (Stasiulis and Yuval-Davis, 1995). Firstly, Israeli Zionism constructed itself as a national movement returning to its 'old' homeland and not just building a new society/nation; secondly, Israel was autonomous from its inception rather than a product of a specific empire, but always had to ally itself with the dominant empire in the area at the time; and thirdly, unlike other settler societies, it does not constitute a clear majority or a minority in the population, and therefore the eventual outcome of the settlement between the settlers and the indigenous population is less predictable.

'A Reluctant Eulogy'

1. I discussed the shaping of the Hebrew accent as part of the Zionist national imagery in Israeli cinema (Shohat, 1989).

References

'The Contaminated Paradise'

Abdo, Nahla, and Nira Yuval-Davis. 1995. 'Palestine, Israel and the Zionist settler project'. In Daiva Stasiulis and Nira Yuval-Davis (eds.), *Unsettling Settler Societies: Articulations of Gender, Race, Ethnicity and Class.* London: Sage.
Stasiulis, Daiva, and Nira Yuval-Davis (eds.). 1995. *Unsettling Settler Societies: Articulations of Gender, Race, Ethnicity and Class.* London: Sage.

'A Reluctant Eulogy'

Jabotinsky, Ze'ev Vladimir. 1930. *The Hebrew Accent.* Tel-Aviv: HaSeffer. [Hebrew]
Shohat, Ella. 1989. *East/West and the Politics of Representation.* Austin: University of Texas Press.
———. 1992. 'Rethinking Jews and Muslims: Quincentennial reflections'. *Middle East Report* (September–October): 25–29.

Six

Existential States of Exile

Esther Fuchs

Exile, Memory, Subjectivity: A *Yoredet* Reflects on National Identity and Gender

—ɯɯ—

1

When I define myself as Israeli, what precisely do I refer to? The national label encompasses a sense of place, of language, of community, of cultural memory. Having left the country, have I not forfeited my claim to this definition altogether? This essay is a meditation on my multiple exiles as a *Yoredet* – an ex-Israeli – a woman, a daughter of Holocaust survivors (Fuchs, 1989: 295–300).[1] As I refrain from fixing the fluid boundaries of place, language, memory I also reject the possibility that one single accident of birth should dominate all other themes of my personal identity. I would like to consider the possibility that at various times, various themes have become more predominant for one reason or another. In avoiding a single clear position, I affirm a post-modern deconstruction of the self and of a stable cultural identity. Yet in moving from one aspect of my collective identity to another, I attempt to investigate my personal interpretation of various 'labels' and to assess the extent of their collision as fragments in a process of an evolving subjectivity. This writing helps me to clarify what I am not, and to emphasise the instability of the very pronoun 'I', taken for granted here as the subject or creator of this meditation. At the same time, I do not reject the fundamental premise of identity politics, that 'categories and labels are not arbitrary and unnecessary constructions, but have a real impact on the formation of consciousness, subjectivity and critical perspective' (Zimmerman, 1996: 214).

2

I go back to Israel once a year, or once every two years. I have an Israeli passport – dual citizenship. I received my green card through the University of Texas when I worked in Austin as an assistant professor of Hebrew Literature. I cannot forfeit my Israeli citizenship, never considered it seriously, though when compelled to pay a special airport tax reserved for Israeli citizens, I am tempted to consider it as an option. As time goes by, I wonder about the meaning of this document, this passport. At the same time, I am still astonished to find my name under my picture in my American passport. I became an American citizen in 1985, ten years after I arrived here. Does this photographic representation of my face really represent me? My Israeli face in black and white reveals a youthful curiosity. My American face in bold colour reveals a somewhat forced smile. Is there a 'real' me here, or two versions of something I have not yet quite learnt to define, something I no longer wish to define, something that is not finite and therefore indefinite and indefinable. Did I leave because America offered security, peace, stability, opportunity, and if so, did I find them in my new country? I left in 1975, not thinking at the time about the political unconscious and its possible role in my decision. This was after 1973, after the Yom Kippur War, when a collective 'withdrawal from certainty' began to take place not just in Israeli literature, but for me as well, personally and politically. Moving to America, have I regained that certainty, or have I merely removed myself from a troubling collective, from an unsettling situation? It was not the military defeat many Israelis perceived in the Yom Kippur War, it was a kind of moral defeat, the questions: What for and why? They were the questions of justifying the war against the Arab countries, and more importantly – the treatment of the Palestinians. Is it possible that we have become the oppressors, the occupiers, the thugs that my mother and father described in their nightmares as I was growing up?

One cannot run from doubt and uncertainty. These cannot be resolved by physical transplantation. And it would take years before I could separate my own nightmares from those of my parents, for in my dreams I saw myself found out, seized and expelled from my new country, my new passport shredded among my other many pieces. This primordial fear surfacing in this most unlikely of places – am I borrowing another's nightmares? Am I not appropriating the nightmare of the Native Americans, perhaps of Palestinians who are not as welcome as I may be in America? And yet Irena Klepfisz, a Holocaust survivor and a daughter of Holocaust survivors, reports having the same fears. As she puts it: 'Has not America had other Holocausts? Has not America proven what it is capable of? Has not America exterminated others, those it deemed undesirable or those in its way?' (Klepfisz, 1982: 48).

3

Of course I still speak fluent Hebrew and I read – after all, I am not only a sabra, what Oz Almog (2000) calls 'the creation of the new Jew' – I am also a professor of Hebrew literature. And yet, as the years go by I am beginning to become aware of a certain lack, a loss, a flattening. I sense the erosion of my natural connection to the language; I do not recognise many of the neologisms in the speech of my nephew and niece. I do not recognise some terms in Hebrew academic journals. I shudder to realise that so much time has already gone by. Most of my academic articles are in English. Recently, I sent off to the Israeli feminist journal *Noga* a review in Hebrew on a new book by Israeli women on biblical women. I began my feminist critique of the Bible as an assistant professor at the Oriental and African Languages and Literatures Department at the University of Texas in Austin. I was invited by the women's studies programme to give a talk on women in the Bible, and since I always considered the Bible to be part of Hebrew literature, I asked feminist questions of the ancient text, an approach that was revolutionary at the time. But what I began to talk about here was my relationship with the Hebrew language. An important scholar will later describe me as a 'lone voice' in the 1980s, one that 'raised concerns about the subtle and insidious ways in which the biblical text communicates patriarchy. Her work has not attempted to reclaim or reform but only to reveal unapologetically the patriarchal strategies woven into the Bible' (Milne, 1997: 47).

It would take another ten years before I finally stopped revising my manuscript *Sexual Politics in the Hebrew Bible: Reading the Hebrew Bible as a Woman* (Fuchs, 2000). The transition from modern to biblical literature was simple. I did not regard the Bible as a sacral text, but rather as a literary text imbued with both a monotheistic and a patriarchal ideology. The radical questioning of the Bible as a political text invested in the future of sons and the memory of fathers, and dominated by the discourse of a male deity, and male scribes and priests, was yet another divestment of what Minnie Bruce Pratt calls layers of cultural identity (Pratt, 1984: 11–63). My kind of questioning will later make it difficult for me to accept Jewish feminist rituals as substitute, because these rituals revert to fundamentally hierarchical and authoritarian structures. This explains my exile as a secular Jew in the context of feminist New Age or Renewal and Reform attempts to reclaim the feminine in Judaism. I find no solace in the feminist Seders, or feminist Rosh Hodesh (New Moon), or any other gynocentric rituals; something for me is still missing. Something for me is still missing even in the most radically feminist rewriting of traditional custom and prayer (Heschel, 1995: 217–80; Falk, 1996). The exposure of patriarchal paradigms at the very root structure of biblical narrative and in the very construction of its literary characters, including

God, makes it virtually impossible for me to reclaim anything at all. And when this much is being stripped away from my cultural identity, what is left? Of course, 'identity' is a construct itself, and so is the metaphor of a 'layer' of identity – is identity made up of 'layers?' I prefer to think of identity as a process, a journey, with each point of departure an understanding of what remains still elusive and unreachable. What remains is the horizon of a new landscape, a new and yet familiar place I may one day consider home.

4

A poem I published in Hebrew many years ago reads: 'The Hebrew tongue and I am stuttering/Landscapes I no longer know' (Fuchs, 1983: 16). I talk about the loss of language in geographical terms, in terms of landscape, because in exile, language becomes a substitute for place. But poetry in Hebrew, my poems, I did not dare write for over a decade, and only recently published yet another collection, entitled *Scar*, my father's facial scar and the metaphoric scar I carried, my vicarious wound, having been born to Holocaust survivors (Fuchs, 1997). The loss of my connection to the language is not merely geographical. It has become ideological. In biblical Hebrew only men 'know' and 'desire', while women appear as the objects of male knowledge and desire (Brenner, 1997). Modern Hebrew, which is a revived version of biblical Hebrew, carries not just images and metaphors but cognates that define women as at best marginal to men. In modern Hebrew I am a *nekeva* – a female – a noun deriving from *nekev* – hole. In Hebrew a man is *gever* – a noun closely associated with *gevurah* which means courage. The grammatical rules of Hebrew compel us to address an audience of women as men, if a single man is part of it. Hebrew language was for generations the sole preserve of men who were educated in the *Heder* and the *Yeshiva*, while Yiddish, the vernacular in Eastern Europe, was the preserve of women.[2] For generations, Hebrew was identified with a cultural tradition of men, an erudite, sophisticated, elite culture, while Yiddish was seen as the lesser language, a hybrid of Hebrew and German, inconstant and inconsistent, the language of women and the uneducated masses (Seidman, 1997).

When Hebrew literature emerged it was the product of elite Yeshiva students who turned their backs on religion and sought to create a new secular culture: the sons rebelled against their fathers (Halkin, 1970; Mintz, 1989; Alter, 1998). Their rebellion notwithstanding, they perpetuated their fathers' traditional androcentric vision of the world. I have recently written about the male-centred representation of women in the first literary generation of the state of Israel, a representation that reserves for men only the role of military hero and defender, reducing women to secondary, mostly domestic and sexual roles (Fuchs, 1999). In a much earlier article I suggest that there is a peculiar association of the mythical woman and the mythical Arab/Palestinian enemy. Hannah in Amos Oz's *My Michael* dreams of destroying Jerusalem's central water supply tower with the help of Halil and Aziz, whom she envisions as Palestinian terrorists (Fuchs, 1989: 212–34). The national enemy – the Palestinians inside the state and the 'Arabs' across the border – is depicted as the collaborator of the Israeli woman. If the literary imagination projects danger on the Israeli woman inside the home, could it be that the national imagination projects danger on the Palestinians inside the state? In my book *Israeli Mythogynies: Women in Contemporary Hebrew Fiction* (Fuchs, 1987) I suggest that the construction of 'woman-as-other' includes both female characters and female authors. If 'woman-as-other' embodies male fear of emasculation, does not the Palestinian embody Jewish fear of extinction, and is there a process of transference here carrying the European trauma of the Holocaust into the new context of Palestine/Israel?

Is there a connection between the increasingly hostile attitude to women and the militarisation of Israeli society? While this process may have begun in the 1930s, in literature women begin to emerge in ambivalent roles in the *Palmach* literature of the 1940s and 1950s and continue to be depicted as dangerous, if not abject, 'others' in male-authored literature of the 1960s and 1970s.[3] Simona Sharoni points to the linguistic connection between two meanings of the word 'kibbush' – the occupation of a woman's body and the Israeli occupation of the West Bank and Gaza Strip (Sharoni, 1995: 38–9). She furthermore argues that Palestinian women's identities and bodies have become the battlefields of both Israeli and Palestinian male national leaderships. 'The Israeli military has used the discourse of national security to justify the massive arrests of Palestinian women and their forceful interrogation' (Sharoni, 1995: 39).

5

I used to go back to Israel once a year, at times for a conference, mostly for family reunions. Since the early 1980s I have visited once every two years. I notice the passage of time in the faces of my nephew and niece. They were children when I left in 1975. Now they are the proud parents of children who resemble them slightly. I go to Israel for weddings and for *Brit Mila* celebrations or *Bar* or *Bat Mitzvah* celebrations. It is of course impolite to ask why I do not have children of my own, and why I have not married. I do not stop to explain that I did in fact get married and that I also got divorced. I do not talk about my marital status, not even among friends or family. But the questions continue to hang heavily in the air, and at moments like these I know why I left Israel when I did. I knew when I left that in America I would not be harassed by such invasive questions. I would not be investigated; I would not be pestered by the anxious concern about my marital and procreative duties. It would take years before I realised that the intense pressure I escaped when I left for Boston in 1975 was a shared experience. It would take years before I made connections between marriage as the 'national panacea' and 'the cult of fertility' and the demographic war against the Palestinians (Hazelton, 1977). I who was a star in high school, I who was selected to represent my school in a foreign student exchange programme, I who competed successfully for the privilege of spending six months in the United States – became in my late teens a liability, an embarrassment. My mother no longer pulled out my grades to show them off to neighbours and friends. Instead she was hard-pressed to explain why I was pursuing a BA at the Hebrew University instead of doing what my sister had done: get married and have children. One could, after all, study after giving birth.

In the early 1970s the concept of autonomous maternity was not as prevalent in Israel as it is today (Kahn, 2000). While in the late 1980s and 1990s reproductive technology in Israel proliferated along with the multiplicity of discourses sanctioning unmarried motherhood, in my time marriage was still considered the *sine qua non* for bearing children. Matrimony and motherhood – both states were a panacea, inextricably intertwined as the desideratum of mature femininity. But there was also a degree of sexual pressure from Israeli men, who could not comprehend my prudishness. I guess these factors must be considered, though at the time I believed I pursued nothing but the Truth. I believed I could submerge myself in this Truth by moving to Jerusalem and returning to my religious heritage. My parents were desperate. While my sister went into the army and got married shortly after she was drafted, I became involved with Gesher (literally, 'bridge'), a group devoted to creating a dialogue between secular and religious Israelis. While my sister gave birth to her first child, I was off to Jerusalem to live among people of faith whom I considered my new, true family.

6

The invasive questions did not stop even when I moved to my new 'home' in Jerusalem – an apartment I shared with an Orthodox girl from England. The pressure to fit in only intensified as I move to another religious group, the Messianic-Zionist 'Kookniks' – the followers of Rabbi Abraham Isaac Kook, who perceived the secular state as a paradoxical incarnation of Messianic hopes (Ravitzky, 1996: 79–144). The last stop in my religious journey took me to the Haredi (Orthodox) college (*Michlala*) for women in Bayit Vegan, Jerusalem. In the women's dormitory, the young women talked about engagement parties. Some girls who had not yet become engaged were anxious and lost. The scholarly debates I was looking forward to, the mystical learning, the textual analysis of Jewish exegesis and ethics, classes in Talmud and Kabbalah – the answers I sought at this ultra-orthodox college for women led to more intensified pressure to get married and have children. My flight from the secular city to Tel-Aviv to the religious world of Jerusalem became a vicious circle. My initial enthusiasm began to wane. When I first joined the Haredi community I was led to believe that any woman could learn the classical texts and achieve a respectable level of interpretive proficiency. The goal of the Michlala was to ensure that graduates would receive a teaching certificate for haredi schools. When I left Orthodoxy, I seemed to have reached the end of the road. My rejection of secular Zionism, my family, my high school and university education came to some kind of an end. I could not endorse the secular culture I left, but neither could I accept the religious alternative. And at this point, only an escape from Israel altogether beckoned as a real possibility. So when Brandeis University offered a scholarship towards a doctoral programme, I did not hesitate.

For a while I enjoyed the media attention I received as a result of my unusual journey from secular life in Tel-Aviv to haredi life in Jerusalem and back (Hanoch, 1975: 21). Leaving for the United States in my midtwenties was a relief. In this new country I would not have to decide between religiosity and secularism, and above all, I would not have to fit in. I was flying from the collective narrative to the possibility of what Yaron Ezrahi will later call 'self-narration'. I was trying to affirm my right to be the author of my own life (Ezrahi, 1997: 78). My best friend, who had read Simone de Beauvoir's *The Second Sex* in French when we were still at the Dizengoff elementary school for girls, did not approve. She dismissed my decision to leave for the States as mere 'careerism', something between opportunism and selfishness. My mother cried – could she recognise that she was in part the reason for my leaving, with her overprotectiveness, her unmitigated demand that I fulfil my marital and reproductive obligation, her obsession with the Holocaust? I tried to flee from my mother, a useless attempt, as I later found out, for imperceptibly her demands and memories became mine long before I left, and a change of place could not mute my mother's voice, the only love I knew. At the airport, she warned me not to become overinvolved in social justice causes and to focus on my own best personal interests – an oblique reference to finding an appropriate – successful – (Jewish) spouse, so I could finally pursue my real mission in life. She was not clear about the value of a Ph.D. and my professional prospects. In a way, she was right to be sceptical. Though I was relatively lucky, doctoral degrees do not guarantee jobs or positions after completion. As many Israeli emigrants do (Shokeid, 1988), I kept reassuring everybody that I would soon be back for good. I promised I would be back soon, shortly after completing my degree. I did not make a conscious connection at the time between the Arab-Israeli conflict and the emphasis on procreation and the security of domestic space. The Israeli feminist movement itself would come to life only in the late 1970s, after my departure, and the basic texts of Israeli feminist analysis would not be written until the early and mid-1980s (Izraeli et al., 1982; Swirski and Safir, 1991).

7

For my parents, marriage and family were urgent prospects. My father had lost a wife and a young daughter – Hinda – in the Lodz Ghetto. My mother had lost her husband of three months. Both survived, but never forgot their siblings and cousins who perished in the war. There was nothing more important for my parents than the reconstitution of their families. My mother became pregnant within a year of her marriage to my father, whom she met at a halfway house for refugees where she tended the sick and the wounded. My sister and I became the focus of their lives. My parents rented a house in Jaffa, and despite their sense of alienation among the Palestinian neighbours around us, they rarely discussed politics. They had more pressing things to discuss – the future of their children and economic survival. They never tried to draw linkages between their status as new immigrants (*olim hadashim*) and their inability to negotiate the self-contradictory directives of an impenetrable bureaucratic system and discourse. My father did not question why he could only earn a viable income as a labourer at Mekorot, the water supply company that needed cheap labour to lay down water pipes in the Negev. But later his lawyer applied directly to Germany for compensation, which insured him a basic monthly sum allowing him to finally retire many years later, after a failed attempt to earn a living selling electrical appliances. My mother let the government take care of her compensation, which is why she received only a quarter of my father's sum. According to my mother, the government disbursed much smaller sums to Holocaust survivors because it needed the money to pave roads and keep up the military, and so used some of the compensation money it received from Germany to deal with more urgent needs.

According to Idith Zertal, Israeli leadership displayed a rather ambivalent attitude towards Holocaust survivors perceiving them as second-class citizens at best. Her historical analysis suggests that my parents' predicament in the early 1950s was the result of a policy rather than an isolated case (Zertal, 1998). As I understand it, Idith Zertal and Dina Porat discuss the ambivalent response of the 'Israelis' to Holocaust survivors in terms of an abjection, a familiarity with and an alienation from a close relative

(Porat, 1991: 157–74; Zertal, 1998: 8). The Holocaust survivor epitomised for the sabra or the dominant Ashkenazi elite the abjection of diaspora existence: passivity, victimisation, and vulnerability – in a mythical sense: femininity. The new Jew, the Zionist, was to be a muscle Jew, self-reliant, strong, a Zionist, a man (Boyarin, 1997). In the evenings my parents would huddle together in the kitchen to figure out how to pay back the debts they incurred, the electricity and the water bill. Their feverish discussions about rent, savings, and interest rates were in Polish, the language they reserved for themselves. When they spoke Polish they knew we kids would not understand. They were not safe in Yiddish, for I spoke fluent Yiddish with my grandparents, who shared the flat in Jaffa with us. My grandparents, who taught me Yiddish, my first language, gave me the parenting I often did not receive from my harried parents. They, with my mother and her two brothers, survived the war hiding under a cowshed, protected by a Catholic farmer who was once my grandfather's employee in the little shtetl of Sterdin. My parents told us we compensated for their losses, and the clear message was that as daughters, we had a sacred mandate to have families of our own some day. Later in life, I learnt that my achievements at school were also a form of compensation. So I worked as hard as I possibly could to erase the memories that continued to wake them during the night.

My parents did not feel secure in Jaffa. Not only did they have to contend with a new national idiom they began to consider their own, they were confronted with a reality they may not have understood. They did not discuss their Palestinian neighbours, though I could sense their discomfort, somehow they felt threatened. Were our Palestinian neighbours not threatened by the new political regime that turned some of them into second-class citizens, and others into refugees? Did they not feel threatened by us, by the 'new immigrants', the *olim hadashim* often derided by the *vatikim* (longtime Jewish residents in Israel) as *olim halashim* (weak immigrants)? We did not ask these questions back then. I remember my Mom telling me that when I was a toddler, she would at times entrust me to the care of Hanna, an Arab neighbour, about whom she spoke warmly. Nevertheless, as a child I was warned not to play with 'strangers' and naturally not to respond to adult strangers, especially if they seemed to be nice. I now think that 'strangers' may have been a sexual (perversion, predatory adult behaviour) and national code. I always ran from adult males, and I began to avoid my Palestinian neighbours, Yaffa and Tamara, the twin girls who lived next door (or did they begin to avoid me?). I could never understand how one of them could have red hair when her twin sister had black hair. After kindergarten I stopped socialising with them.

When the time came to go to elementary school, my mother argued that the 'kids' deserved a better school. After seven years in Jaffa our family moved to an apartment on Dizengoff Street in Tel-Aviv. The bustling town made my parents feel more comfortable. Nonetheless, because I was the younger child, I was sent to the religious school that was within a block of our apartment and did not require crossing any roads. Thus, I ended up in the orthodox Dizengoff school for girls, the only secular girl in my class, while my sister, who was older, went to a secular school further up north. I was ashamed of my family and our tiny flat in Tel-Aviv when I brought friends over. Our flat could not possibly compare with the houses some of my friends had, friends whose fathers had been there before the Holocaust, and who owned factories and had prosperous law businesses. I was made painfully aware of the difference class makes, and perhaps that is why I continued to strive for the coveted A's that won me my parents' approval, increasingly at the price of social isolation. Class and religion did not endear me to the girls at Dizengoff. They knew my parents did not keep kosher and did not observe the Sabbath.

8

In the United States I soon learnt how small a place Hebrew literature occupied in the global map of comparative literature. Teaching Hebrew literature at the university makes me aware of this literature's marginal status within the literary academe. It lives on the margins of a Euro-American literary empire, lacking the recognition minor literatures sometimes receive in a comparative literary context (Kronfeld, 1996: 1–20). For years I did not teach a course in Hebrew literature, simply because I refused to teach male-centred texts, texts that I characterised as 'mythogynous' (Fuchs, 1987). Why teach A.B. Yehoshua, Amos Oz, Yitzhak Orpaz, Pinhas Sadeh, and the Palmah Generation that preceded them, or even Yosef Hayyim Brenner, Uri Nissan Gnessin, or Micha Yosef Berdyczewski? Why teach the Hebrew canon if it is dominated by men and male-centred plots? If the personal-national story again and again revolves around the uprooted young *Maskil* (enlightened Jew) or the alienated and confused *Halutz* (pioneer), or the isolated and noble-minded poet, or the idealistic Israeli soldier who is disturbed by the implications of his military mission?

It would take a decade before a body of feminist critical work made it possible to teach Hebrew literature that would include forgotten women authors and poets and that would address gender issues as central to the literary enterprise (Sokoloff et al., 1992; Diament and Rattok, 1994; Seidman, 1997; Kaufman et al., 1999; Feldman, 1999). With all this wealth of materials, I should be able to teach Hebrew literature in translation without feeling that I am presenting a skewed literary tradition. And yet, is the literary spectrum complete now that we can include women? Of course, the implications of my resistance to the very core of my academic field transcended the purely academic. Hebrew literature for me replaced the religious text I left behind when I left Israel. Hebrew literature, despite its critique of Zionism, provided a modern secular substitute for religious texts that had lost both meaning and relevance (Fuchs, 1982: 1–6). And yet, as I have already indicated, Hebrew literature revolved around the male protagonist, and my feminist approach made it increasingly difficult to accept it as an inclusive cultural paradigm for competing identities. The canon of Hebrew literature we learnt as graduate students questioned the Zionist meta-narrative, and yet it has become increasingly clear to me that the questioning was limited. The canon marginalised not just women, but also Mizrahi Jews and Palestinian citizens (Gover, 1994; Berg, 1996). Israeli culture and literature consisted of foundational Zionist myths that have not been sufficiently questioned or critiqued (Zerubavel, 1995).

My discomfort with the aesthetic standards and formalistic norms that have dominated the field of Hebrew literature was nurtured by a new awareness of the self-serving agendas of the study of Zionism and of Zionist historiography. A survey of diverse approaches within Zionism (e.g. Shimoni, 1995; Halpern and Reinharz, 1998) was not satisfactory, just as a survey of the varieties of contemporary Israeli literature was no longer satisfactory (e.g. Mintz, 1997). Zionist history, Israeli sociology, and other fields were based on a narrative, or a meta-narrative with a political perspective, informed by the interests of an exclusive, dominant Jewish, heterosexual, Ashkenazi, and male elite (Ram, 1995; Silberstein, 1999). The dominant intersecting ideologies excluded voices and perspectives that also made up Israeli identity, voices that were stifled. Women's voices were among these voices. I still remember my early questioning of Zionism when I was a high school student. That questioning came from the Right. After my return from the United States, where I spent six months in New York and Arizona as a foreign exchange student, I began to feel that something was missing. There was something superficial, something incomplete about the education I received. When I reached sixteen, two years into the secular public high school, Municipal High School No. 5 in Tel-Aviv, I began to ask questions. I pestered my history and Bible teachers especially: What was Zionism about, if not an attempt to salvage Judaism for the modern world? And if our mandate is to salvage Judaism, then how can we forfeit the teaching of the Mishnah, the Talmud, Biblical Exegesis, and the study of Halachah? Zionism was a watered-down version of Judaism; it was hypocritical in its claim to the land because it did not anchor its claim in a supernatural source, namely God.

I now tend to see my 'return' to religion as part of a general trend, a trend that was a response to the collapse of Labour Zionism beginning with the Six-Day War in 1967 and reaching critical proportions after the traumatic Yom Kippur War of 1973. I understand my response now as an attempt to protest against the ideological poverty, the empty promises of both Herzl's political Zionism and Ahad-Ha'am's spiritual Zionism, the promise to provide peace and security for the Jewish people and the promise to create a new vibrant cultural centre in Israel. By returning to the 'ghetto', as it were, by returning to religion, I rejected the promises of modern secularism and nationalism and endorsed the kind of Judaism that Zionism set out to replace. I now believe that I was seeking individual salvation in order to cope with the breakdown of the collective ethos of the time (Beit-Hallahmi, 1992). I also believe that my encounter with American Jewry in 1967 awakened me to the realisation that Israel is not necessarily the centre of the Jewish people. At best, Israel is one of two centres, and not necessarily the most 'Jewish' and not necessarily superior; it is one of two worlds of Judaism, one specific experience (Liebman and Cohen, 1990; Gal, 1996). I first rejected Zionism by becoming religious, and then rejected it again by leaving Israel, by becoming a *Yoredet*. Yet, I would not define myself as an 'anti-Zionist' – I abhor labels, I find them all restrictive and misleading. For me the question now is, what remains of my previous cultural identity? Emptied, stripped of so many 'layers' of my upbringing and formative education – what remains now?

9

When a person is stripped of her most basic sustaining myths of collective ethos – the myths that make her think she belongs to a broader community of people, even to a national vision – when she loses the sense of home, a certain emptiness, a certain exhaustion sets in. The keen awareness of the suffering of others and the recognition of the justice of their cause create guilt, a heavy burden to carry for anyone, not just a child of Holocaust survivors whose guilt is absorbed from her own guilt-ridden parents. As an Ashkenazi woman, am I not as well an oppressor in a system of restricted resources? Does my feminist theory have practical meaning? Does it include Mizrahi and Palestinian women (Swirski and Safir, 1991; Izraeli et al., 1999)? I also wonder about my privilege as a white college professor in the US. Since class is a relative category, sure, I am privileged. But to traverse so much distance, countries and states, for a rented apartment in the foothills of Tucson, to have come such a long way for the privilege of realising that a house in this area is completely out of my reach? To realise that the hikes in rent, electricity, and water rates do not equal the occasional cost of living salary adjustments – is this privilege? To pay for hotel expenses out of pocket, because my department would not defray more than travel costs, is this privilege? Or should I argue that as a college professor I should not measure my privilege in monetary terms, that my privilege is a name on a badge in a learnt conference? Will this name buy me the luxury of not moving yet again to another, cheaper apartment, perhaps on the outskirts of the foothills, to keep the cost of rent down? And as I wander from apartment to apartment, I wonder how far have I have come as an immigrant to the land of promise, from my parents who immigrated to the Promised Land. They still reside in the apartment they rented over thirty years ago in Tel-Aviv, and would not move to a house if their lives depended on it. As a *Yoredet* my story includes the exile of both Laura Levitt and Marcia Freedman, the Jewish feminist who failed to find a home in America and the feminist Jew who failed to find a home in Israel (Freedman, 1990; Levitt, 1997). What have I found in exchange for the sabras of my homeland? Are the saguaros greener, and is their prick less painful?

10

As the years go by, I lose names of people in Israel, as well as telephone numbers. I blame my exile for the loss of a community I once had. Though that community was never a stable or constant one, it was there: people who cared about the same ideas and beliefs. And yet, I must confess my ties to individuals or groups were never very strong. They tended to be intense and temporary. I was afraid to create lasting relationships, remembering already as a child that some imminent catastrophe could easily sever those ties. I grew up knowing that it is much easier to survive without ties: to family, to friends, to children, to parents. Those ties could kill. Jews who escaped, who did not let ties hold them back, those Jews survived. Children were lethal. They endangered their mothers; they endangered whole communities, because they cried at the wrong time. It was safer to be single; it was safer to be alone. Growing up in Tel-Aviv, I had few friends. Friends were not a priority. Homework always was a far more serious priority, because grades could magically wipe out my parents' pain.

My American therapist suggested some years ago that I consider the possibility that my emigration rehearses my parents' immigration: my parents had to leave Poland after the war, but I did not have to leave Israel, did I? What was she trying to tell me, I wonder? The more I ran from my mother, the more closely I resembled her, and the more I tried to escape from my parents' legacy, the deeper I became entangled in it. When I left Israel, was it the memory of the Holocaust I tried to escape? It would take years before I permitted myself, an associate professor of Judaic studies, to do a research paper on the Holocaust, or more precisely, on the representation of the Holocaust in films. In a recent paper I argue that women survivors are stereotyped as hideously ageing, stifling, overprotective, mentally ill mothers. I do not see my mother in the suicidal Madame Rosa or the sadistic Henya, the monster mother in 'The Summer of Aviya' (Fuchs, 2001).[4] But even as I deconstruct these films, I wonder about Mother's occasional tendency to dismiss my concerns, her tendency to compare my problems to the 'real' problems of kids in the ghetto – to what extent is this response, too, a scar. For if my complaints are merely expressions of self-indulgent fantasies, how can I trust my intuition, my feelings, my own pain? It is fitting to focus on films, shadows of reality created by imagination and projected on a screen? I cannot write about facts in the Holocaust, only reflections. It is not only because I am a literary critic, rather than a historian. It is because, as my parents kept repeating, I will never know the magnitude, the profundity, the enormity of what happened, so what is the point in attempting to reconstruct the facts? I am content to reconstruct the fiction. After my departure to the US, even as I won an additional fellowship, finished my Ph.D., moved to Austin to teach at the University of Texas, and later to Tucson to teach at the University of Arizona – the Holocaust would remain the single most important topic that binds us together. I report to them about a museum, a film, a newspaper article, and they report about yet another Holocaust survivor, one of their friends who passed away recently. The Holocaust has become a code for intimate conversation. After many years of endless conversations, my mother began to write her memoir (Fuks, 1988; Fuchs, 1999b: 127–33).

11

The ties that bound me to Israel may not have been as strong as they could have been, but they were the only ties I forged, for here in America I find it much harder to belong. The question is, which community? As a secular Jew and as a single woman, I find it especially difficult to find a place in any Jewish community, including the single progressive group led by the only woman rabbi in Tucson. My ambivalent embrace of the local community in both Austin and Tucson is reciprocated. As a professor of Judaic studies, I am sometimes invited to give a lecture at a local synagogue or a local chapter of Hadassah. The audience does not usually warm to my feminist critique of Hebrew literature and Israeli culture in general. They are not interested in a feminist deconstruction of the biblical narrative, either. Some openly ask me why I left Israel. Some keep this question to themselves. The order of the day is the reclamation of Judaism through inventive ritual and feminist Midrash. I teach a course on Women in Judaism, and even though I include theological interpretations, and feminist readings of Rabbinic and Halachic literature (e.g. Plaskow, 1990; Umansky and Ashton, 1992; Hauptman, 1998), the Jewish

communal structure in the US leaves very little for those who cannot affil-
iate with religious or quasi-religious institutions. Perhaps I should emphasise location, though: this is the case in the Southwest and the West.
It could have been different in New York or in Boston.

12

Isolation is part of living in the ivory tower of the academic world. The
Women's Studies Department has become just that – a department, a part
of the university, and as such it cannot become a home, though its friendliness is a welcome oasis in this figurative and literal desert. My courses
on Women in Judaism and Israeli Women are cross-listed with Women's
Studies, but I wonder sometimes why Jewish feminist texts are not featured in the core curriculum (Beck, 1996: 163–77). There is no single faculty member at the English department who teaches a course on
American Jewish fiction or poetry. Jewish literature is invisible in the
graduate programme of Comparative Cultural and Literary Studies. My
course Israeli Women is somehow omitted from the course list of Near
East Studies, my 'home' department. Am I too Jewish, too Israeli for the
Centre of Middle East Studies? In my course Israeli Women we read texts
by Palestinian women like Manar Hassan, Mariam Mari, Saniya Abu
Rakba, Nabila Espanioly, and discuss the oppression as well as the
achievements of Israeli and Palestinian women fighting for peace (Tawil,
1979; Emmett, 1996). In discussing the emergence of the Israeli woman as
enemy in Hebrew fiction of the 1960s and 1970s, I remind my class that in
literature, and in life as well, we create enemies out of fear (Fuchs, 1989b:
268–82). The 'other' is a fantasy as much as the self, whether that 'other'
is defined by gender or nationality.

The possibility that I am constructed as an 'other', as an enemy by dint
of belonging to a group of Western oppressors who have intruded into
the Middle East in order to cause nothing but misery for millions of innocent people, this possibility, this probability, makes me shudder. As a
child of victims, I find it terribly difficult to belong to a group of people
who willingly or unwillingly inflict suffering on another group of innocent people. Even if I no longer live in Israel, I am still part of the imaginary community that is often referred to as a nation, and this nation, my
link to it, continues to shape my consciousness and that slippery thing I
call identity.

Sometimes I doubt the very category of children of Holocaust survivors, realising that much of what I describe is the legacy of many Jews,
including those who were not born to parents who survived the Holocaust. I cannot answer this question yet. At this point I am working with
the category of second-generation survivors as a hypothesis, one that

explains my own personal traumas rather well. I would also like to believe that I belong to the theoretical category of second generation survivors who opt for a universalistic rather than a particularistic *Tikkun Olam* (repair of the world) (Berger, 1997), people who are committed to eliminating injustice for all, Jews and non-Jews, Israelis and Palestinians, women and men. This vision is the horizon, the promising contours of a place I might call home.

Ronit Lentin

'If I Forget Thee ...':
Terms of Diasporicity

—ɯ—

Prologue: (Israeli) Feminist Postcards from the Edge

In January 2001, during the fourth month of the al-Aqsa Intifada, I participated in a conference titled 'Gender, Place and Memory in the Modern Jewish Experience' at Bar Ilan University. One of the participants argued that since too few Israeli places were named after women, an intervention was needed so as to honour more women by calling places after them. I questioned this discussion, which did not mention the complex geopolitics of place names, many of which were hebraicised after their destruction as Palestinian villages. My comment, like my paper for that conference, met with violent opposition. I was told that 'this was not a space for politics', and the conference chose to proceed, ignoring the war waged outside the door. The hecklers' demand that we ignore the very political underpinning of the gender-place-memory nexus would have amazed me, had I not been prepared for what I have dubbed 'the self silencing of the feminist (and other Israeli intellectual) lambs' (Lentin, 2000a) during the al-Aqsa Intifada.

The current stage of the Israeli-Palestinian conflict has found many Israeli intellectuals, including many feminists, confused and at a loss for words. However, the fact that many Israeli intellectuals – authors, poets and philosophy and literature professors – have been supporting the Israeli government and blaming the Palestinians for the violence, is not particularly surprising. Apart from the Lebanon war, each Israeli-Arab confrontation saw the central intellectual players line up in the shadow of the establishment, giving it the necessary legitimacy. An example is Amos Oz's article in *The Guardian*, 'Arafat's gift to us: Sharon', in which he blames the

Palestinians, who, by refusing to accept Ehud Barak's 'generous' peace offering, brought about Sharon's victory (Oz, 2001).

Many Israeli feminists, with the exception of groups such as New Profile, Bat Shalom, the Women's Coalition for a Just Peace – preferred to join other Israeli intellectuals in nurturing Israeli victimhood and blaming the Palestinian leadership, and implicitly Palestinian women, for the current violence, negating the radical feminist mission of transforming society beyond nationalism and sectarianism.

This self-silencing raises a host of questions for me about the true nature of feminism, about ethnocentrism and imperialism within the (Western) women's movement (see Mohanty, 1991), and about feminists' inability to transcend national boundaries. These issues are problematised in the introduction of this volume and in Nahla Abdo's essay. This essay, the bulk of which had been written before the start of the al-Aqsa Intifada, and which I revised a few weeks after Sharon's election victory in February 2001, is presented in the shadow of that silence. The body of the essay is divided according to milestones in my writing career – the 1976 Jerusalem novella *Stone of Claims*, the 1982 *Conversations with Palestinian Women*, the 1989 novel *Night Train to Mother*, the 1996 novel *Songs on the Death of Children* and the 2000 book *Israel and the Daughters of the Shoah: Re-occupying the Territories of Silence* – as the stages of my diasporic journey, but also of my political awakening. I end with some questions about demilitarised zones, the only hope for any sort of future.

In the prologue, however, I want to comment on the reluctance of many Israeli feminists to engage with what I consider to be central feminist issues of difference, sisterhood and gender, as evidenced in the Bar Ilan conference. On 4 October 2000 I invited the Israeli feminist electronic list to discuss the implications of the crisis.[1] The list moderator replied: 'Ronit, while I agree wholeheartedly with your sentiments, this list was set up for specific goals. There are general lists discussing these issues....' Indeed, apart from two brief supportive responses, the debate largely did not take place. Only on 4 November 2000 did Micheline Beth-Levy call list members to debate the crisis as a 'feminist issue': 'I fail to understand how the violence and deaths of the last month are not a feminist issue to discuss and around which to mobilise support, which fulfils the purposes of the list (to discuss feminist issues, and mobilise support for feminist causes in Israel)'. Beth-Levy suggested feminists should look in the mirror and 'determine why the feminist Israeli response ... with the exception of Bat Shalom, has been seemingly relegated to ... feminist individuals within the "larger", very small movement....'

Despite the initial silence by mainstream Israeli feminists, most of whom, during the al-Aqsa Intifada, have identified, more than ever before, with the government, the opposition, or the Jewish settlers, Bat Shalom, New Profile, the Women's Coalition for a Just Peace, and other feminist organisations have continued to work relentlessly against the ongoing occupation and the oppression of the Palestinian population under Israeli closure (see http://www.batshalom.org; see also Gila Svirsky's essay in this volume for a detailed account of the activities of the Women's Coalition for a Just Peace).

However welcome such feminist activities are, initiatives such as 'Let the women talk'[2] evoke questions about essentialist assumptions regarding women's greater ability to make peace. On 2 November 2000, for instance, one such essentialist call for demonstration stated that 'Women make peace, generals do not. We did not get our children peacefully from Lebanon so that they kill or get killed in Judea and Samaria.... We, women, call on the Israeli government to talk, not kill. Listen to the voice of feminine wisdom, because the era of the generals is over!'

This raises important theoretical feminist questions. Despite the allure of such essentialisms, I agree with Sharoni (1992) that in order to understand the positioning of women and men in war and peace, gender must be understood as socially constructed, and that neither the equity position, demanding full equality for women in armed forces, nor the essentialist belief that men equal war while women equal peace, is helpful. The essentialist position may in fact lull women peace activists into ignoring Israeli women being implicated – as mothers, wives, sisters and lovers of soldiers, and as soldiers themselves – in Israeli militarism and in the continuing oppression of the Palestinians.

Another important issue is the invisibility of this feminist activism to the general public. Since the beginning of the Intifada, information about the activities of oppositional Israeli groups as well as Palestinian organisations has been communicated mostly electronically. This alternative, electronic communication network reports what the establishment's radio and television channels (and to a certain extent, also the Israeli print media) prefer to marginalise: the shortage of food, violence by the IDF and the settlers, and the left's protests (Cousin, 2001: 5). Despite its initial reluctance, the Israeli feminist electronic discussion list has been carrying the news from women's groups engaged in coalition and protest work, work which is largely invisible to the general public. Yet incidents such as the Bar Ilan conference remind me of what I already know: most Israeli feminists, like most Israelis, prefer to blame the Palestinians on the one hand and employ escapism strategies on the other, as their preferred responses to the ongoing Intifada.

Introduction: Fatherlands and Mother Tongues

Night.   Jerusalem.   *Yerushalayim.*
Jerusalem.   If I forget thee
Oh Jerusalem   Jerusalem   Hebron
Ramallah Nablus Qattana   if I
forget thee oh Jerusalem
Oh Hebron   may I forget
my own past   my pain
the depth of my sorrows.

> (Irena Klepfisz, 'East Jerusalem, 1987', in Klepfisz, 1990: 240)

I look at exile as human, not only Palestinian fate. Exile is not necessarily the opposite of homeland. Homeland is not defined by its opposite. All people are strangers.... In order to remove the curse from exile and from your treatment as different, you have to say, no ... we are all different and not equal. (Mahmoud Darwish, cited in Natur, 2000: 1)

When I looked back, I understood that the world in which I grew up, my parents' world, the pre-1948 world of Cairo, Beirut and Talbieh, was an imaginary, unreal world. It did not have the objective solidity I wanted it to have. For years I mourned the loss of that world.... But now I discovered the possibility of re-interpreting it. I understood that not only I, but most of us, keep shedding the past. What is forgotten, what is lost. I understood that my task is to tell and retell the story of loss in which returning home is impossible. (Edward Said, cited in Shavit, 2000: 22)

The Jerusalem I have dreamt about for many years while in voluntary exile in Ireland, dreams quite unlike those fostered by my Israeli Zionist upbringing about the 'forbidden city behind the wall' which must one day return to us, 'its rightful owners', is indelibly intertwined with my diasporic condition. A state of mind rather than a city where real people live and fight, love and kill, my Jerusalem epitomises the impossibility of reconciling difference, the improbability of return.

Surprisingly, despite endless family stories about 'there', my Israeli childhood did not signal the centrality the diasporic would assume in my later life and politics. It was, as they say, an 'ordinary Israeli childhood', complete with edicts of the Zionist return to the 'land without people by a people without land'. Palestinians were a shadowy presence in the mixed Arab-Jewish city that was Haifa, my birthplace. Shadowy, because we children saw them merely as labourers, house cleaners and at best Druze (because Druze, remember, were depicted as 'good Arabs' through complex blood contracts between the Israeli authorities and the Druze leadership), but always devoid of full humanity. I was part of the 'new Hebrew' generation, willed to fight and be strong, willed to differ from our diasporic 'Jewish' ancestors. Moving from Haifa to Jerusalem in the early 1960s, the 1967 war, and the realisation of injustice and Palestinian dispossession: these events signalled the first – albeit as yet unacknowledged – part of my journey away from 'new Hebrew' to diasporic Jew.

In Jerusalem I met the Palestinian man I was to call 'George' in *Stone of Claims*, the novella I published in the Hebrew literary journal *Siman Kria* (Lentin, 1976). The 'co-existence' I attempted with George failed because of the oppressor-oppressed power differential, but also because intimations of diasporicity began to mar my hitherto unproblematic, even if oppositional, Israeli subjectivity. In Jerusalem I also met Louis, my partner of over thirty years, with whom I moved in 1969 to Ireland, where I began having impossible (émigré) dreams about Jerusalem. In Dublin I wrote a book of interviews with Palestinian women, the first of its kind in Hebrew (Lentin, 1982), in which I naïvely searched for that very 1970s feminist link between 'the personal' and 'the political'. It was only years later – in two fiction projects, *Night Train to Mother* (Lentin, 1989), which traced the herstories of my Jewish-Romanian foremothers, and *Songs on the Death of Children* (Lentin, 1996), which tells of silences in the life of a daughter of Shoah survivors, and a re-search project on Israeli daughters of Shoah survivors charting the gendered link between a masculinised Israel and a feminised Jewish diaspora (Lentin, 2000b) – that I was able to make a lasting personal and political link with my diasporic Jewish past.

It is not by accident that I cite Klepfisz, Darwish, and Said at the start of this section. All three, émigrés par excellence, have excavated beautifully and painfully the layers upon layers of exile in relation to the land where my people have reimagined an ancient biblical past in modern nationalist form (cf. Anderson, 1983; 1999), complete with a search for essentialised 'roots', away from the 'routes' of our origins.[3]

Said writes about his choice of how to represent Palestinian lives in his *After the Last Sky*, named after Darwish's poem of that title: 'Since the main features of our present existence are dispossession, dispersion, and yet also a kind of power incommensurate with our stateless exile, I believe that essentially unconventional, hybrid, and fragmentary forms of expression should be used to represent us' (Said, 1986: 6). This essay – which links my two complex diasporic trajectories, that of the Israeli daughter of the 'first generation to redemption' to her diaspora Jewish past, and that of the 'ordinary' Israeli daughter of the Zionist dream to her anti-Zionist politics – employs a variety of 'fragmentary forms of expression' – fiction, theory, autobiography – to try and make sense of the indelible link between routes and terms of diasporicity.[4]

My story is but one of many stories of gendered dislocation, where, in that interstitial spaces between national/ist discourses, delicate power matrices are reconstructed. I make no apologies, at the risk of sounding like the Orientalist female voyaging beyond the veil, for including as a central element my attempted – what should I call it? – 'love affair' with

'George', my Palestinian 'other'. It is part of my herstory, albeit long in the past tense. Nor do I apologise for borrowing from Said – his insights into the position of the exilic light the darkness of constructing my own counternarrative to the Zionist narration of nation.

My first meeting with Nahla Abdo in Gaza in February 2000, after months of e-mail contact, strengthened my resolve to underpin the telling of my own story in Palestinian narratives of dispossession. This is not because the Palestinian and the Israeli exilic stories are similar or even parallel – after all, the power differentials are too palpable, too unbridgeable, as the account of Abdo's and my respective exits from Gaza on our way to the Israeli feminist conference in Beit Berl, related in the introduction, attests. Rather, it is because Abdo's (and Said's) anger – not always easy for Israelis to hear, particularly not for Israelis on the so-called 'left' of the political equation, who think that by designing projects together with Palestinian colleagues they are displaying their commitment to the Palestinian cause – is forcing me to tell the story differently. It forces me to reflexively engage with their brand of nationalism, at which, as a member of the (so far) powerful partner of the Israeli-Palestinian pair, I can afford to sneer from my inter-nationalist, anti-nationalist stance.

The story I tell in this essay – and this is not autobiography in the sense of 'life as it is lived', but rather in the sense of 'intellectual auto/biography' (Stanley, 1993; 1996) – is a very gendered tale. Indeed, the exilic in this instance is a woman, a feminist, whose understandings of exile fall somewhere between (Zionist) *fatherland* and (Jewish diaspora) *mother tongue*. Shari Benstock (1989) cites Sandra Gilbert (1984: 194–5), who posits *matria* as the underside of *patria* in the work of exiled women writers. *Matria*, for Gilbert, is 'that which is repressed, rejected, colonised, written over, subjected, erased, silenced'. The woman writer must discover her *matria* by peeling back the layers of patriarchy. For Benstock, however, *matria* is not the underside of *patria*, but rather an 'internal exclusion' within the entire conceptual and definitional framework, the 'other' by and through which *patria* is defined. *Patria* can exist only by excluding, banishing *matria*, *matria* is always expatriated' (Benstock, 1989: 25, emphases in the original).

If Gilbert's definition may describe the Palestinian sense of permanent exile as Said or Darwish would define it, Benstock's insistence on an internal exilic condition as a woman in a masculine nationalist culture fits my own condition as exilic Israeli-Jewish woman, away from the strict fatherland of my origins (despite the obvious power differentials between Palestinians and Israelis, even, or perhaps especially, those Israelis in voluntary exile).

A comment about the very Jewish edict of the title never to forget Jerusalem, which I do not mean as either a religious or a nationalistic dictum on the centrality of

Jerusalem for the 'Jewish nation' (an invented term; see, for example, Eilam, 2000). I have written elsewhere (Lentin, 2001) about the delicate balance between remembering and forgetting the Shoah as a constitutive part of Zionist politics. The imperative to remember the Shoah (albeit according to a Zionist script) was a centrepiece of the Israeli narration of nation-state. In my work I posit a link between the discursive silencing of Shoah survivors and the silence surrounding the dispossession of the Palestinians (cf. Morris, 1987; 1995; Pappe, 1994; Laor, 1995). Memory and forgetting, or *the need to remember in order to be able to forget*, has been a central imperative of the relationship between Israel and the Shoah. In recent years, however, other voices calling upon Israelis *to forget in order to be able to remember* are beginning to be heard. My work engenders the discussion by arguing that Jewish memory is male memory and that the way the Shoah was commemorated and 'memorised' in Israeli society has played into the masculinisation of the Israeli subjectivity, but also of Israeli memory.

Forgetting in order to remember (the Shoah) is indeed a political necessity, but forgetting Jerusalem is quite another thing. I find it hard to forget, but not only because, as the American poet and Shoah survivor Irena Klepfisz vows, 'forgetting the injustices of the present obliterates the depth of past sorrows'. Or because, by adding a Jewish past to my 'new Hebrew' Israeli past, 'I still have not found home in the dia-spora of my own making. Or because in the Ireland of my dia-sporic adult choice I'll forever be a (m)otherless-other, whose memories play a different tune. But, perhaps, because you can only be homesick at home. In that tragic, magic, Jerusalem evening light' (Lentin, 2000b: xiv).

Stone of Claims

In the novella *Stone of Claims* I tried to connect, in fiction form, with post-1967 Palestine, and put flesh on my budding political convictions. Before 1967, Palestinians – whom we called 'Arabs'; the political term 'Palestinian' came into use by (some) Israelis only long after that war – were not only the *'arabushim'* of our lexicon of curses. They were also the exotic 'other'. The story reveals the exoticising ambiguities:

> I was always envious of Yossi and Hemda Klein – they had friends from Kafr Kana and Taibeh.... Knowing Arabs meant eating their roast lamb and salty-sour cheese balls which floated in jars of green olive oil. Knowing Arabs was going to their weddings and telling your youth movement pals that Debka is actually an Arab dance. Knowing Arabs was saying that their music was not that monotonous after all, and feeling slightly sorry for their girls and boys who did not kiss in the public parks and did not neck fearfully under their khaki shirts after scouts meetings.... And later, on campus, there were other Arabs who used to whisper in the corridors and who were said to be a fifth

column and opposition organisations, and about whom we said they had the cheek to study at the expense of the government while hating the paymaster.... (Lentin, 1976: 111)

The story told not only of the friendship with 'George', but also of a (fictional) childhood sweetheart, 'Michael', who is killed after the 1967 war. When I wrote it, some six years after becoming a voluntary exile in Dublin, war, bereavement, sex, and love, both sexual and national, were part of the same story for me. *Stone of Claims* was told as an expression of the compulsion to prove that it could be different: 'the obstinate will to love – just once – an Arab man. Perhaps in order to prove that the hatred on which you were raised did not stick' (Lentin, 1976: 110), but also as a tale of what I thought was at the heart of the Israeli story, where gender and war are inseparable (Sharoni, 1992; Lentin, 1998). Reading the story today, I am somewhat embarrassed by the Orientalist theme of the Western woman and the Oriental man, although I was aware of consciously constructing the script:

> During supper ... sharp smells of pepper, rosemary and cardamom, you were alone. George, his manners perfect, acted the son of the family, moving from guest to guest, offering pistachio nuts, whiskey, Lebanese cigarettes, and helping the housekeeper to serve the food. You enveloped yourself in silence and allowed your eyes to tour the house and take in all the details, as if they were separate from you, like a film camera which takes in everything in order to edit and cut later ... constructing memory, an almost artificial memory which you were creating for some not too distant future. (Lentin, 1976: 112)

Ultimately, my relationship with 'George' fails because the diasporic Jew in me cannot relate to the dispossessed in him:

> 'George', you said softly. 'We *are* an Israeli Jewish woman and a Palestinian Arab man and we both pretend we don't care that we are so different. I don't know about you, but I grew up in an anti-Arab atmosphere since I was a little girl'. And you tell him all the things you wanted to tell him and which you were afraid would hurt him. About Mother who told you how, when she was alone with you when father was in the *Hagannah*, she held you in one arm and the revolver father had hidden for her in the bedroom linen cupboard in the other, whenever there was shooting in Haifa. About how, when fear overcame her, she would mumble to herself and to you, her screaming baby, 'I hate them, I hate Arabs'. About how Arabs were called '*Arabushim*', '*Araberim*', or simply 'filthy bastards' by the young men who queued up in the grocery store in the morning after a sleepless night on guard duty to buy fresh bread and cigarettes. About the joy of independence, the joy of victory, and about the relatively simple life of the 'first generation to redemption'; you, who had not experienced anti-Semitism, and did not understand the persecutions, the pogroms, the ghettoes, who were to grow up holding your heads high, free

from the perils of destruction, in the land of Zion and Jerusalem, the land of the Jews. And all was wonderful; there was nothing like you in the world, Jewish children, Sabras, in the land of your forefathers. No one ever said that there had been someone else here before you, in the abandoned houses, or that your pride was bought at a price of war. You were going to be different, better, the fruit of a long struggle. (Lentin, 1976: 136)

Stone of Claims is a mosaic of memory, told from the vantage point of the exilic: nation, war, love, sex, family, all blur into gendered prisms of 'personal' and 'political', in the realisation, as Said cites Adorno as saying, that in the twentieth century, the notion of 'home' has become marginal:

I suppose that part of my criticism of Zionism is that it apportions too much importance to home. It argues that we all need a home, that we would do anything to achieve a home, even if it means we render other people homeless in the process. Why do you think I am so interested in the idea of a bi-national state? Because I would like a rich texture that no one can understand completely, and which belongs to no one exclusively. I have never understood those who say this place is mine, and you remain outside. Nor do I like the striving for roots, for pure origins. I believe that the worst political and intellectual disasters of the twentieth century were caused by restrictive movements that sought to purify and simplify. Which ordered us to pitch our tents or our kibbutzim or our army here, and begin afresh. I don't believe in it. And I would also not like it for myself. Even if I were Jewish, I would struggle against it. And it won't survive. Believe me ... it won't even be remembered. (Said, cited in Shavit, 2000: 22)

Conversations with Palestinian Women

Living outside Israel did not dampen my political conviction. If anything, my opposition to the occupation was strengthened by living away from the everyday existence of war, reserve service (which the men in the lives of my girlfriends all had to do), and the daily infringements of Palestinians' rights. Maintaining contact with my erstwhile political colleagues, I was in receipt of information about the realities of the occupation from friends whose anti-Zionist convictions did not dim with the years. In 1972, after three years in Ireland, my (Irish-born Jewish) husband and I tried to resettle in Israel. The attempt failed. Israel proved too harsh for him and although I was torn between wishing to remain with him and stay in the country, I returned with him and our Israeli-born baby daughter Alana to Dublin in 1973, just 'missing' the 1973 war.

A comment about 'missing' the wars. Since the lives of Israeli women are punctuated by wars and by the army service of the men in their lives, and since all Israeli women are conscripted, I have always felt outside the mainstream because I was not conscripted at eighteen (because of asthma). Thus, I missed a crucial building block of Israeli identity: while my girlfriends served in the IDF, I went to university in Jerusalem, and while wars play a central role in most Israeli Jewish women's lives (as they do, from quite another perspective, for Palestinian women), I had only a few partners who served in the army. My husband was not an Israeli citizen and my son Miki – because his parents reside abroad – was not conscripted. So, although both my brother and my nephew were and are air force pilots, not serving in the IDF or having a soldier in my immediate nuclear family kept me outside the Israeli-Jewish anxiety circle. So 'missing' the 1973 war, and having experienced the 1967 war as my political awakening, as well as living most of my adult life in Ireland, exacerbated my 'otherness'.

In Ireland I worked in television and freelance journalism, and covered Israel for a variety of publications, making annual visits – I had young children with whom I spoke Hebrew and who enjoyed visiting their grandmother and cousins. It was a former Matzpen colleague, Haim Hanegbi, who suggested that I conduct a series of interviews with Palestinian women for an Irish newspaper.[5] It was an efficient journalistic endeavour – a colleague who worked for foreign television companies introduced me to some of the six women I was to interview: Mary Khas, formerly of Haifa, coordinator of UNRWA's preschool education in Gaza at the time of the interview; Hanan Ashrawi, then a professor of English in Bir Zeit University; Lilly Feidy, a Druze philology lecturer at Bir Zeit; Sahar Khalifa, a novelist and cultural coordinator at Bir Zeit. Another friend introduced me to Raymonda Tawil, director of a Palestinian news agency in East Jerusalem, famous for having been house-arrested by the Israelis. Finally, I met Siham Daoud, a Haifa poet and journalist. The interviews with Khas, Ashrawi, Tawil, Khalifa and Feidy were conducted in English and the interview with Daoud in Hebrew. Trying to focus on the then current feminist emphasis on the link between the 'personal' and the 'political', the interviews, which as a sociologist I would today call 'unstructured and open-ended', covered the women's beliefs about the conflict, about the position of women in Palestinian society, and about the difficult relationship between Israelis and Palestinians.

From the point of view of a sociologist, one of whose research interests is feminist research methodologies (Byrne and Lentin, 2000), it is easy to critique the book's methodology and contents. Situating myself within the process of the encounter with the six women, I disclosed my politics and history in an effort to elicit what I liked to think were commonalities between the women and me, but in the process I was probably guilty of what Bonnet (1999) calls 'white guilt', in trying to ingratiate myself to my interlocutors. For example, I was moved to ask all the women whether they hated Israelis, and whether they approved of 'terrorist' attacks. Today I understand this line of questioning as an attempt to bridge a gap between my Israeliness and my commitment to Palestinian rights. My reflexivity was provisional – locating myself in the process by declaring my politics was less than honest, I know today. Like so many 'progressive' Israelis, I thought that the mere act of interviewing Palestinians meant that I was conducting a collaborative, 'progressive' project, while in fact the agenda was entirely mine, just as the resulting text, published in Hebrew (which meant that several of the interviewees were unable to read it), remained my intellectual property.

Today, my commitment to participatory, emancipatory research strategies brings me to critique that project, at least for its naïveté. Katrina Goldstone (2000), writing about researching ethnic minorities in the Irish context, cites bell hooks (1991) who argues that 'rewriting you' is never either progressive or emancipatory. According to hooks, researching the 'other' often occludes her voice, even when researchers and writers are committed to making audible precisely that voice:

> Often this speech about the 'other' annihilates, erases. 'No need to hear your voice when I can talk about you better than you can speak about yourself. No need to hear your voice. Only tell me about your pain. I want to know your story. And then I will tell it back to you in a new way. Tell it back to you in such a way that it has become mine, my own. Re-writing you, I write myself anew, I am still author, authority. I am still the coloniser, the speaking subject, and you are now at the centre of my talk. (hooks, 1991: 151–2)

I may be harsh on myself. *Conversations with Palestinian Women,* although it presented only voices of privileged Palestinian women, not the voices of peasant or refugee women, was the first book of its kind in Hebrew and struck a chord with many Israeli readers at the time. Today, particularly from the position of a feminist researcher and anti-racist activist in Dublin, I believe that in order for majority members to interrogate the experiences of minority ethnic and colonised peoples, we have first and foremost to interrogate our own identity as 'white', and in the case of the Israeli-Palestinian conflict, as Israeli Jews.

Interrogating the dichotomies of majority/minority status both as an Israeli/Jew and as a Jewish 'other' in Irish society brought my two trajectories together.[6] No longer merely an Israeli whose Jewish past was obscured by triumphalist Zionism, my life as a voluntary exile in Ireland sent me in search of my maternal Jewish-Romanian roots/routes and onto the next stage.

Night Train to Mother

When did the journey begin?
When was the first time you remember being told about there?... Was there ever a time when you didn't journey, searching mother's hand, gasping for air, your asthmatic bronchials rasping to her reassuring voice?... You could have been a child from there, but they did all they could so you would be a child from here, a strong, earth-smelling sabra. The children at school mocked your skinny body and you developed an acid tongue in reply. (Lentin, 1989: 12–3)

In 1984 I journeyed to Bukovina, Northern Romania, my parents' birthplace, in order to research a book on the lives of the women of my mother's family – which, I suppose, I had really been researching since early childhood, when I was doing family trees with Grandfather (my brothers were not really interested) and listening (and not listening) to the stories of relatives who returned, broken, from Transnistria, a little-known areas of ghettoes and camps where the Jews of Northern Romania were exiled during the Second World War by the Romanians and the Nazis (Lentin, 2000e).

Over the years I gradually realised – it is hard to understand, in view of our Zionist childhoods, why it took me such a long time – that Israelis, constructed as 'non-Jewish Jews' actively engaged in what was seen as an existential 'no choice' war against the Arab states and the indigenous Palestinians, were, above all else, diasporic Jews who had returned to 'the land' to realise their Biblical past, thus not only skipping centuries of diasporic existence, but also negating the reality of Palestinian lives. This realisation, and the wealth of untapped material about Bukovina, an area rich in Jewish tradition, and its women, was slowly working itself in my head towards the novel I published in 1989. But it took the journey to the (diaspora) 'place' for the novel to mature. The book's title derives from the night train journeys that went from Bucharest to the north of Romania, where today in the towns once dominated by Jewish trade, commerce and culture, only handfuls of elderly, frightened Jews remain, and from Vatra Dornei, Mother's birthplace, to Czernowitz, once Bukovina's cultural capital, today a provincial Ukrainian town. I was journeying from sabra arrogance to my own diasporic past, but the actual journey was to Mother's life.

Strangely, visiting Vatra Dornei (nicknamed 'Dorna') felt like coming home, something Mother could never understand. It was strange how central Mother's family had been to the region, as I was repeatedly told by the few remaining Jews:

Dorna, situated between the mountains where the Dorna Stream flows into the Bistritsa River, is one of the most picturesque towns in this otherwise grey country.... Down the road is Schiebergasse (named after Mother's family), today Dobreanu Gherea street, named after a Jewish writer.... Here is

Mother's first home, named after her, Villa Lia. Today, it's a tenement, housing several families....

Why do you feel so good here? Why does it feel like home? It is nothing like the Israel of your childhood ... but somehow it feels right, despite the harshness of the present. The journey is beginning to have a sense of destination. (Lentin, 1989: 18–9)

Researching the book included talking to Grandmother, Mother and anyone else who would talk to me. But largely – and this is not authorial arrogance or pretence – the book wrote itself through the voices of those women whose lives I fictionalised, constructing for them love, trade, marriages, sex, loss. The voices came into my head and I was rewarded by family members and friends telling me that 'this was how it really was', making the novel sound almost like a memoir, or a documentary. An uncanny connection was made between those foremothers and their exilic daughter, over Mother's head – Mother who swore she felt no yearnings for the landscapes of the Bukovina 'there' which so fascinated me, her wayward émigré daughter.

I loved writing that book, loved that terrain, the re-memories. I particularly loved the final chapter, which depicts Hetti, Mother's (fictionalised) lame aunt, who lives in a downtown Haifa street amongst Israeli Palestinians, whose losses epitomise our oh-so-Jewish fate. Hetti evokes the spirit of Menashe, her dead communist husband, killed on a labour detail in Transnistria. Hetti, who travels to Tel-Aviv to commemorate the anniversary of the death of her parents and brother-in-law, does not even have a date to commemorate the death of her husband. Hetti, whose only son Yossi has left Israel. Hetti, whose sad life touched me, her fictional creator, most deeply:

Sometimes in the early morning, when she cannot sleep, she imagines Menashe hadn't died. That he is alive somewhere in Russia or Romania with another family. That he was told that it was she who died. But it makes no difference which of them died. And so she continues to live with his fading features and with Yossi's short letters from Vienna and with a scar across her stomach and a brace. And that, as they say, is it.

She decides not to watch television. Perhaps I'll be able to sleep tonight. The cemetery tires me so. I am too fat, too heavy for this long journey. A journey from which I return less and less each time. There are still people who tell her, how lucky you are to have such a wonderful family, such wonderful sisters, such a successful son.

But they say it less and less and she listens less and less. (Lentin, 1989: 215–16)

Night Train to Mother gave me the first opportunity to make contact with my exilic, gendered Jewish past. Re-writing me, not the Palestinian 'you', I no longer need to prove my 'progressive' political credentials through my fiction. When the next stage came, that of researching a doctorate on

Israeli daughters of Shoah survivors and at the same time writing my next novel, I was on my exilic journey in earnest. More committed than ever to equality in Palestine-Israel, I was now delving into my 'whiteness' and at the same time embarking on a new political journey, that of an anti-racist activist in Ireland, where the advent of a small number of asylum seekers (some 27,000 between 1992 and 2000, see Lentin, 2000d) was bringing racism out of the nation's crevices into the media and the high street.

Songs on the Death of Children

As I was researching my doctorate on the gendered relations between Israel and the Shoah, a new book wrote itself. Inspired by the ignorance of most Irish people about the intricacies of the Israeli-Palestinian conflict (a leading political journalist once asked me in all seriousness whether Jerusalem was on the Golan Heights), I began writing about Patricia Goldman, an Irish Jewish journalist who goes to Israel to cover the conflict for her newspaper. At the same time, I was researching Israeli silences about the Shoah, and also about the dispossession of Palestinians, a silence which left no space for Shoah survivors to tell what one of my interviewees, Israeli writer and daughter of Shoah survivors Nava Semel, calls their 'intimate memories'. So I found myself writing my protagonist Patricia Goldman as a daughter of survivors who had never been told about a sister whom her parents had given to Christian German neighbours to mind when they were deported to a concentration camp:

> I didn't ask any more questions. Gaining a dead sister was enough for one day. I felt immobilised by the dead weight Mother had just burdened me with. But I realised now I had always carried that weight, always unknowingly struggled uphill, carrying my pain around my neck. (Lentin, 1996: 31)

As Patricia decides to write a book on Israeli and Palestinian women, and as she gets entangled with Daniel, a married Shin Bet officer, himself a son of survivors who is haunted by his parents' demonic nightmares, she is driven to search for her lost sister.

Patricia's contact with Israelis and Palestinians and, through her Shin Bet lover, with the excesses of the Israeli occupation in all its ugliness, and its messy emotional ties to the political abuse of the memory of the Shoah as a justification for these excesses, drives her to get her mother to tell her about her Shoah past, which was a dark secret presence in Patricia's childhood. She eventually discovers that her sister is Daniel's wife (and learns of his part in deliberately bringing them together):

> I've found her, Mama. Your daughter. Your Hanna.... You didn't think I would find her. You weren't sure what I would say to her. You didn't really want me

to find her, did you? I haven't met her yet. I must think before I make the next move.... How to introduce myself to her. What to say. (Lentin, 1996: 213–14)

The story has no happy ending. As Hanna and Patricia meet, as they tell each other about their silences and secrets, Daniel looks on, no longer able to partake in his wife's, or his lover's, world, despite his own palpable pain as a son of that same survivor generation. I left the ending ambiguous: when Patricia phones their mother in Ireland, their mother refuses to speak to Hanna. When Hanna dials her on the following morning, the phone rings and rings and there is no reply.

Israel and the Daughters of the Shoah

I finished the novel in the summer 1996, as I was working on chapter drafts of my doctoral thesis. At times, as I wandered through the empty house – my family was elsewhere that summer – I wept. The materials I was dealing with in both works touched both my trajectories – that of the diasporic Israeli daughter who had abandoned her (m)otherland and who was now connecting with her exilic roots, and the émigré Israeli woman connecting with the routes of her anti-Zionist politics: roots and routes combining to form my ultimate dia-spora, scattering and sowing, journeying and putting down roots in a foreign land, my night train journey *away* from mother, towards an unknown destination.

The irony is that *Songs on the Death of Children* was my least autobiographical fiction work – Patricia was definitely not me, although my politics, both feminist and 'political', are reflected in the novel. However, the thesis and the book which ensued, *Israel and the Daughters of the Shoah: Reoccupying the Territories of Silence* (Lentin, 2000b), concentrated on the autobiographical implications for me of the materials I was researching: the gendered aspects of the silences in Shoah survivor families and their silencing and stigmatisation in Israeli society. The conceptual link between the terms 'silence' and 'territories' of the title are connected to my own two trajectories (see Lentin, 2000c). Silence – silent Shoah families and the silencing of Shoah families in Israeli society, despite the many words that are spoken about the Shoah and the imperative 'never to forget' – is the central character in the lives of Shoah survivors, both those who are able to tell their stories and those who take their stories with them to their graves, but also in the lives and the fictional and cinematic works of their daughters, as I documented in the book.

I now know that my work, both fiction and academic, has always attempted to give voice to that silence. I began working on the gendered relationship between Israel and the Shoah on a hunch, theorising that Israel was, and is, a masculine construction where, although women are active participants, society is built on axioms of a 'no-choice' ongoing military struggle. Necessarily, the ongoing wars privilege male soldiers who share in the dividends of military, social, and political power, to the detriment of women. Much has been written on both the discrimination against Shoah survivors upon their arrival (e.g. Segev, 1991; Yablonka, 1994) and the masculinisation of Israel (e.g. Hazelton, 1978; Shadmi, 1992; Boyarin, 1997). My research goal was to link Israel as a masculine construction with the stigmatisation of Shoah survivors via 'reading between the lines' of the silences that enveloped Shoah survivors upon their arrival and that still envelop their children in contemporary Israel (although these silences are in the process of being broken, thanks in no small measure to my narrators' works).

Crucially, silencing survivors' Shoah experiences was linked to the silencing, initiated by early statist prime minister David Ben-Gurion, of the 'true story' of the pre-state violent return to Zion, which entailed expelling Palestinians and dispossessing them of their lands during and after the establishment of the state of Israel in 1948. With the years, this silence deepened; it was broken only in the 1980s with new histories of the Israeli-Palestinian conflict (e.g. Morris, 1987; Pappe, 1994). Using newly available archival materials, these 'new historians' produced alternative academic accounts of the history of Zionism and the state of Israel by illuminating the silenced facts of the 1948 expulsions and the 1950s murder of thousands of so-called 'infiltrators', Palestinian refugees stealing across the borders in an attempt to return to their villages. A recurring theme in the writings of these post-Zionist historians was, according to Silberstein:

> the need to open spaces for the voices of those who have been designated as the 'other' in Israeli society, including diaspora Jews, Jews of Middle Eastern origin, Palestinian Arabs and women. Thus, postzionists may be said to be engaged in a 'space clearing gesture', clearing space both for previously silenced voices and for alternatives to the dominant Zionist discourse. (Silberstein, 1999: 3–4)

A silencing similar to that of the Palestinian experience in relation to the establishment of the state of Israel, born out of the refusal to consider a narrative different from that of the 'state generation' – 'those narcissistic and diaspora-negating *sabras*'[7] – also enveloped Shoah survivors as they began arriving. And the monopoly on memory, appropriated by the Israeli state – 'first there was history and later a nation was 'written' to fit this history' (Laor, 1994: B6) – assisted the 'state generation' in nationalising the memory of the Shoah.

What I did not know before beginning the research process, which entailed extensive personal narrative interviews with nine daughters of survivors, was how deeply implicated I myself was in all this. When all the narrators spoke of coming from 'silent families' where one 'knew and did not know' about the Shoah at the same time, I hadn't realised the extent that my own family was such a 'silent family'. Mother's insistence, until a very short time ago, that she never needed to speak of her past life in Bukovina, a life she abandoned at the age of nineteen to go to Palestine in 1941, was beginning to ring hollow. As I began transcribing the narratives, I realised, on the one hand, how much she *did* talk about her Romanian childhood – when I visited Bukovina in 1984, Dorna looked as I had imagined, coming to life through her stories about 'there'. On the other hand, and somewhat contradictorily, I realised just how silent my own parents had been about the Shoah. This, despite having lost several members of their families, while other family members were exiled to Transnistria. Because Mother and her family managed to escape on time, they never saw themselves as survivors – the mantle of 'Shoah survivors' was not lightly assumed. Yet, according to a broader definition of survivorhood, we *were* a family of survivors, and I was a daughter of such a silent family (Lentin, 2000c: 252–3).

I chose the terms 'territories' and 'occupation' for the title because no discussion of Israeli society can be undertaken in isolation from the Israeli-Palestinian conflict, ignored for decades in Israeli social sciences, which, until the late 1970s, were concerned above all with perpetuating the institutions of ruling (Ram, 1993). I concur with Sharoni's argument that the state of Israel can be seen as 'a reassertion of masculinity, justified by the need to end a history of weakness and suffering by creating an image of an Israeli man who is exceedingly masculine, pragmatic, protective, assertive and emotionally tough' (Sharoni, 1992: 457). Because of the ongoing occupation, Zionist ideology has made 'national security' a top priority, offering Israeli men a privileged status and legitimising national, ethnic and gender inequalities. Linking occupation and gender relations, Sharoni argues that 'in a context where every man is a soldier, every woman becomes an occupied territory' (ibid., 459).

The resulting book is an act of 'naming' – naming myself, for the first time, as a daughter of a family of survivors, and also naming myself publicly for the first time as an anti-Zionist. I do not want to overstress the agonising about these two acts of 'coming out' – both are easier to engage with from the distant security of my Irish exile. In *Israel and the Daughters of the Shoah*, my two trajectories come together. I end the book with the words of the exiled daughter who cannot rid herself of guilt for having left home, the home she carries, snail-like, on her back, and who is still full of love for her (m)otherland, her unrelenting *matria*, despite everything:

Journeys end wherever we are. Many endings.
I think I know now what I needed to know when I embarked on the journey which began in 1984 in Bukovina.
Or in 1944 in Haifa, at the end of that war, before all the other wars of my life.

Or in 1992, with the conversations with my Israeli sisters-daughters, about our beloved country, the home we carry on our backs, our imperfect crystal ball.
I needed to put words to the pain that was my beloved country, my beloved evening light. The light which darkened our past, seeking to reinvent it, erasing the hurt of the code words passed cautiously in Grandmother's glass-panelled room.
I needed to have my Jewish exilic past returned to me, my European maiden name returned to me.
And I needed to forgive my Israel for darkening the light.
And to be forgiven – for leaving the only home I have never left.
Even in exile.
If I forget thee oh Jerusalem, oh Dorna, oh Transnistria,
may I forget my past
my home
my exile
my pain, the depth of my sorrows. (Lentin, 2000b: 227)

The Last Sky

Carla de Tona (2000), researching Italian women migrants in Ireland, cites a line about migrants by an unknown poet: 'we are the trees with roots in the sky'. I like this image for the Jews' eternal state of diasporicity, which is, as I see it, a state of eternal otherness despite Israeli Zionism's anti-diaspora claims, which intended to put an end to the Jews' exilic existential condition. But if Jews – and I include my own diasporic existence – have their roots in the sky, wandering, scattering, and sowing their seeds, always somewhat temporary in their countries of sojourn, Palestinians are trees with their roots in the soil. If the diasporic Jew is like Chagall's floating cows, violins, brides, 'fiddling on the roof' of the Eastern European shtetl and the world, the Palestinian is like an olive tree, older than memory, tougher than stone.

Stone of Claims begins with an attempt to sing the sound of Jerusalem's stones:

Stone.
Another stone.
Stones.
Golden, warm, transparent.
In the square in front of the Holy Sepulchre Church, at evening time, there were days the stone invited a touch, with the cool wind blowing a shudder through my body, slipping under the little dress, blossoming in thousands of tiny red flowers. And in the stone, which hugs the sun during the day, there is a warmth which lightens the coolness of the night. (Lentin, 1976: 109)

'The concept of diaspora', writes Avtar Brah (1996: 16), 'offers a critique of discourses of fixed origins while taking account of a homing desire, as distinct from a desire for a 'homeland'. This distinction is important, not least because not all diasporas sustain an ideology of 'return'. Reading Brah, I acknowledge the difference between the desire of exiled Palestinians born in Haifa to return to their home place, precisely because they *can't*, and my absence of longing for 'home' in the sense of wishing to return to the Haifa of my birth, probably because I *can*.

Said writes poignantly about notions of 'early home', which means finding 'the place where originally one was *at home'*, and says that 'those individuals and that "people" best suited to the task are Jews. Only the Jews as a people (and consequently as individuals) have retained both a sense of their original home in Zion and an acute, always contemporary, feeling of loss' (Said, 1979: 62). Said's argument about Zionism's continued efforts to efface the Palestinians, about no human being having to be 'stripped of his or her land, national identity, or culture, no matter what the cause' (Said, 1979: xvi), does not need re-rehearsing. In this essay I have tried to sketch some themes that divide my own *Jewish* diasporic experiences from those of my Palestinian sisters.

Writing about the Palestinian exile, Said (1986) cites Mahmoud Darwish's evocative poem: 'Where should we go after the last frontiers / where should the birds fly after the last sky?' The people whose roots are 'in the sky' and the people whose roots are 'in the soil' do not share the same horizon, the same last sky, and stones are not merely romantic metaphors; they can be instruments of war.

Stone of Claims ends after exile and the failure of love:

> And then – they say that the Sepulchre Church is being renovated and that the old Palestinian guides are being replaced by authorised Ministry of Tourism guides. The shaded yard in front of the church is still lovely and cool, and the icons' gold leaf is still beautiful. (Lentin, 1976: 143)

Epilogue: Demilitarised Zones

Israel is a militarist state (see Ben Eliezer, 1995; Lomsky-Feder and Ben-Ari, 1999) and the road to struggling for the demilitarisation of Israeli society is long and stony. New Profile: Movement for the Civil-isation of Society in Israel does just that. It names militarism as a package of organising principles which guide the Israeli state, amazingly, considering that Jews, until relatively recently, were people 'with roots in the air'. According to the group's position paper (2000), the militarisation of Israeli society is evident in language, politics, and media (the Israeli media, with the exception of Gideon Levy and Amira Hass, both writing for *Ha'aretz*, tend to serve government and IDF views), in the second class status of Palestinian citizens of Israel, the increasing tendency to conceal information (using 'national security' as an excuse), and in the privileging of the IDF's ongoing budgetary and operational freedom (and thus increasing the turnover of Israel's and its Western allies' armament industries).

Israeli feminist groups who keep up the struggle, few as they may be, often differ in defining their political aims. They disagree as to whether the groups are too elitist, too Ashkenazi-based and therefore too remote from the majority of Mizrahi and lower class women (see Shohat in this volume), and as to the final goal – two states for two nations, or one secular, democratic Israel-Palestine, as Nahla Abdo and I also debate in the introduction. Issues of sisterhood, democracy, and equality, as majority world feminists have told us time after time, are divisive and, as Palestinian feminists argue (see for instance, Dajani, 1994; and Abdo in this volume), it is never easy to prioritise between the national and the social/ gender agendas.

I have come a long way in defining my own politics, although the trajectory has not been one-directional or one-dimensional. I have oscillated between the need for a 'Jewish state' for a 'Jewish nation' alongside a 'Palestinian state' for a 'Palestinian nation', and a rejection of all nationalist aspirations, be they Israeli or Palestinian. The al-Aqsa Intifada and the racist, oppressive Israeli response have strengthened my rejection of narrow nationalisms, although I recognise the strong call for national self-determination by the oppressed.

What I have not wavered on, since 1967, is my belief that the occupation is both oppressive and corrupting. The cessation of violence, any violence, is a just demand and should top the list of any political negotiations. However, as Gideon Levy argues, it is hypocritical for Israel to demand that the Palestinian Authority put an end to Palestinian violence without demanding the same of itself: 'For most Israelis, violence is what the Palestinians do to us. Israeli reaction is just that, a reaction.... Israeli measures, from siege to closure, from land confiscations to house demolitions, are not considered violence by Israelis.... When thirty-three West Bank villages are cut off by bulldozer-dug impassable trenches, blocking the passage of ambulances and water carriers, as Israel has just done, the demand for a cessation of Palestinian violence is hypocritical and enraging. End to violence? Why shouldn't Israel, as the stronger side, be the first?' (Levy, 2001: B1). Nor have I wavered on my conviction that victimisation often victimises – yesterday's victims of anti-Semitism and annihilation have become, sadly, today's victimisers – and that, perhaps because of the Jews' self-imposed higher moral values, we must struggle against that sense of victimhood and aspire to the indivisibility of justice and morality.

I would therefore like to end with some questions, because I don't really have any answers. Reflecting on women, war, and peace in the Middle East, I would like to ask whether it matters what feminists do or don't do while the killing continues. Is the self-silencing of Israeli intellectuals a sign of collusion, collaboration, or confusion? Do national élites on both sides ultimately need intellectuals only in order to confirm the institutions of ruling (something I have obstinately refused to do for decades, both in Israel and in Ireland)? Do intellectuals, in attempting to reformulate discourses of national identity, racism, discrimination, or state violence, not merely reaffirm them? The discussion on the role of intellectuals is beyond the scope of this essay, but we, as Israeli intellectuals and feminists, can no longer say that we did not know. We can no longer blame the messenger and ignore the message.

Notes

'Exile, Memory, Subjectivity'

1. The root *yrd* means 'to descend', in contrast to the noun *oleh* – immigrant – whose root derivation means 'ascend'.
2. *Heder*, which literally means a room, refers to elementary education in traditional Judaism, while *Yeshiva* refers to a traditional academy of high learning.
3. The *Palmach* is an acronym referring to the crack fighting forces of the *Hagana* (literally, defence), the pre-state voluntary army in Palestine under the British Mandate.
4. 'Hakayitz shel aviya', directed by Eli Cohen, produced by Gila Almagor and Eitan Evan, 96 minutes, 1989.

'If I Forget Thee ...'

1. iff-l@research.haifa.ac.il
2. haggith_gor@smkb.ac.il
3. Interestingly, Said's *Orientalism* (1978) was published in Hebrew only in 2000 (soon after the publication of the Hebrew translations of Benedict Anderson's *Imagined Communities* and Hannah Arendt's *Eichmann in Jerusalem* – two other seminal texts hitherto ignored by Israeli publishers). Comments on the new translations (Gershuni and Sand, 2000: B13; Sadan, 2000: B13) 'forget' to mention the 1981 Hebrew translation of Said's *The Question of Palestine*, which I translated together with Yahali Amit for Mifras publishing house, which also published my *Conversations with Palestinian Women*. This obfuscation might have to do with Mifras being a (now defunct) 'left wing' publisher, or because the Israeli media needed more time to begin to grapple with the implications of Said's (as well as Anderson's and Arendt's) ideas, which, on various levels, challenge the Zionist hegemony, which has in the past decade been challenged by Israeli 'new historians' and others.
4. Although I was born in pre-state Palestine, and have a British Mandate Palestinian birth certificate, I, like many Israelis of my generation, have designated 'Israel' as my birth place. Naming myself 'Palestinian' is of course politically unacceptable.
5. Matzpen was a Trotskyist group established in the early 1960s, whose politics included opposition to the occupation and a commitment to a secular democracy in the Palestinian-Israeli space.

6. I am, however, aware of the problematic of the majority/minority interface, which reduces the problems of unequal power relationship to one of numbers, with the effect of naturalising, rather than challenging the power differential (Brah, 1996: 186–7).

7. The term *sabra* (named after a desert cactus originating in South America, imported to Palestine some 200 years ago) is used to denote Jews born in Palestine (later Israel) since the 1930s. According to Almog (1997) the term is a cultural, rather than biological (born in 'the land'). Ironically, the Palestinians also describe themselves as *sabras*, and the cactus appears often in Palestinian visual artworks.

References

'Exile, Memory, Subjectivity'

Almog, Oz. 2000. *The Sabra: The Creation of the New Jew.* Berkeley: University of California Press.

Alter, Robert. 1988. *The Invention of Hebrew Prose: Modern Fiction and the Language of Realism.* Seattle and London: University of Washington Press.

Beck, Evelyn T. 1996. 'Jews and the multicultural university curriculum'. In Marla Brettschneider (ed.), *The Narrow Bridge: Jewish Views on Multiculturalism.* New Brunswick: Rutgers University Press.

Beit-Hallahmi, Benjamin. 1992. *Despair and Deliverance: Private Salvation in Contemporary Israel.* Albany: State University of New York Press.

Berg, Nancy. 1996. *Exile from Exile: Israeli Writers from Iraq.* Albany: State University of New York Press.

Berger, Alan. 1997. *Children of Job: American Second-Generation Witnesses to the Holocaust.* Albany: State University of New York Press.

Boyarin, Daniel. 1997. *Unheroic Conduct: The Rise of Heterosexuality and the Invention of the Jewish Man.* Berkeley: University of California Press.

Brenner, Athalya. 1997. *The Intercourse of Knowledge: On Gendering Desire and 'Sexuality' in the Hebrew Bible.* Leiden: Brill.

Diament, Carol, and Lily Rattok. 1994. *Ribcage: Israeli Women's Fiction.* New York: Hadassah.

Emmett, Ayala. 1996. *Our Sisters' Promised Land: Women, Politics, and Israeli-Palestinian Coexistence.* Ann Arbor: University of Michigan Press.

Ezrahi, Yaron. 1997. *Rubber Bullets: Power and Conscience in Modern Israel.* Berkeley: University of California Press.

Falk, Marcia. 1996. *The Book of Blessings.* Boston: Beacon.

Feldman, Yael S. 1999. *No Room of Their Own: Gender and Nation in Israeli Women's Fiction.* New York: Columbia University Press.

Freedman, Marcia. 1990. *Exile in the Promised Land: A Memoir.* Ithaca: Firebrand Books.

Fuchs, Esther. 1982. *Encounters with Israeli Authors.* Marblehead: Micah.

———. 1983. *Tsaleket* [Scar]. Tel-Aviv: Ecked. [Hebrew]

———. 1987. *Israeli Mythogynies: Women in Contemporary Hebrew Fiction.* Albany: State University of New York Press.

———. 1989a. 'Exile, Jews, women, *Yordim*, I: An interim report'. In Mary Lynn Broe and Angela Ingram (eds.), *Women's Writing in Exile.* Chapel Hill and London: The University of North Carolina Press.

———. 1989b. 'Images of love and war in contemporary Israeli fiction: A feminist revision'. In Helen M. Cooper et al. (eds.), *Arms and the Woman: War, Gender and Literary Representation.*Chapel Hill and London: University of North Carolina Press.

———. 1997. *Li Asur Lehitabed* [No licence to die]. Tel-Aviv: Ecked.

———. 1999a. 'The enemy as woman: Fictional women in the literature of the Palmach'. *Israeli Studies* 1 (1): 212–34.

———, (ed.). 1999b. *Women and the Holocaust: Narrative and Representation*. Lanham: University Press of America.

———. 2000. *Sexual Politics in the Biblical Narrative: Reading the Hebrew Bible as a Woman*. Sheffield: Sheffield Academic Press.

———. 2001. 'Women survivors in cinema: The issue of madness'. In John K. Roth and Elisabeth Maxwell (eds.), *Remembering for the Future: The Holocaust in an Age of Genocide*. New York: Pargrave Macmillan.

Fuks, Zila. 1988. *Za'akot lelo kol* [Silent screams]. Trans. Yosef Avni and Asher Shofet. Tel-Aviv: Y.L. Peretz.

Gal, Allon (ed.). 1996. *Envisioning Israel: The Changing Ideals and Images of North American Jews*. Jerusalem and Detroit: The Magnes Press and Wayne State University Press.

Gover, Yerach. 1994. *Zionism: The Limits of Moral Discourse in Israeli Hebrew Fiction*. Minneapolis: University of Minnesota Press.

Halkin, Simon. 1970. *Modern Hebrew Literature: From the Enlightenment to the Birth of the State of Israel – Trends and Values*. New York: Schocken.

Halpern, Ben, and Jehuda Reinhartz (eds.). 1998. *Zionism and the Creation of a New Society*. New York: Oxford University Press.

Hanoch, Amos. 1975. 'Mi Dizengof Lemea She'arim Uvehazara' [From Dizengodd to Mea She'arim and back]. *Ma'ariv* 22 (August): 22–54.

Hauptman, Judith. 1998. *Rereading the Rabbis: A Woman's Voice*. Boulder: Westview Press.

Hazleton, Lesley. 1977. *Israeli Women: The Reality Behind the Myths*. New York: Simon and Schuster.

Heschel, Susannah (ed.). 1983. *On Being a Jewish Feminist*. New York: Schocken.

Izraeli Dafna, Ariella Friedman, and Ruth Shrift (eds.). 1982. *Nashim Bemilkud* [The double bind: Women in Israel]. Tel-Aviv: Am Oved.

Izraeli, Dafna, Ariella Friedman, Henriette Dahan-Calev, Hanna Herzog, Manar Hassan, Hanna Naveh, and Silvie Bijaoui-Fogiel. 1999. *Min, Migdar, Politika* [Sex, gender, politics]. Tel-Aviv: Hakibbutz Hameuchad.

Levitt, Laura. 1997. *Jews and Feminism: The Ambivalent Search for Home*. New York and London: Routledge.

Kahn, Susan Martha. 2000. *Reproducing Jews: A Cultural Account of Assisted Conception in Israel*. Durham and London: Duke University Press.

Kaufman, Shirley, Galit Hasan-Rokem, and Tamar S. Hess. 1999. *The Defiant Muse: Hebrew Feminist Poems*. New York: The Feminist Press.

Klepfisz, Irena. 1982. 'Anti-Semitism in the lesbian/feminist movement'. In Evelyn T. Beck (ed.), *Nice Jewish Girls: A Lesbian Anthology*. Watertown: Persephone.

Kronfeld, Chana. 1996. *On the Margins of Modernism: Decentering Literary Dynamics*. Berkeley: University of California Press.

Liebman, Charles S., and Steven M. Cohen. 1990. *Two Worlds of Judaism: The Israeli and American Experiences*. New Haven and London: Yale University Press.

Milne, Pamela J. 1997. 'Toward feminist companionship: The future of feminist biblical studies'. In Athalya Brenner and Carole Fontaine (eds.), *Reading the Bible: Approaches, Methods and Strategies*. Sheffield: Sheffield Academic Press.

Mintz, Alan. 1989. *Banished from Their Father's Table: Loss of Faith in Hebrew Autobiography*. Bloomington and Indianapolis: Indiana University Press.

———. 1997. *The Boom in Contemporary Israeli Fiction*. Hanover and London: University Press of New England.

Plaskow, Judith. 1990. *Standing Again at Sinai*. San Francisco: Harper and Row.

Porat, Dina. 1991. 'Attitudes of the young state of Israel toward the Holocaust and its survivors: A debate over identity and values'. In Laurence J. Silberstein (ed.), *New Perspec-*

tives on Israeli History: The Early Years of the State. New York and London: New York
University Press.

Pratt, Minnie Bruce. 1984. 'Identity: Skin, blood, heart'. In Elly Bulkin, Minnie Bruce Pratt
and Barbara Smith (eds.), *Yours in Struggle: Three Feminist Perspectives on Anti-Semitism
and Racism*. Ithaca: Firebrand Books.

Ram, Uri. 1992. *The Changing Agenda of Israeli Sociology: Theory, Ideology and Identity*.
Albany: State University of New York Press.

Ravitzky, Aviezer. 1996. *Messianism, Zionism and Jewish Religious Radicalism*. Chicago and
London: The University of Chicago Press.

Seidman, Naomi. 1997. *A Marriage Made in Heaven: The Sexual Politics of Hebrew and Yiddish*. Berkeley: University of California Press.

Shapira, Anita. 1993. *Herev Hayona* [Land and power]. Tel-Aviv: Am Oved.

Sharoni, Simona. 1995. *Gender and the Israeli-Palestinian Conflict: The Politics of Women's
Resistance*. Syracuse: Syracuse University Press.

Shimoni, Gideon. 1995. *The Zionist Ideology*. Hanover and London: Brandeis University Press.

Shokeid, Moshe. 1988. *Children of Circumstances: Israeli Emigrants in New York*. Ithaca and
London: Cornell University Press.

Silberstein, Laurence J. 1999. *The Postzionism Debates: Knowledge and Power in Israeli Culture*.
New York and London: Routledge.

Sokoloff, Naomi, Anne L. Lermer and Anita Norich. 1992. *Gender and Text in Modern
Hebrew and Yiddish Literature*. New York and Jerusalem: The Jewish Theological Semi-
nary of America.

Swirsky, Barbara, and Marilyn Safir (eds.). 1991. *Calling the Equality Bluff: Women in Israel*.
New York: Pergamon Press.

Tawil, Raymonda Hawa. 1979. *Ma'atsar Bayit* [My home, my prison]. Jerusalem: Adam.

Umansky, Ellen, and Dianne Ashton. 1992. *Four Centuries of Jewish Women's Spirituality: A
Sourcebook*. Boston: Beacon Press.

Zertal, Idith. 1998. *From Catastrophe to Power: Holocaust Survivors and the Emergence of Israel*.
Berkeley: University of California Press.

Zerubavel, Yael. 1995. *Recovered Roots: Collective Memory and the Making of Israeli National
Tradition*. Chicago and London: University of Chicago Press.

Zimmerman, Bonnie. 1996. 'The challenge of conflicting communities: To be a lesbian and
Jewish and a literary critic'. In Jeffrey Rubin-Dorsky and Shelley Fisher Fishkin (eds.),
People of the Book: Thirty Scholars Reflect on Their Jewish Identity. Madison: The Univer-
sity of Wisconsin Press.

'If I Forget Thee …'

Almog, Oz. 1997. *Hatsabar: Doykan* [The Sabra: A portrait]. Tel-Aviv: Am Oved.

Anderson, Benedict. 1983. *Imagined Communities: Reflections on the Origin and Spread of
Nationalism*. London: Verso.

———. 1999. *Kehilot Medumyanot* [Imagined communities]. Trans. Dan Daor. Tel-Aviv:
Open University.

Ben Eliezer, Uri. 1995. *Derech Hakavenet: Hivazruto shel Hamilitarism HaIsraeli 1936–1956*
[Through the rifle-sight: The construction of Israeli militarism, 1936–1956]. Tel-Aviv: Dvir.

Benstock, Shari. 1989. 'Expatriate modernism: Writing on the cultural rim'. In Mary Lyn
Broe and Angela Ingram (eds.), *Women's Writing in Exile*. Chapel Hill and London:
University of North Carolina Press.

Bonnet, Alistair. 1999. *Antiracism*. London: Routledge.

Boyarin, Daniel. 1997. *Unheroic Conduct: The Rise of Heterosexuality and the Invention of the
Jewish Man*. Berkeley: University of California Press.

Brah, Avtar. 1996. *Cartographies of Diaspora: Contesting Identities*. London: Routledge.

Byrne, Anne, and Ronit Lentin (eds.). 2000. *(Re)Searching Women: Feminist Research Methodologies in the Social Sciences in Ireland*. Dublin: Institute of Public Administration.

Cousin, Orna. 2001. 'Okef consensus' [Bypassing the consensus]. *Ha'aretz*, 24 January: 5.

Dajani, Souad. 1994. 'Between national and social liberation: The Palestinian women's movement in the Israeli-occupied West Bank and Gaza Strip'. In Tamar Mayer (ed.), *Women and the Israeli Occupation: The Politics of Change*. London: Routledge.

De Tona, Carla. 2000. *Italian women in Dublin*. M.Phil. dissertation, Ethnic and Racial Studies, Department of Sociology, Trinity College Dublin.

Eilam, Yigal. 2000. *Ketz Hayahadut: Umat Hadat Vehamamlacha* [The end of Judaism: The religion-nation and the realm]. Tel-Aviv: Yediot Aharonot/Hemed Books.

Gershuni, Israel, and Shlomo Sand. 2000. '*Orientalism*: Al kocho shel hayeda veal hayeda shel hakoach' [*Orientliam*: On the power of knowledge and on the knowledge of power]. *Ha'aretz*, 15 September: B13.

Gilbert, Sandra. 1984. 'From *Patria* to *Matria*: Elizabeth Barrett Browning's Risorgimento', *PMLA* 99: 194–211.

Goldstone, Katrina. 2000. 'Re-writing you: Writing and researching ethnic minorities'. In Malcolm MacLachlan and Michael O'Connell (eds.), *Cultivating Pluralism: Psychological, Social and Cultural Perspectives on a Changing Ireland*. Dublin: Oak Tree Press.

Hazelton, Lesley. 1978. *Tsela Adam: Ha'Isha Bakhevra HaIsraelit* [Israeli women: The reality behind the myth). Jerusalem: Idanim.

hooks, bell. 1991. *yearning: race, gender and cultural politics*. London: Turnaround.

Klepfisz, Irena. 1990. *A Few Words in the Mother Tongue: Poems Selected and New 1971–1990*. Portland, Oregon: The Eighth Mountain Press.

Laor, Yitzhak. 1994. 'Halashon Hakeru'a' [The torn tongue]. *Ha'aretz*, 19 September: B6–7.

———. 1995. *Anu Kotvim Otakh Moledet* [Narratives with no natives: Essays on Israeli literature]. Tel-Aviv: Hakibbutz Hameukhad.

Lentin, Ronit. 1976. 'Even hato'im' [Stone of claims]. *Siman Kri'a* 6: 109–43.

———. 1982. *Sichot Im Nashim Palestiniot* [Conversations with Palestinian women]. Jerusalem: Mifras.

———. 1989. *Night Train to Mother*. Dublin: Attic Press.

———. 1996. *Songs on the Death of Children*. Dublin: Poolbeg Press.

———. 1998. 'Israeli and Palestinian women working for peace'. In Lois Lorentzen and Jennifer Turpin (eds.), *Women and War Reader*. New York: New York University Press, 337–42.

———. 2000a. 'The (self) silencing of the (feminist) lambs: Israeli and Palestinian women struggling to come to terms with the lost possibilities of peace in the Middle East'. Paper presented at the Euro Forum, Florence, Italy, 22 November.

———. 2000b. *Israel and the Daughters of the Shoah: Reoccupying the Territories of Silence*. New York and Oxford: Berghahn Books.

———. 2000c. 'Constructing the self in narrative: Feminist research as auto/biography'. In Anne Byrne and Ronit Lentin (eds.), *(Re)Searching Women: Feminist Research Methodologies in the Social Sciences in Ireland*. Dublin: Institute of Public Administration.

———. 2000d. 'Introduction: Racialising the other, racialising the "us" – emerging Irish identities as processes of racialisation'. In Ronit Lentin (ed.), *Emerging Irish Identities*. Dublin: Ethnic and Racial Studies, Trinity College Dublin.

———. 2000e. 'Chaotic childhood: Narratives of Jewish girl survivors of Transnistria'. Paper presented in the Seamus Heaney Lecture Series, 2000–1, St Patrick's College, Drumcondra, Dublin.

———. 2001. 'Memory and forgetting: Gendered constructions of silence in the relationship between Israeli Zionism and the Shoah'. Occasional papers series, no. 2001/08, Mediterranean Programme, Robert Schumann Centre, European University Institute, Florence.

Levy, Gideon. 2001. 'Mahi alimut?' [What is violence?]. *Ha'aretz*, 11 March: B1.

Lomsky-Feder, Edna, and Eyal Ben-Ari (eds.). 1999. *The Military and Militarism in Israeli Society*. New York: State University of New York Press.

Mohanty, Chandra Talpade. 1991. 'Under Western eyes: Feminist scholarship and colonial discourses'. In Chandra T. Mohanty, Anne Russo and Lourdes Torres (eds.), *Third World Women and the Politics of Feminism*. Bloomington: Indiana University Press.

Morris, Benny. 1987. *The Birth of the Palestinian Refugee Problem 1947–1949*. Boston: Beacon Press.

Natur, Salman. 2000. 'Review of *Eres Hanochria* [Poems] by Mahmoud Darwish'. *Ha'aretz Musaf Sefarim*, 31 May: 1.

New Profile: Movement for the Civil-isation of Society in Israel. 2000. 'Social and state processes in Israel during the 2000 Intifada, in the light of the ongoing militarisation of Israel'. Tel-Aviv: New Profile.

Oz, Amos. 2001. 'Arafat's gift to us: Sharon'. *The Guardian*, 12 February. <http://www.guardian.co.uk/Archive/Article/0,4273,4133117,00.html>

Pappe, Ilan. 1994. 'A lesson in new history'. *Ha'aretz Magazine*, 24 June: 53–4.

Ram, Uri (ed.). 1993. *Hakhevra HaIsraelit: Hebetim Bikorti'im* [Israeli society: Critical aspects]. Tel-Aviv: Breirot Publishers.

Sadan, Yosef. 2000. 'Devarim beshulei hase'ara haSaidit' [Words on the margins of the Said storm]. *Ha'aretz*, 15 September: B 13.

Said, Edward. 1979. *The Question of Palestine*. New York: Times Books.

———. 1981. *She'elat Palestine* [The Question of Palestine]. Trans. Ronit Lentin and Yahali Amit. Jerusalem: Mifras.

———. 1986. *After the Last Sky: Palestinian Lives*. London: Vintage.

Segev, Tom. 1991. *Hamillion Hashevi'i: HaIsraelim vehaShoah* [The seventh million: The Israelis and the Shoah]. Jerusalem: Keter.

Shadmi, Erella. 1992. 'Women, Palestinians, Zionism: A personal view'. *News from Within* 8 (10/11): 13–6.

Sharoni, Simona. 1992. 'Every woman is an occupied territory: The politics of militarism and sexism and the Israeli-Palestinian conflict'. *Journal of Gender Studies* 4: 447–62.

Shavit, Ari. 2000. 'Zechut hashiva sheli' [My right of return]. *Ha'aretz Magazine*, 18 August: 16–22.

Silberstein, Laurence J. 1999. *The Postzionism Debates: Knowledge and Power in Israeli Culture*. New York and London: Routledge.

Stanley, Liz. 1993. 'The knowing, because experiencing subject: Narratives, lives and auto-biography'. *Women's Studies International Forum* 16 (3): 205–15.

———. 1996. 'The mother of invention: Necessity, writing and representation'. *Feminism and Psychology* 6 (1): 45–51.

Yablonka, Hanna. 1994. *Akhim Zarim* [Foreign brethren: Holocaust survivors in the state of Israel, 1948–1952]. Jerusalem: Yad Ben Zvi Press and Ben Gurion University Press.

Index